KU-736-127

WARREN BEATTY

A Life and a Story

David Thomson

SECKER & WARBURG · LONDON

First published in England 1987 by
Martin Secker & Warburg Limited
54 Poland Street, London W1V 3DF

Copyright © David Thomson 1987

British Library Cataloguing in Publication Data

Thomson, David, 1941—
   Warren Beatty: Two Lives.
   1. Beatty, Warren   2. Moving-picture
   actors and actresses—United States—
   Biography
I. title
791.43'028'0924   PN2287.B394

ISBN 0–436–52015–X

Phototypeset by Wyvern Typesetting Ltd, Bristol
Printed in England by
Redwood Burn Ltd, Trowbridge

LEABHARLANNA ATHA CLIATH
GLENCULLEN LIBRARY
ACC. NO.   0436 52015X
COPY NO.   RB 1002
INV. NO.   732A
PRICE IR£   16.50
CLASS   791.43/ BEA

Author's Note

There are two strands to this book, one biography and one that is fiction. The biography treats a real movie star, Warren Beatty, his life and work and the ways in which he has inspired a part of the romantic imagination of this century. The fiction concerns an imagined star, with the absurd but perhaps prophetic name of Eyes. His story is set vaguely in the future and entirely in legend. But the purpose of his fable is to shed light on a world inhabited by both Warren Beatty and his unknown spectators. For it is in the nature of stardom, movies and our times that bright, photographed faces do coexist with dark wonderings.

"His enemies may say that it is the only thing he has; but to me to have charm is fundamental. That accusation is like saying this fellow is only a genius, or that fellow is only an angel."
– Jorge Luis Borges on Oscar Wilde, *Twenty-Four Conversations with Borges*

"I bet you think this song is about you."
– Carly Simon

for Jim, Robert and David

A Life and a Story

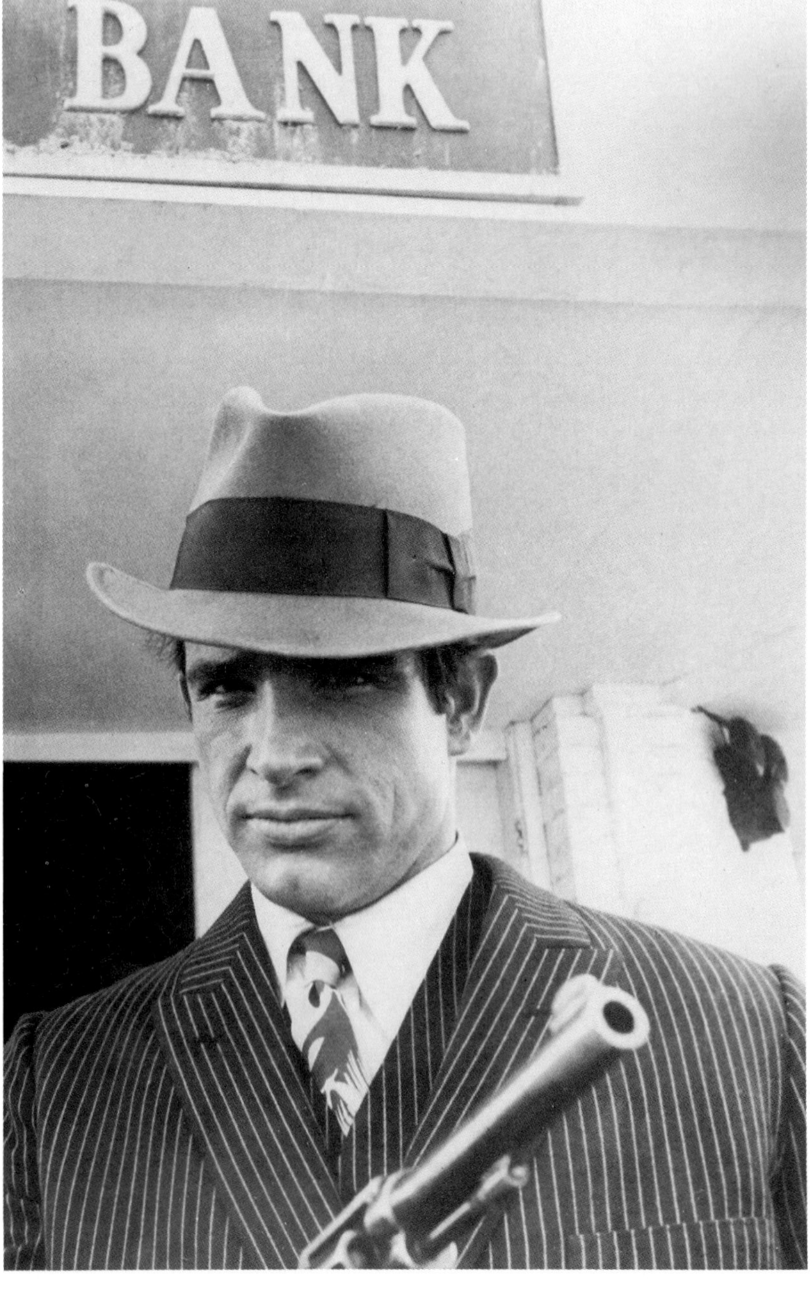
BANK

THERE HE IS

There he is, on what is called the facing page, watching you before you begin, looking to see what you will think, ready to smile as soon as you like him, but quite prepared to be above it all if you're left in doubt. Don't think he's not going to be there looking over your shoulder, or coming up behind you very softly. Don't count on him wearing some obtrusive Jockey Club cologne you'll always pick up. He'll just be *there*, intrigued, suspicious and downright hooked that you're thinking about him. For while Warren is certainly the center of this book, and of his own view of things, there's nothing so attractive in him as his own avid attention – his watching and listening, his being so alert that he takes control of the passing moment. He likes to telephone women in the night and ask, "What are you wearing? Let me guess." And so later they wonder if it is them he likes or simply the phone's authority.

*

Can you attempt the "life" of anyone still alive? Does responsible biography need as a first condition the death of its subject and the stillness of his life? Does an aspiring biographer have to dispose of his target before he can write with a clear conscience?

I began with an essay on Warren Beatty, published in the January 1982 *California* magazine, to coincide with the opening of *Reds*. The article described the making of that film; it had the benefit of telephone talks with Richard Sylbert, the film's production designer, and Jerzy Kosinski, the novelist enlisted by Beatty to play Zinoviev. It drew upon a meeting and several amiable conversations with David MacLeod, Warren's cousin and the associate producer on *Reds*. It had even a telephone contact with Beatty himself, or with an actor claiming to be Beatty. This immediately intimate voice called me, without secretarial

1

threshold, to say that while he appreciated what I was doing he wasn't talking to anyone.

Only high perversity takes the trouble to say that; and only a shell-shocked showman declines to promote the biggest picture he has ever made. He said, "Well . . . If you're going to write this article, I won't stop you. After all, I couldn't." But Paramount, the distributor of *Reds*, may have been begging for it. Movie distributors want us to know their picture is there. And for a movie starring Beatty, as well as produced and directed by him, they might have had cover stories in *Time* or *Newsweek*, as well as a dozen other magazines, not to mention appearances on television, perhaps a privileged hour with Barbara Walters as Warren said what the film really meant to him, giving Barbara that coax-me grin when she urged him, "Warren, you can tell *me*."

Paramount gathered none of these boosts. Yet Warren could tell me, gracefully, that he appreciated but had decided against aiding my effort. *Reds* was not a success. It was well received critically; it was a prestigious film, liked by many. But it did not recover its costs on initial release. It was the first failure of Warren Beatty the producer.

The industry estimated that if he had given more of himself then *Reds* might have stood a better chance of success. For Warren, perhaps, this had to be believed. Otherwise, the picture's failure was incomprehensible. After all, he is famous for his charm and seductiveness, yet he had been turned down by America. A few months later, when he accepted an Oscar for directing *Reds*, he gave an earnest speech about wanting to reclaim a lost chapter of America's history. That same sentiment offered earlier, to Barbara Walters and Walter Cronkite (the three of them in armchairs in the Library of Congress?), might have put several million on the film's rentals. Who can doubt Warren's ability to make Communists tasty for middle America? In the film itself, the Reeds had been made adorable, sexy puppies.

But that campaign could not have saved the film. And if nine-tenths of Beatty was opposed to failure, still perhaps the last tenth was fascinated by it and saw it as the way of doing less in the future. For there is no such creature now as an aging or middle-aged movie star. There is not much left between being Warren Beatty at 47 and Cary Grant at 81. Nothing but the time to fill.

It is Beatty's ambivalence about himself that makes me most interested in examining him. He has a way of catching sight of us looking at him and asking, "You want to be here? If I move over?" Who else has been so shyly conscientious about being the larger-than-life figure stardom requires, yet so irked by its excesses and so determined to withhold himself? These warring impulses make a perplexing result – Warren is simultaneously legendary, yet barely existing. Everyone "knows" him, but wonders what is there. His superiority is what a ghost might command.

If you do not appreciate this phantomness, try a game: imagine Jack Nicholson and Warren. Now imagine each one on his own, in the sancta of their homes (not unalike, not far apart – there is a stretch of Mulholland Drive where the gods live, tended by the same caterers, art dealers and security experts). No one is with them; the homes are ticking over efficiently; time and deals are passing. Just Jack. Just Warren.

Nicholson is all cracks, ledges and handholds for the imagination. I can hear his stomach rumbling: he farts and chuckles at the sweet afterburn of last night's gingered lobster. I can hear him breathing, enjoying the peace of the day, inhaling now and then on a fine smoke he has made for himself. He is a kind of Caliban, a jolly bad boy, scratching on his too-large belly, seething gently with his own good time, crawling over to the bookcase, sniffing at it, and then going pie-eyed over a page of Thomas McGuane or the I Ching, and beginning to suspect he'll be horny in an hour.

But Warren sits in shadow, perched on the edge of a Bauhaus chair, still, tense, poised, not sure he isn't being sapped or sucked on by secret recording devices, even the imagination of the world. He is so paranoid, so intelligent, he *knows* we are there. And so he schools his body to be quiet and reserved. He is a Prospero who has kept the look of an Ariel. But he has too many dreads to be a virtuoso self when alone. He may be as tempting as ice cream; but don't taste, and if you don't, he won't melt. So he finds a young woman (the numbers are all in his head), takes her to a restaurant, and then frets and trembles that his privacy is being jeopardised by the bold stares of other diners saying "Isn't that him?" And he smiles at her, as if to say, "Imagine when we are alone."

I am entering Warren Beatty's life, pen at the ready, to puzzle out his dismay. He has not welcomed me, or sat down with me. And though I asked for that once, I am glad he refused. For I see now how he could hardly listen and hesitate without applying control. And how can you warn someone you like if he insists on keeping power?

He should think of me as a rescuer, not a threat. I may have some understanding of him and his anxiety, and I am drawn to stardom. Hollow as that condition may be in any sensible consideration, I wouldn't mind being there. This ardor drew me once into the romantic assertion that Howard Hughes had arranged to die in the air, the "there" he loved most. Friends who heard this yearning laughed at it. But I think Warren, another Hughes fan, would have understood the principle involved. Of course, Warren is not laughed at much; the lack colours his loneliness a little. He does not let his crazy romanticism show, but keeps it sheathed in grim elegance and holds himself taut and cool. 47, 48, 49 – he begins to look like someone afraid his back could go out at any minute. It is a time of life where grace meets surgical support.

This is not a biography that inches across the knowable facts like a vacuum cleaning the carpet. Such bodies of page-time fall into place after death; and only then because, without presence in the life, a writer proceeds by way of research. The richest biographies concern those who kept diaries, sent many letters and had the wisdom to cultivate survivors. Research bestows order and temporal progress on a life. But it makes muddlers and neurotics seem more purposeful, and it forgets how life can feel empty, untidy and beset by indecision. For it keeps putting facts in order – as if the chief task of the subject had been to put his affairs in order before dying, instead of raising a good mystery. And if Warren wants to be mysterious, then a life written while he lives has the best chance of responding to the puzzle. He may come clearer afterwards. But he may look dull and minor.

"Being Warren Beatty" may be what his autobiography or some posthumous biography settles on – especially if he finds himself caught in some political backwater. "Being Charles Dickens", we may say now, is best rendered by the biography by Edgar Johnson – best, that is, if you insist on not reading the novels. But for Dickens, the part was a ferment of possibility that helped exhaust him. The writing of his novels included everything he omitted as well as what is now the settled text. The life is left standing, but its living was all the effort and hope that sought to prop it up. And the momentary electricity of this desperate being is especially important in a film star's enigma. For great stars change before our eyes; it is their disguise of growing old. Being Warren Beatty is sharing those flickering transitions with millions, sighing to them in the rapture of a close-up, "Imagine me", until the unknown answer, "O Warren, baby, come to *me*."

The image remains for history, but not its intensity. To appreciate an actor you must have seen their work. To know a movie actor, you must have been moved when their films were new. It is impossible now to feel all that Lillian Gish meant before 1920, or Garbo in 1930. The excitement turns camp nearly as quickly as ripe cheese becomes inedible. It is enough to make a picture actor wonder whether it is worth working.

*

There are two lives here. The one is Warren's, or as close as I could get to it in reading, talking to his friends and associates, seeing his films and in simply thinking about him. The other life comes out of all that thinking: it is a fiction, a life one might offer to him, a part fit for him to play. The story helps me explore the Hollywood Warren inhabits – and this is a book about the atmosphere of that place – but it also contributes to the portrait of a man who is always looking at stories, judging whether to give them life, and who may sometimes be uncertain where the facts of his life end and the possible pictures take over.

Beatty sent a message to me once, through a mutual friend, that he couldn't understand anyone writing about someone else without having met them. I sent a message back – that he should think of Clyde Barrow and John Reed. For Warren knew in 1967, in the first film he produced, *Bonnie and Clyde*, that lives, lies and insights abound before an outlaw is shot to pieces, especially if he is capable of that ecstatic, knowing glance – for death and immortality – exchanged between Warren and Faye, Bonnie and Clyde, just before their firing squad. Clyde did not look like Warren; the outlaw's passion on the brink of death is invented. But Warren aspires to art and transcendence, and he has carried Barrow into history with him.

And the potency of movie stars depends on their remarkable bond with strangers. They have established a peculiarly modern "knowledge", that of familiarity without contact, intimacy without experience. Beginning in movies, it has already reached out into most forms of public discourse. The stars may think it crazy for millions of the unknown, people in the dark, to invest so much in imagining them. But there is a matching folly in the stars being so available for the kindness, or the demon, of strangers.

It is a measure of the great stars that they seem to speak privately to the individual stranger: that is their shyness and our sensitivity. For it is essential to the great public show of stardom that it whispers to every pair of eyes in the dark, "Here, here is my secret. For *you*." The secret shines like a gift; the same offer of knowledge and privilege is made in love or seduction. The viewer's enormous desire has been recognised, but the trick is to let him or her believe that no one else has noticed their need. The great show is as furtive, and as bound by loneliness, as every voyeur's pleasure must be.

*

It is all desire at the movies – wanting to get on the screen. Suppose Warren had been drawn to movies once for no better reason than to get into that fame, and to meet women? When the public thinks of him now they feel the undertow of his seductiveness, his longing to be secret. He gazes at desire in the certainty that it can never quite be satisfied, not if the secret is to last. The public may not fathom this, but they see Warren has a design upon them evident in his guarded mind as well as his rationed appearances. So they are wary with him.

There is no welling up of imminent merriment and affection, as there is for Nicholson. There is not the amused respect accorded to Clint Eastwood, the securely unimaginative Clint, safe in his timidity. When Beatty's films are thought of it is in scenes of sexual allure – the orgasm in death in *Bonnie and Clyde* (so stroked by photography and cutting), Julie Christie going under the table in *Shampoo*, or even a poster picture, the angel of death and sex in *Heaven Can Wait*. The public has not quite kept up with his halting career. But they hear the legend of his prodigiousness in love; he is proverbial. They suppose it accounts for the gaps between pictures. He says he has been busy with serious things, like politics; and the public smiles. They know politics have become foolish. They wonder if he is trying to seduce them with his earnest smile. He is so sultry to the public mind he is nearly feminine. Which other actors seem so challenged to make us think of desire?

Give him some credit for the idea's currency. Say you have a list of 792 known women with whom he has had sexual congress; or 1,316; or realise that he is old enough for 10,000. Then look at this abiding youth and feel the mystery. Tell the stories of the several notable and prolonged affairs in his life. And find some decent way of letting the reader feel the heat and theater in Hollywood sex, as well as the sex in most acting. It is a place made out of looking and longing, fearful of physical decay and wear. Still, there *is* the real thing, rising every night like an old story.

There is also a legend to which others ascribe, willingly, helplessly or with envy. It is enough for Warren to keep a demure silence over that, sure that in the end he will be as good as they say he is. For instance, Orson Welles told his biographer, "The only way I can hold Warren's attention is to cease to be a gentleman and trade off marks on the gun, you know. It's the only way an old man could keep him interested. He'll listen for hours to *anything.*" And so Welles told Warren about an actress with whom he had had an affair, until the woman's affections were stolen away by Billie Holiday.

Warren "was so fascinated with it," said Welles, "that he stopped for a week until he got to know the girl and asked her if it was so. He's that obsessed by the subject. It struck him as so exotic and unlikely and probably a lie. And he found out it was true. *That's* all he thinks of, day and night. Oh yes, he's a real satyrite . . . calling different people all morning long to be sure that in the evening there's going to be somebody new. You know, that's the *real* Casanova."

Welles comes off as the Falstaff in the story, or as the fond old fool who has been outstripped. That may only mean there are always roles in Hollywood, and a certain sense of the crown being passed on. His story aids the warm myth that performing genius fucks them all, and has a pistol feathery with notches. Beatty learned long ago not to own up, but to tease and deflect such leading questions. A rumor lurks in Warren's bedroom eyes – don't you wonder if it's all true?

It's an intellectual mystery that beguiles as much as the sensual promise. For it seems to say not just, here is the fuck of your life, but what do you suppose it is, finally, to fuck? If you were sufficiently seduced, or that much in love with love, could you measure the quality, could you tell a Don from your husband? Warren Beatty's eyes allude to the chance that sex is imaginary, whatever its physical antics, and that in carnal knowledge only the knowledge lasts – and sometimes that goes the way of forgetting. He has seldom taken off his clothes on screen. But he has a head and face for dreamers – poised, recessive, lyric and secret. And like any Narcissus, he will keep his looks so long as desire moves him. If that ever goes, if it becomes a mere idea, then youth will be replaced by something like Dracula's haggard smile.

*

You may have come to this book for some fresh-cut slice of Hollywood revelation in which this or that flagrant young woman is tripling with Warren at her conventional bower and Jack at the back door, axing his way in with "Here's Johnny!" You are left to your own imaginative devices, the most solid sharing you will have with Warren, Jack or any of the blatant dames.

There are some films made, but many more declined or lost in delay. It makes you wonder at the other things Warren *hasn't* done. Aren't real lives just as consumed with thoughts of things not done as with the glee or misery that recalls things checked off and done with? Isn't it sometimes – because regret may be so much more lasting than glee – more challenging to contemplate things not done? One might think for many years about a lover never bedded, not even asked. But once the act is managed, doesn't the hope fill a smaller part of the dreamed day?

It's all very well to say that, on the balance of the evidence, it seems probable that Beatty had sexual relations with Joan C. and Natalie W., and so on. But he never "knew" Grace Kelly – did he? Further, I think we can safely eliminate Vanna White, Margaret Thatcher, Marlene Dietrich, Marilyn Monroe, Louise Bryant, Emma Bovary, Miss America, the usherette in Edward Hopper's painting *New York Movie* and Miss Piggy. I can find no jot of evidence that he has had any of those beauties. Believe me.

But suppose you don't. And suppose you have ears still for some whisper of gossip which says, well, with one of them, yes, he has, we'd have to call if f-cking. Whom would you guess? Can't you see how it might have been any of them?

It makes you wonder about other available pursuits. Do we think he has read Gibbon's *Decline and Fall of the Roman Empire*? Has he seen Goya's sketches in the basement of the Prado? Has he drunk calvados in the evenings in small Normandy towns? Did he ever see Carl Yastrzemski go hitless at Fenway? Has he read every book in his house? Has his car broken down on Mulholland Drive? Has he thought of going to a monastery, or some rather less severe retreat, for the rest of his life? Has he listened to Charlie Parker for days on end, been seasick, overslept or spent Christmas Day alone? Will he read this book? Will he think it's about him?

D goes home

D hurried home through gruesome streets, his new script under one arm, its copy under the other. He had had to take one of the rubber'nlead sheets to protect himself. The kopyshops gave them out now because of the radiation in copies. It was a stiff, soiled square with ragged edges. It left his side clammy and hot: his shirt was already soaked and stained from it. Would the cotton disintegrate? Shirts were essential for meetings. So he moved the drab protector and used it to guard the script against a collision on the street.

He could feel the cool pack of pages now against his body. D smiled to think of the rays seeping into his bones with the rubber sweat. He needed his work. What if it did destroy him? He had no age insurance, anyway. Something would happen before he turned old.

Though it was a little out of his way, D did not resist the routing of his legs towards the Eyes Building. He loved its shine, and the idea of it. It was eleven stories, an arrangement of selenium panels, in all of which there was a hinge with a dozen or more panels that could slip forward to help compose the facade. Thus the building had the appearance of a shower of tears. Its firmness as a structure was made poignant by the shimmering mutability in the facade. After all, it was only a building, a front; nothing happened inside.

And what the front pulsed with was the face of that great star Eyes – or the face as last seen in a movie made . . . how many years ago was it now? There were over a thousand panels and every one was a piece of Eyes' face. Since every panel-space had a dozen variants that could slip forward (at eleven different speeds) according to the programing of the computer, Eyes' face was always alive. The building breathed and shifted with the sensual possibilities of his smile or his frown. Even his stillness fluctuated. There were always people watching the building, their attention making a pilgrimage from his brow to his lip. As D looked up, the tongue swept across the mouth – a tongue like Moby Dick – and for a

9

few seconds a dew of readiness glistened on his lips. Another building might have dragged out its foundations and lurched across the plaza to kiss it – the Tuesday Weld Memorial Hall, maybe, from the other side of the street.

It was remarkable what they could do now. D was sure it was not mere partisanship, but truly the color quality in the Eyes Building was the most refined in the city. He felt so proud of his daughter, V, who worked on the process. For the past four months she had had responsibility for Eyes' upper right cheek, where a pink as delicate as Albertine rose had been appearing. D joked that she was the apple in Eyes' smile.

*

The problem at the intersection was no easier. Years ago, as people complained of boredom waiting for the lights to change, the authorities had mounted videos on the traffic light posts. They had changed behavior. People now thronged to the corners to watch; there were scuffles over the best positions. And so, gradually, the vehicles had noticed that people did not cross when they were entitled. Inevitably, some drivers grew impatient and began to go against the red. In a few months, there was traffic anarchy and several pedestrians who had seen an episode already, or who were blind perhaps (one heard only the stories), seeing the green or hearing its meek tone, stepped out and were killed. One had to take one's chance. Reports said that an average citizen was later home by fifteen minutes. "Intersections" did $7.2 billion in the first year. New lights were being pretexted all the time. Fresh, narrow streets were stuck into hitherto solid blocks. Between 52nd and 53rd there was now A as far as F.

D passed the Personal Appearance Arcade. There was not much of a crowd, but several camera crews at the entrance were recording the night's couple. D recognised them. They were actors who had met on a commercial and gone on to several series. She wore a boysenberry-colored fur coat, with the fall of her amber hair piled on the collar. Her lean face and lovelorn eyes turned from one camera to another. Her husband had distinguished gray hair, rimless dark glasses and strands of silver chain round his brandy-hued neck. He wore loafers and a cowboy suit, and held two Dobermans on lurex leashes. These hard brindle animals, pop-eyed in the Kliegs, surged against the wife so that she swayed and sighed. On the video, this tossing and her breathing were clear, but the dogs were out of the frame.

10

D goes home

Interviewers were asking them the secret to their lustrous, enviable marriage, and she was giving the same answer, take after take, for different crews:

"Well, we do it one day at a time, we respect each other, and we have fun. We do."

Another sigh. And the gray head of the husband nodded while the dogs arched against their mistress's fur. D saw the hot-pins of the dogs' penises, and when he looked at their yellow eyes he thought of a scene in which the dogs might rape the lady – and she could dream it was her unaccustomedly ardent husband. You could have her in a sun-mask, so that she did not actually see her lovers. And then pups a little later . . .? D could not decide whether it was a comedy or a grisly.

*

D peeled back the flimsy door to the apartment ready for the assault of cooking, noise and family. There was always too much crammed in there. The warmth, the density of things, the impossibility of being alone. What magic D felt in emptiness. How steadily people of their poverty dreamed of airiness, space and time, of solitude, that lovely suspension that beckoned from films and videos whenever a star was alone with the camera.

The children, their evening occupations, the hungry pets, the cracks and flaws in the apartment ran out to meet him like sour water from a burst pipe. He would embrace them all, letting the stain sink further into him, laughing and chattering, welcoming it all. He could not bear to see how worn he must be, or the shame of tiredness in movie's light. People in the tenements did not often look at one another; they moved like bats, bowed and humble, bumping and apologising, ready to kill, moving away, edging into corners, dreading bare mirrors.

The family fed in a hunched group every evening, like card players worrying over their hands. The meal was consumed in a few minutes to the hiss of soda cans and the discord of three videos left playing. The licence had been halved a year ago if the set was always left on: it played gentle sleeping sounds at night along with shots of colored scarves falling, sinking, on a marble floor in slow, voluptuous motion. D sat up many nights, waiting for this infinite cascade to turn sinister, daydreaming of sleep and new clothes and bumping awake with steel in the morning sky and computer fractions hopping across the screen with tremors of the Market.

The poster for *Heaven Can Wait* (Paramount)

Weegee, *Palace Theater, New York*, 1945 (Wilma Wilcox, Weegee Collection)

While he washed up in the kitchen, he studied the video set in the sink. It was easy, looking down, and there was something whimsical in having the picture swirled by waves of greasy water. The picture was a patio and a lounge, in daylight, up in Bel Air. It was an actress a lot of people were talking about, Arlene Loomis; she had an aching quality, D could tell. In this moviette she was alone in her home, alone with a saluki, trying on kaftans. Each one was lovelier than the last – she went from perfect to plus-perfect. But Arlene became vexed by choice. And so at last she lay on a bird's egg blue sofa made like a moccasin and stroked her sex until she fell asleep with her hand still folded, nostalgically, between her legs, and the saluki's sad head resting on her calf. She was hot – D could feel it. She would be cast soon. He wondered if she was right for the female lead in his script. She was too old, of course – they were all, always, too old – but you got a vivid extra panic if you cast an actress younger than her age.

D walked around the apartment. His dear V, nineteen, had fallen asleep over a half-finished jigsaw of Eyes. Her face rested in the hole in the center of the puzzle and her dribble was flowing onto Eyes' face. D soaked it up with his shirt tail and shut his daughter's mouth. She worked so hard. Little T was asleep at the end of his cot, the Jagger doll on the rubber band above his head. P, seven, was playing a game show with a video, and G, twelve, the studious one, was writing his paper on Wink Martindale.

And so D turned to the cleared table, to play hearts with his wife, C. He did not look at how exhausted she was – she irons transfer faces on T-shirts all day. He knows it is kindness not to let her see disappointment.

She deals the cards from the pack so old that the image of Loretta Young on the backs is scarred and worn in so many ways they can, both of them, identify several of the cards. But they do not mention this, and sometimes play from habit alone, not keeping score or noticing gross errors, but freed from the day and able to talk fondly in the placid rhythm of cards as heavy as skins.

"Did you decide on a title for the script?" asked C, sorting her hand, still believing in shape.'

"Well," said D. He had not made up his mind. He still favored *Imagine Me*. But he suggested, *"The Center of Attention?"*

C pursed her lips and inclined her head, as if trying to name a scent. "I think I like that very much," she decided.

Her pleasure was so brave, D looked into her battered, gratified eyes.

If it had been a movie, he might have wept. C went on, "I know, my dear, this one will be a success. It's the finest thing you have done."

"Have you the two?" D asked politely, ready to scream if their little game didn't start. He wasn't sure if she meant these things, or was an acute parody of his dreams. Did he hear C any longer, or only her lines and her role?

"You work so hard to be famous, we all love you for it. You are our hero. Why, V keeps a photograph of you in her –"

"The three?" he asked.

This might have gone on much longer: they were both void in clubs. But then the apartment door opened and Scrug looked in. "Phone," he sneered, looking at D. "I'll play your hand." He was the building supervisor, a lout they feared so much they lived with unreported breakdowns.

"Oh no," C began.

"Why argue?" said Scrug. "Phone."

So D reassured his C and went out into the dimly lit hallway. *Streets of Fire* was playing on one wall, and the usual corridor porn on another. The phone was dangling; a three-legged kitten was beating at it with its head. As D reached down, the cat clawed him. He looked at the pink raking on his knuckles.

"Well, now," said the phone. "Is that D?"

"Yes," he cried, naked with hope. He could never quell his amazement with the phone, of finding that someone was thinking of him. He was weeping. His tears stang the scratch marks. "D," murmured the phone, privately. "This is Clear. With Eyes. I was wondering if we might meet." D knew he would go anywhere to meet this understanding voice and its easy reference to magnificent authority.

"I believe this may be your break, D," said the phone with a modesty not comfortable with such stale promises, but duty-bound to say it just this once. "Are you there still? Surprise hasn't stunned you, I hope? Not dropped dead?"

LITTLE HENRY

Beatty lacks those handicaps of birth or upbringing so often used to justify ruthlessness in stars, or desperation. He does not come from the wild side; and he never persuades us he might lose control. He cannot turn on some executive in a dispute over terms, or confess to a woman on the beach at Malibu at twilight, "What you have to know about me is I come from nothing. So I have nothing to lose." Indeed, he has more the pinched air of a man who fears some intense, inner theft.

His line will have to be more mysterious, one without much screen tradition – "I don't have to do this, you know" – as if, one day, he might not if the woman or the studio heads don't lay restraining hands and deals on him now. He is going to hint, "You could lose me." And because he lets it be felt that he is in movies out of some private, incommunicable decision, he carries a patina of mysterious intelligence. This is a suspicious commodity in Hollywood. Who else there would bother to have his mind on anything except the place and its contest? And a game becomes philosophy if the players are amused by their intensity.

But in an unreflective setting, he who treasures his intelligence may end up a fool. Next to the raw thrust of Eastwood or Sylvester Stallone, Beatty seems to lack the confidence required in his medium. Beside the younger generation, he looks fussy and distracted. And while Beatty prefers to draw our attention to his loftier purposes, we might ask whether any thoroughly intelligent person could exist, let alone work, in Hollywood?

He is a child of teachers, born in 1937, when the education establishment is inclined to regard Hollywood as a dangerous place, where lies are concocted for the American imagination, and specious dreams divert the people from knowledge, reason and hard times. In 1937, despite Depression and Fascism, Hollywood makes *History is Made at Night*, *Wee Willy Winkie*, *The Awful Truth*, *Lost Horizon* and *A Star is Born*. In 1938, from the Garden of Allah Hotel, Scott

16

Fitzgerald, seeing himself as a cracked-up literary figure, writes to Max Perkins, his New York editor:

"... this amazing business has a way of whizzing you along at a tremendous speed and then letting you wait in a dispirited, half-cocked mood when you don't feel like understanding anything else, while it makes up its mind. It is a strange conglomeration of a few excellent overtired men making the pictures, and as dismal a crowd of hacks and fakes at the bottom as you can imagine. The consequence is that every other man is a charlatan, nobody trusts anybody else, and an infinite amount of time is wasted from lack of confidence."

Warren Henry Beaty is born a year and twenty-four days before that letter is written. Yet he will go on to illustrate its several points, and there are times when he will share Fitzgerald's wounded tone. As if Warren Henry's parents have not filled the house with warnings.

He is born in Richmond, Virginia, on March 30, 1937; in the South, the capital of the old Confederacy, the city where, in the summer of 1932, there has been held one of the last great parades of Civil War veterans. There is then a home for old soldiers in Richmond, where white-haired men run up the Confederate flag and bitterly contest the possibility that a statue of Robert E. Lee can be assigned to a sculptor from Ohio, or that a monument at Appomattox – fifty miles to the west – may bear the healing inscription, "North-South: Peace-Unity".

Richmond then is the headquarters of the cigarette industry and of Civil War nostalgia – a place of smoke and statues, neither of which will impress the boy any more than the considerable conservatism and untroubled racism. Ira Owens Beaty is a respected figure in the town, a teacher who will go on to be superintendent of Richmond High School. He is a southerner, married to another teacher, Kathlyn Maclean, from Nova Scotia originally, not just of the North but Canadian. She is a thin woman, very quiet in the marriage; he is large, authoritarian and domineering.

The father has been a promising young violinist in his home, Front Royal, Virginia. A teacher has heard him playing with the amateur symphony orchestra and recommends special tuition, Europe and a career as a soloist. But Ira Beaty turns the prospect down and, years later, gives this explanation to his daughter:

"The competition was too rough, Monkey. And that would have been no way to make a living. It wouldn't have been dependable. Sure, I would have seen Europe, maybe been wined and dined by royalty, but if I had done it, !

17

probably wouldn't have met and married your mother and we wouldn't have had you and Warren. So I think I did the right thing."

The daughter is never sure her father believes this. In his drinking and in his provocative way of raising arguments which sometimes get to the exposed souls of his family, he seems frustrated and disappointed. His children learn the lesson not to compromise with possible talent, and the son may see in himself the same turbulent mixture of search for glory and the need for security.

Ira Beaty reads philosophy at Johns Hopkins, and he is a professor of psychology and education at Maryland College, in Baltimore, when Kathlyn Maclean comes there to teach drama. They have a kind of sacrifice in common, for she has wanted to be an actress. They fall in love and they marry, despite Kathlyn's sense that Ira has been hurt by an upbringing in which he was dominated by his mother.

At the birth of Warren Henry, Ira and Kathlyn already have a daughter, Shirley, who will be as outspoken as Warren is reserved. Shirley MacLaine will give a portrait of her parents in 1970 like scenes from a family drama about repression and escape. It might be by Ibsen or O'Neill. It is nowhere near as painful or drastic as *Long Day's Journey into Night*; it is lit up with hope and freedom. But it is a play in which the daughter understands and rids herself of emotional shadow by becoming an actress. She leaves a brother behind who, when his turn comes, will also act; but this troubles the brother, for he is never to be a happy actor, sure of having found himself. Warren is part-participant, part-onlooker in Shirley's battle. We cannot tell from her story whether he noticed the same threat, or felt her need to survive it. But just as she presents her father as an obstacle she has to overcome, so it is possible that the strongest force in Warren's early life was his older sister. There is still a look of wistful patience on his face sometimes that has had to wait out the tirades of her quicker spirit, its glorying in earnestness and its certainty that she is a soul who has been many other people in earlier lives. She too is loved by America.

Shirley says she has "loving parents", but then she adds that there are things left wanting – "feelings". The children are caught in "a cliché-loving, middle-class Virginia family", in a house of objects, furniture and possessions too precious to be touched, yet fake sometimes, like the "Chippendale" mirror. She grows up with a sense of fineness in the family, and its aspirations; yet, in hindsight, she sees just "a plain, modest, middle-class, red-brick house – mortgaged and everything". The failure that haunts her adult account is that of honesty and sentiment, and the warping that springs from it which she was too strong or determined to endure:

> "My father was the autocratic head of the family, well educated, with a portly build moving toward rotundity whenever there were peanuts around. He was a stern man with light blue eyes full of suspicion, the censor of all he surveyed, and the guardian of our safety. He was sometimes terrifying, because he always acted as though he knew not only about the 'bad' things we *had* done, but also those 'bad' things we were *going* to do. Then there were times when he was so moved with pride for us that his chest puffed out even further than his stomach. His sensitivity was bottomless, but the fear of his own feelings was sometimes too painful to witness.
>
> "Mother was a tall, thin, almost ethereal creature with a romantic nature, who found even the most insignificant unpleasantness difficult to accept. In fact, it didn't exist – nothing unpleasant existed; it was a mistake or misinterpretation."

In all of this, Warren is a child follower, what Shirley calls her "companion in adjustment and rebellion". She recalls being handed her baby brother wrapped in a blanket – "He spent most of his time yelling, and with growing finesse and sometimes astounding precision, he has been doing so ever since." That is an odd change of tone and time focus in a childhood recollection, a belated recognition of control in the young ally, as if she has needed time to appreciate his mastery.

She says their parents were perfectionists, but that the father was defeated, a man of great ambition who had abandoned his own hopes and become bitter or depressed. It is clear how often father and daughter challenge one another, how steadily the mother observes the fights until she has to say, "All right Ira, that's enough." And that seems to do it; in the end, the Beaty males do not have authority. There is a crucial confrontation. Warren is not there – Shirley remembers this. As an actor, he will not court fights. His eyes can seem stunned or baffled by the pain of others, at a loss to help and so a little more drawn to coldness and distance.

This incident occurs when she is sixteen, and Warren thirteen. It "still blazes in my memory". She is studying to dance, in addition to her regular schooling at Washington-Lee High School in Arlington. She goes into Washington for dancing classes. But she loses the part of Cinderella in a Christmas production, and comes home in tears. Her father witnesses her return and the spectacle of her failure releases his loathing of any type of success (it does require an O'Neill):

19

"He stopped, and with finger wagging told me that that should teach me to stop trying to do things I wasn't capable of."

They are on the staircase, like people in a crisis in a Hitchcock film: "wasn't this episode proof enough for me that, if I attempted to go beyond my range, I would only be crushed? Hadn't he told me many times during my life? When would I believe him, when would I understand that if I tried I would only get hurt?"

Shirley remembers a few years before when his scorn at her performance as Ado Annie in a production of *Oklahoma!* ("I'm just a girl who can't say no") had stopped her singing completely. She says she fell on the stairs, with her father above her berating her. She cries so hard she vomits, but he never stops telling her off. The mother says that is enough, Ira. It's the one line Shirley gives her, and it's as haunting as something from *Long Day's Journey*. And Shirley sees the whole thing in one of those flashes that can be blinding to the enlightened, but never noticed by faraway brothers. It is victory and defeat, a curtain moment:

> "He could see, even though I had dissolved into a little pile of protoplasm, that I would never stop dancing. And he seemed to understand that ironically he, in effect, was teaching me to dare because I saw that he was such a spectacular disappointment to himself for having never tried it. A strange clear look of understanding came into his eyes [this is the passion of movies and movie-going] as he realised I didn't want to be like him. He stepped over the vomit and went to fix himself a drink."

A couple of years after that, Shirley leaves home, with her mother's support, to become an actress. But in the book that includes these family scenes, *Don't Fall Off the Mountain*, she goes back home years later, in 1968, on a visit. She has come from Mississippi, the deep South, where she has been watching voter registration and school desegregation. In 1968, Shirley will be a delegate at the Democratic Convention. At home, her father hears she has been in the company of blacks and – he is a southerner – jokes: "Don't you want to have a nice, long hot shower before you tell us – we just had the upholstery cleaned."

Instead, she tells him, a teacher and school superintendent, about a black girl whose chair in class is spat on by her fellow-students.

"Dad listened to my story about Thelma with clenched teeth and when it was over I could see tears streaming down his face. He slumped deeper into his favorite chair like an old man and said, 'God, I want to change, but it's so hard I think I'll die first.'"

Shirley tries to open the windows in the room, but her father tells her

20

they are fixed shut. It is really Ibsen now – the windows have *always* been closed. The mother comes in carrying meatloaf for dinner.

" 'Why aren't these windows open?' I asked. 'It's hot this afternoon and there's a breeze outside that would help.'

"Her eyes stopped dancing and she quickly darted a look toward my father. 'I don't know,' she said. 'Daddy says they've never been opened.' "

The curtain comes down again, on the frozen scene of father and daughter staring at one another in horror and an airless room.

The set for *A Loss of Roses,* designed by Boris Aronson (Friedman-Abeles)

Clear's appointment

The next day D set out to see Clear. That night, on the phone, like an idiot (how easily one hated oneself), he had blurted out, "I could come now." He took it for granted that this Clear never rested. But Clear had paused, chuckled amiably and said, well, he was in the bath. There was a sound of water stirring, and then a more significant gathering of waves, as if someone close to Clear, in the same tub, had stood up and water had tumbled from their body, rills sliding off their shoulders, scoops abandoned by their flattened belly. It was like darkness broken and pushed aside by the bright face in a close-up.

D strained to picture this person before he or she vanished into towelling. It seemed an impressive figure, if immaterial; substantial, yet only a slip of a thing. It could have been a boss, or a hooker hired for the night. But D could tell that Clear was watching, too: his voice when it returned was upturned and expectant, waiting to see if this other person smiled.

"Come any old time," said Clear. He was so intent, he might have been watching his heart have an attack on a measuring machine.

"*Any* time?" D could not endure such vagueness.

"Call when you're coming." Clear sounded sleepy now.

"I could come tomorrow."

"You could?" Was Clear taking advice? Or watching a toy drift in the tub?

"Easily."

"Why not then? I suppose so."

The click that told D the call was over was preceded – his eager ear was attuned now – by a rising in the tiny lapping of water, as if the phone floated beside ducks, drinks or waterproof volumes of poetry. He could imagine the perfumed steaminess. D felt a little dirty. He remembered that his pants were soiled and no shirt had all its buttons. Could he manage a casual look? For an instant, he wished he lived in the desert and never saw another human being. He was shaking with strain after the call.

"Don't bleed on my floor," growled Scrug, looking at his hand. Of course, the floor was rancid. Just thinking about it made D fear his wound was infected.

"I have an engagement tomorrow," said D, but Scrug muttered, "Swine", out of habit. No one believed D was going to be famous. Even D thought sometimes that his best chance was to kill Scrug and seven or eight others in the building. "Crazed Author Runs Amok!" he could see the headline, and a Weegeepic of himself scathed by flashlight, his face hanging like a rag, his eyes struggling to get out of his head.

Not very cheering stuff, thought D in the fishy morning light. The place that Clear had told him to go was a four-hour walk away, above Sunset. D planned his journey to arrive in the early afternoon. There was no transportation that went there, but D knew the city well enough to avoid the worst climbs and keep to the shaded sides of the street. He would probably arrived soaked in his own sweat anyway.

He wrapped the script in a towel to protect it. Obviously he had to take it. Clear hadn't mentioned it, but why else would Clear call? He hardly wanted to see D for social reasons. D knew he was an embarrassment; he had made up his mind to let it be that way. An agent once had told him he had no charm, not enough to get any invitations. "You would have to write *soooo* well," the agent said to himself, and he had declined to take D. "Go on, viper," he'd said as a joke. "Keep all the loot yourself!" And so D had been without proper representation. "It's a life for strong spirits," the agent had said on parting, the last lash on a flayed soul.

The building at the end of D's journey was made of azure glass: from a distance it was only lines etched in the surrounding sky, a fancy, a diagram. But coming closer, up the last inescapable hill so steep he had to use his free hand to hold on to the ground, he realised it had block, depth and a parking lot. There was a space inside the glass that flung back the world's sated look at itself. He was exhausted, and the last mile was filled with an irrational dread that the script might fall from his sopping grasp, the pages skipping in the fractious breeze. D could never subdue these fears, or shut out of his mind the dazzling, despairing liberty of hurling away this and every other script, all that neurotically numbered paper, with CONTINUED on top of the pages, from the highest hills of the city. Suppose LA smog was really only the waste of all its abandoned stories, all unmade, poisoning the air.

There were colors up there. In D's part of town, you forgot color in the

23

smog; it erased it. But in the lobby of the building there was a pink carpet that hurt his eyes; or rather, not exactly the retinae, but their old association with feelings. Wherever he looked, up here, D saw the surface of desirable emotion. He wanted it all for himself, as well as the girl at the walnut console, a lone lean creature, fiercely tanned, in a black halter top, with fresh black grapes in her hair. She wore moist ivory lipstick, and when she spoke to him a tremor of expectation ran through her body. She was excitement. There was a way people here embodied mood and need. Everyone was a degree of desire. It was the way he remembered old movies, where apples and automobiles, blondes or killers, were all sexy because they were being seen.

"Hi," said the girl. "Like a grape?"

D reached out a wavering hand. As it touched the grape, the firm soft fruit dropped into his palm, and he heard the girl say, sigh rather (the lips did not move), "Oh, you're gentle." Was it an answering machine?

"You must be the appointment for Mr Clear?"

This was marvelous! In a twelve-storey building, to be known and expected. "That's right," smiled D.

"Why don't you take a video? I'll tell his office you're here."

D examined the row of watermelon velvet chairs, each with video in its arm, like a nail on a finger. He sat down and realised that the picture was Miss Grapehead herself. How witty! And when he smiled, her picture looked up and gave a sly wink back to him. The soundtrack had her breathing and the slight flexings of her clothes. He could feel the self-satisfied interplay of her good health and her Frederick's lingerie. He was a fly resting on her lustrous skin, and he noticed his seat was not quite still. It breathed in time with the receptionist! This was like being between her breasts. He felt so rested. The face on the screen looked up at him, and said, "It's D, isn't it? Sure, that's right. Our old fiddle-dee-D. So good to have you," and then, "So sweet," as if treasuring a lost civilization.

A moment later he heard her voice again, but now it was petulant in the flocked air of the lobby. He strolled over to the console, quite impishly for a wreck, saying it was a droll device. But she was altered, unfiltered. She had become a receptionist at the tag-end of a humiliating day. Her mascara had run with her confidence.

"What?" she said, out of patience.

D sailed on, too full of rapture. "To have the seat over there adjusted to your breathing . . ."

She looked at him as if he was mad, as well as ugly. "Mr D, that's quite

24

absurd. This is only a lobby. Do you think people are made of money? God! Go on up, will you." She said it as if he was an assassin. He had ventured out of his shell, and made a fool of himself. From the console, those palpitating seats looked crude and inert, like seats at a bus station. It was late afternoon. The building had turned itself into a place everyone longed to quit.

"The eleventh floor?" said D in a daze.

"That's right," from the snappy bitch. "And don't repeat everything up there. They'll throw you out of the window – if they can get the window open, that is." This seemed to amuse her, but she laughed in a panic-stricken way. D hurried past, before she came to tears.

The elevator was the size of D's living room. He marvelled to think of such a space, empty as often as not, rising and falling through the heart of the building like a pump. How many such rooms were there, all over the city, each with its signed inspection certificate and the chiselled warning that no more than sixteen persons were to be there at one time? D admired the braille dots to show the floor numbers. Suppose there were seventeen blind men in the elevator? Even at the end of the day, bedraggled and daunted, he was a story man. That was the kind of bucking up C would have given him. C, his wife, so far away, in the ironing room, trying to tell the sky from the lead tone in the sweatshop skylight. Poor dear C, with wizened eyes and gaunt limbs. He loved her, he told himself, as the elevator whispered to the passing walls. It groaned and bumped at 11.

He realised as he got out, there had been no video in the elevator. It made him sure that he had been watched. He looked back at the panelled interior. There was no hint of a lens. But who was there to fear these days if they couldn't fashion a spy-hole invisible to the naked eye?

He had to withdraw his searching head as the doors began to close automatically. Wedges of polished steel met in front of him. He saw the frosted outline of a man behind him in the sheen. Before he could turn, hands fell on his shoulders and a close, muted voice said, "It must be D, isn't it? Don't disappoint me." Anxiety is so catching, thought D, as he closed his eyes and made to turn his battered body round.

FEMALE INFLUENCES

When Shirley makes a family drama of the childhood she shares with Warren, then he is cast in the role of her best audience. Their mother is as committed to duty and endurance as the grim scenery; Warren is the attention Shirley looks for, to make sure that her rightness has got across. When Shirley finally leaves Virginia, she says to herself about her brother, "He'll do something. And it will be his way, just as I am going off to do something my way. But I knew that, whatever it was, somehow it would continue to be a joint plan against the established way of doing things.'"

But suppose Warren does not feel all of that jointness, and is not as hurt by the defeated force in the house that drives Shirley away? Suppose he is more attuned to the necessary forlornness of energy and selfhood. Thirty years or more later, Shirley MacLaine is convinced of the reach of reincarnation – apparently so eccentric, so dotty – whereas it is hard to think that Warren believes in anything except what really happens and the decent doubt one retains about even that.

Yet he does follow his sister; he goes off to be in show business. That can only boost her hope that he is her ally. But it might haunt his wish to be his own man. It might make him tactically cold to her, as and when they do meet in their other world, show business. Does he need to say to her, Don't always think you understand me, Don't think loyalty covers everything? He is someone who wants to keep an indefatigable puzzle at his center, even an emptiness that others must try to fill. But if she lectures him when they are children, if she tells him her problems with their parents, so often and with such narrative bravura, then he may be afflicted by the condition of audience and the sibling resentment that feels we were always talking about *her*. No wonder she is baffled at his silent rebukes later: she was brought up as the center of things. She is the story-teller, so Warren cannot escape the meekness of a listener, with the imprisoned needs of someone who imagines more than he can ever

26

describe and who sometimes asks himself why the power and the glory can't come to *me*.

Warren Beatty will make his name in a profession where a very few do and are, and the many watch them doing and being. This is one of the equations of our times, a neon equals sign surrounded by fear and superstitions. It allows that the few have more vivid identity and more public worth than the many. But they are also regarded as vain, unreal and vaguely corrupt. Those human failings actually count as ingredients of exemplary public value. For such figures are loved and despised. A great trouble with actors, you hear it said, is that they are always "on", always performing, with only "off" as an alternative. It is as if they are versions of electricity; and like electricity they are used, taken for granted and then scorned because their light is not natural.

Shirley MacLaine is an example of such brilliant, "electric" presence, a star worthy of the lights that emblazon her name, or some such. She is famous for an energy beyond her years. At fifty, she has an exuberant, "unbelievable" one-woman show. She comes off soaked in sweat, crystalline, as if it was the residue of electricity. Her screen work is broad, explosive, larger than life; she has red hair; she is called outspoken; she struts, she laughs out loud, she bumps and grinds; she pours out her heart. The public is fond of her and sees her "inner life" – the thing about reincarnation – as part of her exalted condition. She could end up another Ethel Merman – superhuman, an immortal, the spirit of show business and America.

These two warm winds become more alike during Warren Beatty's childhood and the pride of stars in uniform. He is seven when Franklin Roosevelt is re-elected in 1944; it will be the first presidential election he notices, and it seems to say that the leadership of America is the focal point in international crisis. That is why this one man goes on being elected, why a man so ill and physically depleted that he has become a photographed figure, a movie man, all shots and close-ups, has defined a crisis that needs him. America knows FDR is a cripple but it is shown what it wants to believe – the pictures of power. There is no sharper time in which to learn about the presidency's modern drama.

Another actor, the young genius of his time, is very prominent in the Roosevelt campaign. We have encountered him already: Orson Welles. He speaks for FDR, on the radio and at public meetings, and he writes in *Free World*. The actor and the president are on friendly terms, exchanging notes. Not yet thirty, Welles has made and acted in a film about a man who sets himself at the highest power in America, *Citizen*

Kane, a film that directly compares politics and theater and shows the same imaginative drive going from one to the other. When Roosevelt wins again in 1944, he writes to Welles:

> "I may be a prejudiced spectator who had a special interest in the action, but I want to thank you for the splendid role you played in the recent campaign. I cannot recall any campaign in which actors and artists were so effective in the unrehearsed realities of the drama of the American future. It was a great show in which you played a great part."

Warren does not know this, of course; or, he does not read the letter. But he is a seven-year-old boy, looking out at the drama and its movies, bathed in their light, and he would know already as part of the great show that a president might talk to an actor, waving to him above the dark throng, winking even, like kin. Long before the voting in of Ronald Reagan, there is a pressure building in America: the natural consequences of its idealism, its dreaming and its media.

Millions partake vicariously in stars' blithe risk-taking, their high kicks, and their willingness to be invented people. Some find it easier to live with Ronald Reagan as president, because he is so good at being president. This is not the same as being a good president; it is to take the role as one laid down in that messy genre made up of the news, documentary and political announcement. The detail of his administration may seem comically inept. But he has made that reality transparent beside the humdrum radiance of his show. He is a star for anxious unknowns or humble tyrants, a model for salesmen, the more removed from criticism because he is so expertly wry and amateur. His administration is the best celebration of ordinariness yet managed by stardom. Like Will Rogers or Johnny Carson, he identifies the power possible in being likeable.

Such a presidency functions like the movies. It takes our minds off our own awkwardness and failure and our fear that perhaps nothing now is likeable. We so identify with him that we can vote for him while ignoring his wretched, irrational policies. This "we" has given up several birthrights – observation, evidence and judgement, at least. For we are believing in the unbelievable. The only compensation is that we have in so doing affirmed imagination. From our own dank place in the dark we can feel for, be with, these electric stars. They do not know us, cannot see us; but we know them as if they were us. Somehow, this presumption of ours fills the empty space they worry over in their hearts. For they let us lead entirely other, phantom lives: thousands of them, as many as a satyr could mate with. And if we elect one star as a lover supreme, it is because we are fucking crazy.

Many people felt better on seeing *Bonnie and Clyde* – more relaxed, more energized, clearer. All American movies are restoratives of a kind: they are ointment and lubrication to the reckless process of imagining that the medium encourages. Stardom gives us fantasy, which is so much more up-to-date than the afterlife: we can have it now. As we sit in the corners of gloom and chaos (remember D), we can pretend we are Eyes (or Mouth). Far from the reckless or irresponsible escapism, this is proof that we have inner potential; it is a fineness that corresponds and communes with the empty, impossibly electric quality of those we watch. This is not really so far from the apparently crazy scheme of reincarnation – close enough to see that a brother might still be fascinated by what a sister believes.

If Warren Beatty is the most intelligent actor in Hollywood, then he must think on these things. No wonder he dines sometimes with Orson Welles and tells him, yes, he is serious about being president. And Beatty will have looked at *Citizen Kane*, taken its love of mystery to heart; he may even have read around enough to find that, reviewing the film, Jorge Luis Borges said "it is a labyrinth without a center". Which could help explain why he acts so seldom, and so absentmindedly, as if the work never convinced him. He has a shyness that suggests he would rather be watching, and that he is not sure why or how he became an actor, unless it was the helpless response to his beauty, his inspiring sister and the way his America is so ready to look at pictures.

The boy Warren Henry Beaty was a watcher not given to opinions. He tiptoed away from what he saw so as not to be questioned about it. Did he really howl as a child, as Shirley remembers, or did he just exist? It is so hard to hear his raised voice or forceful enunciation. His grown-up authority is deferential. Shirley looked at him and knew he was prettier than she could ever be, beautiful in ways that are contingent on silence. Too much talking can tire a face and eat away its calm.

The few things Warren has said about his childhood omit the stresses felt by Shirley – because they are hers alone, because they are too intimate to be revealed, or because he hates being known. He has remarked on his parents' interest in the arts. His mother directed plays, his father played the violin. He felt their wish to have creative children, just as Shirley says they resisted it.

"I never thought I would be an actor. I watched my mother direct, my father

29

play the violin, and Shirley dance. I played the piano; maybe I just waited to spring. But no thought of getting up to perform. I was interested in the theater as a place to control, to manipulate."

Shirley was the best boy he knew. She was called "powerhouse" as a mighty hitter of home runs in softball games. When bigger boys picked on him, Shirley would rush in "like Rocky Graziano". And then "Warren would look grateful but bewildered, because he really wanted to take the risk himself".

He *was* her companion in escapades she designed, emptying garbage on neighborhood doorsteps, ringing doorbells and running away, pretending to drop dead in the middle of busy streets. At home, they were well behaved, hard-working and dutiful, so Shirley says. Yet Warren may have been lazier and more reclusive. His room had a spacious, walk-in closet, with a window of its own. It was a place to hide out in, a place to live away from others. Shirley envied it, and did not seem able to penetrate it. She only learned years later – when he must have told her – how in the empty house, in the basement, when no one else was home, he would be "acting out his soul to every Al Jolson record ever made, and memorizing in detail every play that Eugene O'Neill ever wrote."

There was a Jolson revival when Warren was nine, ten, eleven and twelve. Columbia made *The Jolson Story* and *Jolson Sings Again*, with Larry Parks as the singer. But O'Neill was an odder taste for a boy, unless he too was drawn to some of the unspeakable stories in reputable, creative families with fathers who had been actors and mothers who had to go upstairs to lie down; or unless he was making his devoted attempt to hear and be in the kinds of drama his sister insisted was their lot.

Warren has a forceful father, yet the father's example is one he may decline to follow, more a set of mistakes than a model. And Warren will have a way, later in life, of searching out men's weaknesses. Is he more comfortable with women, and more wholeheartedly admiring of them? He has at least three strong female influences in his early life – not just mother and sister, but his maternal grandmother. She had been Dean of Women at Acadia University, in Wolfville, Nova Scotia. Warren's mother will remember that Warren had a special rapport with this grandmother:

"I remember he used to get all dressed up to come to the dinner table because he knew Mother would be dressed. She never came to the table without having dressed, with a new hairstyle and perfume. And she wouldn't use a paper napkin. She insisted on a real linen napkin. Anyway, as soon as Warren and Mother sat down, Warren would snuggle up to her and say, 'Oh, Grandmother, you smell so good.' He never left her side. There was something very profound between the two of them."

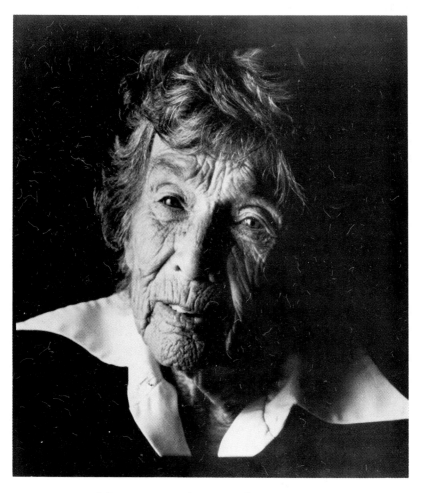

Adela Rogers St Johns in *Reds* (Paramount)

Drew

"*N'est-ce pas?*" Clear asked again at the elevator. His life seemed to depend on the answer, until he saw his reflection swimming in the steel doors. He put up one arm to be sure it was him there. D suspected he had too much to do, and could no longer concentrate. It was a condition that came from lifelong readiness without action.

Clear was tall, yet curved, in an attentive forward droop, like a stick of celery. He wore rimless spectacles and his hair was a fine, brindle cover poised on his lean head. There was no doubting his quickness of thought. But his reactions came a shade slowly and his pale blue eyes had gazed on a prairie where only patience survived.

"It's D?" he hoped. D surged with the great responsibility of not wanting to disappoint Clear. He liked him on the spot, and he was intrigued by the way efficiency and dreaminess met in him but did not fit exactly, like a face cut in half and the halves restored a millimeter out of true.

"D," said D, in as hearty a way as possible.

"Terrific," said Clear. He stuck out a splay of long, narrow fingers. It was a hand to span a dinner plate, with a dry palm that might have given one last caress to a finished statue, as if the sculptor wanted to say, "Well, there you are, that's the best I can do." And now this hand fell on D's shoulder like an epaulette.

"My word. You're damp," said Clear. "Shower? We have everything here."

"Well," said D. He regarded his soiled state as a measure of integrity.

"Why not?" asked Clear. "I have to run out, anyway. My number just came up on television as a winner, if I can get there in five minutes." He shifted from one foot to another to show the boyish hurry behind his tranquil smile. "Of course, it's nonsense," he added. "But I've never won and I'm curious to see what people do win. The procedure?"

"You should go," urged D.

32

"It's not foolish?" The eyes had gone otter gray. The skin near them ran with deep lines. Clear was so willing to be laughed at.

"You'll be blue later if you don't go," said D, out of unexpected wisdom. It didn't seem like him.

Clear's face rose. "That's exactly it. This is the start of a proper friendship, I can tell." And he contrived in maybe thirty seconds to show D the suite, tell him how the shower worked and take a silver tray of canapés from the refrigerator, without seeming rushed or putting his five-minute deadline in jeopardy. D wanted to ask, "Well, why am I here, then?" But it would be unsporting when Clear was so valiant.

"Good luck," called D.

Clear's face had time to reappear at the doorpost, a milky sun of good will. "Thanks so much, old fellow," he said, and vanished.

D stood for a moment, alone in the suite. There was a large reception area with many other rooms leading off it, some doors flung back, others only ajar, but nothing closed. Degrees of daylight from these rooms seeped into the reception area and mingled with the frosted lilac and vanilla of the overhead. All the machines were working. The carpet felt like spring grass. D walked here and there through the reception area, past artwork and copying machines, admiring throw cushions and the telex. Something like pride filled and refreshed him. It was arousing to be alone in such a spanking place. D had the feeling that anything he touched or needed would be new, exact and ready.

He breathed deep the dry gin air of power and command. But the conditioning tickled his throat. He had a panic of choking. How ghastly to splutter in this groomed silence.

As if the place divined his horror, there came the sound of a piano being played in one of the rooms. Apparently in a far corner of that room. The notes were distant, tender and speculative. It sounded like a blind man tip-tapping a way into the tune, not sure if he was composing or remembering. D thought the melody might be "I Don't Want to Play in Your Yard", but he had a hopeless ear.

He wondered if he should go into that room, greet the pianist, interrupt his revery. Whoever it was had heard his frantic coughing. The tentative notes were a message on the wall to the latest newcomer in a prison. It was a way of saying welcome, but warning don't come in here, I'm here, let me stay here, but don't fret, be of good heart.

D realised there might be several people in the suite, quietly engaged in their tasks or stunned by the ebbing of the day, waiting for night. D looked up, towards the room with the piano. The light coming from there faltered or flinched, not naturally, as if a breeze had blown mist across the failing sun, but methodically. It was as if the aperture in the building had been closed half an f stop. D felt dirty.

He went to the bathroom outlined by Clear. It was a compact chamber of self-improvement, hard to determine in size because all its surfaces were black. When D shut the door, it did not smack or boom closed, but met with the sound of bare feet landing on the ground. Light came on, a suffusion of mooniness where the walls met the ceiling. The room was made of black tile. The towels were black, the soap and the toilet paper. There was even a book on the stool beside the black lavatory bowl, an album of Ad Reinhardt pictures. Did the ebony faucets disgorge black water? It would not be much more trouble, or any less fanciful. How might it feel to be cleansed in a sooty cascade? D imagined black lather on his chest, like curls growing beneath his eyes.

As his timid hand touched his own sad buttons and fasteners, he saw a black bowl of black cherries on the table. They were young and cold, but of a perfect softness that perhaps lasted only an hour. He took one and ate it: authentic juice filled his mouth and worked his jaws until only the pit remained. D dropped it in the dish. This small black room had a mastermind undaunted by the pallor of his body.

D turned his back on the mirror where he had been a fearful, scruffy intruder in the room. He let his hateful clothes drop where they would and he turned on the faucets. The water roared, then preened and sighed as he made adjustments. He stepped into the shower, slid the black doors shut and felt the heat on his back like a lover's support. The small of his back swelled with well-being. If he had had any doubts, his hand immediately found the dry egg of new soap in its recess.

He noticed out of the back of his mind – he was too superstitious or polite actually to observe it – that the water changed as soon as he wished. Both the temperature and the force leaped to meet his desire. He played with this facility. He imagined himself for a moment a slave after a day's labor in torrid Macao: the water began to chill, and soon it was a stream of invigorating cold. Then it was Christmas Eve, and he had been out in the snow chopping down a tree. "Into the shower with you" his family urged, snapping icicles from his nose, before he could have so much as a slice of spiced ginger cake. Then the water steamed and he felt restored by its brave warmth. He let his desires roam. He called for the water to stroke him and the filigree of spray made him giggle. Then he willed its fierceness and his skin tingled with the force of so many stinging droplets. He was laughing out loud with the fun when the water stopped and a recorded voice sounded in the shower, "Thank you". Then there was just D and the piles of silent steam in the black room.

Stepping out of the shower, he saw black towels and a black bathrobe, but his clothes had gone. D was concerned lest some system in the floor tiles had vaporised or consumed them. His key had been in his pants pocket. And there was the key, placed on the corner of the black marble table, beside the bowl of black cherries, replenished. The one pit had gone and a new cherry was in its place. The scene was ready to be replayed – taken again.

"Thank *you*," said D, under his breath, slipping into the bathrobe; it was heavy, embroidered towelling, but soft as mother's love. This phrase came into his head as fully formed and unplanned as the changes in the water. His hand explored the pockets. There was a black case filled with unnamed, unfiltered cigarettes and a lighter in one pocket, and a handy revolver in the other.

He left the bathroom, his feet enjoying the lawn-like texture of the carpet. In the reception area there was a young woman, a quite suddenly gorgeous youthful female creature – he was in love – sitting on the floor doing exercises in time with those offered on television. Her body, D did see, was very white. She wore nothing but the black wool leggings that dancers had in aerobics advertisements. They gave the odd impression of her body having been omitted between her capable white feet and all the white rest above her thighs. The black splash of pubic hair was like a hand holding her black and not-quite-there legs together.

She grinned at him, but did not stop her exercises until the television called for a break.

Then, "Hi," she said, "I'm Drew." She picked up a hand towel and dabbed her armpits. Then she stepped into a black leotard, a wisp of cotton that filled with her. She was a dancer, D assumed, with just the stark white bone of her feet, her hands, her neck and the heartbreak face that came up to D and kissed him. At the same time, her hand (so frail) pushed through the folds of his robe and found his thing. Her hands were cool and mastering. There was no complaining.

Drew squatted. D heard the sinews crackle. Her mouth closed on his thing and worked at it. He was on top of his mountain looking down. He saw her hairs on top of her head. The piano-player tested one note. D was just a loyal prop to this ardent action, being drawn out of himself. He thought of hospital. Her taut throat gulped; she took it all in. He wavered and thought he would fall. So weak, so helpless.

Then there was sound and arrival – Clear. D sought to free himself, but Drew was too determined. Clear did not refer to D's predicament. He was interested in the soft toy he held.

"Look!" he cried. "A teddy bear – isn't it? I don't think I've ever had one."

There was a small noise, as of a vacuum being released. A moist mouthed Drew, still crouched, looked up and said, "You had one once, when you were a little boy."

"I did?" Clear was pierced by lost memory.

Drew was already making herself scarce. "I remember from typing your profile. Bye," she whispered to D. He sniffed the breath of his own life. So salt. And wanted to keep her there.

Clear nodded as if it must be so. He was too delighted to worry. It was an orange bear in a green suit. "D," he sighed. "You've brought me luck. And how are you, old fellow?"

It took a moment for D to see Clear was not addressing the bear.

VIRGINIA KID

He is a boy in war, and a youth in cold war. After the family moves in 1946, he lives on the edge of Washington, in Arlington, where the National Cemetery is located. When he is seven, eight, nine, that cemetery has a steady supply of those who have won special honor dying for their country. In 1944 or 5, such a boy cannot know that there are Americans who do not attend to the running of the country as part of their natural responsibility. He will be politically minded in the way a film fan is Hollywood-minded. He will sometimes seem humorless about this, and he may explain that to himself as a measure of his extra seriousness. If there ever comes a moment when he notices that neither Hollywood nor Washington quite merits intelligence or dedication, then he will have to put himself above it all, too solitary to be taken, too cool to back a loser.

He might be president – if he could make it without first committing to the contest. Could he go from that bedroom closet philosopher, with his private window, his books and the stewing envy of his sister, to being the nation's studio chief? Is there a way all the intervening, democratic fuss could be avoided? Could it be managed so that the humorlessness never comes apart in its owner's hands or lap, so that he never has to see that his integrity has been spoiled?

In later years, people writing about him will fall upon his wry remembrance that, "My earliest childhood ambition was to be President of the United States. That was until I was six years old. At seven I decided to be Governor of Georgia. At eight I decided to become an actor. People become actors because of a need within themselves."

That thought is published in 1962, when Beatty is twenty-five, just arrived on the movie screen. At that time he works hard to imagine what reporters want to hear, and so he may try to give himself a Beaver-like American charm. Today, the remark has become prescient, for the years since have provided a president who was Governor of Georgia first. But in 1962 and 1944 (when Beatty is seven), that ambition testifies to the place of the South and civic duty in his mind. Of course, no one interviews kids when they are seven except the kids themselves, lying on the floor in their closed rooms, filling the light of the window with their future, chatting away in their heads or out loud to the only properly respectful world, the one they can invent.

Perhaps the kid has such thoughts, and then thinks of being a bum, a nobody, by the time he is ten or eleven – not a true nobody, but one like Vag, the emblematic vagrant, in Dos Passos's *U.S.A.*, or Montgomery Clift in the movie *A Place in the Sun*, a dark stripling hitch-hiking, backing towards and then turning to face the camera. And the camera says, that's someone. *A Place in the Sun* opens in 1951, when Warren is fourteen.

The new actor in Hollywood in 1962 is organising the way people think of him. But to be famous one day, he may have begun early, talking to himself with the patience of a Washington reporter, schooling his mind in the solitude of his closet on the humble jokes that become celebrities. A kid imagines himself famous already. Most go on to failure and dismay. Yet Warren Beatty has not failed, or has not let failure register. The most intriguing possibility of the 1962 story is that the teller still had some sense of being a destined child. The very ordinariness the story seems to pose and polish could be a role founded in the child's inexperience of being thwarted. The purest power in America is having your fantasy realised. Such hopes can still exist in men far more affected by age, grind and disappointment than Warren Beatty. If Ronald Reagan can survive his errors and unfitness, it may be because the shortcomings never adhere to his dream. In any manipulation of the media, the most vital mind to sway is the first one that will entertain the impossible dream. For if *you* can believe, you can make anyone follow you.

The Beatys are Baptists; they are taught to be truthful, clean and meticulous; they are children in awe of their parents. There is even a year, 1945–6, when the father works as principal at an elementary school in Arlington. Warren is taught to read at four, by his father, so he is able to follow newspaper accounts of Pearl Harbor and keep up with the course of the war, as well as the Little Henry cartoon in the comics section. He is called Little Henry by the family. He is a pretty little boy with a gentle, brilliant smile; his dark hair is parted on the right and much curlier than it will be. He has a large collection of toy cars, and he will grow up knowing all the details of 1950s automobiles. He does his homework, he listens to his parents and his sister; he talks to himself and he absorbs his parents' love of the arts.

His school record is not outstanding. Between them, the daughter and son of two teachers will amass one year of college after which Warren backs off because the educational system is not serious enough. In later years he will be called an omnivorous reader, an extraordinary memory, a tenacious arguer and negotiator. But those who observe these traits remark on the way he imposes his own terms on discussion and dealing. Like the self-educated, with equal amounts of pride and insecurity, Beatty is not always emotionally capable of being defeated. His intelligence has worked towards what we might call self-improvement, not the fostering of general discourse and debate. And for the self to stay improved, it cannot be wrong. This timidity trusts no one else with its education. Years later, on the set of *Reds*, when some people marvel that there is no script, Diane Keaton will observe that Warren is keeping it all in his head. That speaks for the capacity and power of the head, and for its need for advantage and privacy. It also shows an ignorance of how the ordinary educated man may use a library, and know that knowledge is there outside his head – safe, unstealable.

Self-improvement, after all, can be absolute and abstract; or it can be driven by competition. It can be a very American pursuit, idealistic yet paranoid. It can lead to those sad testaments of self-nagging like Jay Gatz's *Schedule* in which the Mid-West nobody who would one day be the supreme but unrecognised host at his own great parties set himself to do dumbbell exercises, to "practice elocution, poise and how to attain it", to study needed inventions, give up smoking and chewing, "read one improving book or magazine per week" and "be better to parents." Little Henry has a grandmother who teaches elocution, and he will be an actor who takes pride in never speaking clearly.

He goes to Washington-Lee High School in Arlington, and when he is thirteen he is challenged by a teacher and a system because he spends all his time with books when he is plainly the best athlete in the school. He switches. He takes up every sport and becomes an exceptional football player. Yet he is not a wide receiver, not a running back or a quarter-back (the position he gives his character in *Heaven Can Wait*). He is a center: at the nub of battering contact, without much chance of touch-downs, visible glory or space in the game reports. But he is over six feet, and his weight is close to 200 pounds. He is a big boy and, briefly, a team player. He makes president of his high school class. Football has become very important to him: it earns him offers of ten scholarships to college, in the era before face-masks. Singer John Phillips, from a rival school, remembers, that, on the gridiron, he was called "Mad Dog Beaty".

It is easier now to think of him as a coach or a field general. If football is ever his game, it must be because of its scope for planning. Yet all a center has to do is urge himself forward across a foot or so of overshadowed ground into the collision with his blocker. The center is a large body the general wants, and can replace. Within a few years, Beatty will scorn football. He does not follow it much now; he does not take an interest in sport. He explains his earlier involvement as "Maybe it has to do with at a certain age in high school you want to prove you're a man."

In 1985, *People* magazine runs a story on misfit kids who grew up to be showbiz stars. It has comments from Cher, Woody Allen, Barbra Streisand, and so on; and it includes Warren. *People* does not get him to speak, but it quotes *the mother of a friend*: "Warren would come to my house, sweep in and give me a big theatrical kiss. He gave the impression of being self-confident; actually, he was essentially a loner, never wanting to be committed and tied down."

People prints a picture of Warren at seventeen, his large, rather jowly jaw, his fat grin and his sultry teen eyes all pressed down by a savage cropped haircut. He looks like a brash stud athlete who could so flirt with friends' mothers that they'd recall a kiss thirty years later and the impossibility of tying him down. In five years' time, on Broadway, Warren will be playing a provincial kid who goes to bed with a friend of his mother. And in 1985, in *People*, the cocky 50s grin is saying, "Is that right, Mrs . . . | I actually kissed you? I did?" When he is famous he will look back on his school years as those of "a cheerful hypocrite".

*

"I think he graduated in . . .," the biographer stumbles. He is not above feigning dullness, for sometimes rescuers volunteer the most.

"55," says the woman's voice. "He graduated the same year as me."

"Oh, really . . ." Oh, really. This woman is a Mrs L-----, secretary now, in 1985, to the principal of the Washington-Lee High School. The biographer has come upon her by chance in an effort to ascertain that Warren's father, Ira, never taught at Washington-Lee. (He didn't; he had given up teaching for real estate.)

"Did you know him well?" he asks his newfound treasure, wondering what "well" will mean to her.

"Well . . . I didn't know him 'well'. He was class president and all those good things."

The biographer sighs. He might call back, of course, might make friends with Mrs L-----, ask for her home phone, or urge her to call him collect when she is out of the office. And so perhaps at home at night she fidgets round her phone until Mr Lasks, "What *are* you doing?", and she explains, and he says, "He'll just want dirt," and Mrs L has to decide whether to betray or whether to admit she was always outside the charmed circle that might have had the dirt. She does not call, and the biographer does not call again.

But he notes the way in which a class president, center of so many "good things", is lost to the school while someone never quite in the swim now works there every day, nine to five, an hour for lunch. Speculate: do not call. This is an imaginative biography. And, anyway, as Mrs L tells the biographer, Washington-Lee has no alumni organization where one might round up the good things gang. No alumni organization? Is that Warren covering his tracks?

*

In 1954, the summer before his senior year in high school, he hangs around the National Theater in Washington D.C. He is hired as the kid who will stay out in the alley every evening to scare off the rats. The theatre has been invaded by rats; an actor has been bitten. And so Warren Beaty waits in the alley, with sticks and stones maybe, a big boy with a Baptist dread of rats, while Helen Hayes works inside on a production of Thornton Wilder's *The Skin of Our Teeth*. The play is a parable about how easily the world might end, and brave families with it, and this is 1954 with Eisenhower president, the H-bomb shared by Russia and America, in the lull between Dien Bien Phu and "Vietnam". It is just before rock and roll and James Dean.

Piano player

D was far from home, even if this splendid suite was only a city's breadth from the apartment where he lived. He might have felt as homesick as an African slave dressed in silks as a lady's toy in a Nash house. Amid such ease and grace – when the flicker of need in his numb head was leaped at by supple bodies – he could not forget the harder lot of those at home. Then again, he had never been serviced so comprehensively as he had been by Drew. He remained puzzled whether he had been technically unfaithful. After all, it had been her idea, her power, with D simply a baby, made all the more absurd because he was giving her suck. But he had been pleased. It perplexed D that he could measure technical ethics where something like desire seemed to have been involved. Nor was he accustomed to lounging in a designer robe with a gun in its pocket, his toes delighting in the carpet and the cool azulejo tiles.

But if ever D feared fainting from embarrassment, there was Clear with some small question – the date of Magna Carta? the credits of Clifton Webb? – to set D on his feet again. And talking of those feet, when Drew reappeared with a silver tray of drinks – she was dressed for company now, in a pink sheath – she looked at the floor in amazement. D thought he must have dropped something. But Drew's voice was somber with wonder.

"Oh, those feet. I don't think I have ever . . . ." The ice in the drinks shivered. "Clear, have you . . .? They are the most amazing, I only just noticed them. Who, I have to know, you have a podiatrist? Clear, have you seen D's feet?"

Clear was smiling with contentment. "Among the first things I appreciated in D." He had the gentlest way of saying this. It seemed to tell the air why, yes, D's feet were majestic; but likely D shrank to hear this mentioned so much; not that Drew should feel brash for speaking; she had only declared her heart, and wasn't that the stuff of life, recommended in Humanities 101 and TV Inspirationals?

Piano player

"Those feet are Praxiteles," said Drew. "Tell me they aren't."

"I won't," whispered Clear. "But the ears are nobler. If you can pick some murderers by their ears, D must be a saint." Drew's gaze came up, like a Grand Canyon telescope, unlocked by a coin, and Clear slipped D away to meet others, leaving Drew in a pose of resolute awe.

Clear seemed to give all his thought to putting others at ease, yet this left no trace of weariness or resentment in him. He was *for* others, a sort of service. D had never met such benevolence.

"Eyes is fortunate to have you," he said.

"Well . . . his sort are lonely, you know – masters of the world, but so shy."

"It's the reticence that is most magical," said D. "In this age of pressing and boosting."

Clear's arm rose and settled on D's shoulder: it was a garland of team spirit. "Just look at that," said Clear, for they were at a vast window, confronting the city.

The last flare of amber fell across the view to their right as the sun dropped into the sea. The buildings were gray and mauve, except when their windows held a final coppery facet of the sun. The streetlights were on and along the highways every vehicle was pushing and dragging its small jewels through clots of smoke and cloud. A fabulous threat fluttered in the view. It was the passion of evanescence, like seeing a face make up its mind. It was in the harmony of twilight and man's lighting schemes, and in the contrast of their vantage and the muddied infinity of the hot, hectic city, a fever of business on the ground and a dust that seemed in danger of being wiped away.

"Now, D," asked Clear, "where are you?"

D reached out for an area of the dying fire beyond the bright light of the smarter zone. "There," he said, as if he was touching C and the children.

Clear peered forward. His nose quietly bumped the glass, and he murmured in amused surprise. The place was a measurable distance away, yet it was another level of location, a part of the far indigo grime from which Clear could now say he had met someone.

"I should be going back, I think," said D. The nearness haunted him.

"Not yet," Clear whispered. "It's too soon."

D looked wistfully at the spot he had picked. How could he admit it all looked alike from here? He had insisted he knew where home was; it had such desirability when he was away. He felt warm tears of separation sliding down his face.

43

"D," said Clear, full of soothing discretion. "Please don't fret. We'll have you there very soon. It's touching that you miss them. Why, the last fellow we had in, he looked me straight in the eye, and do you know what he said?"

D shook his head: it made his teeth ache.

"He had a family or some-such out there, and he said, 'Mr Clear, call me callous, but do away with them. Please. You want, I'll go there and do it myself. But I can't take this failure much longer.' He was garish. Not a bad writer, though."

"What did you do?"

"Oh, we hired him as a bodyguard. I told him it was nothing to be ashamed of. But we do keep an eye on him. I'm not confident he wouldn't go out there on his day off and slaughter them all. For attention. There is often a suppressed killer in a good bodyguard."

"I guessed the same." D nearly said it to himself.

"Why, of course you did," Clear remembered with pleasure. "It's one of the scenes we most enjoyed."

"You've read the script already?"

"Oh, yes. We get instant print-outs. You can't wait for final submissions these days. I was reading it as it was typed. Typists have their little side-lines. May I say, here and now, without prejudice to any future negotiation – a work of genius, D." Clear licked his lips. "And as you know me better, you will find I do not use that word lightly."

"Has Eyes read it?" asked D, sticking to the straight line.

"Not yet. No so far. Or, I don't believe so."

"He must be so busy." D was furious with himself for having presumed.

"In a way," Clear agreed.

"Is he here? This evening?" D ventured.

Whereupon Clear lightly struck his brow. "Good Lord, I never thought to say. D, what have you been thinking? I haven't even introduced you. I tell you – and please don't tell another soul – I have too much to do. You find me at a vulnerable moment."

"I wouldn't say a word."

"That's your quality, your rareness. Others, of course, would expose me."

"Loyalty is the ticket," said D.

"You must meet Eyes," Clear had made up his mind. This was the best reward he could imagine. "Did you hear him earlier?"

D had been on the track all along. "The piano player?"

Clear chuckled. "You're too sharp. He's there now, I think. Come along, won't you?"

Like a messenger from some outer part of the empire, D followed Clear into the most private lounge. There was a white grand piano on the far side of the room, and someone sitting at it, but hidden by the raised lid. Drew was squatting on the floor, easing away hard dry skin from the player's feet with pumice stone. There was a worldly tilt to her lovely head, as if she dreamed of greater feet. The piano player's right hand was drifting idly in her hair, as the left picked over the pieces of a melody.

"Here we are," Clear announced, and then, "No, don't go," as Drew made to disappear from the big meeting.

She settled again and the legs above the bare feet she had been grooming straightened. A blinding image of a man stood up. He wore white slacks and a cream shirt. He was the right sort of height and build; with the same aura, more or less. His head seemed to have been dipped in aroused, headstrong hair. He had a tip-top air of retiring grandeur. He was emphatically *there*, yet receding, sentimentally drawn to vanishing. It looked like Eyes – as far as anyone can look like a picture. The spectacle had all the poignance of the real thing at last revealed, like Angkor Wat still there in the jungle, secure and mysterious.

But . . . wasn't the context more persuasive than the image itself? Was this Eyes or just the mask of beauty, incapable of his authentic, devouring look?

FRESHMAN

Why does he go to college in September 1955, and why is he no longer there a year later? Is this part of a plan already, the traces of solitariness or reluctance to work with others? Does he calculate in advance that he can spare one year of "waste" so that, in years to come, anyone may look back and hear Warren Beatty muttering to himself (at a School of Speech) that the system is not good enough? Is a part of him already living in reverse, arranging biography as a mystery, with the wishfulness-waiting-for-genius of a kid piano-player taking apart tunes?

Some young people go so automatically to college, they do not have to absorb its philosophy. They go because it is there, and has been expected of them, and because the going averts some tougher choices waiting in the dark. College can be a safe way of leaving home; in the mid 1950s it has the promise of smoking, booze and sex, accretions of illicit worldliness. Some American colleges are the slackest way imaginable of carrying the young forward into the national dream of success. Whatever else they teach, they instil an hysterical approach to learning that crams and forgets, and an air of casualness that could go on forever. It is a moment at which absurdity can enter American life, and middle-class repression explode in indulgence, all in the name of making good minds.

It is not easy in an American college to explore intelligence without feeling opposed to the system. That is one more of its crippling conditions, something contributed to by any student's share of flat, passable classes and back-slapping alumni organisations hitting him for donations as soon as he graduates. You learn those economics, whatever your major. You see that higher education can be a transaction in which a degree is purchased by so much accumulated tuition and residence, with courses and grades to suggest you got this or that percentage of the product. It is a process not designed to make you think, but to prepare you for process. And we are talking of the middle 1950s, of the Eisenhower era, before alternative curricula, student government and a world panorama to make America doubt itself.

This is a general description few feel driven to make in the 1950s. And if the American college was then, and is still now, indicative of the business ethic, a kind of societal and work preparation program, then we may consider the possible virtue in one kid, raised to it, the son of an educator, breaking away after his freshman year.

Warren Beaty enters the School of Speech at Northwestern University, at Evanston, Illinois, a northern suburb of Chicago, to be a drama major. An attraction of the school is the drama teacher, Alvina Krause. But Northwestern is not an acting school or a place that offers professional training. It is a university that requires a liberal arts major to meet basic standards in English, mathematics, a foreign language and to have had some experience with science and social science. Charlton Heston has been there, and in 1955 he is playing Moses in *The Ten Commandments*. No student can spend all of his or her time in the theater, and no would-be actor can escape the assumption by the institution that he or she will be a better artist knowing about the world.

It is reasonable to propose that an actor should read novels and history, listen to music and watch dance; that he may understand the ways of rendering character better if he is acquainted with biology and biochemistry – what is happening in Iago's brain and Hamlet's body chemistry?; that he will be more alert in Strindberg if he knows Swedish history and geography; that he can bring more to Restoration Comedy if he knows what was being restored and why; that he can be a surer Moses if he believes in the Law; that he can hardly be serious in experimenting with the psychology of characters if he does not read Freud; and, finally, how will he play Shylock if he does not grasp the principles of interest?

An actor could know all there is to know . . . or does he only need to sense the range of everything in which he can create his particular person on the stage or screen? It is a problem like that of the biographer, torn between research and writing. But people anxious to know as much as possible about everything, and people dedicated to stringent application of the laws of evidence, do not seem to go into acting. It has a better record with liars and dreamers. The stage does beckon those with a special, heightened mixture of insecurity and arrogance, knowing nothing but the lines, their part and the cues. They want the stage, they want to take it over, so their pain, their indecision, their pause, can reign there.

Actors want to get on stage and do it; they want the lights, a scene, the dark, an audience, applause and a pay check. They will tolerate a script, a character, a director, other actors and quite extensive theories if they can get on stage and act. But they soon learn the need to know agents, producers and contacts as well as Aristotle and the texts of Antonin Artaud.

The actors who do make it will range from those who regard thinking about what they do as like walking under ladders to those who can talk-show for a year and a day on stage stories. But in 1955–6 there is in America a passionate fusion of practice and theory, a way of justifying self-absorption. If we think of one college student facing it, in 1955, it is not hard to see the Method as harbinger of all the intensity of self-determination that distracts American campus life ten years later. And to the extent that Lee Strasberg's Method acting is a celebration of movie presence, there are Method politics, in which our votes may fall, with our sympathy, into those wry presidential shrugs, shucks and pauses that fill television. Here is the apotheosis of not knowing but winning. Ronald Reagan has no superior at offering problems a cheery, polite "God bless". Much Method acting has been more agonized. It is still the case that the Method and the close-up have made the act of thinking hallowed, and given it a potency that goes far beyond the reach of thinking itself. We are talking about the desire to know, as romantic as knowledge is realistic. And we are trying to explain the look on Warren's waiting, intelligent face.

There are always reasons for dropping out of college: you can easily suppose you are wasting your time if you accept the college-based theory of the measurability of things; you may be irritated at the humorless way in which the Introduction to Drama always starts at 10.10 a.m.; because you are a freshman you may get no parts in any production, or because you are afraid of being rejected you may not try-out for parts; you may realise that you are part of a community in which most members are trying to become like one another; you may notice that, whatever their claims and hopes, teachers never have enough time to teach enough; you may worry that you are not out in the world, but enclosed in a place for which the term "intramural" was invented; you may want a way of rebuking your parents' expectations; you may be a lazy no-good bum more interested in laying a wider range of females than coeds constitute; you may have been struck rigid that a few days after you began your college career, on September 30, 1955, James Dean was killed, aged twenty-four.

At Northwestern, Beaty dates some, especially a girl named Ellie Wood. He knows athletes, but he doesn't do sports himself. He sings a song in a show. He lives in a dorm, he takes classes, and then he gets out. In the years since, he gives two oblique commentaries on his departure. He says that the Northwestern approach to acting was "slovenly, lackadaisical". And in 1967, he tells Rex Reed about one encounter with a jock:

> "A guy actually became an all-American. He was big and he was tough. He was from Ohio. I rather liked him. One night I came home late to a freshman dorm and they said, 'So-and-so is really sick, got drunk tonight, and he's asking for you. He vomited in the mens' room.' 'How sick was he?' I asked. 'Go in and see.' I saw, for one second, a whole cabbage, a carrot, an unchewed lamb chop – I said, 'Man, I'm too sensitive for *this*!' And I quit."

So he has very little of what is called a higher education – which may mean he knows he must learn on his own. He flinches from packed male company – he does confess to being more at ease with women. That he is, for a time, a drop-out, may account for dismay in his parents. That he becomes, so soon, a success could obscure the fact that he may have been ready to stay a drop-out. The sequence helps him believe in himself, and in no external entities. There may be no alternative for him to being a king or an outcast, best of all a role that partakes of both. To be alone, to stay private, becomes more appealing as the crowd presses in, more dense, more likely to vomit. But what a pressure on this loner if he also wants to be famous. He may smile as he hears of Dean's death, seeing past our loss, knowing now Dean is famous forever and free from the vomit. He may imagine himself as Dean, enjoying the nihilistic liberty, hurrying away from the bogus camaraderie of college.

*

Years later, the biographer calls Northwestern University. He is put through to the Evanston campus, and then to the office of the Registrar, which listens to his query and says, "You need Verification." It is clearly a capital V, no matter that that department or resort turns out to be a smart, amused kid, someone on work study and maybe going through *Madame Bovary* with a yellow underlining pen as he mans the phone. He has, perhaps, just remarked on "Emma was like all his mistresses; and the charm of novelty, gradually falling away like a garment, laid bare the eternal monotony of passion," with a note to himself that this is more than just French, when he gets this guy on the phone asking about Warren Beatty at Northwestern.

The biographer has to stay on hold for several minutes before the student comes back, sauntering, cockily, let's goose this guy, with, "Sir, I have an H. Warren Beaty, one t. Did you know that?"

"Aha," the biographer sighs. And, yes, a year, fall 55 to spring 56, in the School of Speech. "What courses?" the biographer wonders, a little shocked to hear himself prompting garrulousness.

"Oh, I couldn't tell you that, sir."

The biographer has expected confidentiality, and has no wish to trick it. But the kid at Evanston is quite a character; one can hear his grin. It's the voice that goes with that highschool picture of crew-cut Warren. And so the biographer murmurs something about whether H. was in good standing – and would be still, presumably, could go back and pick up where he left off? The kid might like that: "Hey, Warren, split a brew?" The quality of those freshman grades is what the biographer is wondering about – not so much the specifics as their tone.

"Well," the Evanston Flaubert hesitates, surveying the old grade card and grinning again to see courses that are still torture, "he didn't do so great, but he didn't fail anything." There is a pause, as two innocents wait to see how worldly they can be. "All right?"

And the biographer does not even have a name to add to the Acknowledgements, even if for an instant it has *been* Warren, or at least H. Warren Beaty.

Wheel of Fortune

D never knew it, but Clear stayed outside, peering through the door's crack to see if D would pick up the trick.

There was a video camera aimed at the piano player at his white piano and at Drew, attending to his feet. Its pictures played on a large television screen set just inside the door and in the pianist's easy line of sight. D perceived the triangular arrangement, the hallowed "there" being repeated on the screen, like a nose pursuing itself across a cubist face. He moved aside so as not to impede the star's view and stepped round the prow of the grand. Looking to make sure the screen was visible, he saw his furtive self slip into the picture.

"There you are, kiddo," the man sighed. He was happier talking to the image of D. The frame was pleasing, with most of the piano, the man at its controls, swivel-faced D and Drew's delectable head at the bottom of the frame like the silver ball in a puzzle that one must coax into some shallow hole without disturbing the other elements.

"Well then, D," said the man. "Old Didi," he crooned. "Dee-dee-I-oh. Diddle di-dee fiddle di-dee. Dee-dipity-dee. Dee-di-daddy-o." And then a lengthy amount of yodelling on the dee-dily-deadly scheme, rising to a climax with "Yes indeedee!" D was horrified; there must be a mistake. This wasn't Eyes.

"That's neat," murmured Drew. She was bowed over, moving so slightly, as patient and painless with his horny feet as water depleting rock in the Dordogne caves. D could see the tranquility in being slave to a god on Earth. He noticed, not for the first time, the appeal of inventive forms of imprisonment. Liberty had had its historical rage. Most slavery could be adjusted to if it was not rushed. Only suddenness alarmed.

D wondered if the actor was contemplating the role of Gershwin, Liszt or Liberace in a biopic, judging how he might look in a keyboard shot. Key-bored, D decided. This man was stagnant or stupefied. As the scales were eased from his feet so they seemed to have formed on his soul.

There was none of the liveliness of the real Eyes, only glossy, stale resemblance.

With a lunge and a snarl, the man's hand came up from the keys to a channel-selector. He cut from the lulling self-enshrinement to a game show. The tense noise of a studio audience filled the room.

"Wheel of Fortune," the man announced. It was like telling the time.

Drew looked at the host in his plaid soup jacket quivering in the electric storm. Then she smiled at D. He was struck that she had more focus than the piano man. She was attentive; she had interest and warmth; she saw feelings pass. Was she a better actress than the star? D looked at this alleged Eyes: the head was transfixed by the game show, but so slow, so coarse. D had to face his disappointment. Then he looked at Drew again. Did she read his reading? She was inspecting the piano-player in a sly and mocking way, her brow furrowed with the labor of his thought. And then she winked at D, as if to say, what a stiff, this "Eyes", and what fools they were to go along with him.

"It's a phrase," said the piano-player, nodding with the explosive discoveries of the game show.

Wearily, Drew gave another glance to the screen. D looked, too: it seemed polite to join in. Surely, soon, this dreadful, unlikely Eyes would want to discuss plans. He would probably dismiss Drew then, D thought gloomily. There was something necessary about her. She might be sewing down there on the floor, stitching up this unresolved scene.

The game was hanging on a four-word phrase:

T-- ---T-- -- -TT--T---

"Shit," said the piano player. "This is hard." Drew smiled in an absent-minded way.

Then a contestant, a flight attendant from Buena Vista, called for an N and Vanna White swished forward in her cherry-colored slant-cut dress, and Ns rattled into frame against a crackle of applause:

T-- --NT-- -- -TT-NT--N

"That last word's giving me a headache," the man cried.

"I think it's ATTENTION, baby," said Drew, studying his feet. Did she have the image screened for her in his big toenail?

"It is? Yeah? It could be."

"So," said Drew. "What's the first word gonna be. Gonna be an article, don't you think?"

Another contestant, a black schoolteacher from Palms, asked for an H, and the first word could only be THE.

"Only one H, though," the pianist grumbled, and he urged the players to buy a vowel. But they pushed on, sportsmen all, until the third of them, a body-builder and encyclopedia salesman from Lancaster, hit on C:

TH- C-NT-- -- -TT-NT--N

"I know!" he yelled. "The Country of Attention."

"I don't think so, honey," said Drew. "It doesn't fit. I think they want an R."

"Yeah?" he struggled with this clue. His face crinkled, like the land mass in a time-lapse movie about continental cooling. Then he bounced on the piano stool and shouted out "The Central is Attention!"

Drew laughed, as if a ghost had tickled her. "That's not a phrase," she told him.

"The Center of Attention," said D, quietly. He had not meant to speak but the coincidence would not stay modest.

"I bet you're right," said Drew. She was looking straight at him, not smiling, but entirely concerned to see what was happening to him. He faced her, but her gaze was too strong for him. D blinked. His head dropped. He was such a sissy. And the piano player was bellowing, for he and the flight attendant from Buena Vista had solved the puzzle. His noise precluded the risk that another had been there first. He stood up and moved forward to look at the prizes. His feet gone, Drew looked at the window and the night, an estimating smile on her face. Was she seeing all the way to the desert where the night was an hour older?

The flight attendant was claiming her bounty: kitchen machinery, a year in Hawaii and a jigsaw puzzle of the home of Wayne Newton on which his face was superimposed. It looked like a puzzle testing enough for all that year in Hawaii while the kitchen steel festered.

"Pussy time," announced the man. He had to have some prize.

"Not now," said Drew, but she was warning D. He heard her fear of the star's brutal whim.

With one quick movement, the man brought down the lid of the piano. The room vibrated with crushed notes. "Up you go," he said, and Drew was dragged onto the smooth white surface.

"D shouldn't –" Drew began.

"He stays." The man's blunt finger prodded D's papery chest.

D could only watch. The man's hands tore away the pink of Drew's clothing; she was left as pale as the white lid. He dropped his head into her profuse dark bush. His head was lost in it. No wonder he sounded afraid.

He was eating, lapping, snorting over her. Drew's face was only a foot from D's hand. Her eyes were blank; he wanted to tilt his face to see if there was any expression. But soon her face could not resist the tremors coming from his animal intrusion. Her light body was bubbling on the piano. When the player looked up for air, drool was hanging from his gunmetal fillings. Then he plunged down again and Drew groaned. It could have been the piano's broken chords rising to protect her. But the cry that came next was hers.

She was sliding helplessly towards a climax when her gaze caught D's and looked at the channel selector. D understood. But how did the tool work? He struck at it until he found the answer. On the set, across the room, the game show was wiped away by a diagonal spectrum and replaced by the old standard, the piano, and Drew's turmoil. Sounds of feeding and surrender came from the set. Drew's head turned to watch herself. The scene went on, all its action and terror. Her face was contorted, but her eyes rose in sympathy: she had become the show.

D could not stay there. He staggered away from the piano – the man was too intoxicated to notice – and he went out into the larger room. There were several more people there now. But D did not look at any of them. He was walking, he did not know where, when Clear's arm stopped him.

"What ever –?"

"Horrible! That man . . ."

"Yes?"

"It cannot be Eyes. I may be a fool. But this is a creature without tenderness or spirit or . . ."

"Humor?" suggested Clear. "Of course it isn't him. This is his idiot stand-in. And you knew it, you champ." He embraced the trembling D. The two men swayed together, and D thought he must faint. But over Clear's shoulder, D saw the naked scrap of Drew in the doorway, so weak she clutched the door, but eager to see what D thought and felt.

HEALTH

He goes to New York. In 1956, in all of America, where else can a Northwestern drop-out go and expect to retain the least reputation for seriousness? And wanting to be taken seriously is already palpable – it may be a little like fear in combat or the guarded edge that makes women believe he is interesting. He wants to be taken seriously; he wants to be respected. And so he makes himself aloof, as if to say, look, he doesn't care about those very things.

No matter that he gives every indication in the next few New York years of wanting to be an actor, still at the time and years later he says he is not/was not ever sure. Maybe it was a director he was going to be. Don't mark him down. Don't be sure you ever know what Warren's intending. It is so much harder to fail if your own needs stay masked. Other people do not see your depression or disappointment. You may even keep your own simple limits for yourself if you can believe you are so clever a fellow you have ambitions intricate enough and necessarily veiled so that no one knows them. The country and the leader secure against espionage is the one who has no plan. If there is, finally, nothing final to be found out, why, possibility goes on forever. You can get a reputation for being dreamy, floating somewhere between the sublime and the downright humorless.

"You know, I think there is no such thing as reality," Shirley MacLaine says in her one-woman stage show. It's all a matter of perspective. That very same principle could be the motto for a handsome, formidable, very intelligent ghost. In 1956, we are on the edge of an age where being thought of will come to rival being. Acting, for that sort of philosopher or adventurer, could be less a profession than a kind of yoga of the soul, and a way towards flexibility and emptiness. Sometimes the very great personalities feel most conscious of their own nothingness.

"I don't think either of us ever seriously considered that we *wouldn't* be able to make something of ourselves. We *had* to; it was the only way we'd have any respect for ourselves. We *wanted* to live up to whatever our potentials might be. The frustrating spectacle of people who hadn't, who had been afraid to, and were bitterly disappointed in themselves as a result, had been crippling to us in many ways as we grew up; but, on the other hand, their failures and frustrations had been so clear that Warren and I had a precise blueprint of how *not* to be."

That is Shirley, years later, thinking about her parents, herself and her brother. She had gone to New York in 1952. She had an apartment at 116th Street and Broadway, a succession of roommates, crackers and honey and auditions. She was broke by the time she got an audition for the Servel Ice-Box Trade Show which was going on the road. She got noticed.

" 'You mean me, sir?' I asked timidly.
" 'Yeah. What's your name?'
" 'Shirley Beaty, sir.'
" 'Shirley Batty? That's a funny name.'
" 'Not Batty. Beaty.'
" 'Yeah, that's what I said: Beauty.'
" 'Not Beauty, Bay-tee.'
" 'OK, so it's BAY-TEE. Don't you have a middle name or something?'
" 'Yes, sir – MacLaine.'
" 'OK, Shirley MacLaine, you're hired.' "

So those long legs go on the road to arouse gatherings of travelling salesmen to the virtues of refrigerators. With such nightmarish confusion of being hot and cold, it may be as well to reassure yourself you are nothing but a figure in the light going through those motions. No, it's not me; it's just the part.

By 1954, Shirley had got the task of being understudy to Carol Haney, one of the leads in what would be a hit show, *The Pajama Game*. It opened when Warren was 17, and then Carol Haney broke her ankle. In going to New York, in the family, Warren was showing his foolishness. One child had gone into show business – against advice and tradition – and she had been a success. But she had striven for it throughout her childhood; she was so outgoing; and she was a girl, pretty and vivacious. Warren had always seemed so much more serious and reticent. There had been talk of him becoming a lawyer. Did he now expect that the mad future that makes a success in show business – not to mention stars – would hit on one small family twice? Shirley must have been asked to dissuade him. He must have been warned that he was making a fool of himself; he must have wondered if he was so immature, so under-developed, that he could only see the path that his sister had pioneered. And could aloofness work where she had needed all of her drive and all her great appetite for change?

But he went to New York and, like a cool guy who didn't dance, he took acting lessons at the Stella Adler Studio. This is the short hard time of Warren Beatty – the second "t" comes in in these years – in which he has as the center of his life something that doesn't pay. In a few years' time, by the time he is twenty-five, he will be considering and refusing offers that would look magical to the peanut-butter-sandwich brigade who want to be actors. And by that stage, he will no longer have interest in being a theater actor. For this kid "makes it" not in a hit show where the star has a mishap and youth is thrown "on", with the audience's applause ready to mingle with the cheers of history and posterity, already attending to the larger show. No, Warren Beatty is in one Broadway play, a flop, in a company that goes away convinced of his intractability, and he has never yet tried another play. He is not quite the trouper, not exactly like the sister who, at fifty, is doing eight performances a week of her one-woman show in the course of which she tells the audience that you're cheering or you're not, you call a glass half-empty or half-full, and that you have to love yourself before you can love others, whereupon a female voice in the audience shouts out "Don't tell Warren," and Shirley says, "You have great taste," and the audience laughs so warmly that maybe even Shirley thinks it was a warm remark.

So Warren lives in a room on West 68th Street, a furnished room for $24 a month. "It was a junk heap," he said. "I mean a real junk heap because a junkie had lived there before. And the smell was still there." Did the kid who flinched at a football player's vomit lie awake warm summer nights inhaling and reeling in that sinister smell? Did he know what it was? Do junkies smell more than or different from other deadbeats? How do out-of-work actors smell? Or is it a line from a picture about a kid who has really lived, had it tough? Is it a line dropped in a reporter's notebook with a wry grin?

He works at this and that, apparently: he washes dishes, helps a brick-layer, he is a sand hog in the Lincoln Tunnel, one of the crew carving out its third tube – or so it is said – this is back-flap territory, the early life of the later great that lists so many unlikely jobs and which might be God's truth or the bitterness of fame that has known anonymity and says how much nonsense will these idiots take. It is the

Catherine Deneuve in *The Hunger*

Andrew Dasburg in *Reds* (Paramount)

short life in which I once saw that William Faulkner had been a factory caretaker and wrote *As I Lay Dying* between midnight and two a.m. Just one two-hour slog? I thought. It is a short book, and I knew what I was meant to expect of genius.

But Warren has to have money for the rent, the acting classes and the peanut-butter sandwiches. So he does this and that, and maybe there is some money coming from home or even from Shirley. By 1956, she has made *The Trouble with Harry, Artists and Models* and *Around the World in Eighty Days.*

It seems a little more interesting that occasionally – it may be no more than once or twice, and even unpaid – he plays cocktail bar lounge piano at Clavins on East 58th Street. He does play; he enjoys jazz. And in all his later work, the aroma or aura of these shabby days in New York City is captured only once, in *Mickey One*, one of his stranger, least known pictures, in which he plays a nerve-racked nightclub entertainer, a comic and a piano player. *Mickey One* is a low life picture about a kid who goes undercover in some unnamed city (a city out of Kafka by Orson Welles) because he thinks the mob, or even the Mob, is after him.

Is it? Who knows. Reality is wondering. In *Mickey One*, Warren is unshaven and dirty. It is a black-and-white film, with a feeling for exotic poverty and human wreckage. But it ends with the camera craning up above a penthouse where Mickey - rehabilitated, cocky again – is hammering out chic jazz, like Erroll Garner in a Concert by the Night. More of the film anon, but it is a window on Beatty's sense of the lustre in performing.

And he contracts hepatitis at this time, and is so sick he has to go home to Arlington to be looked after.

*

The question of health arises. The young man has made his attempt on fame and been compelled to come home with a serious illness, one that can leave lasting weakness in the organism, and one supposed to accompany reckless and unhygienic living. "You've not taken care of yourself," he is told, and he has to work out a reply about the risk if he is to protect his dangerous ambitions.

He has worked in tunnels and lived in rooms sour from junkies. What happens to a face deprived of sunlight and washed over by junkie atmosphere? What happens to any face that grows old, exposed to the elements of unhappiness and failure in which the face is known only to those who meet you and see you in life? This is the kind of face a mother looks at every day to judge whether the yellow is receding from the eyeballs. It is a face that must look up at the inspection of the mother, whose face "no one" would recognise. Real life, ordinary life, is truly the secret territory for those whose faces are famous.

Suppose he takes a safer line with his life, in real estate or business? Suppose he becomes an unhappy drunk? It would make his face sag or turn scarlet; it would strain the blood vessels, the eyes and the hopes behind the eyes. "I was born tired," Warren's father says, "and every morning I have a relapse." By forty, the hair might recede, the face flabby and the eyes ringed with the stains of depression. Or it would be collapsed from the worry of taxes, children and holding its strained substance and security together. It could be a face like yours or mine, and by forty we are content to have it not much known.

At forty, Warren Beatty will be making *Heaven Can Wait*. When that film opens, it is said how beautiful he is, how well preserved. He plays a Superbowl quarterback and a sweet absent-minded millionaire. This man wins the love of Julie Christie, eats health foods and has his own accidental death corrected by Heaven's bureaucracy. He looks as good as any man of forty can look – ideal or exquisite – while playing out the fantasies of someone only thirty.

By 1977, it will be clearer in how many obvious and subtle ways Warren Beatty has taken care of himself. He has not smoked, drunk or taken drugs. It is not that he has never done these things. But in the context of actors, obsessives and Hollywood people, it is notable how little of them he has done.

His weight does not fluctuate. He has resisted anything like his father's weakness for peanuts. He has not rivalled the Brando, huge with dismay and idleness, likely to be "taken" against his will by scandal-sheet photographers at airports. He has disdained being a Jack Nicholson, prophet of commonness at $4-6 million a movie, prepared to let his lovely gut hang out in view of the camera. It is hard to imagine Warren doing what Robert De Niro did for *Raging Bull*, stuffing himself for the character. Warren would have known that even if that new weight was shed again, the face would never be the same. De Niro may be nearly as thin as he was, but the face cannot recover from the excess and the tiny shifts in bone structure to hold it. Nor can it erase the indignity and the repression in the diet that stays with you and makes you look like a fugitive from the law. What is most special about Beatty's face is still that it is not haunted. It is the face of someone who thinks well of himself, without being a fool.

So Warren takes care, and knows he merits the care. Yet few see the strain of such effort. He does not run like Bruce Dern, or jump up and down at basketball games like Jack; he does not ski Redford's slopes, or swim and play tennis like Robert Towne. And on those very few movie occasions when he has to run or fight, he looks like someone embarrassed by the actions, who would prefer not to be seen exerting himself.

He has private ways and tricks. ". . . it's something I got from Warren," says Nicholson, "a trick he learned in English theater. If you're going to be lit for a photograph, you put dark powder here [points to hairline] because it keeps the light from making the hair you do have disappear. There are certain things Warren is just not ashamed about, but I am." Warren is loyal to a movie code from the 30s and 40s, in which the parts were subservient to an actor's glamor.

There are several aspects to this process. The most obvious is to play roles younger than oneself, and have no one remark on the gap. When John Reed died, he was thirty-two; when Warren plays Reed, he is forty-two. Movie lends itself to this by the bold lies of casting, the soft deceits of make-up and lenses, and the simple phenomenon whereby an actor can look back at his films and see himself younger, cheating death.

The next is to be good-looking. This is where physical well-being and thinking well of oneself come together. For in movies, beauty is inseparable from moral worth. It is a form of idealism; we know it is irrational and contrary to life's evidence, but we adhere to it helplessly. We think beauties reach the greatest heights of passion and compassion. We think Garbo's elevated face was the imprint of her fineness. And so Garbo did not play Mother Courage or Baby Jane, and she retired from pictures when this idealism put its greatest test on photography, when she was thirty-six. It tends to happen ten years earlier for women than for men.

Today's movies do not pursue perfection as devotedly as once the medium did. Film has lost primacy and confidence; it is in advertising now we see the richest display of "good-looking". But screen actors still prefer to play "good" characters, those liked by an audience; for they want to be seen in an agreeable light. They cling to the notion that the look is substance – it becomes part of their diet or regime.

Photographs and film have taught us a kind of beauty and goodness that are only photographic. I mean a tone and texture to the skin, a shine in the eyes and mouth, not observed in life. They have to do with light, emulsion and the quality in prints called "glossy". These measures do massage age, but that is a minor effect. The larger achievement is a look that enshrines health, and adds this to the definition of "good-looking" – that it feels good to be seen. Because all photographs are still, this aura lasts. There is a vague hope of averting decay in wanting to look like photos. Glossy prints have a radiance beyond fingerprints or aging, fatigue or infection. Was it into a version of photography that Howard Hughes hoped to escape?

There is a climate and a place in photography we aspire to; it is our mythic kingdom. For the photographed are at a different level of existence, poised, friction-free, alive and unaging. They are seen and imagined but not lived with or in. They are proof against time, preserved in a situation and a pose emblematic of their whole being. Star photos are the stars' hope for themselves. They are the uplifted moment that transcends ordinariness, just as any still has won an edge on death. If you regard death as natural and proper to life, then they represent a peak of health verging on insanity. But they are the most subversive cultural influence in a society far from sure now that death is necessary.

The smallest family snapshot begins to make the life-like more impressive than life. The close-up in a movie drama projected to the height of two or three storeys is so potent it is hard to grasp the discrepancy. Those images have been made by the best film-making skills. None has been passed unless it is free from error . . . or illness. Movies want to get everything right. That means saying the lines correctly, with the intonation that is revelatory. But long before the actor acts, the camera has been cleaned, fresh film has been loaded, the lights have been set and the camera has been put in what must seem the only position. The result is a record of appearance and a piece of the story. But it is also perfection vindicated. Even villains seem resplendent with health; they are right on. The lack of doubt is monstrous.

Most people, given the option, would rather not be photographed. How remarkable then if someone believes his nature deserves this gigantic, broadcast photography. It is not enough to call the confidence "vanity", though there is vanity to the point of delusion in some movie stars. One of the most intriguing implications in Warren Beatty's career is that he persists in being a star, but worries at it, and would therefore often rather not work, not be seen. He is like a man who makes a great quest for treasure, but who has an urge to back away at the threshold – as if he knew the quest was more precious than the jewels and the gold. He seems drawn to find out how long the very famous person can remain invisible. He has a sense – far more profound than his evident talent as a director – that the ultimate force of movies rests in the things unseen.

Of course, in his real life, he does show signs of actual decay or neurosis, the ordinary failures in fineness. One lover who meets him again after several years notices:

> "Alas, his college boy looks were becoming slightly crumpled. The eyelids were heavy, the cheekbones mottled. Much of the charm was still there, but the old magic was missing. It looked like Warren had made himself too available: it seemed to me that practically anyone could have him."

That could be spite: Britt Ekland is not what she was herself. But she is not just talking about the audience having Warren come to them, like a dream. And Beatty has not posed for formal still photographs since 1978 and *Heaven Can Wait*. He has rationed his film appearances. No one thinks he is anything but very healthy, yet he handles his reputation with something like the first fear of invalidism. Is this coming closer to Howard Hughes? Is it being so intuitive a magician of well-being that he resembles a witch doctor?

There is an old story about Warren. It has him crossing wires and overhearing a telephone conversation between strangers. He listens as one man tells the other about his symptoms, and what the doctors reckon they amount to.

"No," says Warren. He interrupts; he emerges from the silence. "It's not that, it's — ." And he names another rare illness that his private research has studied. He proves correct. It is magic.

He deserves this story, even if it has no basis in fact. And that is one reason why we can believe nearly anything about the great suggestive faces.

Stand-in

Coming out of the music room and falling into the arms of Clear, D realised the turn his life was taking. He had a huge wish to say, "Let me go home, now." But it would seem craven to burst into tears. Spoiled children cannot run this world. It did occur to D that he might not see home again. How easily one could fall off the carpet. He had been sucked into this sinister party where death was sipped from canapés and wounded sexual eyes.

But Clear was not inconsiderate. He had the remote compassion of an overworked psychiatrist. He sat D down on a sofa so charcoal it was scarcely visible in the twilight.

"D, a wicked game has been played on you. Well, not quite wicked – "

"Oh, it was, it was!"

"My dear, good fellow, do shut up." Clear said it in such an easy way.

D did as he was told and he heard stealthy chuckles in the rest of the party. Was he on show?

"Eyes," said Clear, "is not here. Eyes is often not here. He is there, you see." And he nodded with his head towards some other level of being.

"He is ill?" asked D.

"No, very fit," replied Clear. "He jogs an hour every day and, for a man of his age, well. . . ." He waved a hand in the air, as if reputation was enough. "No, it is the danger. Stars are inviting targets. I daresay you've felt the itch to stone some lustrous vapid face."

"I see the prudence," agreed D: there is a policeman in anyone who lives in fear.

"Moreover, he is an artist."

"I was going to say –"

"And he needs peace. Therefore, we employ Chuck – you met Chuck – as a look-alike, a live-in."

"So if there is an attempt on Eyes' life," D hoped, "this Chuck will get it?"

"No one wishes Chuck less than the best. He takes the risk."

"He is *like* Eyes," D admitted.

"Well," Clear searched for the word, "only like him."

"It's merely a resemblance."

"You felt the difference," Clear reminded him. "Between ourselves, D, he is a bore. It is good for the rest of us; it makes us more appreciative of the real thing."

D could not conceal his further questions.

"You're wondering how much Chuck does? Appearances – he opens malls and charity benefits. He takes young actresses to restaurants and has apparent liaisons at discreet hotels. After months of work we have got him to do a fairly respectable absent-minded routine in this or that lobby with some model on his arm. We do not let him say much, and this restraint meshes intriguingly with Eyes' own. . . . You will like Eyes."

And then, as if to say too much talk was morbid, Clear stood up and did five fast knee-bends. There was no effect of exertion: it was like a tic. "I've not had my squash today," Clear remarked. "I feel the loss immediately. When the body is finely honed, it can notice an ounce of fat on an angel's wing. Who said that? Was it Julia Child or Victoria Principal?"

With that question, Clear whirled and headed for the party. Yet he stopped and held out a white hand at D. "Come, let's mingle. These are your new friends."

The place was becoming crowded, shadows moving to the shuffle of a samba and the aroma of snacks. A spiffy young restaurateur, Stephen, was presiding over the eats, and the three gaunt waiters he employed. Stephen, Clear said, was the group's chef and picnic-man. Whenever there was a gathering he would bring in his latest nouvelle outrages. Tonight he was offering a lamb pâté cut with ginger and served in a vinaigrette of white tomatoes; there was a salad of eleven different leaves in walnut oil with crumbled pieces of old Turkish delight; and a bloody swamp of sun-dried tomatoes – "Tenderised, slightly chillied ears from El Salvador, try them yourself," quipped Stephen.

Stephen had a lacquered head like a barber's mannequin advertising hair-dressing. His baby face moved in and out with snide jokes, and he left the impression of being a cocky eleven-year-old close to ruin. He was bold, undaunted by a discard's future. So he did whatever came into his head and dressed it with crackling devil's patter.

66

Then there was Doc, a gangling gray-haired figure, who strolled around forbiddingly, a learned amateur in matters of health who, it was said, had polished up or reworked key scenes in just about every interesting movie of the last fifteen years. He had a windswept look and a philosophical gaze: aging swiftly, he might have played the Astrologer in an adventure set in Tibet or Nepal.

And so on . . . writers for the magazines, fashion consultants, agents, lawyers, accountants, automobile repair experts, gunsmiths, tennis professionals, masters of the hunt, gallery owners, dealers, crooks, whores and lyricists, all in the soft gray light where business was done and promises shared over quiche.

D was assaulted by names and brief lives, as Clear led him around, always saying "And this is D, who is going to be very important." At last the circuit ended. Clear had business to attend to. "But I want you to tell us the story of your script. Pitch it for us. It's the nicest way for everyone to know you. Do it after *Network Superstars*." He nodded at another room where the TV's light flared.

And so D withdrew from the rush and smartness. He backed away until he felt the softness of a body at his side. It was Drew. She seemed fully recovered. D would notice here that women had the capacity to restore themselves to a pre-sexual state, groomed and ready, as if nothing had happened and anything could happen like new, for the first time.

"Same shit," said Drew quietly.

"Isn't it?" D agreed. "Are you feeling better?"

"Oh sure."

"How can you be?"

"I'm not, but I say I am. It's what they expect."

"Why do you do this?"

"I want to be in a picture with Eyes." She took the last dead embryo in cilantro aspic on her plate and put it in her mouth. "We're alike, lovebunch. Wouldn't you kill for a break?"

FIRST PARTS

A would-be actor is desperate to have the small opportunities to be other people for money. He inhabits a folk-lore that says if you have real talent you will make it, or that talent is never enough – you need perseverance, the absolute readiness to humiliate yourself, and blind luck. It is out of your control, or it is something that only you can change. You must regard yourself as a helpless leaf or as the wind.

If you have been brought up in an educating household, and if you have dallied with thoughts of a career in law, it is like going over the edge into voodoo and darkness. Rationalism and intelligence do not sit well on actors; in the eyes of casting directors, agents and other actors, they may be taken as marks of coldness, lack of insight, reservation about commitment. Actors live with legendary tales and rumors – that, say, one in a hundred young people who seek the stage will make it; that one in ten thousand hopeful movie-players will ever have their pictures sold to the public; or that it should be one in ten thousand and one in five hundred thousand. You are gambling without any accurate sense of the odds: the mythology says merely that it is impossible. There are drunks, derelicts and the dead to point to, people who had one great review, who seemed poised on the edge of eternity, but who could not go all the way; there are ex-actors selling insurance in Des Moines, working as a mental nurse in North Carolina, or just gone, vanished. If you fail as an actor, you may at least have learned the tricks or picked up the illness that keeps you from being a fixed, findable you. So you dissolve in and out of many different lives and personae and you go missing and roaming, a person without identity but vivid to all who see you pass by and who offer you the chance of a passing performance. People may tell you, "You should have been an actor" as if *you* betrayed the trust, the talent and the arrangement of destiny.

You could drift between bottomless cynicism and demented faith; you might be alienated and superstitious, at a loss as the fierce member of small, intense religious cults. You could be killed, or a killer. You begin to resemble a coin.

If you fall ill, with hepatitis or acute depression, you do not so much blame bacteria or chemical imbalances in the brain; you try to feel out the pressure in the occult scenario that brought you these burdens. So intent on getting into stories, you cannot help but see yourself moving in a stream where fiction is the best version of current. Actors take acting lessons, they may have their noses and their teeth corrected, they may go into analysis. But they read horoscopes, they have their fortunes told, they live for coincidence – and, if it occurs, they wonder whether it is lovely or horrific. They may watch religious shows on television: there is work there, and the message of such shows, the strange pattern of anonymity and celebrity, speaks to the loneliness of their lives. Actors believe in gods, seldom one, but many of them; actors collect horoscopes, like line readings, sure that truth is in the collage. And if you know all your possible star charts, then you may imagine that you can control their real course. "If I know everything this character might do now, then I can decide what he must do." Or, "Knowing all the possibilities, I am helpless in the face of decision." In movie acting there can be an intense hiatus, a depth of being that will not speak, move or decide, where the actor's presence opposes itself to the machinery's need to move forward and says. "Wait. I can suck you in." It is observable in the young Warren Beatty.

Your world cannot make up its mind what it thinks about actors, which in itself supports the dread that the life is dangerous and daft. It has an age-old faith that actors are what they are because they have no real person to be – and the 1950s is a time strong on "real" people. It thinks what actors are paid is ridiculous, a travesty of sensible careers and proper work ethics. It believes that show business is a mess of falsehood and corruption; it assumes that actresses sleep with the system before they sell themselves to the larger public; so in popular fiction, "actor" or "entertainer" are synonyms for whore. Acting and pretending are symptoms of madness; the stable, sleeping world cannot forget that the performance is a lie, no matter that it lives it every night for its dreams. Liars are scoundrels, aren't they?

Yet in the 1950s, for the first time, acting has broken out of the bounds of its business. It is everywhere. There are fewer films being made, but television is devouring American attention and it will provide far more work for actors not just in *its* films and series, but in commercials and in all those interweaving moments and situations when people have to go on the small screen and project. In a few years' time, the American presidency will be won by a man hooked on movie stars and successful (so they say) because he was better on camera. Where do they say it? On television. At last, "good-looking" is taking on a natural, metaphysical depth at a national level. The president will very soon be the person who is photographed to denote certain formal state occasions. The televised press conference will become the central governmental process. A public that once saw a couple of movies a week is well on its way to witnessing, or accepting, a couple of movies' worth of screen time and imagery a night.

*

Warren Beatty looks for work, for parts, for jobs. He must recognise the likelihood of failure, of being turned down and sent away. Very early on, he elects for himself the posture of one who will not abuse himself, who will not be comically ingratiating, who will not take too much shit. He says to himself that *they* will be lucky to have him. It may be the only way to maintain dignity – or to overcome the terror – in the situation of going for auditions. He will say of his studies with Stella Adler, "She equipped me with a certain amount of arrogance – arrogant self-confidence, I should say – which enabled me to bluff my way through a few sidescrapers." In the next few years, he will earn the reputation as someone likely to walk out on auditions if he dislikes the atmosphere. When one director criticises him for mumbling, Beatty hands back the script and the role without a word. It is a great gamble – if it is all trick; but the situations are so testing that a young actor must believe in the way he is playing. The pride, the difficulty, the aloofness, are heartfelt. They are dignity coming to life.

He gets small parts in television and in local stock. He works on an early morning religious show; he has parts in Studio One and Playhouse 90 for CBS; he plays the lead in *The Curly-Headed Kid* for Kraft Theater and NBC. And there are two New York-area theaters where he plays in repertory: the North Jersey Playhouse in Fort Lee, New Jersey, and the Gateway Theater on Long Island. He has parts in plays of the time – *A Hatful of Rain, The Happiest Millionaire, Visit to a Small Planet, The Boy Friend* and *Compulsion*.

He is acting hard; the work will never be as intense again, if we think simply of the number of roles. This is also the effective end of whatever formal training Warren Beatty has as an actor – which is to say, part of a

70

year at Northwestern and some classes in New York. It is not much, not if one compares what young actors must submit to with the training of musicians, dancers, painters, or even writers. But, of course, in Warren's time there is a way of believing that actors in America function rather less through craft and steady work than by touching their own deepest and most neurotic inspiration. It is in their nature and their liberty that they should not have to submit. This can lead to the modern appraisal that Marlon Brando is a great actor who stays away from the corruption of work.

We do not have to accept that trust in magic, or conclude that Beatty is anything but an able and professional actor like all the others. Still, the thing that he does is something he does rather seldom. By the age of fifty, Warren Beatty will have appeared in some ten plays and in just seventeen films. At the same age, quite apart from many roles in school, in training and in repertory before he was twenty, Laurence Olivier has played in over sixty stage productions and starred in twenty-eight films, three of which he has directed. Cary Grant has made fifty-seven pictures.

Elevator

D detached himself from the party – he was a professional story man, if he ever earned anything, no one people wanted to meet. He felt hideous among the smooth beauties. All he wanted was an empty room, somewhere he might wait until the socialising died down. Solitude was the only answer to mortification. But he could think of nowhere free except the elevator. He was not sure he dared occupy it, with all the risk of being found there, so evidently hiding. Unless he could suggest that elevators were a hobby or a fad, a perversion these people would understand. He decided to work there; wouldn't that be honored? So he took his script and a pen and slipped away towards the elevator.

Barefoot still, he approached so silently he did not disturb Drew who was sitting in the corner of the elevator reading a paperback – *The Eye of the Beholder*, by Marc Behm. He paused to examine her, holding his breath. It was delicious, she did not know she was being watched. Her diligent, sexpot face flickered with the developments in her book. He could see every sentence wriggle, like a snake across a pond.

"Hi," she grunted, never looking up.

"I didn't mean to disturb you," said D.

"Looking for a hideout?"

"Well," he didn't want to offend, "this isn't quite my sort of thing."

"You'll fall in that well," said Drew, gloomily.

"What?" He saw a figure falling down an empty elevator shaft.

"Don't worry. I don't mind it. I kind of like it."

"What are you talking about?"

"Saying 'well' before you say something. It's like a doorway, something you're behind."

"It's just that I don't know what I should say."

"You'd rather say nothing."

"Sometimes." He couldn't tell if this dialogue was gaining momentum, or she was teasing him.

"Rather be writing scenes."

He shrugged, he did smile, he was blushing, "Well –"

Drew laughed and D felt the warmth.

"You look very beautiful here, on your own," he whispered. "I spoiled it for you."

"Certainly did not. Who knows I look good if you don't come by?" she asked him. "That's the problem," she added.

"What problem?"

"Being alone but being seen. That's the trick. That's what Eyes is so damn good at." She assumed it was all clear to him, and he didn't want to seem stupid. "Won't you come in?" Her small hand patted the floor beside her.

D felt he was getting into much more than an innocent elevator – not that he trusted that one's simplicity. But he went in, and Drew pressed the doors shut.

"You want to ride?" she asked.

He grinned in agreement; it all seemed so playful. They sat in opposite corners, their toes close but not touching. He saw that hers were bent and smudged.

"You see, writers," she told him, "they're always thinking pictures and story and construction and character motivation and dialogue that fits together. The whole dramatic thing. Right? I'm not saying that's not important. You have to have it. But it's not all. You know what actors like? They like scenes like 'She is alone with the camera'. Now if the writer writes that he feels like a jerk. Right? What does that mean? So he writes a whole lot of extra stuff about what she's thinking. But the actress really gets off if the script just says, 'Alone with the camera.' She loves it. So she just prowls around her room, lazy but loose, lights a cigarette maybe, straightens an ornament. She's doing nothing whatsoever for the story. She's like the music and the light. No lines, no interaction. Yummy! It's immense, total. And audiences love it. They just float on it, watching the beast up there on the screen. It's the most erotic thing. I wouldn't even have to do any flesh. I just let the camera see me, and I don't know it's there. You know, D, if I had one good scene like that, a minute, thirty seconds, I could make the world fall in love with me." The shine on her eyes left no doubt about her capacity for so much admiration.

"Oh, yes," D breathed. He could see it, better than he usually saw anything, as if he had been given new glasses that made him younger and more hopeful. She was captivating. He was already envisaging a whole film about her, a meditative epic in which she met not another soul, had no need of any, with her own sleek surface to buff, an egg or an orange to eat and a book to be stirred by. She could sing beneath her breath, and audience hearts would fly up to the illusion of her skin, like sparrows going after bread. Well, D gave in, it looks like I'm in love.

"Of course," Drew laughed, "there's maybe ten million girls in the US who could do it, too. And you'd fall for all of them."

"Oh, no," said D, "not nearly so many."

"You in love with me?" she asked, and then before he could begin, "Don't say 'well'."

So he said nothing. However astute her analysis, this strategy had not occurred to him before. It gave him a strange sensation, as of shedding gravity or his body. But it seemed to work.

"Bet you are," she probed. "I just bet you are. I can tell. Oh, you're wicked." She was grinning; she had seen what he was up to. "You really not going to talk?" It irked her and made her move for him. She was no longer poised in her corner, confident about letting his gaze wander over her. She looked at him, and looked away, trying to hook and scramble his concentration. Her knees came up, and then slipped sideways as she shifted her position. It was a test of wills, and she had become a plucky girl, ready to cry with frustration or peal with laughter at the heady game.

"Tell you what," she said, "I'll do something I've never done before. I mean it. I'll tell you a story about my life. And it's a great story. I just need someone to write it, to *see* it properly, and put it down on paper. Then I could play it. All right? I'll tell you." Her voice dropped and her eyes swung away to the corner of the elevator – bright and empty. "You'll be the only one who knows."

The elevator stopped. "Why, there, you see," she was not surprised. "It heard me."

"Where are we?" said D. His alarm always let him down.

"Oh, you spoke!" Drew was petulant, but she was pleased not to be thwarted any more. She came across the floor on her knees and put herself between D's legs. She fitted so easily, like a letter put in a book. "There," she said, looking at him. "Oh, and there," she remembered, seeing something within the fold of his black robe. "You are awful," she warned him, as if he was invading her. Or telling dreadful things about her.

"Your life story," he said, trying to distract her.

"Oh, yeah. Some other time."

"You said –"

"So." She was insolence. "That was to get you talking. Now you're talking. Love me?"

"When did you meet Eyes?"

Her hand had been penetrating the robe, but it stopped. She considered his question and all the ways of answering it. "I don't usually talk about him," she said. She was disappointed.

"But he must be an important part of your story," D told her.

"Oh, you think so?".

"I daresay he made you lovable," D suggested.

It went home. He saw her appreciate that he was more than she had reckoned on, a stooge maybe, but someone who could see. "That's real smart," she said. "And it's right. Know how he saw me? I was kidnaped up in New Hampshire. Yes, I was. That's where I came from. This creep up there he went crazy one winter and took me off to his cabin. He was a packer at the IGA."

"Against your will?" D asked.

"In a way. Yeah, it was really."

"But not quite?" He was trying to be adult about it.

She looked at him and rolled her eyes. She seemed to say, guess, sucker, to suggest that maybe she and this madman had had some bizarre thing together and what a fox D was to work it out. But D wasn't sure she had not been carried off, raped, whatever, but only now made the incident more vague, more suggestive, for his benefit and her own sense of story.

"Well," she decided, "I was rescued after a while. And there were police and everything up at his cabin, and there was TV – not that I saw it then – what are you looking at?"

"At nothing." He kept his face straight.

"Oh, you cheat, you slut," she murmured. "Anyway, there was coverage. I was national. And Eyes saw it. There was this shot of me being pulled both ways, by the guy and by a cop. That cop was hot for me, I'll tell you. And Eyes said the look on my face stopped what he was doing." She grinned. "I don't know *what* he was doing."

"You never saw this shot?"

"Yeah, I saw it. Later."

"And?"

"I don't know. It was OK." She thought about him. "You want me here, D? Now?"

"What did Eyes do?" D did not answer her question, but he got up and while she started to answer, he merely urged Drew onto her back on the floor. She never altered what she had to say.

"He called me and said I should come and see him. If I wanted. Because he'd been so impressed, you know."

D put his hand inside her clothes. She had changed again, but it hardly mattered what she was wearing. The clothes were just clues or signs to follow. He found his way between her legs, and she was moist already, sure all along that he would get there.

"So I went down to New York city on the bus," she was telling him, but her eyes were already reacting to where his hand was. "He wouldn't send me a plane ticket. Get that. I went to his hotel. Oh yeah, and you know what, on the telephone I had talked to him and we'd made a date and I was so nervous I said, 'How will I know you?'" She laughed out loud; the floor hummed with her mirth. "And he loved that. He said he thought it was the wittiest thing he'd ever heard. You listening?"

D was looking directly into her face. But he had his whole hand in, the fingers moving as if she were a ball in there that he was deciding how to throw. And the back of his hand rode against her so that she breathed quicker and was becoming slowly thrilled and shuddery as if the torture could not be escaped.

"And he, he said I had a skin so white. It shone. From the winters."

"Your skin is still very white," D told her.

"Yeah?" She was anxious for it all to be true. "And I became his lover and he made me feel so good about myself. I never had. For all of February."

"But he never put you in the picture."

Furious, she shook her desperate head. "Not yet. Get in me. I want you. Don't you want to?" He saw her mind accelerate. "You can tell yourself it's somewhere Eyes has been before you. Don't you want to be there?"

And D knew he did, and would be, and though the elevator suddenly resumed its progress, he knew not even that would deter him.

"Can you really write?" she hissed in his ear.

But he chose again to answer her without talking, and he rocked her to the timing of her gentle, stricken cries there in the stuffy space of the lightly rising elevator.

DISCOVERED

Discovery is a vital moment in the self-sustaining ritual of show business. It enables everyone involved to believe that they are involved with magic and excitement. If the world is seething with those ready to be discovered, then boredom is staved off. And if all those participating can believe in the fact of talent, its mystery and its fateful manifestation, then it becomes rather easier to live with and overlook the mass of hard work, sacrifice, corruption and mere chance that also goes into the making of stars. After all, if you are a member of a religion, you want to believe in our ability to recognise the god. One of the benefits of divinity is that the gods carry the responsibility: if we don't notice them, then that is part of their design. We don't have to realise that we are stupid. Show business would be harder than it is to endure if you believed that quantities of talent missed the net, smashed up on the rocks and just went unnoticed. Stars have to believe they deserve their stardom, and the business clings to the divine right of true stars. Otherwise the shit is also a bagatelle, and perhaps unforgivable. Whatever happens then, is divine and designed: if fools and monsters thrive, and fine young people kill themselves . . . that's show business.

You may do nothing, or you can try to manipulate every last taxi ride and telepone call – it does not matter, profoundly, because discovery depends upon some higher, deeper purpose. You may be resigned, or you may be the most fearsomely ambitious creature anyone can remember – still, discovery absolves you from your own way towards the light. You may be infinitely ruthless and calculating, and still think you did nothing. In the end it is easier to think you are blessed than talented. For talent is a matter of skill, sensibility and unending pursuit. It is a good that might be lost. If you trusted talent, you might end up hopelessly anxious and neurotic. But if you think you are blessed, then "it" does not go, and does not involve your unceasing effort. You have only to be saved. Anxiety may be replaced by madness: it is the difference between being Marilyn Monroe and Norma Desmond. And whereas a Monroe must have known how easily she might have been missed, and lived with the daily fear of being dumped, a Norma Desmond knows no luck or gratitude.

Warren Beatty is discovered twice at once. Two people see him in the same small part in *Compulsion* at Fort Lee and are moved to action. For it is just as moving to discover as it is to be discovered. It is another heartfelt part of show business mythology to know when your robe has been touched, to look into mid-West beauty contests, chorus lines, summer stock or casting photographs and say "that one". It is another way of wanting to be magical to aspire to magical insight. And the business is thrilled by stories of discovery, not just for the unknown, but for the director or producer whose vision crystallises in the nick of time. God needs to be identified, too.

We know Josef von Sternberg as the man who found Marlene Dietrich for *The Blue Angel*. We remember the story how in the early days of shooting *Gone With the Wind*, David Selznick turns away from the lurid lights of his burning Atlanta and is introduced to Vivien Leigh. In the Cukor *A Star is Born*, James Mason goes in search of a singer who rescued him at the premiere and finds her after hours in a club, singing "The Man That Got Away". He knows, and his life is going to be saved for love and purpose. It is the moment in thousands of movies and perfume ads when he or she stops and notices he or she and the cutting and the music sigh with rapture or "I want to fuck you". The movies, more than all the rest of show business, believe in magic noticing. And he who notices is given bliss, power and a kind of parenthood in picking out the new wonder. It is a very erotic siezure, even if the two people on either side of fate's margins do not couple.

Joshua Logan notices Warren Beatty. He is a director and a producer, a man of fifty-one in 1959, who started in pictures in the 1930s, then moved to Broadway and directed the original productions of *Annie Get Your Gun, Mister Roberts, South Pacific* and *Picnic*. Then in the mid-1950s he had gone back to movies and directed *Picnic, Bus Stop, Sayonara* and *South Pacific*. It is notable that in the movie of *Picnic*, he has "discovered" Susan Strasberg and given Kim Novak an opportunity denied her in her earlier work; and in *Bus Stop*, he has so earned Monroe's confidence and recognised her strength that the picture will survive as one of her best. Logan is a writer and a master of big shows, but his work shines with affection for players.

In Fort Lee, he wonders if Beatty could be right for a new project he is supposed to make for Warners, a picture called *Parrish.* "I sent for him. He was all a director could hope for: tall, humorous, extremely male. He even sat down at the piano and played and sang. His name was Warren Beatty, and I decided to use him though he had never been on the screen before."

Logan had Beatty fly to Los Angeles where he screen-tested him with another newcomer whom he had thought of using in *Parrish,* Jane Fonda. It is impossible now to think of those two, both graced by family connections, on the wrong side of success, caught in the same waiting room. We can only imagine them as stars pretending to be ingenues. The story is that they kissed in their screen test and could not be stopped, or awakened, by repeated calls of "Cut!". Why not? They wanted to be remembered, noticed. You may not do just as you are told if you are desperate to be remembered. You may change your lines, pause until the camera comes back to wait for you. The two of you may say to one another, "let's show them", or one of you may plan to surprise and ravish the other. Perhaps they both surprised each other, and went off afterwards in laughter and in love. There is eroticism left over in filming, not least in tests, for it to change the real lives of actors. But people talked – the crew perhaps, crusty, unsentimental types who know it is their duty to propagate that very sentimental mode of rumor, legend.

But *Parrish* doesn't happen. Warren Beatty's first movie is one he will not make. When the script of the film arrives, Logan does not like it. He asks Warners to reassign it. It is made by Delmer Daves who casts his hot discovery Troy (*A Summer Place*) Donahue in it. That picture opens in 1961, and it begins to suggest that Donahue's discovery has been an error. For the business believes that it can disappear people as easily as it can discover them: if they will let that happen, if their magic is not strong enough.

Instead, Logan agrees to make a movie of *Tall Story*, about a college basketball star and a cheer leader. He sees Jane Fonda as the female lead and he thinks of using Warren Beatty opposite her. But Logan's short-term personal contract with the actor had lapsed, and he was persuaded to cast Anthony Perkins in the role instead. This does not work out perfectly, for Perkins persuades Logan to let him and Fonda rehearse the love scene alone.

"They worked very hard," Logan writes later, "devotedly in fact, on their intimate scenes. When they showed them to me they were strangely slow and full of pregnant pauses, but apart from that quite attractive, so I filmed them as rehearsed. Unfortunately, when cut into the picture they were endless and, I think, hurt the picture almost more than the charm of the two people in those scenes helped it."

Tall Story is at least the second picture Beatty does not make. "At least" because he spends a few weeks in Hollywood, long enough to inspire a five-year contract offer from MGM starting at $400 a week, and long enough, no doubt, for him to be surefire casting for this movie over dinner, or that movie over the weekend. "Discovering" does not wait for divinity. There are just as many matchmakers as there are suitors. Beatty will discover that there may be twenty projects talked about and believed in for any one made. The amazing possibilities of sweet deals are always circulating. To be in the city is to be a piece that might be fitted into any of them. To this day, Beatty's aura and reputation are just as much those of a piece as they are those of a maker of films.

MGM has a first picture to go with their contract offer – *Strike Heaven in the Face* it's called, the last great 30s title of the 1950s. He turned it down and got out of the enclosing contract. He went back to New York, too smart to see his "big break" or already a better reader of real opportunity than most people in the city. For someone else had noticed him in *Compulsion*, the playwright William Inge.

Ham and cheese

Chuck was sitting on the floor in front of the television, eating cream of wheat. He turned to look at them as Drew led D into the room. The party was listless and broken, here and there around the suite. The night was complete now, a black-brown cloth like Guinness with a sparkling head of traffic and night trade. D traced the lines of the streets until they vanished. He imagined C putting together the humble evening meal, wondering where he was. He wanted to wave and say, "Don't worry, I'm here." And he imagined her amazed, foreboding "There!"

"Hey, buddy, don't jump," said Chuck.

"Oh, I had no intention —"

"Plate glass. You'd just bounce off." Chuck snorted to think of the wasted energy. "Not ordinary glass. New stuff. They tested it. Got a kamikaze plane to hit the window. Wham!" His hand described a rebounding arc. "Just caromed off, like a little bee. It was on *Real People* when they built this building."

"Did you keep bees?" D asked.

Chuck's face fell half an inch, or rather the clench of eagerness slipped from perplexity. He seemed shorter.

D tried to be conciliatory: "I wondered if as a boy perhaps you had a hive."

Drew was crouched by the television, in a lotus position, "He's just asking if you kept bees, you jerk, back in De-troit City."

"Shit, no," said Chuck, aghast at where small talk could go. "They sting. What do I want with 'em?"

"Honey is super virile," suggested Drew. "And that Queen Bee jelly, oooh," she shivered thinking of it.

"Yeah?" said Chuck, and he turned to D, "You a diet doctor?"

"D is a writer, Chuck," Drew enjoyed explaining. "He has done a new script, which I hear Eyes is crazy for."

"Isn't he always? That guy uses scripts like toilet rolls."

81

"This is a special script" She was guiding him along, like a mother making sure he finished his dinner. "Doc has been looking at it already."

Chuck grunted. He was impressed. It was an early mark of trust in a project if it had sicknesses enough for Doc's attention.

D was just as surprised, and more alarmed, but Drew had a quick private smile for him, "Don't worry. It's a good sign," she said.

"Wouldn't it be something to be working again?" sighed Chuck.

"Everyone's excited," said Drew.

"Training all the time's brutal for the body." Chuck had his problems.

"Oh sure," said Drew. "All foreplay and no coming gets you muscle-bound."

"Kid!" scoffed Chuck, and he threw a playful hook at her jaw. D winced for her, but it was an old routine and she knew how to ride the haymaker. "You're all right," he told her.

"Thanks Chuck." It was a sweet answer, without irony. As D would learn, remarks there drifted into the air like chlorine in a pool without the cultural guarantee of being heard.

"Listen, D," said Chuck a moment later. "You want to watch some TV with me?" It was something he had been planning, a way of getting to know an important writer better. D was nervous enough from the strain of this new world to swim in the lines a little. Chuck gathered arms of cushions and the two men stretched out in the light of the screen.

There were two shows Chuck was watching, and he went from one to the other with a proven instinct, seldom missing big moments and managing a rhythm, like that of a large yacht in a heavy swell, that was invigorating without being frightening. The shows were *Family Feud* and *Network Superstars*.

In the one, a Mexican family from San Diego was competing with a Swedish family from Solvang, and the crisp-haired Richard Dawson was giving them just three seconds to say what things a husband and wife do simultaneously. A hot pepper seventeen-year-old daughter had X'd out on a giggly "Kiss?" and Lars, the cousin from the old country, whose sandpaper face was tuned pale cherry on the Sylvania, got all the money with "They sleep, I tink, Richard."

And in the other, at a sun-drenched college track, there was a steeplechase in progress in which men raced with women on their backs. D noticed Doc Severinsen, hardly able to toot beneath the soft statue, Loni Anderson; Jim Palmer and Mary Lou Retton; William Shatner, puffing a mite but dignified in conversation beneath Dr Joyce Brothers, her thighs gripping his jowls in approved Eastern-taught riding style;

and Carl Lewis, with Brooke Shields up. Al Michaels (on a ride-along camera car) was interviewing the contestants as they plunged through the water jump.

"Make one of these shows," said Chuck. "Boy, that's it!"

"The rewards?" D surmised.

"Unbe-fucking-lievable. You've got a prize for this meet, has to be two mill. Then there's the play-offs, and the endorsements. And the winning couple get a series." Chuck whistled at the way a few sportsmen had it soft.

"So, anyway, D," Chuck began, "this scripteroo . . .? The real thing, huh?"

"Well. . . ."

"All the signs are good, I hear."

"You hear that, too?"

"What she, what Drew just said."

"Ah," D was feeling his way. "And if it's done, that will be good for you?"

It was obvious to Chuck. "Gets me visibility. The stunts, the stand-in stuff. Eyes doesn't take no risks, now."

"Of course not," said D. Just the bits alone with the camera, so peaceful and so insurable.

"I have told them all – Clear and the high command – we should take some of the action pictures. Those offers don't go on forever. Eyes takes his time, that's OK, that's his thing, but we get offers it's dumb to turn down. It's spitting at money. A lot of action pictures, they could send me out and who knows?"

"The audience would think it was Eyes?"

"Right. Adventure pix, they're heavy into long shots, anyway. What is so hard for Eyes' integrity we pick up some cash and give people a good time?"

"Those films are popular," D admitted.

"It would broaden Eyes' appeal. And the exercise would be good for him."

"But," said D, "you would be doing it."

Chuck wasn't deterred. "Oh, right. Anyway, why not? I'm off four weeks, no more. No sweat. Eyes has to take some of his ass out to eat at Michael's, Spago, wherever, himself."

"You often do that for him?"

"Do I? It's freaking my body."

"Too much rich food," D could imagine.

"And all at once. Secret is, little and often. You have to break your slavery to the meal. I dip. I keep a bag of nuts and dried tomatoes with me. And sitting down when you eat is worst. You ever think what is occurring in the lower intestine and the colon when you sit down?"

Whereupon, Chuck stood up and started running on the spot. One of Stephen's young fauns had just entered with a tray of canapés. Since this was not a full meal – and was plainly little things coming around often – Chuck took a miniature kiwi quiche with a slice of foie gras on it, a pasta horn filled with red caviar and a piece of marinated raw goat flesh.

"Don't you want something?" Drew asked D. She gave the impression of being anxious about his strength. "What would you like?"

"Well . . . do you think a ham and cheese sandwich?" D hadn't had one for years.

"You have to be kidding," drawled Flex, their waiter.

"You don't have it?" D was unhappy to make trouble.

"They can make one," said Drew, defiant.

"Would you like that with a, with a pickle?" asked Flex, not bothering to hide his amusement.

"Could I?" D wondered, and Drew kissed him on the cheek.

Flex went away, churlish and subservient, and then Clear came into the room with all the pleasure of reunion after many a long year. He embraced them all, but kept his best hugs for D, who saw Drew's smile as he was held tight against Clear's fine cold-stone ear.

"It's nearly time for your story," said Clear.

"Have many read the script already?"

"Very few," Clear promised. "Think of us all as virgins. It's more lively that way. Just take charge of us. Put us in the palm of your hand."

Flex reappeared, carrying a silver tray. On the tray was a folded white napkin, on the napkin a plate, on the plate a sandwich, and on the bread, still damp, a pickle.

"Ham and cheese," said Flex in a sultry way, "on rye. I held the mayo. Until it wept."

D thanked him and took the plate. He picked up the sandwich and brought it to his mouth. Then he caught the old wolfen scent of Drew's sex, like rich land where water must lie, or was it bodies buried in the woods? The smell was so close to life and death.

"What's the matter, old chap?" Clear saw any hesitation.

"Oh, déjà vu," said D. And he bit into the several textures, tearing at the ham, his eyes watering from the Dijon mustard, his nose in ecstasy at the hard, dry decadent tang of the Swiss. It was the best sandwich he'd ever had.

What a whirl! The picture business! Here was D, hours only away from dingy home, eating a rare sandwich and remembering the stealthy musk of his lover's cum, about to pitch his own story to a round table of Hollywood excellence. He let the mustard excuse his tears, and saw the fluctuating Drew coming up to him and kissing him. She couldn't get enough.

"There," she said soothingly. "There, there."

It did seem as if he was there at last. Now all he had to handle was the being here, too.

LOSS OF ROSES

KENNY: I want *you*, Lila. I can *talk* with you and feel at home with you.

LILA: Kenny, you don't mean those things you're saying. You shouldn't talk like that to a woman if you don't mean it. Things like that excite a woman, so much more'n you know. They raise her hopes, and then, when you don't mean them, those hopes have to fall again. That's happened to me, Kenny. It's happened to me several times. And each time, I think I'm gonna die. I even *pray* to die. Don't tease me, Kenny.

KENNY (*Believing himself completely.*): Lila, I never talked this way to anyone in my life.

— William Inge, *A Loss of Roses*, Act 2, Scene 1.

William Inge is forty-six in 1959. He is from Independence, Kansas, where he has acted in college plays and summer stock. This settled, provincial world, and the effect of loving, smothering families, is the material of plays that change his life after the end of the Second World War. He goes from being a teacher at Iowa State College to arts critic on the *St Louis Star-Times* to successful Broadway playwright. He differs from Tennessee Williams and Arthur Miller in being closer to the American heartland and to that point where small-town romanticism takes fire with Freudian insight into the parent-child relationship and the perennial struggle between stability and adventure.

He writes *Farther Off from Heaven* in 1947 (which is filmed in 1960 as *The Dark at the Top of the Stairs*); *Come Back, Little Sheba* in 1950; *Picnic* in 1953; and *Bus Stop* in 1955. Their terrain is Kansas, Oklahoma, and the period is often set back a little from the present, out of nostalgia and the need to explain how a middle-aged man feels now. An abiding theme is the longing to get away, to fall in love, to take a risk and escape the sober, sedate mid-West upbringing. The plays are poignant studies of happiness missed because of ordinary failures and everyday insecurities. The Beaty household in Virginia in the 1940s would have been ideal Inge material. This is not said casually: Beaty moves and inspires Inge, and Inge more than anyone helps launch the young man

86

on a transforming career. And even if Warren will become a cosmopolitan hotel-dweller, he never shakes off the wholesomeness or the bourgeois politeness that speaks of the influence of Home. No Inge play quite realises it, but when his characters do break away they begin to remake the kind of life that was so recently suffocating. In revolution, they lose their edge. The John Reed of *Reds*, twenty years ahead, is an Inge character. Beatty, after all, grew up in the 1950s, and we never escape the dramatic atmosphere of our own initiation.

At the end of that decade, Inge is hot as a writer. It is an odd state of glamor which moves the rather depressive, kindly Kansan more than he can say or show in his life. He has a Pulitzer for playwriting; his plays have made successful movies – *Picnic, Bus Stop* and *Come Back, Little Sheba*. In early 1959, Inge is writing a movie original (his first), which will become *Splendor in the Grass*. Beatty is one of several young actors talked about for its male lead.

Splendor is being developed by Inge and Elia Kazan, who in 1957 has directed *The Dark at the Top of the Stairs* on the New York stage. The two men become friendly and want to work together again. Inge tells Kazan a number of possible stories and Kazan picks one that comes from Inge's own life. But the picture is postponed because Kazan is busy with the Broadway production of *Sweet Bird of Youth* and another movie, *Wild River*.

But Inge has seen and been impressed by Beatty, and when the actor returns to New York after his first period in Hollywood, the playwright backs him for the role of Kenny Baird in his new play, *A Loss of Roses*. It is set in a small town outside Kansas City in 1933. Kenny, aged twenty-one, lives with his mother Helen in a modest but cosy bungalow. Kenny is written to be "a nice-looking boy who wears a mysterious look of misgiving on his face, as though he bears some secret resentment that he has never divulged, that he has perhaps never admitted to his consciousness." The father has been dead for years: Kenneth Sr drowned, saving Kenny in a swollen river.

The Bairds are comfortable together – Kenny is willing to be mothered for ever. He is turning into a lazy, dishonest lout, ready to live at home and be spoiled. Helen has no other life, except for the Church. But the play seeks to touch on a buried level of love – Helen has gone cold after her husband's death, and she and Kenny are living in peaceful ignorance of how far they have become unadmitted sexual figures for each other.

Then Lila comes to the house. She is in her early thirties, "a small-time tent-show actress," who was once so friendly with the Bairds that Kenny called her "Aunt". Helen decides to take her in until she can get a job again. In fact, Lila is a failure, someone who is never going to be discovered, who has had breakdowns and who is close to making the shift from show business to prostitution. She is the catalyst in the action: she sleeps with Kenny, even dreams of marrying him. Then she moves on, fatalistically, to a sex show. But the action has been enough to make Kenny leave home, too.

The play proves to be Inge's first great flop; and it is a production marred by disputes in which Beatty exercises a power quite unexpected in someone making his Broadway debut. The play no longer reads well. It seems both over-obvious and too discreet, as if stagecraft was covering up the depths possible in the mother-son relationship. Indeed, there is another, avoided, play close at hand, in which Kenny might sleep with Helen. But a pall of decency hangs over the dangerous prospects. Even so, when the play is published, in 1960, Inge says in the Foreword, "I have never gone into a production with a play in which I had such complete confidence."

The director is Daniel Mann, who has directed both the stage and the screen versions of *Come Back, Little Sheba* and *The Rose Tattoo*. To play Helen, Shirley Booth is cast, the star of *Sheba* and of another film directed by Mann, *About Mrs Leslie*. In addition, Mann has directed the movies of *I'll Cry Tomorrow*, *Teahouse of the August Moon* and *Hot Spell*, the cast of which includes Shirley MacLaine. The part of Lila is given to Carol Haney, who has become famous with the "Steam Heat" number in *The Pajama Game*, and whose broken ankle has afforded a big chance to MacLaine. *A Loss of Roses* is Haney's opportunity to play a big dramatic part, though no one could call her "an extraordinarily beautiful woman of thirty-two, blond and voluptuous" as described in the play. She is not the last actress who may feel daunted by the looks of her romantic partner when playing with Beatty.

A Loss of Roses has textual difficulties. Inge, as he admits, is prevailed upon to do a lot of rewriting, even to the point of making the play's climax Kenny's decision to leave home, rather than Lila's crestfallen but brave acceptance of a career in polite pornography. "I can't remember why all the changes were thought necessary," Inge writes in 1960, "but working under the pressure that exists in the theater today, people become excited and mistrust their best instincts."

The great crisis occurs after a week's try-out in Washington D.C. – at the very theater where Beatty has been hired to watch for rats – when Shirley Booth quits the production. This may be because she is unhappy with her part and with the play as a whole, but she is also troubled by the influence exerted by Warren Beatty.

Beatty and Mann are not getting on, which does not mean a lack of communication so much as persistent attempts by Beatty to stop to discuss every detail. There are stories, too, that he is coming to rehearsal late and then questioning everything possible about the play and its direction. This could be wilful sabotage; it could be the decision to impose himself at all costs, or to impress Joan Collins, often a visitor at rehearsals; and it could be chronic indecision in need of more support and conference than anyone else is disposed to provide. Mann is taken aback by his arrogance and vanity: "I have to say that Warren was one of the few problems I've had in a forty-year career, and I've directed actors like Anna Magnani, Marlon Brando, Vanessa Redgrave, Susan Hayward and Elizabeth Taylor."

Mann keeps Beatty's understudy, Dennis Cooney, in rehearsal too, and entertains the thought of firing Warren. But Beatty has Inge as his warmest defender, and Inge is not only the author. He has put $100,000 of his own money in the production. When Booth walks out, she is replaced with Betty Field, and Inge undertakes rewriting that builds up the role of Lila and plays down that of Helen. Mann says, "Warren won't listen to me, he's going to do nothing until opening night and then he'll play on the sex appeal and charm and all the crap and do something on-stage we don't even *know* about."

Apparently, Beatty will not settle into a way of playing the part that other actors can depend on. He is improvising, or – without the inspiration – shifting, hesitating, brooding, letting his doubts take over the production, like Dean drawing a scene into himself in *East of Eden*, treating a theater as if it were a camera.

A few months later, Inge tries to defend Beatty:

"Warren is really kind of like a young colt who's out in a new green pasture. He's nervous about making a picture and it brings out a most self-protective quality. As a result, he's very reluctant to trust people in charge. He has the feeling he has to design the set, the costumes, the make-up, and sometimes you want to say, 'Oh, shut up and do your part.' But he's basically a very fine kid who will eventually learn a way of working with people."

Inge does go on to publish a "restored" version of *A Loss of Roses*. But if he ever feels unduly influenced by Beatty, he never turns on him. There are two more collaborations ahead, and two roles that are undoubtedly enriched by Inge's chance to observe the actor. Still, a few days before Broadway opening – at the Eugene O'Neill Theater on November 28, 1959 – Inge knows *A Loss of Roses* "was not happening on stage".

It closes after twenty-five performances and an opening night on which, according to another actor in the production, "Warren changed lines, business, blocking, and completely screwed up Carol Haney so badly that she ran into her dressing-room in tears".

There's no reason to think Beatty knows this will be his final stage appearance, late in 1959. (Even now, in 1986, we cannot rule out a return to theater – though we may bet against it.) *A Loss of Roses* is a tumultuous experience, but he may not notice that or regard it as a cause for regret. If he does not trust, he may not sympathise. At the same time, it is a career failure, despite his own good notices, and a failure that owes something to the shortcomings of the play. And it is a play about lost hopes and social fear. When a movie is made from the play a few years later – *The Stripper*, with Richard Beymer and Joanne Woodward, the first film directed by Franklin Schaffner – it is not a good film, but it is about sex. It is possible that, on the stage, Beatty feels himself labouring with Inge's evasions, with the plodding uncovering of unsurprising things and with an actress he is not attracted to. Perhaps he is not excited, and cannot pretend arousal, no matter that Kenneth Tynan, writing in the *New Yorker*, can see that he is "sensual around the lips and pensive around the brow".

Does that face think the world must come closer and doubt be made a part of the material? He is an actor who prefers to be invaded by the perplexity of a moment, and this is something the camera delights in. It fosters the skin's worry about what to say, the eyes' uncertainty; and it is close enough to hear sighs and breathing, not just the script you have to learn – as if anyone in life, Warren says, *knows* the lines. Yet such a doubting actor is a tyrant too, not just determined to have his way, but incapable of bending to the necessity of collaboration, performance and giving to order that constitutes theater. For on the stage, the actor is servant to the play and the public – it is not him on show but his pretending. But in the movies, it is all him.

Tusk & Zale

D would never have guessed the ritual with which these major motion picture people regarded his script. For him it was a recent labor in which he hoped the regular pages, the carefully checked typing and the complex lay-out were compelling without being distastefully anal. There are so many things that can be wrong in a script – the numbering of the scenes, the use of capitals for every character, the consistent indentation of dialogue, not to mention the proper use of technical terms and the leanness whereby 120 pages can be scanned in thirty minutes without loss.

A writer is intent on correctness, on eliminating errors, typos and blemishes in his paper. The bound block of pages must be without guilt. It is mortification to have someone show you a "freind" on page fifty-six, or a "MICHA@L" at the point of climax.

But here, at the apogee of the movie pyramid, D was expected to tell the story to some faces he recognised from the celebrity press, and others full of sultry spite or lavish innocence current in fashion and fitness imagery. He had kept to himself his bewilderment at how Clear had cognisance of the script. D concluded that the Eyes' organization had access to the computer xerography he had employed to make copies of his script. But with the load of scripts being prepared in the city – D had heard as high as 77,000 a day – no human reader could have picked his out. No, Clear's computer must have seen his script's absolute correctness, been triggered by its title and passed that on for eyes which noticed the desirable male lead factor. Of course, D had used the approved system of color coding – red for violence, blue for talk, silver for motion and white for nakedness. Clear might have seen an intricate print-out – an emotional map, or a wave involvement profile – but he had probably not read it.

Such thoughts were soon confirmed. For Clear took D aside into a smaller and noise-reduced room that had no windows. There was a

John Gutmann, *Cynics, Hollywood*, 1944

severe and exquisite white table in the middle of the room at which two men sat in sharkskin suits, vests and ties. Clear introduced them as Zale and Tusk, lawyers to Eyes Enterprises. They greeted D slavishly, and had him sit facing them. There were no papers, no cases, no folders, no phones on the table. Business here was as ideological as torture.

"D," said Clear, "a *petit* formality."

"A dull preliminary," added Tusk, while Zale studied the corners of the ceiling. As his partner's attention slowly sank, Tusk teased, "You're not going to be difficult?"

"Certainly not," D assured them.

"Because you have a lot to gain here," Zale said.

"Exactly," Tusk noted, "and we only need you to sign an agreement that we and all members of Eyes Enterprises have not seen your script . . . what's it called? My head is jello, today."

"*The Center of Attention*," supplied Clear. "Such a good title."

"You think so?" asked Zale.

"Don't you?" Clear asked.

Zale considered. "Seems cold to me. Of course, my wife's the title man. She knows as soon as she hears them. She writes titles, you know. Likes to have something to do in the day."

"It's the only way," said Tusk, "otherwise the bitches start fucking the gardener, the plumber, the chimney-sweep --"

"You have chimneys still in Brentwood?" Clear wanted to know.

"Just for decor," Tusk told him. "But if you've got 'em, clean 'em, is what I say."

"You want I should call my wife?" Zale asked. "She was the one who did *A Virtuoso Personality* and *Everything That Goes With a Kiss*."

"I don't know those," said wide-eyed D.

"Never made," said Zale. "But they got heavy development. They were very big for a time."

"So," said Tusk to D, "we just want your John Hancock."

"However," D began, and the room went quieter. Nothing else in the world could be heard, and D's bold point of view dropped to a whisper. "You *have* seen it."

"Well," Clear simpered, indulgent of technicalities.

"We are *discussing*," D explained.

"He's trouble," sighed Tusk.

"You have expressed *interest*."

"Not a warm enough word," Clear smiled.

"We have talked of *seeing Eyes*."

93

"Very soon." Clear stood up and strolled around the room. Zale and Tusk never took their eyes off D. "You are a breath of fresh air, if that doesn't sound patronising."

This remark didn't trouble D at all; he had always thought well of fresh air, but as seldom as he thought of living in the South Seas.

"I believe we are going to make this picture," said Clear.

"It's 80:20," said Zale.

"85:15," was Tusk's estimate.

"Let me add," Clear went on, "that I have never known these two so bullish at this stage of a project."

"That's true," the partners confessed, and D saw that, if the optimism was rare, the two hardnoses were not ashamed of it.

"Still," said Clear, "experience has taught us it is injudicious –"

"Very dangerous," said Tusk.

"A no-no," was Zale's rule.

"– to be seen to have seen a script," Clear finished.

"Ah," said D. It was all he had to do to give a rhythm to the explanation.

"Open a package," Clear speculated, "slip off a rubber band, return a script with thanks but no thanks and we are open to the charge of having read it. Then years later perhaps, if a name, a line, a situation crops up in some other film – and nothing is ever utterly original – we may be liable to a hole-in-the-wall verminous lying whine that we stole it. I abhor the cunts!"

"Clear has suffered for this," said Zale.

"It gets him wild," said Tusk.

"Fellows," Clear was his old self again, "you are salt of the earth. But still, D, I hope you see the problem. We have been hit for a great deal in the past."

"Mucho cash," said Zale.

"Not to mention professional respect," was Tusk's unhealed wound.

"As a result," Clear picked up the ball, "it is our policy when entertaining a project to first get the writer's signed statement that we have not seen the script. Then, if by any chance, we do not make the picture, we are not shitface down the road."

"We have the papers here," Tusk added, sliding three copies of the one sheet from a card-thin drawer in the white table.

"Now, D," said Clear, "I am your friend, and I should tell you that you might seek advice at this point."

"Oh, Cleary," groaned Zale.

"I don't care," said Clear. "D is special, and I value his trust."

"Fiddle-de-dee," said Zale, looking the other way.

"Of course," Clear admitted, "delay can spoil a mood. And this is a moody art. Hesitation could also mar what promises to be an exciting night."

"I don't want to hesitate," said D.

"This is an intelligent man," Tusk noticed.

"Though I should see my family."

"Oh yes," Clear dismissed the delay, and then to the lawyers, "Isn't he a brick?"

"I suppose I should sign," said D. "But –"

"You want an option?" Zale knew it.

"Well –"

"It's not unreasonable," Tusk agreed.

"D *is* coming to meet us," said Clear, "and I daresay a little short of funds?"

"No funds," said D.

"You could buy some things for the little ones," said Clear.

"My wife has a gift boutique on Camden," said Tusk. "If you'd like to look. Here's her card."

"So the feeling is for some modest passing of . . ." said Zale.

"Money?" Clear filled in the blank.

"Done and done," said Zale. "Give us your signature, kid," and he rolled a pen across the table to D, who signed the three pages with the best writing he could muster. Not that D is a rich name calligraphically.

Tusk returned the three sheets to their drawer. He then stood up and, as it appeared, broke a corner off the very table!

"Hurrah!" cried Clear.

But D saw that Tusk had not a broken, ragged corner of the table in his hands, but a clean oblong. The corner was a separate piece waiting to be detached. It was a slender briefcase, which Tusk now pushed across the table towards D.

"Enjoy yourself," he told him.

One white catch secured the case. D pressed it and the lid bounced up. He felt a cool air come up from inside the case. He wondered if he was gazing at salad, lettuce, cucumber and so on, there was such an impression of green and white. But it was money. Six packs of bills, all with Benjamin Franklin on them, his wise face unflustered.

"Fifteen thou," said Zale.

"For starters," Tusk reminded.

D heard a click in his rapture, then a rattle. By the time he looked up, Clear was able to present him with a photograph of an amazed face. His. He looked like someone in a comedy.

"Your first souvenir," said Clear.

JEWEL IN THE NAVEL

Joan Collins is close to twenty-six when she first sees him. She is English, married once to another actor Maxwell Reed, divorced and upheld by the judge as not having to pay him support. She has made pictures since 1951, and her late teens. But in 1954, she has her big break, playing a vicious wanton in Howard Hawks' enchantingly silly *Land of the Pharaohs*. Not the least point of note about this film is that in her abbreviated costume, Joan has to wear a ruby in her navel to satisfy the censors. She has a very taut stomach, and admirable muscle control, but still a little glue has to be employed to hold the jewel in place.

She plays with Errol Flynn and Bette Davis in *The Virgin Queen*; she is Evelyn Nesbit in *The Girl in the Red Velvet Swing*; she is under contract to Twentieth Century Fox and they put her in *Island in the Sun*, *The Bravados* and *Rally Round the Flag, Boys*. She is attractive; she can be "sexy" in that rather deliberate English way that can never quite take it seriously; she has a sense of fun, and she enjoys herself in Hollywood. Her money comes and goes; she has several boy friends. Fox are not likely to renew her contract. She has had her moments.

In a restaurant, La Scala, with friends, she realises she is being studied by a young man at another table. "That boy who's looking at you," says the friend, "is Shirley MacLaine's brother, Warren something or other."

This is the spring of 1959, during Beatty's first visit to Hollywood. He is an actor without any movie credits, a pretty face most easily placed in a possible scheme of nepotism. Living cheaply at the Chateau Marmont Hotel on Sunset Boulevard, he had seen photographs of Collins, been interested, and gone to see her in *The Bravados*, a Gregory Peck Western. That disappointed him: it is a man's picture, and Joan has little chance to look glamorous in the glaring sunlight. But then he sees her at La Scala. He is with Jane Fonda – they may have just done their screen test, or perhaps they are on their way to it, plotting that impacted kiss.

Joan notices that she is being noticed. This may not be her chief reason for eating out, but she is like any movie personality in that she can eat and chat with a friend while registering everyone who comes and goes in the dining room and what attention they pay to her. If you are not of the business, you may think such a personality is neglecting you. But they can tell you everything you have said; they can break away and still pick up the old conversation a moment later. You may feel slow, dogged or limited, but they will not admit shame or ambition. It is their life to be seen, and they see themselves as if they were on a screen. Technical details so preoccupy them that vanity seems eclipsed. They are not always quite there. Their loveliness is there, their presence. But their inner being may be removed, watching how the show goes. Their presence is hugely sensitive, as the body and the image must be when they are detached from the soul. It is like a child's first adventure without parents.

Joan looks at the other table and sees: "He was about twenty-one or twenty-two. Blondish slightly curly hair, worn rather longer than was fashionable, a square-cut Clark Kent type of jaw with a Kirk Douglas dimple in the chin – rather small greenish eyes, but a cute turned-up nose and a sensual mouth. From where I sat it looked as though he suffered from a problem I had once had – *spots*! He wore a blue Brooks Brothers shirt and a tweed jacket. All in all, he looked rather appealing and vulnerable, and my interest was somewhat piqued."

He is talking all the while to Jane Fonda, and she is listening to him intently. Perhaps he looks away sometimes, into empty space, as he schemes the kiss of their futures, the better to see whether Joan is noticing being noticed. There is a moment where he raises his glass to her in an unspoken toast, a movie gesture in which the code of seeing and being seen has been formulated and broadcast for forty years already.

Some days later, Joan is invited to a Beverly Hills party at the house of Debbie Power, the widow of Tyrone. It is crowded when she gets there – "The usual mob doing the usual things – drinking, gossiping, talking box-office grosses, whiling away another forgettable evening," – but she realises that someone is playing the piano rather well. It was Warren something-or-other, doing imitations of Oscar Peterson, George Shearing and Erroll Garner. She drew nearer – Warren at the piano, intent on the keys, but looking up at the dark-haired beauty (who happened to be wearing Bermuda shorts, a shirt, a ponytail and no makeup – "A cross between Jackie Cooper and Betty Coed."). He looks up, notices her and smiles, "but he appeared totally absorbed in his music."

With Joan Collins

The next day, Sunday, Joan goes to the beach and returns to her Shorelawn Drive apartment to get ready for a cocktail party. She checks her answering service and discovers that a Warren Beatty has called six times from the Chateau Marmont. She wonders how he discovered her number. The calls are better than roses. She puts down her phone, and, like magic, it rings again.

"Hi, did you get my messages?" says the voice, without identifying itself.

It takes movie people, ardent for magic, to cling on to the transcendent intuitive power of the telephone. They do not take it for granted. They realise that two people talking on the telephone are like two close-ups, two streams of film, that could be cut and blended together in the flow of a love scene. The phone is better still for movie lovers for the close-ups stay intact. When at last, in film, two faces kiss, they so easily squash and obscure one another. It may be most romantic for a picture to pause on the edge of the kiss, the two beautiful faces still alone in narcissistic splendor. Let the audience go home and kiss.

This may sound fanciful, yet the dynamics of the phone conversation are very close to the grammar of movie sequences. Infinite use of the telephone is a measure of wealth, and of feeling ignoring budget. And the phone call that finds you unexpectedly may be as sudden and erotic as a hand coming to rest on a thigh in the dark. The love affair that follows between Joan and Warren is an experience of two would-be stars, of sex appeal, of fondness, of a fellow-feeling for publicity. It is all of these, surely, but it is the phone speaking, too. For the telephone is, among all other things, the instrument of intimacy for those who may not want actually to be with one another. The service, and now the answering machine, are further manifestations of the power it offers.

Joan is near the end of an affair at this moment with George Englund, a producer, who has talked about but never quite managed to leave his wife Cloris Leachman. Joan and Warren have a Mexican dinner that Sunday night at Casa Escobar, and he follows her back to her place in their separate cars. He goes up for coffee.

"We became inseparable." She thinks they have everything in common. They talk all night and make love and when she goes to work on her current picture, *Seven Thieves*, she looks the worse for wear. Friends tell her he's too young, too blatantly ambitious, probably using her to get ahead. But she likes him, his attentiveness, his talk, his quiet mind and the way he understands her. She's sure he will be a success without her. She goes to meet Englund at the Cock and Bull, to end that affair, but she kisses George in the parking lot and when she gets back to the apartment Warren is not there. He comes in in a moment, throwing off his jacket and his glasses. She remembers he tipped over a stool without those glasses. He had followed her to the rendezvous, driven around the Cock and Bull for two hours, seen the kiss. They have to make up. If they could either of them admit it, they do not want a settled life, for it would seem to negate ambition. If they fight a good deal, it may be vital to all their loving.

They are committed to each other before he has to go east to rehearse *A Loss of Roses*. "He plunged into rehearsals with enthusiasm and optimism," she remembers. When *Seven Thieves* is completed, she joins him in Washington DC for the try-outs. They stay at the Willard Hotel, but she meets and likes his parents. No matter the problems with the Inge play, Warren has time to advise her. Jerry Wald has just offered her the part of the older woman in his forthcoming picture of *Sons and Lovers*. It is the most demanding part she has ever had a chance at – it will win Mary Ure an Oscar nomination – but Warren tells her she shouldn't do it. He doesn't like the script and he doesn't want her leaving now for England. "Don't go, Butterfly," he begs. "Don't leave your Bee."

They go on to the Blackstone Hotel in New York for the opening of *A Loss of Roses*. When the play fails they stay on over the holiday period, after eating at the Harwyn Club, which gives them free meals for the publicity.

Then early in 1960 they return to Los Angeles. It is an election year, and John Kennedy is running. They live in an apartment at the Chateau Marmont. Warren works with her on scripts, they get into a health food diet and they prowl drugstores looking for pictures of themselves together in the magazines.

A film is being talked about for Warren – *Splendor in the Grass*, written by William Inge, directed by Elia Kazan. She says he was on the phone all day, to his agent and to Inge, who was pressing for him to be cast. "He was never happier than when he was on the phone, and he didn't need a phone book to remember the important numbers he constantly called." So he telephoned, she read scripts, and they made love – four or five times a day. He would take calls when they were in bed, when he was in her, rolling aside a little to make them both a little more comfortable and so that he could look away at the wall to concentrate and imagine. On the other end of the line, people noticed his pauses, the sound of his breathing, as if he was doing something else. The legend of his prowess was being bugged, at his own instigation. As

Joan remembers him, working with her on a script, "He was an excellent director and a patient teacher, with an intense and intellectual approach to exploring the depths and details of a characterization."

The pitch

A whimsical equilibrium had overtaken D. He smiled when he noticed it. He had these tidy white blocks under either arm: the script and the case of money. And since the two looked so abstract, D thought of himself as a jockey carrying weights in his saddle for a handicap. So far, his story seemed worth its weight in money.

D recognised that the bulk of the $15,000 could have been avoided. A check might have come in an envelope, no thicker than a Valentine. But the system had a sentimental side; it appreciated measure for measure. And D realised that, just as they did not want to look at his script, so it would be vulgar in him to open the case and peep. It was enough to know what was there, a solidity of cash. He might slide it into a vault and never touch it. He would die a pauper, a pauper with a happy dream, knowing the dry, green paper waited in its darkness. Money! D whispered, under his arm like a new girl.

And so D followed Clear, Zale and Tusk into the large room. The people there were deployed as if to indicate trepidation that their entertainment had depended on the legal negotiations. There was a smattering of applause as D emerged in which he heard well-bred restraint and sheer lust for sensation. To have money and be wanted, he thought; it was enough to make one beautiful. And D noticed now that not one of the handsome men or women skipped over him. They looked at him, their eyes brimming and fascinated.

"Take it away, D, baby," a soft voice called out of the twilight, and D noticed an elan coming over him, a vibrance he had always wanted. Perhaps he *was* made for show business. Still, he wished he could absent himself quickly for a wee-wee. He hardly wanted to spout his story standing cross-legged.

Zale and Tusk were supervising the setting up of a video camera in the corner. A younger man was in charge of the equipment, but the two lawyers were fussing to be sure its lens swallowed the whole assembly. D guessed his talk was to be taped, and perhaps sent on to Eyes, who must be too busy to be there himself. How inventively the new technology let the busy become busier.

The people in the room turned towards the camera, and in a low but clear voice – not stale from habit, but reverent, like nuns saying grace – they chanted, "I swear that, despite any information or anecdotes being shared in what follows, I have not seen the screenplay of *The Center of Attention*. Furthermore, I attest that I will in no way seek to sell, offer or report on the story of the script. So help me, God. Now this."

Like any good grace, it was appetite-whetting, a proof of readiness and spirits open for wonder. D had not been prepared for the simple disclaimer – he could hardly join in it himself, though (like a good Jew in a Catholic Church) he was sufficiently moved by the sense of the congregation that he might have joined in to be sporting.

"D," said Clear, "I think at long last we are ready for you."

"Well," said D, stepping forward with a will.

*

"Go on," said Clear.

"What was that?" asked D. Something in the fundament, he thought, had shifted.

"Did the earth move, D, honey?" a droll female wondering came up from the cushions.

"It's your excitement," Clear ventured to explain.

But D was not convinced. He had felt a bump, as when reels change, even reels on a fresh print, and his inner eyes had seen the two blobs in the top corner of the screen, sunspots in the brightness. Had anything altered? As if he owned the place and the entourage, D strode to the window and looked down on the city. His Drew came to his side. The buildings were as they should be, erect in their places, poised and unmoving like the advancing gang in grandmother's footsteps. The traffic was burning out the dark core of the highways.

"Tell us your story, D," said Drew, a child disturbed by talk of trouble.

D was not scared, no matter his certainty that something had happened. He looked out towards the horizon, the twinkle of lights going so valiantly into the tawny black of the sky, and there above, the crinkled edge of ground, a few stars. He felt Drew's tentative hand on his arm, and it did not stop his imagination soaring out there to the desert, to the supposedly devastated lands which somehow seemed more tranquil and possible than this jittery city.

*

He walked forward to the shack where the equipment was kept. It was cold and the wind tugged at his fine cotton slacks. He should have put shoes on.

"What was it?" he couldn't walk all the way, not in the dark, with scorpions about.

George's studious voice came back from the shack, "Four seven."

"I knew it," said Eyes. "I can feel 'em."

*

There was an anxious hush in the room when D turned round. Not one of them, maybe, had noticed anything, but they could not dismiss the force of his intuition. The storyteller always knows. Clear came up to D so filled with scrutiny that D felt like a large, late Rothko, or a two-way mirror.

He could see Clear was too much in awe to speak.

"There is the look of an adventurer on your face. Like a deep, prosperous tan," said Clear. D smiled and looked away at Drew who appeared as struck by his unwitting grandeur.

"By the way, what time is it?" D asked.

"Just past eight," said Clear.

"Nine in the desert," murmured D.

He was about to reclaim the center of the room, but he paused very near Clear so that no one else could hear them. "You understand, this thing, the entire enterprise – chaff in the wind."

"Oh, absolutely," smiled Clear, and D realised that this master of poise had a touch of desperado in him. Or desperation.

"Let's start, then," D decided.

He stood for an instant, considering how to tell the story. Then the story came up behind him like a wave and it told him:

There is a young man, an orphan, brought up by an uncle and aunt. He has not found a persuasive course in his life, one to match his uncle's success in business or his aunt's glory in charity.

So the young man spends his time at one of his family's homes, a modernist mansion in the West.

It is a house in the high desert, still, hot and dry, and the young man does little except shoot pool, confront the view, talk to the black man who looks after him and watch television in the basement.

This black, who is fond of the young man, is beginning to think the young man's mind is disturbed by the solitude and the emptiness of his days.

The young man has taken to recording the appearances of a beautiful young woman weathercaster. He has a three-hour assembly of her forecasts.

He writes to this woman at the network that employs her. But the letters are not answered.

He tries to telephone her, but the calls are not taken.

"Why do you like her so?" the black man asks.

The young man points to the screen. The woman is saying, "torrid winds tomorrow".

He learns that the President of the country is in the habit of riding in a nearby valley in the mornings.

He goes there at dawn and sees a figure riding, probably the President, guarded by an entourage. Up and down the valley.

Then he writes again to the weathercaster saying how much he wants to be with her, and how he knows where the President rides. But this letter is not answered.

There is a day in the mansion when the kindness of the black man, peppery enchiladas and trick shots at pool cannot lift the young man from his depression.

The next day the young man goes to the nearby valley at dawn and fires at the President with a rifle, wounding him.

The young man is instantly apprehended by the President's guards.

There is a national frenzy at this latest violence, the threat to the presidency and the sinister influence of television on a deranged personality.

The officers of the network that has the woman's weather are savaged in the press. The woman is cast in a movie.

"I never knew him," announces this new actress.

"We are mortified," say the aunt and uncle.

The booming of editorials is heard in the land.

The black man says, "This is a sad kid with a great hurt."

The President says, "He only winged me."

The actress's secretaries discover letters from the young man in the rooms of unanswered mail.

The pitch

"I admire her," says the young man, "and I wanted to get her attention."

The actress visits the President in hospital.

The young man is examined by psychiatrists, who decide he manifests an inability to recognise obstacles to desire.

The young man is tried for attempted murder and found guilty but insane.

Restored to work, the President reaffirms policies of eliminating the deficit by growth, says he feels niftier for the rest and reckons that America is getting happier than ever.

The actress's film does poorly. Entertainment pundits believe it is because of public reaction to the "example" she set the young man.

The uncle says his nephew should be shot, while the aunt wonders if he had adequate love or understanding.

The aunt calls on the President and they are photographed.

She visits the actress and they go on *Donahue* together.

An article is written by a film professor on how the affair is a consequence of stardom and imagery's generation of a supra-human identity for the weathercaster.

The actress's agent and personal manager devise a plan whereby – with full coverage – the actress will visit the young man in the hospital, proving to him that she is an ordinary young woman.

The aunt asks for the young man to be restored to her custody so that she can re-initiate the process of love and maturation left lacking.

The uncle says justice has been travestied.

The President admits he doesn't understand the fuss.

The actress does visit the hospital and she is allowed to meet the young man, but neither can recognise the other as dull or ordinary. Instead they fall in love.

Enlisting the aid of her personal bodyguard and saying he can come along to make sure she is not in danger, the actress engineers the young man's escape from the hospital.

The three of them go away to the parks of the West pursued by the authorities, the security forces, doctors and lawyers, the uncle, the aunt, the President and sundry movie deal-makers.

"Mad Lovers in Desert" say the headlines.

And D paused there. He knew the resolution to the story. But in the telling, he had seen the desirability in movie stories of having no ending, the plot left in suspense, so that the story can go on forever. Movies, being a medium that shows things – which sometimes threaten to show everything, or to arrive at a reality in which nothing exists if it cannot be seen – secretly aspire to enigma and the unseen. There is no moment so precious in a film as that in which terror is promised but not yet disclosed. And so D learned from this opportunity to tell his story the special potency of the answer withheld.

So D waited and looked at the begging faces of his listeners. There was a faraway rumbling of thunder as if the dream he was telling snored or groaned in the slight ruffling of its sleep.

In his retreat in the halfway high desert, Eyes pondered the prospects of the erstwhile weather woman and her young man blown across the landscape by love and flight. And he wondered if he could be young again.

NATALIE

A moment in the TV night: a segment from *60 Minutes*, on the famine in Ethiopia, with Mike Wallace at a relief settlement center in Bati, being shown around by a white Catholic priest, assessing the drought, the failure of harvests and the many hundreds of thousands who make their way across the barren veldt hearing the rumors of food, a baby born in front of the camera, somehow no larger than a hydrocephalic embryo, and then wrapped in rags, the children's eyes on sticks, the folds of unfilled skin, the heads like cellophane stretched around the ovoid skulls and always the eyes, not like parts of their devastated bodies, but creatures unto themselves, the body eating itself and the certainty of permanent brain damage in the babies from the malnutrition, the possibility of a generation of idiots if they survive, the home of the dead where the bodies are brought every day, the one doctor and the four nurses, and the children as thin as spiders staggering across the grassless plain, and the priest saying to Mike Wallace, "Do you know the President, the President of America?" – this is greater than CBS – and Mike says yes and the priest says tell *him*.

Into the announcer's voice and the flourish of music: "Tonight, Charlton Heston, George Kennedy, Ava Gardner, Lorne Greene and Geneviève Bujold face the natural disaster we all fear the most. It could happen anytime. Tonight on Channel 2, *Earthquake*. Portions of this movie may not be suitable for young children."

*

In the early part of 1960, Joan Collins realises she is pregnant. She and Beatty talk of marrying, or of having the child and then putting it out for adoption. But they settle on an abortion, and Beatty calls friends in New York to discover the best operative. There are moments when Joan changes her mind and wants the child, but he dissuades her. She says he

109

tells her, "Butterfly, we *can't*, we can't do it. Having a baby now will wreck both of our careers – you know it will."

So they fly to New York together, where he will soon start filming *Splendor in the Grass*, and one day he drives her to a high-rise in Newark. When they get there, she notices that he is sweating with anxiety. They comfort one another that nothing will go wrong. She has the operation and they spend a night in a cheap hotel as she recovers. In the course of the next few days, she discovers that her diamond necklace is missing. In her book, *Past Imperfect*, Joan Collins surmises that it was probably stolen by a hotel maid.

The couple take an apartment on Fifth Avenue and Warren begins filming *Splendor in the Grass*, with Elia Kazan and co-star Natalie Wood. A little younger than Warren, Wood is already a veteran star. She has begun in movies as a child, playing in *Tomorrow is Forever*, *Miracle on 34th Street* and *No Sad Songs for Me*. Her own teenage years coincide with the explosion of interest in adolescents in films, and she has had success and a kind of immortality by playing opposite James Dean in Nicholas Ray's *Rebel Without a Cause*, the essential Dean movie in that its setting and its melodrama of teenage frustration are contemporary.

Thereafter, for Warners, she has appeared in John Ford's *The Searchers*, she has won the part of *Marjorie Morningstar* and been borrowed by Frank Sinatra for *Kings Go Forth*. But nothing has had the raw emotional impact of *Rebel*, and nothing has yet established Wood as a mature, disciplined actress rather than a desperate risk-taker who responded to the mood of *Rebel* and the authority of Dean. Her career is at a turning point, and in *Splendor in the Grass* she has by far the most complex role of her career.

Though set in Inge's Kansas again, locations for *Splendor* are found on Staten Island and Long Island, and interiors are filmed at New York's Filmways studio. Joan Collins sees a few scenes being filmed and envies Warren having such a celebrated director, probably the best living director of young actors, for his first film. But she has to give most of her time to taking Italian lessons, for she is due to depart for Rome, where her career has worked its way around to *Esther and the King*, a biblical epic.

Before she goes, she and Warren become engaged. As she describes the proposal it is as charming as a scene from a 1930s romantic comedy. In the middle of the afternoon, as she is reading the *Esther* script, he says he fancies some chopped liver. There is some in the refrigerator. Joan gets up to find it, he waits and calls out, "Does it fit?" He has put a gold ring with diamonds and pearls in the chopped liver.

"'It's your engagement ring, dummy,' he said, grinning like a Cheshire cat. 'I figured, since you're going away soon and we'll be separated we should um, well, um, you know . . .' He shuffled embarrassedly. Took the glasses off. Put them on again. Grabbed a couple of Vitamin C tablets and crunched them. 'Get – well, engaged. What do you think?' He looked anxious.

"'I think it's a great idea – just terrific,' I squeaked happily. 'Are you sure you really want to – I mean you're not just doing this to make me feel secure, are you?'

"'No, Butterfly, I'm not – you know I don't do anything unless I want to . . . and . . . um . . . well . . . um . . . I guess I want to. We . . . er, could get married at the end of the year.' He took his glasses off again and we burst out laughing."

If it *is* a movie, anyone saying "you know I don't do anything unless I want to" is testifying to his own insecurity. For a young actor, like any actor, is hoping to be liked, hoping to be hired and then told what to do and say, which way to look, when to smile and pause, and hoping in all of this performance that he will be good and that he will be liked . . . It is a natural part of that insecurity for a young, decently attractive and reasonably sexed young actor to fall in love with his leading lady, not simply out of proximity and kissing scenes, or because their roles are those of people forever thwarted in coming together, but because they are both in the same dilemma – hoping to be liked – and in a predicament where they are the most likely reassurance for one another. Elia Kazan may have a hunch, and a hope, for the good of his picture, that Beatty and Natalie Wood will have an affair. There's no reason for him to think it need outlast the filming; he does not care for them as much after that, and it is not callous to be so devoted to his project. It is important for him that the kids look loved, and in love. Movie acting sucks on the real personality of the actor; the emptied areas are sometimes filled up with vanity and insecurity. For in acting, and American acting especially, there can be a nearly complete confusion of the character's aspirations and the actor's professional desire.

Kazan can explain this, in terms of theory: "There's a basic element in the Stanislavsky system that has always helped me a lot in directing actors in the movies. The key word, if I had to pick one, is 'to want'. We used to say in the theatre: 'What are you on stage *for*? What do you walk on stage to get? What do you want?'"

Actors fall in love with actresses for so many reasons – they may have to kiss each other over and over again, and the practice can make perfect;

their success in the fiction depends upon the expression of yearning in their faces; and desire is the engine of movies, the energy they cling to. There is another reason, nearly occult: actors are worthy of each other, they have the same rating in the currency of fame, and it endangers stardom to seem happy with unknown people. No one knows of a lengthy relationship in Warren's privacy-seeking life that is not with a famous woman. There is a caste system, and Natalie Wood is at his level and moment.

She has played the child who didn't believe in Santa Claus in *Miracle on 34th Street*. But in her own life, she has never realised that one has a choice about being a movie star. Her mother has done everything possible to foster her career – she is photographed wherever she goes, and she is encouraged to look on Dennis Hopper, Tab Hunter, Elvis Presley and others as possible boyfriends. When she graduates from Van Nuys High School, there are movie studio photographers there ready to transmit the event to the fan magazines. She is internationally famous, yet she is the princess of a small principality – greater Los Angeles, the very backdrop for the drama of *Rebel Without a Cause* – a bride for its courtiers and its lights.

When she is nineteen, she is married to Robert Wagner, a perennial Prince Charming of Beverly Hills who will never manage to get character into his acting or the little boy out of his face. Wagner is in his mid-fifties today. He was eight years older than Wood, but a less forceful screen presence. When Wood is shooting *Marjorie Morningstar* in the Adirondacks, living at a hotel with her mother and her sister, Lana, Wagner joins her and sleeps with Natalie in one suite, with her mother and Lana next door. According to Lana, their mother quells any doubts and serves the young lovers breakfast in bed. When he proposes, Wagner calls on Natalie with a bottle of champagne and two glasses. The engagement ring is waiting at the bottom of her glass. Everything sparkles.

They go by train to Florida for their honeymoon. But Wagner has allowed one photographer to ride with them and, though he tells Natalie the pictures are private, for their use alone, still they get into all the papers. There is no reason to doubt that Wagner and Wood are in love, but just as little to deny that in the principality such a union is a dynastic offering to the media. It is one thing to surmise that professional show people, that actors, do not have any sense of privacy. It is another to wonder whether we are already the self-righteous advocates of privacy because we know we will never achieve fame. It is the culture of movies that has led us to respect intimacy being posted up on a screen twenty-feet high.

How does one describe such marriages as that of Wood and Wagner except to say that its mythic appeal for the lovers themselves was so great that they would need to do it twice? Natalie spends time and money decorating their Beverly Hills home in white and gold, and becomes a talk of the principality because her taste is less than exquisite. The bride is terrified of all the pressures in her life. She takes sleeping pills, because it is important that the camera sees her untired, but also because at her level of the principality you do not have a problem without seeking recourse in purchase and action. She goes into analysis, against Wagner's wishes. It is possible that a famous actress is close to being a human wreck, and that her desirability on screen is the consequence of her vulnerability. Perhaps the analyst has thought of telling her to give up acting. But if being has not yet been worked out, what else is there? And analysts are like Los Angeles High Schools, they are eager to keep famous names on their rolls.

No one has ever thought to look upon Warren Beatty as a human wreck. It is the measure of his distinction, his dark understanding of Hollywood and his superior intelligence that he has taken care of himself. But he will be, and he certainly wants to be, the closest thing Natalie Wood has encountered, since his death, to James Dean. A princess only knows it is her duty to find a prince; analysis may also tell her it is her freedom and her nature to be royally joined.

*

Elia Kazan is known for his work with actors – Brando, Steiger, Dean, Clift – but he believes he is most sympathetic to actresses:

> "I'm better with actresses. And I think your remark about the tenderness is true because for me it's part of sex. I like womanliness, I like character in a woman."

Directors do not always sleep with actresses, and actresses do not fall in love with every director – at least, not every actress. But I doubt that good, vital films – I am trying to edge around the unerring erotic part in the life of films, which has as much to do with their invocation of voyeurism as with working affairs – are made without the possibility. The actress needs to trust the director, to believe that she is better understood, more seen into, more naked, more honestly presented, than she has ever been before. The director needs to see the actress as potentially veiled or obscured and to believe that at this moment he can decently undress her. It is not unlike analysis, and if either party is ever disconcerted by the closeness of an affair or of the way seeing is standing in for fucking, then they can use the process as a version of therapy, a step towards inner cleanliness.

Something intriguing happens during the filming of *Splendor in the Grass*. The film has a scene in which Natalie Wood has to cry. She tells Kazan she doesn't think she can do it. Whereupon, Kazan asks Barbara Loden to join them. She is an actress playing a smaller but striking part in the film, that of Warren Beatty's sister. She is blonde, not quite beautiful, but with a bitter, wolfish, intelligent face. Kazan asks her to cry for Natalie, on the spot.

Loden lowers her head and puts her hands over her eyes. In less than a minute, she looks up and tears are pouring from her eyes. Kazan asks Wood what she thinks of that. Natalie is very impressed, and jealous. "But did you feel anything?" Kazan asks. "No," says Natalie, "I was in awe of her being able to do that. But I wasn't moved."

"Exactly," says Kazan. "Barbara can do it in an instant. She has a special ability. But she was just doing it, just showing you. There was no emotion involved. As long as you are honest with yourself, as long as you show genuine emotion, it won't matter if there are tears or not. The scene calls for you to show pain, not necessarily tears. Show pain, Natalie, and if it is real it will be all that is needed."

When Natalie plays the scene, the crew gives her an ovation. She will be nominated for Best Actress Oscar; I think *Splendor in the Grass* is the best thing she ever did, and I am sure that owes something to the affection and trust shared by her and Kazan, as well as the stimulus of Warren Beatty. But the story also helps show the movies' manipulation of feelings, as well as their sometimes desperate insistence that they deal in the real thing. Barbara Loden never made it as a movie actress; that face was too sharp, too hard in its refusal to try to be lovely. But she directed one very fine film, *Wanda*, before she died, a low-budget, 16 mm, independent picture, not very well known. By then she was married to Elia Kazan, for his first wife had died in 1963 after a long illness.

Word of mouth

The premises of Eyes Enterprises were now beset with word of mouth. Even deaf, you would have recognised the fever people breathed in one another's ears. Wherever you looked, in corners or corridors, in camera or in conclave, heads were turned, face to face, like flowers gossiping over some panic their roots had felt in the ground. Mouths moved, heads dipped and swayed, and as eyebrows arched so hands came up, lifting the weight of amazement. There were already discreet lines at the phones as word was passed out, around the town, to brokers, agents, career-makers, hairdressers and astrologers.

D wondered about the communal oath taken not so long ago, and now tossed to the wind, like confetti. He was stirred by the tribute to his story. But it impressed him that the ceremony of the vow had all along fostered loose talk. It had initiated the low, superstitious murmur. In Hollywood, censorship has been among the greatest stimuli of the creative process. And while there is an intimacy thrilled by "just between you and I", "strictly off the record" and "don't let this go any further" – like the caressing of a private part – still, it is a world in which the urge to be seen must broadcast its privacy. It is a precious gift to these people to be told a secret, and ordered not to divulge it. Word of mouth is bearing witness, and so secrecy is a convention or a genre, like sincerity or the Western, archaic but admired.

A cynic or an outsider might be scornful of such deviousness. But that misses the idealism in word of mouth, and what it reveals of the religious instinct in the community. For they long to believe; and nothing fires the longing better than the prospect of a great film.

D saw faces transformed by his story. They were younger; they were in love. Eyes shone in the dead, handsome faces. People were approaching him all the time with their touching attempts to convey the effect he had had on them. He felt like an evangelist. He wanted to bless them and assure them that everything would be all right soon. Was there ever a people so anxious to have their lives and their exhausted bodies massaged by the wind of fiction?

"D, it gave me hope."

"It did?"

"I see a colossal first weekend, and I know it has legs."

"We are all very eager to make sure of the legs."

"There are Oscars here. This is the one that makes Eyes untouchable."

"He does deserve it."

"D, you're a genius. No, don't blush. You are, you really are. And you're cute – I saw it before the others, I said so. Why don't you come to my aerobics class Tuesday, and maybe my lime sorbet after?"

"I'm not entirely clear about Tuesday."

"So, name your day, D. Who's proud if Jesus is in Town?"

Chuckling helplessly, and backing away with his hands raised – like someone in a dream who finds himself before a firing squad – D realised the need to urinate. He recalled the black bathroom; it seemed an age ago that he had showered in there, and come out to find Drew ready with her last rite. Still carrying his two white packets, he stumbled towards the bathroom, praying it would not be busy. He was beginning to feel the close horror of having to pee in a sink or even, hissing and steaming, on the carpet itself, his performance slowly stilling even word of mouth. If only he had the nerve. He should have done it as he told the story, without pausing. It would have been a sign of confidence to those people. He would have had their hearts forever. "I was there when D pissed," old ladies would treasure it in the rest homes thirty years from now.

The black bathroom was empty. D looked in all its dark corners for some chat about *The Center of Attention*. Nothing. No one. The bliss of an empty bathroom. D knew he could live in a bathroom the rest of his life, saying "just a moment" to every knocking, knowing he would never emerge. He talked silently to himself in bathrooms, about how he would guide the Lakers, master the stockmarket, run wars on the tiled floor or steer his family's way to safety despite the collapse of world order and the cracking apart of Earth.

D had just unzipped, and the first fall of his golden piss was on its way to the sloping wall of black porcelain above the oval of flat water – D did not want a noisy splash-down – when the door to the bathroom opened and Doc came in. He sat on the vanity, blinking, and started to talk.

"Young man, I have been in this business so long I tell myself I must love it."

"Oh," said D.

"And I do, don't misunderstand me. I'm saying this because I want you to know this isn't some old lady telling you that was a great story."

D tried to turn to show Doc his grateful smile.

"And I have worked on most of the best scripts since – "

"I know, I know," said D.

"God, it's a wonderful thing," said Doc. "I'm honored to think I'm going to be working on it."

"You are?" said D, surprise making his cascade waver.

"Clear says Eyes wants me on the rewrites."

"Rewrites?"

"Only the good scripts get rewritten. The bad ones, they make 'em straight away."

It was difficult to hear these unexpected developments while emptying a bladder that he had trained over the years to be commodious in case of emergency.

"How do you feel about Joan Collins for the aunt?" asked Doc.

"Well . . . " said D. "I hadn't thought about that." In truth, he had, and his heart was set on Mercedes McCambridge.

"I got these flashes of Joan in black underwear and the young guy weeping in her lap. I think the aunt wants to fuck him, don't you?"

D thought as quickly as he could. "I did want to suggest that the aunt and uncle have not given him a full measure of affection."

"Sure, sure," said Doc. "Jesus, kid, what have you got there, the Colorado River?"

"I beg your pardon."

"You piss for ever. Never seen anything like it. You get to be my age and it comes in dribs and drabs, like the dialogue in an Eastwood picture. You piss like Orson Welles selling sherry."

D laughed nervously, "It just keeps coming."

"Thing of beauty. I have to tell the others."

"Oh no, please," D cried, but Doc was unhearing; and though he tried mightily, pushing on his river to end it, D's fine arc was still there when several others crowded into his bathroom.

"What did I tell you?" Doc asked them.

One lady moved to get a side-on view. "Oh, I've only seen anything as fine from a Navajo guide I knew in Monument Valley. When he tinkled it was D. H. Lawrence."

"You better join the Fire Department, D," joked Chuck.

"And it's a pretty dick too." This was Drew, squatting down so close she could have trailed her hand in the spray. D was so startled by her coming up on his blind side he could not stop himself turning towards her, a movement that would have drenched her if her sure hand had not reached out to stay the swing of his admired part. "It's warm," she said, sentimentally.

At last, D felt an easing in the flow. The curve began to droop. He had to lean towards the bowl. Like a ship docking after a voyage, the slowing went on a very long time. Then there were tardy passengers, until the last ashore, one pinging drop that fell into the inch-deep amber froth. There was a clatter of applause in the black room, and Chuck whistled in approval. When the noise subsided, Doc said:

"How about this for a scene? Our hero has to take a leak. He goes into the men's room and he's got his dick out. He's got a bag with him with something special in it. Secret stuff. And he's put it down beside him, and just when he's in full flood a thief comes by and snatches it. The guy wants to chase but he can't stop pissing."

"Oh, wow," said someone.

"That *is* neat," said another.

"Now, I don't know if it would fit," Doc admitted.

"In *The Center of Attention*?" D asked.

"It's a good scene. We're going to need a few of those."

"What would be in the bag?" D was aghast.

"Who knows?" said Doc. "I'm just making pictures."

"It *is* intriguing." This was Clear's voice. D was horrified that *he* should be taken with it. He choked.

"D, what is it?" asked the solicitous Clear.

"Nothing," yelped D bravely. "A minor mishap securing my zip."

"Oh no!" cried Doc. "Don't hook that fish." There was laughter, and many pats on D's patient back. "Hey, remember?" Doc asked of Clear.

"What's that?" Clear wanted to know.

"Don't sell that cow," said Doc wistfully, and the black bathroom filled with the good cheer of former triumphs.

SPLENDOR

The tragedy in *Splendor in the Grass* is of a desire which cannot find fulfilment. Deanie Loomis and Bud Stamper are high-school seniors in south-east Kansas in 1928. The kids are in love, still on the virginal shore of sex. But they are compromised by the screen presence of Natalie Wood and Warren Beatty, twenty-two and twenty-three when the film is made, lush, carnal and very likely their own lovers by the time the shooting is complete. Yet their characters are fearful of going all the way with anyone they love. There lies abortion, divorce and disgrace. Boys can use whores, and girls must tame their needs by telling themselves that sex is a nasty tithe they pay for marriage, children and respectability.

But the anxiety about this beast sex seems all the more dementing because the leading actors cannot – no matter how well they act – lose their sexual assurance. There's an irony of more potential than Hollywood could handle that, as Wood and Beatty beat their heads on the sets with pretend sexual frustration, so they get hornier over the real bodies they might get to feast on, once relinquished by the roles.

So *Splendor in the Grass* is period distress brought to hysteria by conscientious acting and Kazan's feeding of its fires. It is also a touching picture, never as solemn as its makers might hope, but never simply ridiculous as some critics have claimed. Whether or not it is plausible for such lovers to refrain from sex, the clash of desire and what is allowed has its roots in cinema. That these lovers come so close to madness – Deanie spends two and a half years in a mental hospital when all she seems to need are the lays that Natalie Wood's false eyelashes know – is part of the awkward but heartfelt attempt to trace such repression to the stupidity of parents and the Crash of 1929. *Splendor in the Grass* thinks bad sex, or the lack of sex, may be what cripples society. For Warren Beatty, the thematic righteousness of his first film is an emotional pointer in the direction of *Bonnie and Clyde*.

119

More accurately, it is a film about acting: so often with Kazan, the story and its issues are pretexts for performance. His great talent is in making actors work. Wood was the more experienced of the two, and the picture is set up to be about her. She has the several virtuoso scenes (she was nominated for an Oscar), and the Wordsworthian title runs in her head. We remember the film for her in a red dress seemingly walking through a waterfall, nearly swooning with dreams of orgasm and guilt in the steam of her hot bath, and suddenly discovered up to her neck in a cool lake, letting the water subdue her heat. She is the water nymph who will not swim and who therefore thinks of drowning herself.

She is very good, even if she is a young actress seeking to regain what was raw instinct a few years before. She is at her best when alone, a face thinking of what she wants but cannot have, an icon beset by the imagery of water and agonising that Kazan pumps in. She seldom shows us the kind of sudden, shocking "mistake" in performance, such as illuminates *Rebel*. She is too accomplished now to give way to nervous breakdown, except that the script calls for it and Kazan has conjured up the set-pieces of would-be drowning for her. We never quite believe Deanie has thought of them.

Beatty seems to be her support. The credits say "and introducing Warren Beatty"; the posters add, "in his very first picture – a very special star!". He is paid only $15,000 for the picture. On the other hand, the story is based in William Inge's own life, and may be intended from Bud's point of view. There are signs of Inge's interest in the young Beatty: Bud is a high-school athlete with an older sister urging him to break away from parental control. But most important, in its subtlest moments, *Splendor in the Grass* is a film about Bud in which Beatty's acting is the more intriguing because it is less spectacular.

The debut is not always comfortable. There are moments when Beatty cannot handle long lines, because of an attempt at regional accent, or even a small lisp of his own not quite smoothed away. A mix of narrowed eyes and open mouth conveys meanness, excessive suspicion and sheer monotony. There are scenes where he is too busy – dropping his gaze, turning his head away, groaning, fluttering his eyes, putting a hand to his head. If movie acting is allowing the camera to inspect your thoughts, Beatty seems untrusting and eager to escape. There are times when his cheeks bulge and his face shines in a disconcerting way. Is he forcing himself to look frustrated? Is there a humor native to him that wants to deflate the portentousness of Bud's situation, a grumbling that cannot quite credit the forbidden fuck?

Still, Bud determines the action. He is the son of a vulgar oil man, carrying the burden of his father's search for more success because his older sister Ginny (Barbara Loden) is a rebellious outcast. Bud wants to marry Deanie, but his father tells him to go to Yale. That is why he drops Deanie, the perfect love who won't put out, and instead dates the famously "loose" girl in class. As a result, Deanie goes to pieces.

Beatty's Bud is a miscast hero, angelic-looking, but unable to meet everyone's expectations. Early on, he mouths silently as his father talks to him. He cannot always finish or grasp what he wants to say. He turns away physically from situations that baffle him. He tends to violence because of the confusion, and he has a habit of shutting off – when his schoolmates discuss girls in the locker room, Bud closes his eyes and lets the shower water flood his face.

He is browbeaten by his father; he is mocked and effectively castrated by a more sexually knowing sister ("If you weren't my brother you wouldn't come near me," she tells him. "I know what you nice boys are like. You just want to talk to me in the dark."). And Bud is overawed by Deanie and the force of her loving refusals. The film does not state this explicitly, but perhaps their frustrated need has bred the fatal, maddening love between them. Deanie is a romantic, and Bud a down-to-earth fellow who cannot fly at her wild heights.

Everyone "remembers" *Splendor in the Grass* as a Wood–Beatty love story, the plot so compelling the actors were carried away. Yet, in truth, they are uneasy together. It is hard for such ambitious actors to play people so much more naive than they are; and so in the love scenes they seem to condescend and watch themselves. Kazan crowds them together, kissing, petting, flustered by touch. He does not let the lone faces watch – and that is the movies' height of love. Natalie is outgoing, and Warren reticent. But Bud needs to be seduced, while Deanie wants protection. So there is a stand-off between them, as when he has to look up, archly, so she can only kiss his neck, and he taunts her, "You're nuts about me." In one of the fullest love scenes, he pushes her to her knees and she says "I'd do anything for you," as if to hint at fellatio.

As soon as Bud moves out of Deanie's aura, Beatty becomes more penetrating. His dismal time at Yale is beautifully captured in a scene where he comes back to his room, contemplates his desk, then calmly sweeps its contents onto the floor and begins to play solitaire. It is the first quintessential Beatty moment in which an unlaughing but amused fatalism refuses to accept the world's clutter. He is more grown up, alone with the camera, than ever he has been with company. He laughs like

With Barbara Loden in *Splendor in the Grass* (Warner Brothers)

someone not just touched but discovered when the dean at Yale says of his father, "He isn't a very good listener, is he?" For Beatty in this first film establishes his skills in that very area. He listens, he watches: he takes it all in.

This reaches its height in his scenes with Zohra Lampert, the pizza waitress Bud meets in New Haven and marries. He is sitting alone in the restaurant when she talks to him. There is no tension or anxiety, just an immediate conversation. She asks him what Kansas is like, and he says, as if just realising it, "It's very friendly. That's what it's like." This is Beatty's best moment; at last a real Bud emerges from the flux of others' influence and the melodramatic set-up of the piece.

In the film's conclusion, Bud is married to the waitress, a farmer, with one child and another on the way. He has become quieter and stronger. He is dirty from his work and tanned by the sun. Deanie, out of the hospital, comes back to see him. It is the one passage of the story that deals with adults, and it comes as welcome relief to see compromise working. The marriage is ordinary. The ex-waitress feels what Deanie meant to Bud, and Zohra Lampert registers the helpless concern more effectively than Natalie Wood does anything in the picture. The Wordsworth runs over Wood's face as she drives away – about growing up and growing sad.

The fine ending exposes early limits and strains. *Splendor in the Grass* is too narrowly about sex to be as erotic as it hopes; and too ready to settle for half-baked equations of sexuality and politics. But it is in Beatty's troubled, cautious display of a mind working at its problem that we glimpse what Kazan said about his own movie:

"As for Bud, you want to know the truth? I think he is sort of scared of her (Deanie), after she comes out of the institution. She is too complicated for him. I think he felt, 'I've got a nice wife, she doesn't make any demands on me, we help each other, we have some aspirations, I'm comfortable here, what the hell do I need more trouble for? What do I need romance for? It's bullshit!' He's happy that way. I think he realises: this is what I want. The American notion, that love is the solution of all life's problems, is only true for an inhibited society. Even if you get the right woman you still have the same problems: you have to solve them within yourself."

Death of air conditioning

No matter the soothing onset of money and success, or the tingling unsteadiness whenever Drew's lissome, casual body pierced his vicinity (she *was* the shiver in his cold), D was anxious to make some contact with his family. As well he might be. After all, this city – as C, his wife, saw it, from their abode – was a cyclorama of peril.

"But you're perfectly all right here," Clear began again. "I would have thought things were more uncertain . . . over there." His hand waved in what he recollected of the direction.

"Exactly!" D was quivering. But it was Drew's fingertips xylophoning his vertebrae.

"Anyway," Clear sighed, "there's a party for the famine tonight. We're all invited to at the Lighthiser house on Mulholland. Cy will slay me if I don't bring you."

He did not expand on the prospect; he was having to shepherd guests out of the building and into a necklace of jet limousines for the trip up to Mulholland Drive. D was again struck by the limitless patience and tact in Clear which never let him appear as a hack or a crawler. Who would want to manhandle a score of piquant personalities, many of whom had calls to make, bathrooms to visit and petty delays if their feelings were not to be crushed? Yet Clear made them all sure that his destiny was to cater to them. He was not unlike the black bathroom, for he met everyone's desires. It crossed D's mind that he might be a warm machine, a very subtle, fleshed-out robot. But no chance: Clear had humor; he saw how silly he was – that was his redemption.

Doc rode down with D in the elevator, as D tried to recall just how Drew had presided over its floor.

"Been thinking about the script," said Doc.

Doc thought as he spoke. It was like jazz, assertive but vulnerable, and an essential defense against interruption. "Let me say, it's a hell of a script. Hell of a basis, anyway."

"It needs more work?" D asked.

"I don't know about work. Concept, perhaps. We have this guy who shoots the President?"

D nodded vigorously.

"We're imagining Eyes there?"

"Well – "

"Ah, you see. You hesitate. I like that, it's a mark of quality. This is not exactly Eyes, is it?"

"The part is somewhat younger," D conceded.

"I don't mean that. We could age this guy up, and you'll be amazed what Eyes can do when he goes into training. But shooting at the President."

"He's mentally unbalanced," D tried to explain. "Obsessed with being famous."

"I get that. And the actress is going to save him. That I like, and Eyes'll be crazy for it. But does he have to shoot at the President?"

"He doesn't kill him."

"That's something," Doc supposed, not convinced. "But it could throw off a lot of public sympathy. I wonder if Eyes – our character – could simply *oppose* the President on some more politically appealing thing."

"Like what?"

"Save the whales, do you think? Or defending a hospital for poor black kids. Orphans?"

"Shooting is much more filmic."

"Well, theoretically, I have to agree. But you see my worry? I don't know if Eyes sees himself as someone who'd shoot at the President."

"So much of my subject here," said D with a zeal that did seem strident in an elevator, "is the matter of fame and death, desire and immortality."

Doc was sheepish: "Well, sure, in the Aristotelian sense you're on the money." He reflected more. "Just suppose Eyes played the Pres, and we built *that* part up, and the girl rescues the President? A youngish President."

The talk went on, repeating itself, and D and Doc rode up and down in the elevator. There they were, amiably argumentative craftsmen, until they realised that the office suite was empty. Whereupon they went down again and out onto the street, where Clear was checking off names on a list.

There was a dense, disconcerting air in the street. It was turgid and static, as if an ominous dung hovered only a few feet above human heads. Two dogs were fighting, and D saw flecks of red in their jaws. Some curse in the stagnant air had destroyed their urge to run away yelping for a better day. They were killing themselves.

It was like the death of air conditioning, but etched with some greater loss, as if oxygen had been made into char. When you moved, you felt the urge to push aside curtains of dust. Your movement set up a rolling wake so that the waves of congealed air fell dead and silent against the buildings. It was like a dream in which you are dying and, when you wake, you believe the dream's plan is carrying over. D shuddered, and heard Clear say something about the Santa Ana imprisoning air up in the canyons until it frets and stirs. He wanted to reach up and rip the sky apart, letting breeze or change in. He felt they were in a picture, a painting, *Evening in L.A.*, being poisoned by the oils.

"May be fresher in the hills," said Doc, looking for a limousine.

D was following, when Clear called out, "You're over here, D. Drew wants you to ride with her." Clear winked at him; it made his face seem mechanical. The wink could not match the rare sensitivity, the delicacy, between him and Drew. And then D thought again, recalled his distant C, and wondered if there was an understanding that could be delicate.

A limousine door was opened, and a long, bare arm beckoned. "Hurry, D," her voice called. "We're going to a party."

Closing his eyes, for who could see in its smoked dark?, D ducked into the aroma of new leather until he pressed against Drew's pliant delectability. His coming released sighs of jasmine perfume from her.

"There you are," she crooned, and her arms reached across him to the door, to shut him in. It closed with no more sound than a safety catch makes in a long shot, and Drew's arm came back to rest on his thigh. Thank God, he still had his script and the money, thought D, as the limousine crept forward and those inside it raised a low, camp cheer like hunger sniffing food. Drew's hand moved up his thigh, and in, and D calculated the distance to Mulholland Drive.

MOMENTS

Biography is supposed to gain in pace and detail as a life comes into its own – as if the famous really did more, or had more minutes in their hours than the unknowns. In the summer of 1960, Warren Beatty makes his first movie; it will prove a considerable success, and it is talked about a good deal in the year that elapses between principal photography and actual release. He knows famous people: he is caught in love affairs with two actresses better known than he is. It is in the nature of things that he acquires an agent, a publicity representative, would-be managers and advisors, as well as lawyers, accountants and people who will be pleased to be known as his tailor, his barber, his mechanic, his tennis coach or his man for all those little things he cannot entirely manage himself.

His life is led day by day. It is as well to remind ourselves of this, for the legend and the dynamics of a movie star's medium let us believe in the power of cutting – instantaneous transports and alterations in which desire or a whim are accomplished in a twenty-fourth of a second. It is the wondrous or magical nature of a movie star that he has the potential to be everywhere – in 2,000 theaters across the nation, opening this Friday, on the upper East side of Manhattan and in Midwestern malls, his fiction unwinding 2,000 times at once; or he is "seen" by gossip columns simultaneously in London, Madrid and Los Angeles – for, after all, a busy man might sit down in all these cities in one twenty-four-hour space, if he was peculiarly driven by being busy or by ample credit card aimlessness; and anyway, in a movie he is everywhere – he is sitting sad in a New Haven pizza joint, in the end alcove, and he is the picture being studied by his old amour as she lies on a couch and talks to her analyst. A movie star is someone whose vital parts we can take home with us after the movie, in the Midwest or in the suburbs of European cities. Which leaves him, the other him, with a day-to-day existence that may seem faintly, comically absent or immaterial. How boring it may seem – how unnecessary? – for these great figures to live minute by minute when they have seen the force they can convey in a five- or six-second take or cut, recorded in the summer of 1960, held in the dark and in the cutting room for a year and then released in darks all over the world as a kind of recurring eternity. To be wonderful, could you have the patience, the stamina or the spiritual persistence to tie your shoes every day? Or won't you opt for slip-ons, and leave broken-backed shoes in the hotels and boudoirs of the smart world so that sometimes, in amazement, you notice your own barefootedness and wonder about a movie that begins with a beautiful, and beautifully dressed amnesiac, wandering into the Pierre Hotel in New York, or the White House, with some intense message, meaning or plot the size of which is mysteriously promised by his having no shoes on? If you are dreamed about, here and there, how long is it before the pressure of these fictions enters your own sleep?

Yet stars must observe the verities of time and place. If you slept last night with —— at her beach-house, you have to drive back to the Beverly Wilshire (if your car starts, or when the cab comes), shower and change into fresh clothes that will please the other lady you are lunching at 12.30 at . . . where was it, Michael's or Spago? And you have to know how long it takes to get the car out of the Wilshire garage, how long it takes to go down from your floor to El Camino Real where the car will arrive. You have to judge how many of the accumulated calls you can answer; you have to shave – you must do it yourself, you cannot rely on the mirror and the presence of so-and-so for Men simply dissolving that monotonous rash of bristle away. And can you find the clean shirts, or has the laundry screwed up again? When can you find the time to sit down and really assess the pluses and minuses of laundering your shirts or simply and only ever wearing new shirts? You are late. You are always late. You had better develop and cultivate the reputation of being late, ambitious, unreliable, impulsive. And who is this woman you're having lunch with? Didn't you fuck her in Rio five or six months ago – wasn't it her? – and didn't she become a slightly more conventional and clinging goddess after you'd made love? So why not call the restaurant – no, you can't do that – better send five dozen orchids to her, at her table, with a note, a note from . . . Valparaiso (the florist can do it) saying gosh, darn it. It will be the greatest moment of her life, the poor bitch. She may get a part because of it, some producer seeing her, levitating in all those orchids, knowing that even in Chile – it is Chile? – you did not forget her.

And you can get a club sandwich or room service and watch game shows, and sleep, and when you wake at last the laundry will have come,

and you can sink your head in the fresh white shirts and feel restored. There is a screening at five; another at seven; dinner dates, two at nine and one that is rather more supper at ten, and there is a call from Jack which you know is an invitation to see a Lakers game. It is nearly his best part, you know, Lakers fan – active, urgent, crazed, merry, a man of the people. Jack is ready and happy to let himself be watched watching. And so you may stay at home, watching the minutes creep away, feeling the pathos in a movie star who is bored and empty. So much later, in revery, you turn up somewhere, anywhere, and you find three women whose names you don't know. The reality is sustained because they know who you are. One never tells a soul, hoping you will value discretion and call her again. One does tell, but she is notorious in LA as a liar, and another makes mocking allusions to the occasion for the rest of her life, so no one ever knows. There will come a day when neither you nor she will ever quite know if you did it, minute by minute, or as in a movie, momentarily and forever. Do you come instantaneously, like the light, or never, as in a powerful promise?

What this means to say is that biography is a literary form in which dates, times, references, source notes, quotations and verifiable sources conspire in an illusion – that, yes, life was lived day-by-day, moment-by-moment, and this is how it was. The strong line of narrative gives the writer and the reader confidence: it keeps them both going. But it is as well to remember that the life they are insisting on reading had no such decisions to make. It was helpless: it was there, in a jacuzzi where time was the water.

A movie star leaves more records than most people. He leaves parts of his life on film and tape. Beatty, before *Ishtar*, has acted in sixteen films, the accumulated running time of which is 1,809 minutes, or 30.15 hours. Now, of course, he is not on screen for every one of these minutes (I would need a special research grant to give you *that* figure). But we may overlook that discrepancy in view of a much larger and vaguer figure: the total time in minutes that Beatty has had recorded on film. For in respectable film production, the scene chosen to be on screen is the best of all the times that scene was filmed or taken. There is a term, the shooting ratio, which is the amount of film exposed on a production in relation to the length of the film as released. A 10:1 ratio is uncommonly low in Hollywood. The production companies would have records of all the film shot somewhere. But it would need more research grants still to discover them, and I am not sure that it would be using our time well.

I prefer to consider that somewhere, probably, the discarded footage of these sixteen films still exists, in cases, in vaults, in dubious safety and preservation, perhaps. But exists. If we suppose an average ratio in Beatty's films of 15:1 (high for some, maybe, but very low for others, like *Reds*) then we can propose a round figure of 27,000 minutes of Mr. Beatty's life preserved in silver acetate – nearly nineteen days of second-by-second imprint of smiles, scowls and the hoverings between the two.

An eternity of presence, of which a fifteenth (by a formula which, I repeat, is modest) constitutes his screen career, his Work, his oeuvre, that which may yet win lifetime achievement awards (with perhaps another three or four days to be added to the eventual total).

There are so many other ways of tracing Warren Beatty. How many still photographs have been taken of him, how many times 1/100 or 1/50 of a second, decently enough exposed for there to be no question of who it is? Of course, not many of those pictures have a calendar in them so that we can ascertain his exact whereabouts for those moments. Still, the world in which he moves is more generous to the latterday researcher than you might suppose. There is a photograph of Beatty and Joan Collins together at a dining table. There is an ashtray in front of them with a crown motif on it, and a name, "The Harwyn". This was a club that allowed the young couple to eat free, says Joan Collins. So we might suppose that a manager of or agent for the Harwyn pushed the ashtray into the picture, checked that it was in focus and in frame, and maybe then went so far as to give the couple cigarettes, so that the ashtray should seem reasonable and familiar. But the legend says Warren Beatty does not smoke, despite the cigarette in his hand. Is this why he is smoking with such superiority. Did he know we would be coming, and had he seen that early that there is not a photograph taken that is not designed and directed?

There may be a reservations book for the Harwyn with "Beatty 2, 9.30" here and there, and some appointments crossed out. The data bank of the world's airlines would have his flights – he must have frequent flier bonuses akin to the GNP of small states by now. There will be credit card records, hotel bills, telephone bills – which university press will publish those six or seven volumes, properly annotated, I trust? There will be other records – more or less unquestionable – of where and when he was: a matter-of-fact litany of commotion.

There may be records a little more uncertain and without a doubt illegitimate. Who knows how many friends have recorded Warren at parties – this is a community so adept at recording machines, small tape geniuses that could fit in the pocket, video cameras in the corners as if the house was a bank. Imagine all the telephone answering machines – wiped, or held in perpetuity – that have something like "Hi kiddo, I'm thinking of you, but I'm off to Helsinki," which might be Warren, as well as decent boyfriends having a little fun with their lovers. Think of all-night parties where the coming and going was preserved on videotapes that no one yet has had the time to examine. Consider that some ladies may have had the foresight to flip on some hidden tape recorder just before they felt their last self-control slipping away (and yes, some, later, find that, in the dark, they had had Warren on fast forward by mistake). Moreover, how many agencies, agents and whatever may have attempted to tap Warren's calls? Presidential offices? He was an active campaigner on behalf of Richard Nixon's opponent in 1972. Movie business rivals, jealous husbands, eager biographers, or Warren himself, quietly aware of a duty to posterity?

The bank of all those records might go on forever, taking far more than one normal life to type or read, and it would simply say how minute-by-minute Warren Beatty did this or that. And it would give no adequate hint of how much he was at a loss, of how far his experience was always hanging between doing everything and nothing.

Like a movie

It was like a movie. Wasn't it? That's what Doc had been saying all along, get it like a movie and then it goes of its own accord.

Imagine you're D, Doc had said.

Imagine I'm me? D started to giggle.

And Doc said right, make that separation, see yourself in the car going north on Beverly Glen, climbing and twisting. You're there, inside, like a vine growing on Drew. But you're outside, too, sucked along in the slipstream, catching the scene.

And D got the odd hang of it, being in two places at once, protagonist and voyeur.

What do you want? Doc asked – the car, the night, this amber-bodied, kiss-me, love-me girl? You want music on the radio, a ball game in the dark? Blossom Dearie, Dodgers and the Mets? You can play with the arrangement, have D say this, do that, polish the lines till they shine like the green clock on the dash.

Getting used to it, D looked at himself in the limo, saw himself locked in that rush of immediacy, the now-ness, and felt himself the spectator. It was uncanny – the dark and the cabin of light hurtling along, side-by-side, the show and its secret watcher.

Anything? he asked Doc.

Sure, there's nothing you can imagine that it could not become. That's what It is, said Doc.

It?

Sure, said Doc, what Hollywood used to say was sex, Clara Bow on a tiger rug. But there's a bigger it than little Clara, or even Drew now. It's watching, don't you see? It's being there and watching at the same time.

Oh yes, sighed D, I see. And he laughed out loud.

"Share the joke, D," said Drew. The line was tipped with her mock lust. But that was how D heard it, how he reckoned she had played it. That sweet Drew might never quite greet you with spontaneity again.

You wondered who set her up to this, who cast and wrote her? You never shook that paranoia.

"What?" asked D, just a small peak of worry on the optical track.

"What are you on, D?" Chuck leered from the black-bead gloom beyond Drew.

"Doing stuff?" Drew asked. And you look at whatever packet they have of this drug or that, and you laugh because what I'm on is I'm not here, I'm out there.

The car goes through curves like liquid taking the line of flow – we'll do it Steadicam at 32 f.p.s., says Doc. There is no shock or jolt from the steel rectangle fighting the arcs of highway. The limo is a motile S, and so the space inside seems to flex at its joints, the walls closing in and oozing out.

Arrange it however you like. Have total dark in the car, a swaying uncertainty and just the wriggle of Drew's fingers opening you up, freeing the cavalier, the feather in her hand. You could wonder whether her other hand, the left, is not another scurrying monkey for Chuck. You could speculate about Drew's handedness, and which one is closer to her soul.

The soul is tough in movie, says Doc. It doesn't photograph.

But she has one, you say, and Doc looks at you with what could be pity or envy.

Or there could be deadpan chit-chat between you and old Chuck, not such a bad guy, men of some world together, as the so supple (you can hear her sinews stretching) Drew bends to your two horsemen. And the two stupefied fellows could look to heaven or the satin roof of the limo without disclosing the intensity of the sensation. To be a you there, you must meet triumph and nirvana with Apache impassivity. You know you are being watched, so give nothing away. Don't look at the camera.

There are other sights to glimpse along the way – the topaz light from pools wavering on adobe walls, the blooms and blossoms like flesh in the streetlights, and the shimmering shapes of people seen through the half-shut Venetian blinds. You could have a three-legged dog lurch across the road, its tail drawn between its legs in terror, and the driver could surmise in walk-on Latino, "I tink I see it onze b'fore, in Monterrey before the – ", but you do not catch the last word in the cha-cha-cha on the radio, and when you look at Drew her nostril is crystalline with too much right stuff. You wish it could be only you and her, curled up under a rug, like lovers riding in Central Park, clip-clop, kiss-kiss, on an endless summer night of personal learning experience.

Like a movie

You cheat! You are an actor, watching what you're doing. Why should anyone ever trust you?

"The car's dying," said Drew, and so it was, drifting into the incline just short of Mulholland's crest, its strength ebbing. The car stopped. They felt the handbrake save it from further indignity. Then they heard the wind searching along the ridge of the hills. You could imagine wolves, or worse, loping along, looking for you.

Couldn't you?

Nastassja Kinski in *Paris, Texas*

LOVING EVERY MINUTE

The family of Natalie Wood lives at this time in a house in Sherman Oaks. One day – it must be 1960 or early in 1961 – Natalie rushes in, in tears, an emotional escapee from the house she has lived in with Robert Wagner. Natalie's sister, Lana, eight years younger, remembers her sister's hand is bleeding "because she had squeezed and broken one of her cherished crystal wineglasses". Wagner has left their home; the marriage is at an end.

When the shooting of *Splendor in the Grass* is beginning, observers reckon that Natalie is in love with Elia Kazan. Why not? This is a movie about desperate love and its thwarted consummation. The actress must be brought, time and again, to a peak that never breaks, never gives her release. Kazan is older, wiser, cunningly skilled in drawing an actor's personality into that of the character they are playing. He is attractive, ugly, physical, dynamic; he has magic, and he makes actors believe he can urge it upon them with his pushy, zealous eyes and his strong brown hands. Any actress needs to think that she has some hitherto hidden power that this director can set free. But then, it may come to pass that she sees how far the director is already a little bored with her and the tricks he can make her play, and that he was always there to escort her towards the young actor whom she kisses in the picture. If the director is very clever, the camera will see the instant at which these two recognize each other properly for the first time.

It may not always work out so tidily, or so well for the picture; and whether or not it does depends on the kind of romanticism in the minds of the actor and the actress. Something like infatuation develops on the set of *Splendor in the Grass*. Falling is so natural a response if you feel raised up by adventure and art, if you are exhausted and insecure, and if you have been brought up in the codes of the Method. Kazan may tell his young players they are doing well, he may bolster them with reassurance; or he may choose the opposite ploy, exposing them, goading them with a disappointment he cannot conceal – which director is a poor actor? But nothing will convince Natalie or Warren more than if they, the real selves, as well as Bud and Deanie, fall in love. And in this, Warren Beatty is the less experienced. Bud will not have Deanie in the film, but suppose the actor can lure the actress away from her husband? This is not cold-blooded, it is passionate. But it is also something that an unusually intelligent man, or one as much drawn to retreat and skepticism as to magic, will one day see as ridiculous.

And life is not straightforward, even if it passes hour by hour. The telephone is always at hand, offering whispered exchanges across 8,000 miles, transformation and betrayal, the sound of static and the little coughs when the medium clears its throat.

Joan Collins is in Rome, on *Esther and the King*. Along with all the other Biblical costumes, she wears the engagement ring that Warren has given her. He has asked her not to live in a hotel, but in the apartment of a friend – there she is less open to temptation, closer to a known phone, and so much less surrounded by anonymity and discretion. He sends her many letters and telegrams, though I would suspect that the letters (needing seven or eight days) are quickly made archaic by cables and phone calls. It may be that a letter arrives with sentiments, beautifully expressed and carefully thought out, but made redundant by a breathless phone confession of five nights ago.

Joan is moved by how much he misses her – "he sounded so forlorn and depressed." She surprises him by flying to New York for the week-end. They spend the time in their apartment, and she watches him filming before she flies back to Rome. When she gets back there, Warren writes with amusing comments on "How to make a Biblical film," for they have agreed that her project is junk. The points are discerning and sarcastic; they show someone already scornful of the way most pictures are made:

"1. It is always best to try to show as much emotion in all scenes as possible. It is generally best if the actor cries in each scene, taking special pains not to be out of control or realistic to the extent that members of the crew or other actors will be made to feel embarrassed. All gestures and facial expressions should be worked out in front of a large mirror. These should not be deviated from. Remember that the audience is not involved until the actor cries. Be very careful not to let the mascara run.

2. In doing Biblical pictures it is best to try to imagine how Jesus Christ would have said the necessary lines and done the prescribed movements and then to emulate his work.

137

3. Never change the words in a movie script. These have been written by great creative forces.

4. Do not challenge the director, or especially the producer. These are dedicated men.

5. Do not tire yourself out with thinking about the script between takes or at night away from the set. This destroys spontaneity."

We are cross-cutting as we advance, as in any Hollywood story about a fellow with two girls: in 1960, in Hollywood, it could be Tony Curtis in the lead, with Janet Leigh and . . . Joan Collins as his two loves. In the summer of 1960, Beatty and Natalie Wood are being seen about together. When reporters catch up with them they say they are just friends. At times, Warren blushes and laughs, just like any other shy fellow in love, and spied upon by journalists.

There are sequences of these times available to us like passages of film, and who knows exactly their proper order? Montage – that rapid, giddy, exhilarating editing style to cover a passage of time – is but one of the ways in which Hollywood asserts that atmosphere, energy and momentum are more important than history.

Joan Collins has suspicions in Rome. The telephone is as available to malicious friends, gossips and provoking reporters as it is to lovers. She wonders about Warren and Natalie, and she recollects the opinion of her astrologer, Ben Gary, that Warren is "stubborn and aggressive, but he is unyielding in his ambition and because of his tremendous drive and energy will have an early and immense success." And, after all, says Gary, he's an Aries, "Ruled by their cock. How delightful for you, my dear."

Warren hears that Joan is being seen with an Italian actor, Gabriele Tinti, and when he calls her she is on the phone for hours at a time. He begs her to go to New York again, and she goes. Years later, when she writes her book, *Past Imperfect*, she recollects sadly that Warren never went to Rome.

After *Esther and the King*, she returns to America and she and Warren live together again on Sunset Plaza Drive. Perhaps, now they are reunited, they think nostalgically of when they were forever quarrelling and making up on the phone, when they knew the local Alitalia numbers by heart. The wedding dress, designed and purchased, lies carefully wrapped in the closet.

There is a brief intrusion from the mundane world: military service. Beaty, Henry Warren (or 44.9.37.130, as the Selective Service regards him), has been classified 1-A since June 1958. But in February 1960, when he takes his physical, he is classified as "Accepted", one level below "Qualified", indicating some imperfection. We cannot say what it is, for the relevant remarks in his record are destroyed under the authority of the National Archives and Records. And so, in March 1960, Beaty is classified 1-D (member of a reserve component).

This takes him to George Air Force Base in Victorville, between Los Angeles and Barstow, on a three-week tour of duty. As soon as he is there, he frets and hates the waste of time. He starts to send cables again and to monopolise Joan's phone, "expressing his misery, loneliness and undying love. So why did he fight with me and harass me all the time when we were together?"

Joan Collins says she was too independent and aggressive. And since he was insecure and determined to have his own way, they make a volatile couple. She has the added difficulty of being dropped by Fox and having to look for work. That is no problem for Warren. He is in great demand, and he reads the scripts offered her as well as those sent to him. He tells her hers are rubbish, and he throws them in the wastepaper bin. He can hardly fail to notice a career that is slipping.

It is February 1961, and in the London Clinic Elizabeth Taylor may be dying – in which case, Twentieth Century-Fox want Joan as her replacement on *Cleopatra*. For a few days they live by the phone. Warren has to go out and find another phone for his calls. Then the word comes that Elizabeth is getting better. There are situations in real life too, where some training in talking (and thinking) like Jesus Christ proves its use. "It's showbiz, baby," says Warren, "as in there's no biz like it."

Warren has a second film, *The Roman Spring of Mrs Stone*, and it will be shot in London. With nothing to do for herself except see her family, Joan goes with him. They rent a home belonging to the director, Peter Glenville, just behind Harrods. She visits the set at Elstree and sits in the dark watching Warren's character, Paolo, in the brightness, making love to Mrs Stone, played by Vivien Leigh. Joan is well aware now that women are finding Warren attractive. When the three of them take lunch in the studio restaurant, Leigh deplores Joan's dress sense and advises her to invest in jewellery. She says Joan looks a little like a man.

"What do you think, Warren darling?" she asks her co-star.

Joan looks at that gentleman as he considers how to answer: "His hair had been darkened for the part of the Italian gigolo. He had a deep tan, which, although it was out of a bottle, looked as if it came straight from

Portofino. He wore a beautifully cut beige silk suit from Brioni, a cream crêpe-de-chine shirt from Battaglia, and a brown-and-beige St Laurent tie. No wonder half the females in the restaurant were tripping over themselves to get a glimpse of him. The Warren Beatty sex-symbol was beginning to emerge. Women adored him. He was loving every minute of it."

Limo death

The limousine swayed off the road and was stilled in the incline of red earth and shale. It had stopped thirty yards from a telephone – just a pole, a perspex hood over the instrument and a light above it. It seemed a recent installation, a fresh, clean phone, put there that morning perhaps. Drew poked with her toes at the arrowed heart and initials put in the cement by a laborer's quick finger. But the crusts stayed hard. She was carrying her sandals, flimsy silver platforms, walking on the warm pavement.

Stretch, the driver, got the hood up. The light from the phone shone into the bed of glossy, succulent machinery. There was a scent of newness under the hood, as sweet as the leather inside. D was backing up the hill to study the view. Chuck threw rocks out at the darkness.

This was not far short of Mulholland, not that late in the evening. When they looked down at the city they could still see movement and intelligence there. How could a stranded car be forgotten up there in the desolate canyon where the air felt thick around them? A phone call would do the trick, wouldn't it?

Drew was jittery at the lack of motion after the serene journey: it was like finding herself in a crack in the desert after panning the spider-trailed floor from a cruising 747. It was like having the movie stop. Drew had had a fit once when the projector blew out during a movie. She had had to be sedated. She had played on it afterwards and said the doctors told her she was subject to fits if the 24-a-second rhythm was interrupted. It was a lie, but one she liked. And now, she did feel rattled, ready to sit down and rant at the sky.

"Call, won't you?" she nagged Stretch.

"I can handle this," the driver's voice said, under the hood. She saw his white cuffs in the car's black stomach.

"No, you can't," snarled Drew. She sounded hideous, and in one bold swing the heel of her palm knocked the wing mirror from its mounting.

141

Stretch looked up at the jolt and ping in the heavy car. He giggled stupidly.

Drew crossed the road, the angry mirror of her face like a baby she was carrying. She found a space of hard, clear ground in the light from the phone, and set the mirror down.

From higher up the hill, alone in the dark, but seeing all of them, children playing in the light, D saw Drew take a packet from her bag. She tipped white powder on the mirror: there was no breeze. Her hand worked over the powder. She must be holding some edge too fine for him to see. The mirror was white. Then Drew made brisk movements that left white ridges on the glass.

She saw the stripes across her watching face, bent down her head and sniffed the three lines up into the mirror and into her face. The glass was clean, and she could see the first smile falling down from the brain and the bone, into the lowered look of Drew. What a sweet smile. The pain dropping too. This girl could be something. Her face in the mirror was liquidising with hope and the hit. Cocaine made you long for your own next minute; it let you feel your heat.

Without bothering with his consent, Drew spoke quietly and firmly to D, never looking away from the mirror, "Come along, come and get it."

D edged forward, to see if he was in the mirror yet. But there was only black around her brilliant face. Did the silvering etch her features with glamor, or do all instruments of seeing polish what they see? D had never seen Drew so desirable, doting on her own intoxication, gossiping with her reflection.

Stretch was sneering at his passengers. "This won't take a moment," he warned Drew.

"You're going to have to call," she sang back.

Chuck had picked up the mirror. Holding it like a pizza to go, he shook cocaine on it. The powder spilled. He groaned and swept some away. It fell to the ground in a shimmer. Then he put his nostrils to the mound, snorted crudely and blew away as much as rushed into his black nose.

"Pig," Drew noted calmly. And then, looking up, pretty please, "D, you have to try. At least, you should try."

Chuck laughed. "If he's never done it, don't let him try this stuff."

"I'm gonna make D a special line," crooned Drew, "just a very thin line, a very short nice line." She was as diligent as a mother picking a baby's first oyster – not too startling, large or odd, an oyster that might be a jelly baby, one that would release its meaning beyond the child's nervous throat, so deep within the system that he felt safe.

Limo death

"D's going to be very fixed up here," she was murmuring – it was wicked and irresistible, the model of the age. "D is going to be in heaven," she was saying as the razor blocked off a line as thin and crisp as thread. If only more personal, less chemical pledges could be made, D thought. He would take it if he must, if it was a way to win this girl's nervy interest.

He held the tube. He was nervous of botching it. But as he moved it down towards the line, he saw the end grains lift and dither towards it. They were so eager to please, they rose and hurried like white balls in an educational movie about busy atomic particles. He was whole and handsome in the second it took. The line filled in his nerves, a Pac-Man gobbling up doubt. He floated back on the ground and looked up at the stars, cold and amaretto in his mouth. And he heard the thrilled company of Drew's body like surf bursting on his own. The two of them, side by side, and Chuck and Stretch at the phone, beggars at their feast, looking stupid and ill-fed.

He heard Stretch on the line asking for rescue. Chuck was doing wind sprints into the peak of the hill. And Drew was romancing him, her trusty tongue inside the mansion of his mouth. D closed his eyes and the slumbering roll in the ground seemed part of his being with Drew. But when he opened his happy face, Chuck was sitting on the ground up the hill, holding onto the pavement as if it had billowed and tried to escape, and Stretch was clinging to the phone, a man overboard.

"The ground moved," said Drew, bleary in her several worlds, but certain and unsurprised.

ROMAN SPRING

Not every movie contrives so grim an overlap between its story and the lives of those making it as *The Roman Spring of Mrs Stone*. But hardly a picture is entirely free from that peculiar haunting.

Joan Collins, when she is in London, watches Warren acting with Vivien Leigh, and wonders whether her fiancé is actually involved with the forty-eight-year-old actress whose marriage to Laurence Olivier has just ended, at his request, with Olivier planning to marry the much younger actress, Joan Plowright. It has been a tormented marriage for many years: she is unstable, depressive, drawn to many affairs, disappointed in her career. Perhaps she is mad – acting is a profession and a life in which that illness is hard to detect or prove. Vivien Leigh believes by 1960 that several irredeemable forms of ruin have overtaken her, not the least of which is age and its effect on her looks.

The Roman Spring of Mrs Stone, from a novel by Tennessee Williams, concerns an actress, Karen Stone, aged about fifty. She has a disaster, trying to play Rosalind in *As You Like It* – the production comes to a grinding, out-of-town halt at the Washington Theater! She decides to retire. Her husband, an older, wealthy man, takes her to Rome for a holiday. But on the flight there he suffers a fatal heart attack. Mrs Stone settles in Rome, an angel of death in attendance in the form of an impoverished but beautiful young man who watches her apartment and follows her.

Karen Stone is "drifting," not really aimlessly, but like a leaf on a river feeling the quickening in the water as the weir approaches. She is fixed upon by the Contessa, a pimp who provides Italian gigolos for older women, generally Americans. One of the Contessa's boys is Paolo. She trails him before Mrs Stone until the ex-actress is helplessly in love. Paolo is a cunning, narcissistic opportunist, played by Warren Beatty. It is to the credit of those making the film that his character is never softened. Not for an instant do we think that the male prostitute has been

144

compromised, or deepened, by feeling love for this forlorn woman. Instead, there is a sense of ritual. He is the man who will destroy Mrs Stone's spirit, so that she is ready for the other young man – who appears before Paolo – and who will fulfil or execute the role of killer that Paolo casually describes to her one afternoon.

The film is all the more acute and troubling in that it is not simply the story of a romantic woman's tragedy in which Paolo is the cruel instrument. It is also a story about acting and ambition, for Paolo will not remain a Roman gigolo, one of the Contessa's hirelings. He wants to get into the business of acting which Mrs Stone has quit. His final betrayal of her is presented as the rite of passage of a shameless, beautiful young man into movie-making.

As Karen Stone becomes infatuated with Paolo, she gives him clothes, jewellery and a movie camera. He plays with it. Then the Contessa – out of sheer malice and the destined urge to destroy Mrs Stone – tells Paolo that their affair is getting him the right sort of attention. He is on magazine covers with her; he is being talked about by film people. There is a young Hollywood actress in Rome at the moment, Barbara Bingham (Jill St John), and she has set her eyes on Paolo, if only to vex and thwart the older, stage actress.

A small but exquisitely dreadful party is arranged at Mrs Stone's apartment – for her, Paolo, Miss Bingham, the Contessa and a couple of the rich ghouls from this cut of *la dolce vita*. It is a party to view the home movies Paolo has shot with his camera. The group is more interested in seeing the shots of Paolo than those of Karen: it is clear which one the camera loves. There is a shot of the statue of an Egyptian god. Across the hot, active projector, Barbara Bingham asks Paolo:

"What's he holding?"

"er . . . That's a cornu-copia. Horn of plenty. There's a lot of . . . Karen before we get to me. Why don't you come outside – I show you the seven hills of Rome."

They move out to the balcony – the facet of Mrs Stone's apartment that Paolo most envied on his first visit – and Karen can no longer deny her love or Paolo's heartlessness. The young couple leave together, and Mrs Stone tosses the key to her apartment, wrapped in a loose handkerchief, to the killer waiting patiently outside. The humiliation complete, she is ready to play out her death scene, as foreshadowed in an earlier scene with Paolo, one of the best in this very dark movie:

PAOLO (seeing the younger vagrant in the street below): Who is this boy that follows you?

145

KAREN: What?

PAOLO: You must have noticed him. He's everywhere we go. Come here.

KAREN: I never saw him before in my life.

PAOLO: The trouble is, you make a spectacle of yourself.

KAREN: What do you mean?

PAOLO: Spectacle? That's something that's conspicuous. You. Your photograph in the magazine pointed out on the street.

KAREN: And you adore it. It's you they look at, Paolo. Not at me.

PAOLO: Ah! You don't hear the comments.

KAREN: Oh, yes, I do. *Che bello uomo* – what a beautiful man. That's what they say on the café sidewalks. And you bask in it like a sunflower. If I'm conspicuous, it's because you've made me so.

PAOLO: It's no use contradicting you. An American woman's never going to admit she's wrong about anything. But you don't hear all the comments. Last week I was compelled to challenge a man to a duel on account of a remark he made.

KAREN: You fought a duel?

PAOLO: I sent a challenge and the man left Rome.

KAREN: And what was this remark?

PAOLO: Too disgusting. I can't repeat it. Hasn't it ever occurred to you, Karen, that women of your kind are very often found assassinated in bed?

KAREN: What?

PAOLO: It's true. Only last week on the French Riviera a middle-aged woman was found in bed with her throat cut from ear to ear. There was no broken lock, no forced entrance. Just stains of hair oil on the pillow. Obviously, the lady had asked the assassin to come in.

KAREN: Does this mean you're going to kill me?

PAOLO: Ay-eie. That's right. Make a joke. Show your sense of humor. And in three or four years I pick up a paper and read about your death.

KAREN: Three or four years is all I need. After that, a cut throat will be a convenience.

Vivien Leigh dies in the summer of 1967, aged fifty-three, about a month before *Bonnie and Clyde* opens. She has made only one other film after *Roman Spring* – *Ship of Fools*.

If *The Roman Spring of Mrs Stone* is not quite a vehicle for Vivien Leigh, still it is the work of three men who admire her very much – Tennessee Williams, in whose *Streetcar Named Desire* Leigh has won an Oscar; screenwriter Gavin Lambert, and director José Quintero, who has lately directed Leigh on the London stage, in Giraudoux's *Duel of Angels*.

Beatty is the interloper. The first plan for *The Roman Spring of Mrs Stone* is that it be shot in Italy with a young Italian playing Paolo. But Warner Brothers are anxious to put a starrier figure opposite Vivien

Leigh. Beatty has seen the script. *Splendor in the Grass* is a Warners picture, and its director, Elia Kazan, may have spoken on Beatty's behalf.

But Beatty decides that he must convince Tennessee Williams. He may be encouraged in this by the story of how Brando won the lead in *Streetcar Named Desire* by meeting and impresssing Williams. And so he puts on an Italian suit and olive make-up and goes in search of the playwright in Puerto Rico. As Beatty describes his conquest: "I walked up to him in a gambling casino and began to talk to him in an Italian accent. In fact, I brought him a glass of milk on a tray, because I had been told that he had ulcers from his reviews of *Sweet Bird of Youth*."

He proposes himself for the part, and he reads for the writer, with accent and without. Williams is charmed; he says sure, why not? There is a coda to this story, told by Dotson Rader, who only meets Williams years later. He says that Tennessee tells him how, later that night, Warren comes to his hotel room wearing a bathrobe. Williams sighs and he says, "Go home to bed, Warren. I said you had the part."

Then Beatty has to win the favor of Vivien Leigh, who has casting approval. She is charmed by him, too. José Quintero is over-ruled. It will be speculated subsequently that Beatty may have given himself in sex to Leigh: his Paolo does have an icy humor that regards everyone as waiting to be used. But nothing is established; the casting is forever tinged by rumor and Williams' instinct that the Puerto Rican gesture showed Beatty's suitability. Perhaps Tennessee sees a grin of danger beneath the make-up and feels that heat of reckless ambition.

The Roman Spring of Mrs Stone does not fare well at the box office but Williams regards it as the most faithful screen adaptation of his work. The picture is not helped by the late decision of producer Louis de Rochemont to shoot it in London, instead of Rome. Screenwriter Gavin Lambert, barred from the set by de Rochemont after three weeks, remembers "the difficulty of creating a Roman spring in the deadly foggy English winter, with a producer as sullen as the weather". This hurts Beatty especially, he thinks, for it prevents the actor from absorbing the life of Rome, seeing real Paolos and hearing Italians speak English.

Lambert thinks that Beatty's Paolo sounds more Mexican than Roman. The voice does fluctuate, but most of all it sounds like an actor experimenting. No transcription can convey the sound Beatty makes before saying, "That's right. Make a joke," in the scene quoted. It is credibly Italian. But it stays in the mind because it seems like narcissistic cunning caught playing with itself. This is not merely an actor at work, but a man who knows everything is always an act. The sound itself lets us know that this Paolo – too cowardly for a real duel – has himself thought of murdering Mrs Stone.

Roman Spring has poor camerawork and studio sets that never seem a part of the sweaty, sexy Rome that would make Paolo more credible. The film is stagy: Quintero is a fine theater director. But it is Vivien Leigh who presents most problems, I think. She *is* the role, painfully so. But she has a tendency to posture whenever her character is most hurt or moved. She is excellent when quiet, watchful or thoughtful, but vague and melodramatic when put to the greatest ordeal.

There is a story told about Lotte Lenya (the Contessa), amused and gloating over her chance to steal the picture because Vivien Leigh was so smitten with Beatty. I think that is ill-founded. Lenya is excellent in what is a rather easy part, but there are really no moments where the three of them are playing together and a scene can be stolen. The true theft is more a matter of Beatty's own lust for the nastiness of Paolo overwhelming Leigh's uncertainty.

He is very good in the part. The inconsistency with the accent actually substantiates our feeling that Paolo is a fake, and draws attention to those moments when he is lying or making an appealing spectacle of himself. In effect, Leigh's voice is like a classical statue, while Beatty's is somewhere between a worm and a serpent, slithering over and around her, letting us feel a constant awareness of Paolo's Machiavellian traits. This gigolo acts with the heart, but never stops thinking and planning. And Beatty was apparently ready to be such a character, never flinching, never clutching at a moment that will let the audience like Paolo.

The movie might be better if its narrative fixed on the way two actors cross paths. If there was one good scene in which Mrs Stone coaches Paolo as an actor, this theme would be stronger, and for a moment at least Paolo might love a true teacher. As it is, the cold-blooded detail is superb. He is sleek, if a little too fleshy for a Roman who might starve if he can't sell himself. His mouth parts like a polyp, and the serene inaccessibility of his face becomes bogus whenever it smiles or frowns. For both are shows for the world: Paolo is really as deadpan as poker. When Mrs Stone gives herself to him sexually, he comes into her bedroom, in a black shirt and black pants. He drops his white jacket on a chair, he closes the drapes, he surveys her and then as he approaches the bed he goes into silhouette. It is a cultivated performance, without warmth or spontaneity, by a man always thinking how he is looking.

One cannot say, of course, if it is the actor's skill, the director's grace, or the simple nakedness of the man pretending to be Paolo. More than the stage, films study that balance of nature and artifice, and in playing an intelligent man, for the first time, Beatty touches on the impossibility of real feeling.

There is one breathtaking scene in which that question exactly coincides with the drama. Paolo is on the phone to the Contessa: she is hinting that he may have a chance at a movie career. The camera is in his lap nearly, as he leans back in an armchair. He is listening to her, thinking, stroking his tie absent-mindedly, his hand cocked, the phone curved around his face like a caress. His eyes dart back and forth, as if watching a fly. It is all brilliant and incisive; it is selfish, rapid thinking made manifest. And if it is acting – if the gesture with the tie was calculated, not thoughtless – then it is just a deeper, darker lie that it can seem so natural. But does this young hustler know when he is on, and when he is not? Or has he taken an imaginary camera into his solitude for company?

*

When the shooting of *Roman Spring* is concluded, he takes a vacation – in Rome. He is in a café there with the actress Inger Stevens when he meets Susan Strasberg, the daughter of teacher Lee Strasberg and another actress. (Does he let them pass him on? Or are there chambermaids and housewives who also catch his eye?)

He is still wearing Paolo's costume from the picture and Strasberg asks if he can sit down in such tight pants. They go out to dinner, and hit it off so well he moves in to her Rome apartment. "I found him charming and intelligent," she says, "with a tremendous need to please women as well as conquer them."

They go everywhere in Rome together, including the salon of Luchino Visconti, the film director. Visconti is "surrounded by priceless antiques and a handful of beautiful young men, while advocating Communism for the masses". A little more scarlet than red, perhaps, the connoisseur Visconti is attracted to Warren. After a little of this directorial scrutiny, Warren elects to visit the bathroom. He whispers to Susan on his way that she is to linger a moment and follow him.

Soon, they are in the small interior. You could safely imagine marble, rare lotions and elegant luxury, if it helped. She asks what they are doing there, *there*, in the john, and he says he'll show her. There is a

149

breathless, cramped and necessarily ingenious twenty minutes before the two Americans stroll back to the salon and all the ardent, waiting gazes. Those eyes have their reward, for Susan has not noticed, she says, that her blouse is still unbuttoned. Or has Warren written the scene and schooled her in the proper display of carelessness? "I wasn't quite sure how to act," says Susan, "but Warren beamed, at one and all, an enchanting, ingenuous smile."

In 1962 (Don Cravens)

Truth and other tales

A wind had sprung up, searching through the canyons. It was not a prevailing wind, but a brief panic in the air, the stir of some pressure in the ground, like the gasp after an explosion or a sunspot's belated gale. D shivered in the wind. It was such a mourning sigh of the faraway, it left him wistful. He was, he admitted it, a failure, a chump who grew sad listening to the wind. Such a pitiful romantic. But what could he do to stop fate dropping him in love with this unexpected and disarming Drew? Was he to blame? Wasn't it absurd to posit moral order or responsibility when this city could be wrecked in a commercial break? And wasn't D there just because he had striven to improve himself – never giving up? He had to learn to regard himself as the ball on the roulette wheel, falling where it might, ready for another play, free from regret or triumph.

"It's stopped," said Drew. She sounded disappointed.

"I suppose the earthquake must come one day," said D, trying to be fair with such hazards.

"I want it," Drew whispered. She was looking for fresh chasms or dust in the air from landslides. Far away the city twinkled on. The surface of Stone Canyon Reservoir was a sleepy sweat in the moonlight. The noise of the city was the familiar tiny booming, the old beat. It all went on, one minute after another, the cars slipping from third to top, the pins being reset after a strike.

"I want it all gone," she insisted.

"How can you?" It was the disbelief he felt someone ought to voice.

He saw her hair shift, like breathing. "I want to see the hills splitting and the reservoir spilling into the city. If this whole city got shaken up," she was straining with the thought, "anything could happen." She laughed as it struck her. "I could get my chance then." She turned on him; there were suspicions in her eyes. "Don't you want it?" She knew his answer. "I don't care! It deserves it." That was her clincher.

152

"It?" asked D. Perhaps she was religiously inclined? So many actors believed in long-shots bets.

"The city, the business." For Drew there was an "it" in there – the power by which the house rigged a game D accepted as open. "It" was the demon of her paranoia, and she wanted it revealed. "When it starts to shake," she tried again, "something in me says, 'Go on. Don't stop.' I want to be the cave woman in the new world." She smiled with relief, for she had got it clear as a role: the ruined city, and Drew in tousled hair and scorch marks, a marauder.

She was so much more molten than he was. D saw how, in life, the manner of actors could seem loose and distasteful, a little demeaning. He led her to a flat piece of ground and urged her to lie down.

"Won't there be snakes?" Her eyes were darting into the darkness, past the clumps of bush and weed.

"Surely not." D hoped the odd rabbit might hop past to live up to her fever. He told Drew to rest. He watched over her stern face, younger once her eyes closed, trying to sleep but growing tense again.

"Know what I did once?" Her eyes opened, grinning already, eager to see how he would take it. It made D think a story was coming, or at least a treatment.

"In Miami, I got in with some guys. They liked to have me lie down on the floor so they could putt golf balls at my pussy. On the carpet in a hotel. For gambling."

He waited. He never knew what traps she had. "That's horrible," he said. The line had been shaky the way she said it, but he wasn't sure whether this was the line's lurid flatness or her shortcomings as an actress. Yet she did not mock his upset. She tried to explain a certain ordinariness in the Miami scene.

"They weren't so bad. I like golfers. They've never let me down, you know." D could see the men, in shirtsleeves, with beer, studying their lie and tossing bills on the table.

"These weren't professional golfers?"

She hooted. "No, you bunny. They were just people in the business. You know who Truth is? A wrestler. He had handmaidens, two of us, dressed like slave girls and he came into the ring carrying us, one in each arm."

"You didn't wrestle?"

"That's death to a career. I wore a veil." Drew smiled at him, remembering the camouflage. "I even wore it to the gym for rehearsal."

"Where this Truth trained?"

"He didn't train. He walked his wife's dachshund. Truth was fifty, easy, and he wrestled three, four times a week. He used to specialise in beating Spanish kids. The Mexicans hated him. Their women called us whores – Cherry and I." He could see those old days jazzing past her romantic eyes.

"One night one of these young Mexican wrestlers took it to him. See, you can hurt someone if you want to, and if you're smart you can make it look like a mistake. This kid broke Truth's leg. Crowd went mad. Truth was weeping, sitting on the canvas. And you know what the Mexican kid did? He smacked Truth in the face, sitting there, so the blood poured out of his nose. It was like the kid thought the crowd wanted blood. But they didn't. They went absolutely silent and I hit the Mexican in the face with a bucket. They loved it. They roared. I just knew it was the time to take off my veil. You wouldn't believe it – the cheering, they threw flowers and the women blessed me. Anything like that happen to you?"

She could see the answer in his face, and so she hurried on. "I was on the Carson Show one night. One of the girls they have who bring out the new products? I wore a white bikini and I had a cake mix."

"And Carson flirted with you?"

"He's a frost."

"Still, the *Tonight* show."

"Yeah, but the white bikini didn't help me. My thighs had built at the gym. I should have had a black one-piece. I could have made it then."

"But Eyes saw you?" D presumed.

"He'd seen the pictures I did."

"Pictures?"

A gleeful idea surged across her face. "You think they were porno."

D blushed, "I didn't know."

"You kinky little D."

"I meant no such thing."

"You thought it. You thought private blue movies for Eyes alone. These were stills in travel brochures. Mexico, South America. Beaches and hotel pools. I was in a lot of those. And Eyes collects brochures. He found me through the agency. Just called me one day. Know what he said?"

"I'd never guess."

"He said, 'Hi'" her voice dropped down to her knees, "'this is Eyes. I just wanted to say I think you have terrific skin.'" Drew laughed, not sure whether to be proud or play the story for absurdity.

"Well, so you do," D told her.

154

"Yeah? I'll tell you about skin some day. Here's the car."

Another limousine was coming up the hill, slowly, looking for them. D brushed the dirt off his clothes, "We didn't have wolves."

"Oh we will," said Drew, "don't you worry."

"I'm puzzled." D had to say it – there is a stickler in him. "There was the New Hampshire story?"

"What?" Alarm loomed up in her guessing face.

"How Eyes saw you on TV, torn between that man who abducted you and the cop."

"Oh. That." It was an old story. She looked like a girl reminded of having to see grandmother when Randy Red Raider has just called.

She was so pretty a thing, such a scrap of dark foreboding. And when she stood, her body arched like a bow his love was pulling back. But D had lost track of how to humor or reassure her. She wanted very hard to be appealing, to have sway, but D could see that she was too desperate. It was her protection against a life of having to be liked. He knew she was more dangerous to his wish to be reasonable than snakes or wolves. Because he had the sense to shun those creatures.

As they gathered to transfer to this new car, D thought of travel brochures and all the young women you saw in them, sophisticated at the casino or sunning by the pool. He had regarded them as a Kodak army, alike, bronze, slender and blank in their wish-you-were-here. He thought of the determination in Drew that had lifted her out of that army.

"I'm glad for you that you are with Eyes."

"Oh sure," he heard her hurt. "Lucky me."

Another kind of slavery? He considered the allure of being a cave woman in this city, rendered back to chaos and primal struggle. D had the first unequivocal sense that he might see the end of the world. As if she guessed it, Drew took his hand and said, "Hang on, dearie. We're going to the party."

JOAN AT THE STAKE

Warren Beatty's attractiveness is being talked about as if it is a great talent, or a phenomenon apart from his character. People encounter it long before they meet him. A movie star never meets anyone to whom he is a stranger or a newcomer. His picture has been seen and appraised in magazines; if he has given interviews, they have been read and allowed to grow in the readers' minds; and in his movies, by giving several seconds at a time of his presence, his watching, listening, waiting self, he has allowed absolute strangers to develop a peculiar sense of familiarity with him. It will be particularly charming or offensive to anyone who is uncertain of himself to find that people he meets believe they have met him before, that they know him, and that when he smiles or jokes they knew he was going to do that. It may leave him suspicious of being, and in certain moods he may make a lavish, exaggerated, self-mocking imitation of this version of himself known in advance. And sometimes that act will go undetected. There may even come a moment in which he can perhaps be "Warren Beatty" in public – it satisfies so many, all the strangers checking in with the freak – and explore himself quietly, secretly, behind the closed doors of his smile. It is something all celebrated actors are likely to encounter, and it has the appeal of seeming to give the person control of a mad, frivolous world. But it is a kind of madness, too, for it initiates a split in the self that can become so constant it will not be noticed. And so you may some day read this or that about yourself, and chuckle, and say, "Look what 'Warren Beatty' is doing today. That rogue, that actor."

While they are in London and he is filming *The Roman Spring of Mrs Stone*, Joan Collins lives with Beatty. They may tell one another that they are in the greatest intimacy either of them has ever known in life. And he is learning lines for the next day, watching himself in the mirrors in the apartment or in the warmth of her responses. The role he is hoping to perfect for the film is that of a young man who exploits women. There are scenes in the movie where he is affectionate to and considerate towards women, where he makes love to them, with words or with his body. Then there are scenes where he is alone, or with men, with whom a quite different scale of candor is in order. He goes to the barber, and there he discusses his looks, his women and their gifts to him with a gloating, "professional" manner. He is the character and the actor in control of the character in *The Roman Spring*.

There is a moment in the barber shop when a waif-like young woman supposedly sauntering past on the Roman street sees this gorgeous young man through the window and stops to look at him. The actress playing this part has no lines. She and Beatty's Paolo are only cut together, each of them looking at the other. But the woman has a lean, wide-eyed face, and long hair that she tosses to him like a fisherman's line going out on the water. It is Sarah Miles, aged twenty, before she is known, before *Term of Trial*, or *The Servant*. For her it is only a day's work, but perhaps she talks to the star of the film between shots, perhaps he says to her, "What do you do?" and she says, "Oh, I just look at you." Perhaps there is no meeting. Joan Collins will wonder every day, and he can tell her, "You know what movies are like. Don't you trust me?" All actors are learning the facility that can make responsibility as slippery as soap in the shower.

Joan and Warren go to Paris for a few days, and they spend some time there with Joanne Woodward and Paul Newman, who is making *Paris Blues*. One night the four of them go to the Carousel, a gay night club in Montmartre. The acts at the club involve young men dressed as women – female impersonators, trans-sexuals perhaps. In their performance, the look-alikes for Marilyn Monroe, Ava Gardner, and so on, flirt with Newman and Beatty. One of them sings "Diamonds Are a Girl's Best Friend" and draws her boa across Warren's shoulders. The men blush, the women feel upstaged.

Then, at the end of the show, the performers invite the movie people backstage. Warren is a little nervous, but Joan says she urges him to go. And in the dressing room, attention shifts. The men are in various stages of bold undress, and they dote upon Joan and Joanne, professionally alert to *their* clothes, *their* hairstyles, and their interesting example of famous, beautiful women. How long is the career of female impersonators? Long enough, perhaps, for someone in Montmartre to be doing an outrageous "Alexis Carrington" still based on memory.

Joan and Warren live together again in Los Angeles after *The Roman Spring of Mrs Stone*. But it is not going well between them. It is her home, but he is irritated when her mother and young brother arrive from London on a visit. She tells him to stop being such a rat, and perhaps he blinks at that word and its failure to mesh with his vision of what is happening.

"It was obvious I had to be the one to end it with Warren. He seemed content to let it drift sloppily along. What happened to the glorious romantic fun we used to have? Why did all of my relationships with men turn sour? Was it my fault? Was I too strong? Or was I too weak? Or was it – and this I knew deep down to be the truth – that I really *wanted* only the neurotic ones, the men unable truly to love, truly to support and truly to give. Only by gaining the love of one of these impossible men could I prove to myself that I was a worthy person."

Joan is offered the female lead in *The Road to Hong Kong*, a reunion of Hope and Crosby. It is fifteen years since the last Road film, and this one will be filmed in England. "It's crap," says Warren, tossing the script aside. "Why do you need to do it?"

"Two reasons: for the money – and to get away from you." He had become a man and almost a star, says Joan, and I had marked time.

But her career is not quickly saved. Indeed, she will never make another good or significant movie again. She works all over the world in quick adventure films, empty comedies and in soft-core pornography – *The Stud*, *The Bitch*, *Nutcracker*. For theaters or television, she lists twenty-six films starting with *The Road to Hong Kong*. Beatty, in the same period, will make fourteen pictures. She exemplifies the kind of career he dreads – forever slipping, but never giving up, taking anything to keep in work.

There may be times in later years when she would go out of her way to avoid a meeting, and to hear his polite questions about what she's doing, knowing she's still doing what he regards as crap. Of course, she marries twice in those years, and she has three children, one of whom suffers but survives a serious road accident.

And then she becomes utterly famous again. In 1981, producer Aaron Spelling offers her a role in the soap opera, *Dynasty*. She says she'll think about it, and she accepts. In the next few years, she becomes one of the best known women in the world. The show is a hit, still running high in the ratings in 1986. Her character catches the popular imagination and "Joan Collins" becomes the epitome of a wicked, scarlet woman. At Christmas 1983, she is on the cover of *Playboy*, and inside, revealing not quite all, but far more than most fifty-year-olds would feel comfortable about. Her cheerful, disarming autobiography, *Past Imperfect*, published in England in 1978 but withheld in America – she is paid $100,000 for this discretion – appears in America in 1984.

In November 1981, already a hit as Alexis, Joan appears at Radio City Music Hall in the "Night of 100 Stars". There are actually over 200 stars, and Warren Beatty is another of them. They are on the same crowded stage for a few moments, and the camera does catch a suave grin thrown in his direction. He looks tired: *Reds* is a month from opening.

There is no simple rivalry in such careers. *Reds* is not *Dynasty*. But there are no actors so sophisticated that they do not feel the raw power of celebrity. And *Reds* is not really so unlike *Dynasty*. They work according to similar rules of storytelling and casting. Of course, more people see *Dynasty*. And if it is crap, then it may be that a cheerful, middle-aged actress would ask isn't most of show business crap? No other woman in Warren Beatty's life seems to have survived his quiet judgment so well or so merrily. An inspired producer would try them together now, in comedy. It would be for Warren to have to consider such an offer.

Lighthiser house

The Lighthiser property was on the southern side of the ridge, and not what you'd expect at the end of a dirt track that straggled away from the smart curves of Mulholland. It looked like a spur that must narrow and choke in weeds, just beyond the blind bend that was all anyone could see from the road. D supposed that it was contrived to look as shabby as possible, with the undergrowth raised to be daunting. He remembered that Cy Lighthiser had made his first fortune in LA as a florist and landscape gardener. This was just a little touch of wilderness in the theater of the Santa Monica Mountains.

For as the limousine wallowed in the dune-like sand, it soon bit on a deeper layer of gravel, and D could see in the car lights ahead a wider swathe of cultivated drive. Through the back window, beneath the clouds left by the car, he saw its deep tire tracks in the act of vanishing. Subtle vents at ground level, hidden in the chaparral, were blowing away all traces of their entry. In a moment, it would look like a dead-end again. D wondered if there was a sound system in the undergrowth that played those small, indistinct hisses that might be animals only a step away. After all, the movies were an art and a technology in which reality had been commandeered for atmosphere. One never knew in Los Angeles which street scenes were spontaneous, and which the sport of story-telling.

The drive now was broad enough to accommodate flanks of parked vehicles and two lanes of traffic in between. There were Mexicans in white, moving in and out of the headlights, to supervise parking. Some of them had rifles strapped across their backs, bandido style. D wondered if brigands were ever hired for the night to come across the hillsides in threatening forays so that guests could be thrilled by the crackle of firing.

They parked the car and stepped out into the warm dust, fragrant with jasmine and mesquite. There were eucalyptus trees farther down the track and D could smell their pungent, mentholating resin. He felt how easy to float down to the party, or to negotiate the distance on a cut. But Drew wanted to walk, barefoot, and D did as she asked. He took off his shoes and socks and left them in the car. Even dowdy D had an inkling of how this abdication enhanced his "look". On impulse, he borrowed a wide-bladed knife from one of the Mexicans and slashed at the ends of his pants to still their forlorn straightness. Drew studied her new pirate.

"You need a bloodstain," she reckoned, and as he was saying, "Do you think so?", he felt a slip of blade scathe his cheek and then stood patiently as Drew arranged a few drops of blood on what had been, at best, D's gesture towards a fresh white shirt – ironed, how long ago, by C, with typewriter white-out to cover its threadbare edges?

"Perfect," said Drew.

He felt the damp drying on his face.

"Act as if you hadn't noticed it," she told him. She was, in her way, as caring as C. Yet she had been armed with that tiny sharpness. D could not recall any pointedness in C; she had been his soft cushion. What a pity she couldn't be there to enjoy the eucalyptus and the trepidation.

"I think this is near the Bugsy Siegel house," said Drew, as they sauntered along, beckoned by the sounds of music – the bass of dance – glasses kissing and the torn strips of laughter.

"Is that so?" D liked to have historic sites identified. "When was that?"

"Oh," she moved away from him, "I don't know the dates."

D had intimidated her. In truth, he believed the Siegel home had been farther over, nearer Silverlake. But he did not want to deter Drew from stories that might be quite as revealing as the facts. So he said, "You could easily hide out in these canyons."

"I know it," she asserted. "I was up here one summer with Eyes. In a world of our own." It was like a caption.

"Near here?"

"Near here," she allowed. "Bugsy Siegel," she decided to say, "he used to dress up and go out, and no one ever recognised him. And then he'd answer the door at his house as the butler, and he'd say, 'Oh no, regrettably Mr Siegel's gone away, out of town – he's in Africa, or he's in jail.'"

"He had an amusing name," said D.

"He was Benjamin really," Drew volunteered.

"I didn't know that."

"Oh sure," Drew paused. "He was only forty-one when he died."

"As young as that?"

"Know what Bugsy said?" The little girl was pleased as punch now. "He said, 'I never thought I'd live to be forty.'"

"Ah," said D. "Forty is a serious step."

"Eyes and I used to picnic around here," Drew was saying. "We'd sleep out nights and make love under the stars."

Was he meant to ask for more, or show some flickers of jealousy? She stooped to examine him. Her old child's face noticed his muddle.

"You could go home, you know. Whenever you want."

"I don't think so, not now," he admitted.

"Don't think of me," she warned him.

"What does that mean?" He was haughty, he knew, trying not to break.

"Don't believe in me, that's all."

D knew there was blunt, inescapable advice in this, amply evidenced by the veering of this slick kid. But her miserable way of saying it made him feel protective of her. The prettiness was so shadowed by fatigue in its act – it looked like illness sometimes.

Then a Mexican came up behind them, polite but not to be refused. "Senor, senora," he said, "you hurry on party. These hills scary at night."

"Of course," said D, and he winked at Drew. "You never know who's sleeping in the undergrowth."

The gallantry touched her. One eye became a tear that slid onto her face. "It really happened, D. Eyes was so bright then. He could have saved the world."

"I know," said D. "I had an idea once for a story for him – he would have been a derelict who discovers a power of healing, and he becomes a famous evangelist. Yet he never knows whether his power is real."

"Oh yes," said Drew – she could see it. "That's a great seventies picture."

SUITCASE LIFE

Maybe Joan Collins throws him out, or is it just that she's left with the impression that she threw him out, while he believes that she was going to England so he didn't see any point in hanging around? This is not a community or a business where very many people break down and tell you, "I was the fool." And it is not that they are necessarily lying to you or themselves. They have got into the habit of seeing how they are on top. They are like Clint in Clint Eastwood movies, always thinking out those cutting one-liners that have an air of being in charge. But Clint uses those lines on other people. Most people talk to themselves with them. Of course, it is not exactly a community or a business. It is more of a séance.

And he is disinclined to unpack. Whether they are living in places she has taken and is paying most of the rents on, in borrowed apartments in London or in hotels, he tends to live out of a couple of suitcases, flat and often open on the floor. The clothes go from the cases to his body to the laundry, and they come back pressed and folded like new shirts so they can go back in the cases again. He knows were everything is – that's why no one else is allowed to touch, because that will disturb the order or further the disorder.

So when the time comes it is going to be a little easier for her to know she kicked him out because she can say to herself, "Just zip your bags, buster, and on your way." It's not that he's picked out magnolia trees for the garden and fed them a little mulch every day. There aren't any evident emotional investments. And if he is thrown out, he can always remind himself that he wasn't ever really, or thoroughly, *there* – not a resident, but someone who was staying there, waiting. It's no humiliation; he was going anyway. Couldn't she see he was his own man? Couldn't he see she knew he was scared?

Not living anywhere, or not having a home, is a strange condition in the extensively middle-class world from which Warren Beatty makes movies. Most of the audience has a home; it is the place they leave to go out to the movies. It is the firm site of security in the lives they expose to fantasy at the movies. If the picture lags, they may get to wondering whether the babysitter is molesting the children, or whether they are being robbed, or how they are going to finance the new room for when the kids get to be of an age when they've gotta do those things – like laying one another, or smoking grass – and you'd rather they did it in the safety of the home, but somehow out of sight.

Most movie stars have homes, eventually; they all die, too, of the same withering and merciless failures. And there have always been magazines that take you inside the homes of the stars, just as there are bus-tours that will lead you past their barred and walled properties. But it is sad to see exactly how a star lives – even if it is Edward G. Robinson with a Gauguin, or Debra Winger with Christmas stockings hanging all year over the hearth. Because it ties them down, it confines them. It is wonderful for a moment to have the detail, but then you realise you have lost the infinite possibility.

So, finally, living out of suitcases, living everywhere for no matter how long as if the place were a hotel, is a form of imaginative complicity with the audience. It is the self-denial of a pilgrim, the rootlessness of an actor who is happiest in the dressing-room, living like a slut, but emotionally secure in the eternal readiness for change. There is a frontier of not having which has a unique appeal to those millions who will be mulling over what they have left at home, worrying so much that a part of them would feel lightened if the message was flashed up in the middle of the movie – "Mr —— come home, your house has burned down."

So Warren moves in with Natalie Wood. Which complicates relations between Natalie and her sister Lana, eight years younger. Lana is not happy at home, and when Natalie leaves Robert Wagner, to live first in Bel Air and then in Benedict Canyon, Lana is around enough to have a room of her own. On Lana's sixteenth birthday, Natalie gives her a Jaguar XKE convertible. "All gold," says Lana.

Sometimes the girls play together, dressing up, exchanging confidences. But then, suddenly, Natalie is a sophisticated young woman with an affair and a kid sister – and an attractive kid sister who in a couple of years will outrage Natalie by posing for *Playboy*. When Natalie makes *Gypsy* – at the same time – she never takes *her* clothes off.

Lana says Warren moves into Natalie's home – the one in Benedict Canyon in which a waterfall outside is made into a stream that runs through the house, complete with mosquitoes – because their love is so intense. "Together in public," says Lana, "they were something to behold: beautiful, exciting, sophisticated." But at home, they fight and live on different tracks. Lana says Warren would talk about his dreams of producing and directing. But then there is a night when the sisters are together, and Natalie is becoming tense. She and Warren are expected at a party, but he has not come home. (They are an evident couple. Norman Mailer will report them at a party at Peter Lawford's Malibu home, which Marilyn Monroe leaves hours before her death.) By the time he returns it is too late, and Natalie is too overwrought for anything but a fight. So he storms out again, and Lana is there to sympathise, to blame him – though she has noticed that he sometimes looks at her – and to save it all up. One night Lana says that Warren is "only chronologically" older than she is when Natalie orders her to apologize to him.

"They occasionally had friends to dinner," Lana will say in her book. "But more often than not it was Natalie and Warren and, on weekends, just the three of us. It seemed to me that whenever Warren was in one room, Natalie was in another. Natalie would lie by the pool in the sun for an hour and then when Warren would appear in his trunks, his usual book tucked under his arm, she would get up and go into the house. It wasn't hostility, it certainly wasn't disinterest, and I have since come to think of it as two lives coming together briefly, but always at cross-purposes. There was always a distance between them."

There are incidents not likely to improve trust, such as the story of Warren and Natalie dining together at a restaurant. Warren's eye is captured by a hat-check girl. Not that Warren comes with a hat. It might be a waitress or a hostess; it might be another diner. But in the version that casts the hat-check girl, Warren excuses himself in the middle of the meal, finds the girl and persuades her to give up her job. They go off then and there, leaving Natalie alone at the table, with a hat-check costume tossed on the dressing-room floor.

Who knows now exactly how or whether it happened? It may have been only a meeting at the restaurant that developed into something later. It may be that Natalie did not know where Warren had vanished to for seven days, without his usual book. The story may be correct, or nothing more than a fabrication Natalie heard being spread around town. Whatever, she knows she is with a man who is the quicksilver center of more stories than she has dresses; and it plays upon her insecurity. Stories are torment to the imaginative. And if she asks him to explain, she can expect a shy denial – as if he is too proud to act it out well

With Natalie Wood

for her. "Well, of course," he can say finally, "if you don't trust me . . ."
This is how the wanderer gets left.

It lasts about a year, with many storming outs as well as plans to make
a picture of the Neil Simon play *Barefoot in the Park*, about newly-weds
in New York. (Several years later, Jane Fonda will make this film with
Robert Redford as her husband.)

Near the end of the year, Natalie has to go to New York for publicity.
She invites Lana on that trip, to be a fellow-shopper. One night they are
to have dinner with the journalist Tommy Thompson: Natalie is having
a "brief affair" with him. Then Warren invites all three to dine with him.

It is an awkward meal, with arguments and silences between Warren
and Natalie. At last, she and Thompson leave to go to their suite. Lana
remains at the table with Warren. She knows he is a philanderer, but she
says she is astonished when Warren suggests they adjourn to her room.

> "He told me I was always provoking him running around Natalie's house in a
> bathing suit, that even though I pretended not to know what was happening I
> knew exactly what the score was. I smiled sweetly – and insincerely – and
> said it couldn't be so because I was never interested in him and, in fact,
> considered him the cause of much of my sister's unhappiness."

But she has him take her back to her hotel. She asks him to get her room
key from the desk, and while he's away she telephones Natalie for
sisterly advice. She asks to be taken in for the night, but Natalie can't
manage that. Warren reappears with the key and Lana tells him no, she
can't do it. The hotel room is a convenience, but it is an institution. It is
somewhere where, whatever happens, it need not be regarded as a defeat
on one's home turf, an action embodying commitment. It is a
well-appointed stage, with room service and fresh linen, in which the
desperation can seem like freedom.

Same old party

The closer D and Drew came to the sounds of the party, the more likely it seemed that the house was not quite there. For they felt themselves close to the brink of a cliff or some drastic collapse in the land. They could feel that coolness which promises there is no ground to warm the air a few yards ahead. There was a point of utmost illusion at which they were hesitant to step forward while hearing phrases from conversations ahead as well as boredom and curiosity in the languid voices.

Then suddenly the house and its garden were beneath them on a last shelf in the hillside. It was a white-walled hacienda with a red-tile roof. Music and amber light were spilling from it onto the first of two terraces where people were dancing on a swimming pool. Yet it was a dancefloor made like a pool, the couples turning to and fro, partners offering and withholding on a surface of rippled turquoise, lit from below so that they did appear to be stepping on water. The Latin dance band was deployed on the three levels of diving board.

But on the second terrace there was a true pool. Guests were swimming there. There was a tang of chlorine and the noise of splashing lifted up by the canyon draft. For beyond the second terrace there was nothing but the vague forms of trees on the valley slope beyond, their top leaves gilded by moonlight. The estate was on the edge of inhabited land. The drop may have been only several hundred feet, but at night it seemed more complete.

There was a large video screen at the entrance to the house, set up near the statue of Aphrodite that Cy Lighthiser had brought back from Florida and surrounded with a bed of roses. The floodlighting made it difficult to distinguish the colours of the roses – they all resembled flesh – but the scents were so astonishing that no one went too near them. The video showed Lighthiser and his wife, the actress, Claudia Cannon. He wore white evening dress, without a tie, his swarthiness protruding at the cuffs and throat. And she wore a jungle green dress from which her

168

shoulders rose like volcanic peaks. Standing between Cy and Claudia was an African couple, in rags, the woman holding a hydrocephalic child. These natives were smaller than Cy and Claudia – like matted-in figures from another movie, taken on a different lens. The hosts ignored the couple: still, they were there, a point of tacit reference in the video.

CY: Hi. Welcome to our home.
CLAUDIA: We thought that as the crowd grew we might have trouble meeting every one of you personally.
CY: So we've chosen this unusual hallo. There's no reason for the party.
CLAUDIA: Except to say that somewhere else others are less well off.
CY: So, eat and drink.
CLAUDIA: And dance and play.
CY: And if you see anyone around who looks like us.
CLAUDIA: Don't be afraid to talk, or touch.
CY: Just don't forget we live in a large world. And don't pick the roses.

Whereupon, his lime-colored consort shivered with laughter. Then they both smiled during an undue delay, like a newsreader waiting to go to pictures, before the image went blank and was replaced with clips from Cy's latest movies.

"What a chic occasion," drawled Clear, coming up to D and Drew. "The Ethiopian pledges, I hear, are enough to have made a mini-series." He had the same wry smile, patient enough to do without obvious irony.

"What about our earthquake?" asked Drew.

"Did you have one? I don't think we felt anything here."

"Our car died," D explained, and Clear smiled again as if he understood all the reasons to stop along the way. "And there was a quake?" he asked politely.

"How's this party?" demanded Drew, disdaining detail.

"Same old party, if you know what I mean. Pasta salads and shoptalk. Some bright young things. A few deals closing before morning. All the old folks cracking the same jokes. The party that moves around town."

"Why do they come if it's not so special?" asked D. To him, it looked as perilous as a zoo where the visitors were expected to stroll in the same paddock as the animals.

"It would be rash to miss it," Clear explained. "You see, giving and going to parties here is like charity in other empires – gifts to the gods. Our starving Africans are the ultimate celebrities. That's why you won't be introduced."

Clear was so alert to the folly that D had to ask, "Eyes will not be here?"

"I doubt he will. It wouldn't be the first time I'd been wrong. He'd be

169

more likely to drop in if he knew I was handing out his regrets. But with parties, in general, Eyes has slowly detached himself. Though, I remember when he was partial to intimate dinners – six or eight people, good talk, that sort of thing."

"Well," said D, not wanting to think badly of this pomp, especially if he was a guest, "it must be better than the Black Death."

"Oh, that's good," said Clear. "We should tell Cy that. I think he'd like it. Look, I have to take a call. Drew, circulate D. Show him the sights. There's anything you'd want." He spread his hands in an air of amiable defeat. Then he moved on, brushing cheeks as he went, and backhanding sly fives.

"Always working," said Drew, bitterly.

"He is agreeable, though."

"Do you think so?" she wondered. "He only carries the messages."

"He has been very kind to me," D assured her.

She considered what this opinion revealed. "You shouldn't be here," she told him. "These people could feed you to the fish."

"I don't think so." D laughed boldly. He wanted to be up to it all.

"Or make you fall in love with them," she murmured. "Would you bathe naked?" This question came so quickly after the barbed remark, D could not deal with both.

"In the pool," Drew nodded her head, leaning that way with a body that wanted the cool in her armpits, between her legs, in the spaces between her toes.

"No bathing suits?" he asked her.

"I told you about skin. Come and watch. There'll be other old gentlemen."

"Is that what I am?"

"I'm fond of old gentlemen," she said. She made him think they were always the most knowing.

"I might watch."

"That's riskier than swimming."

"Don't you want me to watch you?" Was it the tenderest question he had asked her?

"Why not?" said Drew. She looked at him as sad as if he had come along too late, but wondering if there might yet be a best to be made of it. "I'm a slut," she added.

"This is a splendid evening," said D. He wanted her to know how eager he was.

"Until you're sick to your stomach," she threw in.

ALL FALL DOWN

Sometimes an alchemy appears in the early careers of stars. From one picture to the next, a mood hangs in their air as if to say these movies are not really separate, individual dramas in which a Warren Beatty happens to have been cast, but stages in a conspiracy or a cult that *is* the actor. Sometimes this is the shared wisdom at rival studios that he is especially well cut out for some moment or stance that fits easily into many dramas – a way of seeming to arrest the action, looking up at the other characters and at the entire process of the film, saying, "What did you say?" or "You mean me? You think that's me?" Sometimes it is the actor and the actor's agent besieging a project with pleas for a scene they know he looks good in – a star has to realise how he should be photographed, he easily acquires the code for his own looks, and he is likely to chat casually, on a man-to-man basis, with directors of photography ("Lionel, how are we today?" – when he means by "we" the photosensitive pact in which the two are furnishing a kind of religion). Or it may be chance, an unavoidable, rising nature seen and used by different people, without prodding or prompting, just as – it is alleged – some great natural discoveries are made simultaneously all over the world.

Early on in *All Fall Down* there is a scene in a bar in Florida. Clinton, in his late teens, has come south from the family home in Cleveland, looking for his older brother, Berry-Berry. Clinton has brought $200 that was meant to help his brother get set up in business; but is has to be spent to get him out of jail. Berry-Berry is a loner, a drifter, a wastrel, a womaniser. "If he was my brother, I wouldn't brag," someone warns Clinton. But the kid is too much in awe of his brother: they are Brandon de Wilde and Warren Beatty, wide-eyed love and wonder and the narrowed face that hates itself.

So the brothers go to a bar – fond, related, but with nothing in common and no evident thing to do except for Berry-Berry to disillusion the kid. A rich young woman comes in, Mrs Mandel. She is played by

Constance Towers – tall, blonde, a little bitter and repressed – it is one of those many fine performances that seem stimulated by Beatty's presence. She talks to the barman first:

"Good evening, Mrs Mandel."

"Good evening, Tony."

"Are you leaving tonight?"

"Yes, we're going on a little cruise to the Bahamas. My husband's had a terrible time finding a crew today. They all want such enormous wages. Shocking."

The cutting and the framing of the film have already alerted Mrs Mandel and Berry-Berry to one another: it is a medium hooked on attractions. Faces look and the leap of editing gives their ardor an object of desire. It has to, otherwise the film falls apart. Berry-Berry moves over to be nearer, but this is as much an effect of breathing as of real motion. The medium lets him come closer, and Beatty is already an actor in whose sagging mouth breath is the most intense physical activity. His voice comes from his nose – it is crucial to his sexiness.

"Lady, if I had a yacht, I wouldn't complain."

"Do you resent people with yachts?"

"No . . . Just that I got an old man at home who talks about a share of the wealth, and all that."

"Oh, I'm perfectly willing to share any of my possessions," says Mrs Mandel, and she opens her white cardigan on that line. This is the kind of effect – so "right," so slick – that we must begin to feel that people are already helplessly in the debt of movies they have seen, and of their codes. And yet, something in the actress, a certain innocence, still makes the director's touch poignant. We are seeing a frightened woman pretending to be brazen, a woman claiming to be an actress. It is sexy because of this insight into pretense.

She goes on: "Perhaps you'd like to join us? You might enjoy the Bahamas." (There is something wonderful and surreal in movies before the end of sexual censorship – that this cool white sweater holds semi-tropic isles, with the word "Bahamas" on the sound track, passing into radio's eroticism.)

Berry-Berry considers and then says something utterly out of keeping with the compelling naturalism of this scene, but something so right if it is really a scene about actors: "How do you know I'm not some dangerous maniac that goes around killing beautiful women like you?"

She relaxes; the threat is balm because he has noticed her greatest worry, he has called her beautiful. She is stupid for him, and he is in control. *All Fall Down* does not much like women: "Well, in that case, I won't have to take a sleeping pill tonight." This is why the picture is in black-and-white, and is years ahead of anything that could be made now, more than two decades later. It has a lucid pessimism, not flaunted and not evaded, a quiet terror at the way people are and at their destructiveness.

"Well. These are the only clothes I got," says Berry-Berry.

"I think I can find a pair of trunks that will fit you."

"Well, I've got another problem here," – power in pictures always humiliates others – "my kid brother, I gotta take care of him. Need about fifty bucks to get him home."

Mrs Mandel hands over the money: it is her body printed in neat, flat, oblong forms – Grant's tomb.

"Be down on the pier in half an hour. If you don't come I'm going to have to have you shanghaied."

Berry-Berry is a gambler, and a self-destructive. Even the "golden" offer is one to take risks with: "Didn't I hear you say you had a husband?"

And the film leaps with danger, as Mrs Mandel has her moment: "Oh, I do, but I don't think he'd appeal to you at all."

All Fall Down is two films that never mesh. It is the story of the Cleveland home, of parents who insist that their sons call them by their first names as if to ignore their constant need for infants. Ralph and Annabel (Karl Malden and Angela Lansbury) are failures: he drinks, she nags; they are craziness kept decent by domestic habit. And Clinton, their son, has been driven to spying on them and recording their conversations on his way to being a writer: *All Fall Down* was first of all a novel, by James Leo Herlihy. Clinton is a sweet hero, who loves life. Will he survive this family?

Berry-Berry is another film, that of a sexual roadie whose dark hair has golden ends from the Florida sunshine. He lives off fools and women. He beats them, because he hates life and himself. He could be a good deal more depraved if the film were bold enough – he might sleep with Mr and Mrs Mandel, he might be an adventurer a little less burdened by self-pity and a little more capable of true intelligence.

But Berry-Berry is there to teach Clinton about life in the kindly, conventional and circumscribed scheme of William Inge, John Frank-enheimer and James Leo Herlihy. And so he must behave so badly that Clinton sees the light. Berry-Berry comes home. You mustn't ask why. The family's house guest, Echo (Eva Marie Saint), falls in love with him.

She is a thirty-one-year-old virgin of the kind that Hollywood keeps in the trunk next to the one for drifters, wastrels and womanisers – just so long as the two breeds can sniff each other's begging blood. Echo gets pregnant. Berry-Berry wants his freedom. She drives off into the night and the rain and crashes. The studious film has already established her as a good driver.

It may be the craziest measure of *All Fall Down*'s "family virtues" that this young mother's suicide is utterly condoned. Like most of Inge's work, this movie wants to tear the family limb from limb, but it can only sit there in its awful shadow, suffering. Annabel loves Berry-Berry but the emotion is repressed. It is a far better film if Berry-Berry offers sex to his mother. Beatty seems just as interested in Angela Lansbury as he does in Eva Marie Saint. Their love is a plot device in which love-making is dissolved with shots of swans and emotional embraces so much less acrid and pointed than the talk with Mrs Mandel.

Beatty is on screen for rather less than half the film. He cannot handle the implausibility in his actions. He never makes us believe that he loves Clinton or Echo. Nor is Beatty remotely successful in either a final tearful breakdown or a devilish, laughing display of nihilism. It is clear here how far – in a certain professional sense – he cannot act: these are types of scenes in which his effort is merely perfunctory. When he has to cry, Frankenheimer despairs of the actor moving us and employs a series of cuts moving in on ever closer shots to register an intensity Beatty cannot give the lens.

It is the "sincerity" dearest to this concept in which Beatty fails. It is as if the real man in the actor is too guarded to play such revelatory scenes. Warren Beatty has extraordinary screen presence, but it is confined to situations of thought, guile and artifice. He has to play an actor. He does not believe in the generosity that gives of the self. Given that in Beatty, Berry-Berry should only come to the Cleveland home like a terrorist, bent on ripping away all its veils of disguise.

The film is an interesting failure, then. But in its first half, it has two of Beatty's best scenes. The first is with Mrs Mandel, where the game and the act are everything: indeed, they are the best sex Mrs Mandel is going to get, however many garments she is ready to open up for him. The second scene comes when Berry-Berry has moved on to work at a gas station. It is just before Christmas when a woman comes in for a fill-up. The actress is Barbara Baxley, and it is the best thing she will ever do on the screen.

"You new here?" she asks. Her voice is shifting from the tired, thin

Southern scream of a teacher who no longer believes in talking, to the deeper, more careful delivery of someone who knows she may be on the verge of a "great scene." Now she is becoming the teacher who always wanted to be an actress.

"I'm just helping out for a while." He hasn't noticed her yet.

"I wondered. I drive here regularly, and I knew I hadn't seen you before. I think I would have remembered you if I'd seen you before. I mean, you're not the kind of young man one expects to see in a job like this." She is already essaying the Blanche DuBois no one will ever ask her to attempt.

"Why's that?" There's the line, sighed to the car as much as to her, but coaxing the picture to address him.

"Well, if I were a young man, and I were as good-looking as you, I think I'd go to Hollywood. Try and get in the movies." In Beatty's career, no subject will ever loom larger than the career itself, and we are left as cultural explorers wondering whether such a scene is conscious or natural.

"That where you're headed?" He is saying so little, working on the car, while she is talking. She is like an actress auditioning for him, and he is too busy and callous to give her all his attention.

"No, I'm going to Louisville for my Christmas vacation. I'm a teacher. I have three weeks' vacation. I'm going to Louisville. I have a sister there. I hate to drive all the way to Louisville by myself. I don't suppose you know any young man who'd drive me, do you? Somebody reliable? Who'd be a kind of companion, too."

"I don't suppose you'd like to change your mind by any chance and go to Cleveland?"

"Cleveland! I don't have any relatives in Cleveland." There's a tremor in the air, disturbing her small hopes, saying just how much would you give up for the part? Order? Sanity?

"Well, what if this young man didn't have any bread. He couldn't afford a room?"

"Bread?"

"Didn't have any money."

"Oh, well, teachers aren't ever rich, but I'm sure I could afford a room for him some place. As long as my vacation lasted. And provided he'd drive me back. And if he'd take me a few places in Louisville. My sister and her husband don't go out very much, and sometimes I get very lonely." The would-be actress wants the play to be about her; it may be her miracle play.

"You got yourself a driver." She will never catch this blunt pace. He will come and come again while she is getting in the mood.

"You mean you can go?" (The actress is exquisitely good: we know exactly how far desire's dream is destroying her philosophy.) "You mean you can just pack up and leave? My goodness. You can't just go, right now. And leave the station without anyone to take care of the customers."

"You want me or not?" This is Attila at the gates of her vagina.

"Well, I'd be delighted if you took the job, but I don't want to inconvenience other people."

This is the peak of *All Fall Down*. There is a short scene to come, in Louisville, where the teacher knows she has been humiliated and where Berry-Berry hits her because, "You made me do it. I didn't have any choice." But it is unnecessary after the dark comedy of the pick-up which lets us imagine all the damage to come while never losing the acidic mirth of the spider keeping the fly in the corner of its wicked mind.

It is telling that Beatty so wanted to play Berry-Berry and to emphasise his waywardness. When people saw (or see) *All Fall Down* they cannot like Berry-Berry at the level of the movie's conservative consciousness. But they cannot forget Beatty because while he is poor, abject or nearly non-existent in several scenes, still he is the heart of the movie's best scenes, those in which it has the power available to the medium.

It might be a kinder world if movies awakened us to human depths that let us behave better. But they are more concerned with power, glamor and seductiveness, and that is why they can make danger and darkness so attractive. Movies always say do you want me or not?, and now, not just when you're ready. Movies race on at *their* pace and energy and they say leave your belongings and your attachments. On a cut, let us go from Florida to Louisville, or from propriety to desire's nakedness. Berry-Berry knows the energy of the medium: its fuel is his air and nothing is as frightening or as exciting as this readiness to go now, leaving the dull, real world for what it is.

The medium celebrates such drifters, however much the script scolds them. Perhaps William Inge knew why Beatty's own family experience equipped him for *All Fall Down*. Maybe he wrote scenes for the young actor he liked, and feared a little. But we must remember that Inge's world wants home and family to work, and it could be that Inge himself would have gone crazy if he had ever had to live out of a suitcase or literally give up the ship that placed him in the world. *All Fall Down* is the worried lament of middle America, too nervous to really use the animal it half-wants as its nemesis. The movie is still disturbing just because of that conflict of wish and energy. It is the kind of failure that can enhance a career.

Drew dives

Drew was in her dive, a twist and somersaults, the whorl of pubic hair the screw fastening her to the scene. D would have watched her all the way down. But the tall woman in black went on talking to him. "Mr D, I'm telling you about my art event," dragging his head away from the leggy spin his naked Drew made in the floodlight before the streak of body cut the water and an uncomplaining lifeguard went in after her. She was a spectacular diver, but she could not swim, and had to keep a certificated man around.

D could not take it all in, along with the silver trays of canapés, the ever-fresh tulips of champagne, or the smoldering joints. He was not accustomed to parties: he was like the Ethiopians, and he wondered if his eyes were as terrified as theirs. His head was swivelling. Yet he was aware of all he was missing.

The party was one space, not with precise distances between the magnolia tree and the parrot on its perch, but an inner montage in which these images were superimposed. For he was always in one place, with his attention in another, shutting down talk at his ear to pick up whispers over there. And he could alter his tuning, just as he could believe that everything was happening at once, that the party was not a night or several hours, but a bulging instant.

At the pool, Drew met several children putting a kitten on the water on a square of white styrofoam; and the kitten was clawing at its small raft, destroying it. So Drew chided them and lifted the cat to safety. But its hair-thin claws raked her arm, and the children oohed to see blood. It was like chocolate in the floodlighting.

Then it was teenagers, hard with muscle, impervious to the fudge sundaes they were eating. They ganged up on Drew, and tossed her in and out of the water. She was their ball, nearly sick with laughter. Then at last she was left hanging on the rail in the water until one of the boys swam back to her, stood behind her and drove her flat against the wall. D was left to wonder if he was penetrating her. She tried to beat at him and he knifed away through the water like an indolent shark. Drew sagged from the rail, her eyes shut. He saw her mouth muttering. D had done nothing but watch.

He attached himself to a ring of savagely attractive faces and their conversation:

"So I will have this affair with Teddy," said a woman in orange hair. She had the air of being dead, examining her old life.

"Not Teddy! I hoped he was gay," said the man with her.

"Of course he is. But he wants to humiliate Maxene."

"I know I'm going to kill Maxene," another woman promised them all.

And another man, "Have you forgotten? I did kill her a year and a half ago, but then a few months later she just came back from a trip, re-cast and no one bothered."

A butler brought D a white telephone: "For you, sir."

"How can it be?"

But the fellow only smiled and put the phone to D's head.

"Having fun?" said the voice on the phone.

"Well," D tried to explain. "It's extraordinary." He had just noticed that another group was exploring the floor of the valley below with a laser beam. The small lemon of light pierced through woods, patios and houses. It found a couple asleep. The light stopped. The woman stirred. The light had focused as a pinpoint in her open armpit. She tried to get away. D felt her agitation. She never woke, but the intrusion reached into her sleep.

"I've been talking to Eyes," said the voice.

"Who is this?" asked D.

"Look up towards the house," the voice told him.

D did as he was told, and he saw a man by the terrace balustrade, looking down, smiling at him. The man was on the telephone. The man was Clear.

"No, stay there," said Clear on the telephone, as D looked for the steps so that he might be with his colleague. "It's easier like this. Anyway, I talked to Eyes about the script."

"Is he here?"

"The telephone. He loves it – I told you that – but he puts his finger on something that troubled me."

"What's that?"

"Well, it does rather dwell, in terms of time and space."

179

"I see," said D. He could not decide whether this was a mortal problem or akin to an unpleasing color in the paper.

"We weren't sure," said Clear. "So we called your wife, and she concurred."

It was a shivery knife in his back. He looked up and Clear was still amiable – thank God now for the distance of the phone. Clear must have foreseen this.

"You could reach her?" D felt sick.

"By good luck. We called and some rather grim man answered. He got her to the phone."

"Scrug," said D. The man was menacing at night, when he might have been taken from some favorite show.

"He seemed very nasty," Clear recalled.

"And she agreed?"

"You don't mind us asking?" Clear's voice wormed into his ear.

"She does know the script," D reasoned.

"And your pluses and minuses. Anyway, think about it. Let's talk soon."

"Soon?" D asked. In ten minutes or later in the year?

"I have to run." When D looked up, Clear was gone.

He returned the phone to the rest, and noticed a silence crowding in on him except for the voice of a woman, who, apart from being rather overdone, looked like Barbara Howar. She was saying, "But even at a party like this, entertainment business goes on and the hopefuls may find out whether this is the place for them or whether they should get the next Greyhound back to Omaha."

There was a camera pointing at him, as well as lights. D read "Entertainment Tonight" on the camera. He looked again and it *was* Barbara Howar, not exactly overdone but in the swing of her indefatigable desire to catch the system at work. D felt mortified. He was sure people were laughing at him, yet he tried to find out from the crew what night this segment might be shown.

SOUR APPLE

It *feels* orchestrated, even if there has been no master plan. "Warren Beatty" bursts upon the world like a campaign. His first three films open in the period from October 10, 1961 to April 11, 1962. Initially this is because of the unusual interval between the shooting of *Splendor in the Grass* and its release. But it is also because other pictures feel they may be harboring a phenomenon to be exploited immediately. And so, *The Roman Spring of Mrs Stone* opens three days after Christmas 1961, in time to secure Oscar possibilities for that year and to catch the wake of interest left by *Splendor*. *All Fall Down* is pushed out early, in part because MGM have a disaster in *Four Horsemen of the Apocalypse*, but also because in early 1962 people are talking about Warren Beatty. There are the films, and there are the love affairs; and if it may sometimes trouble an earnest young romantic to see how the two are confused, still the careerist has a complete understanding of how seductiveness works. But if he *is* a romantic, he will dislike himself for his cool calculation. And if he is Warren Beatty, too, he will see how far his own sensual presence, his uncanny need to be alluring, and his own wish to be in control of it all, leaves many people disliking him. There are moments when it could put a kid off romantic life for good.

All Fall Down is a severe failure; *The Roman Spring of Mrs Stone* does not do well; and, while it is well reviewed and is clearly an event, not even *Splendor in the Grass* excels at the box office. These are all despondent views of life, grim, sad or resigned. They are the natural material of novels or plays trying to find outlet on the screen, but never convincing the American audience. For, all too plainly, they deal with reality, and both the entertainment force and the artistic achievement of American films have always and will always depend upon turning reality into energised metaphors – they are called genres – that take the crowd for a ride and let the moral sink in peacefully.

In the early 60s, the picture business in America is going out of

181

control: nothing else may irk Warren more. The studio system has broken down, just as the mass audience has given its imagination to the small screens. Hollywood is making hugely expensive throwbacks – like *Cleopatra* – or small, old-fashioned, literary studies of harsh reality, like *All Fall Down*. Neither works. We are still a few years away from the reclaiming of movies by the young as a vital American form and from the new forging of American genres, something that prevails from, say, *Bonnie and Clyde* to *Taxi Driver*, a period in which Warren Beatty is a clear leader and a figure of unquestioned charisma.

There is no reason to think Warren foresees all this: the story goes dead if he does. But he knows things are wrong in the business he is entering, and if he and that business do not get on well in many ways it may be because his skepticism keeps nagging at its failure to understand and change. He does not trust the business to run his career, and he does not see the sense in the inane round of empty interviews entailed in promoting a film. So he angers the studios and the press – all of which makes him more desirable, and surely schools him in an insight which may never have been far from his nature: that it can be seductive to stay silent, to be difficult, to treat your admirers badly. The seducer despises his conquests, for they have failed to see that the charm was just a trick, the play of an intelligence that does not much like life or the world.

When *All Fall Down* opens it gets reviews that manifest the nation's urge to confuse the star and the characters he is playing. When we are sensible and pious we always deny this; but it is central to the nature of celebrity as it attaches itself to movie actors. In *The New York Times*, Bosley Crowther says: "Everybody in the story is madly in love with a disgusting young man who is virtually a cretin. At least, Warren Beatty plays him so he seems like one. This persistent assumption that everybody should be so blindly devoted to this obnoxious young brute provokes a reasonable spectator to give up finally in disgust. Surly, sloppy, slow-witted, given to scratching himself, picking his nose and being rude beyond reason to women and muttering about how much he hates the world – this creature that Mr Beatty gives us is a sad approximation of modern youth."

Film criticism is doing just as badly as the business in the early 60s. Yet Mr Crowther inadvertently touches on a mysterious appeal in pictures – a puzzle that fascinates, which is, who picks his nose? Is it Berry-Berry, or Warren Beatty? There is no answer; it is the question that is most relevant and illuminating. For the audience and actor alike there is a freedom in letting it be both at the same time, and it is a liberty

182

that works best in the deserted intimacy of the movies, where "he" is "here", "now" and never here, never now, never knowing us, his watchers. You can show the spy outrageous things about yourself if you are certain the spy cannot warn you he is there.

The press grumbles about Warren Beatty in the way Bosley Crowther preaches against the character he plays. Even those who work with Beatty despair of him and sometimes turn on him with the kind of rejection that the Willart family realise is all their Berry-Berry deserves.

In 1962, the Hollywood press give Beatty their Sour Apple award for being uncooperative. That covers everything from rudeness, silences, evasions when he is being interviewed, to doing all he can to avoid and deny the press. The particular section of the press that covers "entertainment" is not known for its intelligence or its restraint. And Beatty will not have to wait long to discover how far he is wasting his time and his thought on them, especially if they keep asking about his plans to marry or his special intentions towards a few specific ladies – questions he cannot solve when the ladies themselves ask. So he has reason to be aloof or uncooperative.

But John Houseman, the producer of *All Fall Down*, sees someone who is also intensely ready to sell himself. It is Houseman who has asked MGM to let him turn the James Leo Herlihy novel into a film. "Almost against my will", says Houseman, the cause of Beatty for Berry-Berry is promoted. William Inge is the actor's chief spokesman, a writer in whom at the time Houseman sees a depression that sometimes becomes suicidal. Houseman allows that Beatty himself has done the rest: "In an astonishing campaign of self-promotion this young man . . . had managed to get pictures of himself, together with feature articles, into every major magazine in the country. Using charm, sex and unmitigated gall, he kept the country's female columnists in a tizzy".

Houseman remarks on the fact that Beatty has made himself a name and a personality that quite outdims more experienced professionals like Karl Malden, Angela Lansbury and Eva Marie Saint. And he attests to something not easily believed today – that Beatty at the start of his career is interviewed all over the media. That he is sometimes morose and difficult in those interviews does not contradict the zeal with which he and his agents go after them. His reticence toward the press in later years might be explained as the rueful lesson of those early years. But that has to suppose that Warren is not in charge. If he seeks interviews and then plays difficult – as if that was his role – then it is in character that, after a time, he decides to withhold himself from the press. The control is *not* complete: there is a pathology beneath control, the one area it prefers not to notice. But there is always an experimenter at work in Beatty, watching and refining the alchemy of being liked and hated, known or forgotten.

He may have to put up with more lovers than friends. "From the start," John Houseman says of the making of *All Fall Down*, "our most serious problem was young Mr Beatty. With his angelic arrogance, his determination to emulate Marlon Brando and Jimmy Dean, and his half-baked, overzealous notions of 'Method' acting, he succeeded in perplexing and antagonising not only his fellow actors but our entire crew."

Houseman repeats that the cameraman Lionel Lindon – the one I imagined Beatty attempting to charm with, "Hi Lionel, how are we today?" – grew so enraged that "he flew a camera-bearing helicopter within a few inches of his head". But Houseman knows Lindon as "Curly". Perhaps Beatty is too shy, too hip, to know how to talk to a veteran. Maybe he is seeking friendliness when he calls the gaffer "kid", only to alienate that grizzled stalwart. It is hard to be easy with the crew, to pretend there are no gaps, when they are dowdy technicians to the glossy dream.

At the end of location shooting in Florida, the crew and the local police plot together, and Beatty is left to spend a night in a Key West jail cell. This is exactly where *All Fall Down* discovers Berry-Berry – the ironies outlive the laughter.

The reviews are not all bad. In the *New Republic*, Stanley Kauffmann admires Beatty's Berry-Berry: "Physically, Beatty has the requisite magnetism; emotionally, he has the coiled-snake tension of black lower-middle-class frustration. What he needs now, as an actor, is to develop a more reliable voice, with a wider range."

At this point, a certain kind of movie star biography would launch out on that widening range to see the actor growing. But it has never happened. Warren Beatty acts less now than he did in the early 60s. But when he does and when he is good he is exactly like his Berry-Berry, watching himself, dark, fatalistic, as fascinating as a cobra, and in charge.

The young man does not accede to all the best hopes around him for how he will grow up. And he stays young: approaching fifty, Beatty is still a Kid. His greatest denial or refusal is towards the leavening of experience, or even towards its risk.

In January 1962, an interview appears in *Cosmopolitan*, conducted by Jon Whitcomb. It is far from the toughest or coldest Beatty gives. When the tape recorder is turned off, Whitcomb recalls, Beatty expands, relaxes, grins and talks like a kid. But while it is on, he is grudging, suspicious and difficult, like a kid paying James Dean lines:

"To break another silence, I asked him how he happened to meet Mr. Inge.

"'I met him for *Splendor in the Grass* in a most conventional way. My agent introduced me to him.'

"'Had he seen you?'

"'Who, my agent?'

"'No, Inge.'

"'No. He was trying to cast this picture, and I was introduced to him by my agent.'

"'What sort of play was it?'

"'What play?'

"'*A Loss of Roses.*'

"'Well, I met him for *Splendor in the Grass.* Then the picture was canceled, and he had this play, so then I did the play.'

"'What was your role like?'

"'You're trying to get me to say something I don't wanna say?'"

Later in the same piece, Whitcomb describes a talk with William Inge. It is full of insight: Inge anticipates that Beatty may give up acting; he speaks of his instincts and his conscience. The remarks reveal Inge as a sad, hopeful, kind man, a man moved by Beatty, knowing him well in some respects, seeing but perhaps too afraid to look all the way to the end of the tunnel:

"This young man is still high, still exhilarated at the turn his life has taken. His birthday comes early in the summer, I think, and he's just turned twenty-four. I think he may start closing the doors on the press pretty soon. I doubt if he will give interviews at all much longer. When I first met him he seemed marked for success. He was the kind of boy everyone looked at, knowing he was going to make it big . . .

"I don't think he knows how he acts. He's hard-working and instinctive. He's got a healthy ego. And a good ego, a really sound ego, has its negative side, too. There's an awful lot of negativism in Warren, but he has real intelligence. And he has a basic self-confidence that's made of iron. Indestructible! . . .

"He's been so intent on his career that he's devoted his entire self to it. He's just sitting around now, waiting for the rest of his life to come back to him."

Thinking of running

D was worn down by the gaiety on the terraces. He was like an electrician who ruined every shot by being caught on camera, endeavoring to conceal a cable or scrim a brute while the beautiful action went on. And so he wandered, to avoid attention. He had time to appreciate how every scooped surface on the property was filled with humus so that some velvet bloom could be reared there. No one but D examined the flowers, he was solitary enough to be a connoisseur. He grew dizzy dipping his head into all the startling scents, and even a little sick.

These "grounds" were not as substantial or as organic as that word suggested. There was an odd sensation in having the ground beneath one's feet, of coming upon rock gardens, streams and trees, yet feeling exposed and thrust out into the canyon. At the very edge, by peering over, he discovered that the Lighthiser property was all on a platform. There might be twelve feet of earth or fill on top of a base which jutted out from the hillside and was supported by steel struts. There were large birds swooping between the stanchions. D guessed owls, or carrion crows, waiting for chicken thighs to slip from the careless fête.

He looked farther down and heard a breeze grazing on the invisible canyon floor. Or was it a more full-bodied roar? Was there a river below, or a factory busy in the night? D had never known what happened in the folds of these hills. Being there only heightened the mystery. How rare for such uncertainty to prevail – no wonder the area was so desirable.

Looking into the prickling darkness D was ready for monsters to rear up or for sprites to beckon him down. What a spot for suicides – it was so tempting to step up onto the balustrade and walk into the solid, balmy night. Stunt men, D decided, were mystics as well as droll mechanicals perplexed to have so many women around. They had their affair with impossible ventures. They dived off cliffs, time and again, so brave but such insiders with death.

There was a rumbling in the valley, several ridges away. Then, quite distinctly, he heard a cry rise up from the canyon, full of despair. Half a mile away, D knew the person would never heal the wound that had sent up the cry. He had heard anguish tearing. It was as if the person had accidentally found the complete betrayal of their life. He waited, but there were no further cries. He knew he would have to forget the cry.

He wandered into the house, in and out of different lounges, and found Doc alone in front of a television set that was following some late election results.

"You got the whole damned thing laid out tonight," said Doc, in the spirit of a soothsayer ignored by his age.

D looked at the picture: the numbers changing, the disarray of campaign headquarters, exhausted kids who had forgotten their foolish, sloganising clothes, and studio pundits talking it all to sleep. It was vaguely political, D supposed, with brash art and color.

"I didn't know there were results tonight," said D.

"Every week now there are some run-offs or other," said Doc. "Contests, prizes. Where democracy meets the lottery."

"It's not popular where I live," said D.

"It's sleepwalking, that's what it is."

"That too," D agreed.

"Anyway, he won."

"He was cheerful?"

"He was hunky-dory. He's an amiable guy."

"I find myself liking him," D admitted.

"Don't you, though?"

"It makes you nostalgic."

"This city has perfected it," said Doc. "It's the swansong of the easygoing pal. There used to be a kind of pal in adventure pictures – it was just casting. No writing or direction. The guy had to watch the hero, grin and talk to him, say 'OK, Jeff', back him up in shootouts, agree with him. Just a soldier ready to do anything because he wanted to be liked."

"And cast?" said D.

"Exactly! The same urge to please on the silly face. And now it's a dry old-timer who doesn't know much and makes knowing look stuffy. And he just darned well refuses to see that it's difficult or impossible. He just says 'Have a good day' to whatever it is and takes you to the zoo instead, and you feel like you're four and he's grand-dad with a warm brown hand for you to hold on to."

"Yes," D knew that satisfaction. He could feel the comfort, and he remembered the ease in going out with his own grandfather, and of riding serenely in a tobacco haze, confident about where he was being taken. It was puzzling, for D had not known his grandparent.

"There was a moment tonight," Doc wanted to talk. "He was up in his hotel suite, and she was down at the headquarters addressing the people and there was this great screen on the wall behind her. It was like her insignia. And some of the time while you were watching they put the faces of people listening to her on the screen. And sometimes there were vistas of America – the cornfields, the Mississippi, the steel mills, the Rockies, the malls. But then, when she finished, there was cheering, the screen cut away to him in his room, on the sofa, and there was a camera crew there with him and after about five seconds the old fart got it that he was *on, there*. And he waved, and she waved back. He was so tickled, and the noise got louder and he and she were grinning away at each other. 'Hey, look! We're on TV!' Straight to the heart."

D was excited by Doc's treatise: "If only the people could hear you say that."

"I'd sound crazy. You start analysing TV and you look fatuous, a spoilsport. You sound like thought – you'll pardon the expression – it's poison. That's why Eyes doesn't have a chance."

"He is thinking of running?"

"The whole time he's thinking."

"Ah."

"Eyes is always going over the arguments. And that shows." Doc was gloomy and clear about the dead-end.

"Aha."

"No one will trust him. The intelligent look wicked on TV. As if they're plotting against us."

"That's it!"

"Anyway, he'd never stand to be on TV, just grinning there, walking from the helicopter, riding his horse. No, you got him, D."

"I did?"

"Absolutely. He's someone who might try to shoot the President – just to see if he was real. I have to admit it, Eyes could be our assassin."

"As a matter of fact," said D, "I understand he's having some doubts now himself."

"You bet he is. Did you ever meet anyone that thoughtful who didn't have a lot of doubts?"

"I suppose not."

"What did he say?"

"It was rather vague – too much dwelling on space and time."

Doc reflected. "He read that somewhere. Or he dreamed it. He could have woken up with that line in his head."

"What do you suppose it means?"

"He expects you to tell him."

"How can I?"

"He's like a Pharaoh who wants his dream given footnotes."

"This could hold up the deal?"

Doc was smiling. "Something has to. Eyes and I have a project – seven years old – but I can't crack his worry."

"What is it?"

Doc grinned, admiring the trap he was in. "He says, 'You don't think I'm too old for it?' How do you like that?"

D nodded ruefully. It was good to have this professional fellowship with a veteran like Doc. "What a strange business," he admitted.

"It's a madhouse. And we're lucky."

"Yes?"

"Eyes is head and shoulders the thinking guy in town. He'll headgame you till you're as stuck as he is. But he'll pay you while you're figuring the answer. So long as you don't ask."

DOING ... NOTHING

It is something like the privilege of being at your own funeral: being a movie star, but doing nothing. Consider this parable – there are two young men who meet in acting school, or in summer stock. They tell each other how much they want to be actors; they both impress their various audiences, on and off the stage. The one is truly addicted to acting; he is not comfortable off the stage; he pursues work, sometimes in defiance of poor pay and billing. It is said of him, as he says himself, that he loves the theater. He comes in time to be regarded universally as a master actor. Late in life, when he has married again and had children, and when he has had several illnesses, he does television commercials and what he admits are bad pictures because he needs the money. But it is a great deal of money that comes in, and yet he goes on working. If he is a great actor, perhaps it is this insecurity that drives him. He would rather act than be, and so he happily adopts disguises and character parts. He is never, quite, a star: he never takes the risk of saying "Here I am, let *me* be famous."

The other does not work as hard at acting. He turns down interesting low-money offers; he is determined on the best billing. He never lets his looks change on the screen. He does not much enjoy acting; he does not really have a rich technique. But he is a star. And being a star was always so much his only ambition that he wants to see if he can be only a star – not a star kept alight by regular work and appearance, but a star who exists according to the self-perpetuating mechanics of stardom. There is a power in going on stage, commanding the silence and attention of strangers, and bringing them to tears. There is another power in being known, in being known to be *there* by millions of people. Where is there? It is stardom, and it is located on the edge of some Los Angeles pool. It is a place to be for ever, or for as long as you can manage – well, at least for twenty minutes. One of the most beautiful, heartfelt pictures of Hollywood I have ever seen is of Faye Dunaway, the morning after the

190

1977 Oscars, when she won for *Network*. It is a sunny dawn and she is sitting besides a pool with her Oscar on a table. Maybe they have to get up very early to get the picture. Maybe there is a throng of friends, servants, gigolos, pool-cleaners, renters, process servers and shy assassins they have to clear out of the sight-line to get the right, splendid aloneness. But it is a picture the actress needs. It shows her on the edge of a mythology she believes in as much as anyone. "I was there," she can say when she is old and ruined. It is a small trinket against death, her most precious jewel.

Hollywood is a very hard-working community – if waiting, talking, dealing, planning are work. But there is no peace, no leisure, not if a career is as desperate and ruthless as it must be. There are pools as little used as Gatsby's, except that they constitute the "there" that journalists, producers and the family can see when they visit from the East.

Warren Beatty does nothing – so to speak – from late 1961 to the middle of 1963. By which I mean to say, he does not shoot a film, his apparent line of business. Of course, his days and nights are full enough to account for some of his bad temper. He reads many scripts, and some of them he reads several times. He travels, he sees women, he discusses projects. He is in and out of grand hotels, he is giving interviews, he is going to parties, there are days when he gets to sit beside some of the several hundred thousand pools there are in Los Angeles, and maybe dozes with a book folded on his dry trunks. There is possibly a moment in this time – it could even be in October 1962, as the TV gets ready for a war, the big one, for Cuba – that he realises how, in a way, he is doing nothing, just to see whether it can be done. He laughs to himself, for he has proven how absurd this world he has conquered is. But then he realises he must take a firmer grip on himself, for a man could easily go crazy so angelically poised between such heavy things and nothing.

He is not under contract to a studio – such pieces of paper still exist, even if they are no longer identification cards for an industry. Beatty does not commit. He has one agreement, with Elia Kazan, a personal service contract of a kind common with big directors who reckon that they are the ones making the new stars. It talks about other projects, but none ever comes along and nothing significantly disturbs Beatty's line (over the years) that Kazan is a great director, or the best.

As yet, he has been paid only $105,000 for his three pictures – $15,000 for *Splendor in the Grass*; $30,000 for *The Roman Spring of Mrs Stone*; and $60,000 for *All Fall Down*. And he does not get all of that, of course: there is an agent and a secretary sometimes, and he has to consider whether it is worth hiring a lawyer to save him money with the IRS. But, despite the generally poor box office of the three pictures, he is asking $150,000 for his next movie. His expenses are going up, after all. And his reputation is going up, despite the reviews and the bad press. A true star does not have to make good or successful films. Hollywood has always told itself that was not so: failures vanished, three strikes and you're out, as good as your last picture. But Hollywood is changing. Different perceptions of how to place works are becoming possible. One crucial law in the famous breakdown of old Hollywood is the notion that it was a business run on hard facts and common sense. This was never the case, but now it is becoming easier to see that Hollywood was always an inane business, just as dependent on superstition and magic as on the numbers. Even the numbers are not firm. The numbers are like songs, a way of keeping cheerful.

And if you are asking $150,000 a picture in 1962, and turning down scripts, you can charge anything you want in LA. People sometimes stay there a year in the grand hotels, the bills waiting on the deals that are known to be coming. That is why the deals are so important: they determine whether you can live day-by-day. Warren Beatty will die with a record in which deals out-number finished films four or five to one. That is how one kind of inflation works; the overhead has to eat all the incomplete development deals. So he rents a pink stucco house – not large – above the Sunset Strip, and moves his suitcases in. One day as he lifts one of those cases, thirty-five uncashed checks fall out, along with some unpaid bills. He may not need a bank account or a credit rating; word-of-mouth will be enough. Alexander Korda, the Hungarian producer, once gave this advice for handling LA – move into the best hotel, be seen with the most beautiful women, charge everything and harbor any cash for lavish tipping. Wait for offers.

The scripts flow in to Beatty. Sometimes, not scripts, but ideas. He and Natalie Wood are talking about *Barefoot in the Park*. There is word that he is offered a lead in *The War Lover*, John Hersey's novel about American pilots in Britain during the Second World War – Steve McQueen and Robert Wagner end up playing its two leads. Which is Beatty offered? Which do you want, Warren? He could have had the part taken by Alain Delon on Luchino Visconti's film of *The Leopard*, shooting in Italy, being dubbed, working for a prestigious foreign director, spending more time in his bathroom.

In the middle 60s, the American director based in Europe, Joseph Losey, develops an espionage script set on the Russia-Finland border –

The Most Dangerous Game, written by John Paxton. Beatty is to play the lead, but the script is never quite right and the location presents serious weather problems. The snow and the ice will have to wait for Warren. At another time, Losey will think of doing William Faulkner's *The Wild Palms* (a novel of parallel stories), with Warren, Julie Christie and Elizabeth Taylor.

Moss Hart's autobiography, *Act One*, is to be filmed by the one-time MGM boss Doré Schary. It is a best-selling book about a showbiz hero. Beatty is interested, but in the end the role has to make do with George Hamilton and the picture is a flop. It is a mistake to deduce that Beatty could have rescued the film, or that it would have been made with him. Casting is the Hollywood stock exchange. Everyone is considered for everything. Someone would have been ready to make *The Godfather* as *The Godmother*, if Barbra Streisand had said yes, and the songs were right. We only see the pictures that are made. Bad as many seem, they have fought through the jungles of those only thought about. Beatty does a few projects that are simply demonstrations of his power, films that would not exist but for him. Some say he turns down 75 scripts a year. Casting is more vital than actor-director rehearsal; that is one reason why rehearsal is dying away. It is a vagueness that lets a Beatty believe he might have been in 80 per cent of the pictures of his time.

So his agent, Charles Feldman, is on the phone to him a lot. He gets used to having Warren answer, "What's new, pussycat?", a line he has used for the many women. And when Feldman becomes a producer, he adopts the line and its life-style and sets up a picture about a fashion editor with more lovers than he can remember. But Peter O'Toole plays the part in a movie that is Woody Allen's first script credit.

*

The next famous refusal concerns *PT 109*, a movie about John F. Kennedy's alleged wartime exploits as the commander of a PT boat. The Kennedys are movie mad. They have made pictures and had actresses as mistresses for a couple of generations. No matter that he knows how generously exaggerated the original book was, John Kennedy is not averse to the picture being made. (After all, it will open in 1963, just before re-election year.) Warner Brothers persuade themselves that it is a hot property. They put veteran Bryan Foy in charge of the picture. And Foy was irked to find that Kennedy's quiet choice to play himself when younger and glorious was Warren Beatty. Pierre Salinger, the presidential press secretary, acted as envoy. But Beatty doubts the chance of war pictures, especially this script, and may flinch from playing so well-known and so apparently real a personage. Cliff Robertson gets the part, and the movie fails. But before then, a part of the press have treated Beatty's refusal as arrogance and even lack of patriotism. Bryan Foy says, "Actors today will drive you crazy if you pay any attention to them."

Beatty extends his circle. He goes to meet Jean Renoir, the French film director who lives in Beverly Hills, and he probably sees a few Renoir films. The French New Wave – Truffaut, Godard and so on – are having an unexpected commercial impact in America, and they all vow the greatness of Renoir and his influence. A friend of Renoir's is the playwright Clifford Odets. Beatty collaborates with him for a time on a screenplay, and probably listens to the older man's stories about the Group Theater, about true work and selling out, about being married to actresses and loving them, about Luise Rainer and Frances Farmer.

The press portrait of a sulking Adonis builds up. The story goes around that when Beatty made *All Fall Down* at MGM he got a star dressing-room and then posted the name Gregor Krocp on it, so that he could sleep undisturbed. Is this star behavior or is it satire? In England, the press are similarly agitated when the Beatles simply refuse to be interviewed "properly". It's what comes of having a president who cracks jokes at a state banquet; it's a new, cool style; it begins to look suspiciously like the 60s.

In July 1962, the *Saturday Evening Post* carries a profile on Beatty, "Brash and Rumpled Star" they call it. The writer is Joseph Laitin, and early on in the piece he has Beatty turning on him, "I've given you too much of my time, much too much. All you're interested in is the neurotic side of me. You don't want to write about my work. You haven't asked me a single question about my ideas on acting, about the theater or anything I consider important. My childish ego is excited by the prospect of your writing a story about me, but all you're interested in is trivia."

Laitin is chastened. He does his best to give Beatty's point of view, and he tells the story how in New York a few months earlier Beatty had spent days at the bedside of an old friend from the theater until the man died.

Then he says that, in the middle of a conversation, Beatty vanishes and comes back in his swim trunks. Then he goes out to the pink pool, brushes away some of the leaves that have accumulated there and discovers a dead lizard. The young actor pokes at the reptile's corpse,

sighs and maybe takes a grip on himself. He has a great line to deliver:
"If Natalie knew a lizard died in this pool, she'd never swim here again.
. . . Let's go over and use Natalie's pool."

Pool life, from *Sunset Boulevard* (Paramount)

Cy

Some people had quit in an hour of goodbyes, fur wraps unwinding from closets, and dust in the headlights down the drive. But this evacuation passed, and there were still fifty or so who showed no sign of leaving. A game of pun charades occupied the terrace. D kept away. Its howls signalled a ruthless cult.

"Can't you smell the hostility in the air?" said the man in the kitchen, lopping flowers off broccoli. "I take a few crudités around this time of night. Flushes out the system."

D knew it would be easy to sentimentalise raw vegetables in this luxurious setting. He thought it wisest to be casual, so he nibbled at the rugged greenery.

"You don't know me?" It pleased the man.

"I don't know anyone here," D confessed.

The man chuckled. "I know you. I been looking for you, D."

There was only a worktop light on in the kitchen. The man's smile was in half-shadow. "Cy Lighthiser," he explained, but it sounded equivocal, as if the pun charades had come inside to eat away all assurance. "Would I lie?" This was a slim, wiry man, hair receding, in slacks and a sports shirt, cutting up raw vegetables. He was so much more commonplace than the man on the screen who had welcomed guests to the party.

"Disappointed?" asked Cy, his head tilted to study the grain in a root of fennel. Then he attacked it and came up with a white moon hanging from his knife. "Try it," said Cy. "Today, from Frieda's Finest. I like it quick roasted in a walnut oil with fresh pepper. But I don't know how this range works." He indicated the gunmetal chambers where cooking could be done.

"This is not your home?" asked D.

"We're not here a lot. Claudia gets spooked if she's up here on her own. So, if in doubt, don't eat cooked things. And what's the oil going to do but coke your arteries?"

197

"The oil is not good?"

"We eat like decadents," said Cy. "The red meat, marbled with fat." He pinched the items between his fingers. "The butter, the sauces. Night before my heart attack I had three servings of a creamed scallop bisque you could have built on."

Cy crunched a carrot, reflecting. "Life's too precious. I'm not going, you know." His voice dropped, "And I don't believe we have to."

It took D a second to see the destination Cy was ducking.

"My heart. It didn't work. New parts. They can do it. They don't boast they can do it, they're going to be mobbed. Listen, D, this is as hard a business as it gets. It's not the Sistine Chapel. But for worry and heartbreak it has no match. So . . . exercise, diet, relaxation, only let pure things into your home, and your body is your best home. Be tranquil when you can. Then do your work, screw the slimes when you have to. No desserts. A little grain, fibre, a lot of salad, toffuti. I'm still here. I'm better than ever. And I tell you – this is not just my opinion, read the trades – I'm making better pictures. These guys fuck with cigars, cocaine and red meat, they're making crap. Nouvelle cuisine, nouvelle movies. Claudia, now – she has our new kid – she is breastfeeding. Her, taking that risk with her gilt-edged. You can hear that mother's milk flowing, and she is sexier than ever. She stinks with it. The camera never really gets all of her. There's magic left. That's the kick in knowing her. She and Eyes, they gotta work together. And Eyes, he is all yeast-shakes and nice light meals with roughage. What ruined Monroe was not her pussy, it was the calories: ice cream, Danish and lamb chops. I've known sweet kids – I won't name 'em – dolls, Miss Cutesville, and I've seen them eat steak dinners with éclairs to follow. Your liver can take only so much. And it makes a pit of the skin. Your stars that last have skin like photo paper, and they never eat all they'd like. It's will power. You end so hungry you want to kill. Anger!" Cy Lighthiser's eyes shone. "It's the best diet."

"It has always intrigued me, the dilemma of staying a star," said D.

"It's a duel with death."

"As much as that?"

"That's what movies are. The defiance of death. Think about it. It's a magnificent thing."

"A legendary quest," mused D.

"That's very true. So, how is our old Eyes, the monkey?"

"Oh," said D, indicating how hard it was to be sure.

"I hear he's hot for your script. That it?"

Cy

Cy's eyes went in as fast as Duran to the body to the script still tucked under D's arm. "I know you shouldn't ought to let me see it."

"I shouldn't," D agreed.

"So why not maybe put it on the counter. I'll hit the fan, and the pages riffle by. While we're talking. I can sometimes get the taste of a script that fast."

"You are interested in it for your wife?"

"I don't see it, I don't get to touch her, know what I mean? Otherwise I have to go out get a hooker." He stopped chopping. "Unless we have some here. Did you notice any?" He was deadpan, as if the talk concerned the first swallows of summer.

"I'm not sure I would know them."

"John Public," said Cy, pointing the knife at him.

"Me?"

"Sure. The wonderful thing about the picture business is the audience never recognise the whores. Put it down." Cy smacked his hand flat on the counter top.

"I shouldn't," said D. "I couldn't."

"If I was you I'd want my work seen. There are scripts Eyes has bought and paid for, he makes paper airplanes out of them."

"But sometimes – "

"An unmade Eyes beats a Lighthiser?"

"Well – "

"I know. He's a pathfinder. But the pathfinder – "

"Can get too far ahead?"

"Out of sight is what he can get. Is he coming tonight? I got flim-flam from Clear."

D could not resist the momentum of all this sliced and curving chatter: "Clear's a lot of air – but I like him."

Cy caught the shift, and made a little swastika of celery sticks. "We all had aides like Clear, we'd be collecting Nobel prizes. He's a saint. He is also an empty space when he has to be. What I'd like to know is how he'd turn out if there was nothing he had to be."

"Burn off by eleven?" D wondered. How quickly his allegiances could switch on cross-talk. He was a slut. He remembered Drew saying it of herself.

"We asked him tonight, of course," said Cy. "He said he'd call back."

"He doesn't go out much."

"He likes to refuse. 'I'd rather not.'" Cy said it in mockery of the loftiness. "He has this thing for refinement. It does credit to us all."

"A man ahead of his time."

"This business is garbage, and you should never lose the feel for dirt. Maybe he stays out in the desert or wherever, balling young girls and thinks he's a prince of darkness. That's not. That's just horny. There are bankers in this city married to schoolgirls, still paying for their braces. You get outa touch – know what I mean?"

"Living with reptiles – " D began.

And Cy was with him, " – is just a matter of practice." He was already scooping untouched crudités into the waste disposer. It ground down on the stalks – "This house pees V8," said Cy – when they heard the scream from outside and realised what a hush had befallen the pun charades.

LILITH

Lilith is the best film Warren Beatty has made at that point in his career; you could make a case that it is the best he will ever make. A failure in its day, the picture grows more profound and beautiful as the years pass by. It is a lake that resists every effort to plumb its depths. It is not easily explained, critically or intellectually; it is a rapture, just like the madness of its central character. And this sense of belatedly revealed tragedy is surely enhanced by our knowing what became of its actress, Jean Seberg, and by the realization that this was her best work and that she was wasted and rebuffed when at her best. But Beatty does not like the film. After it opens, he calls it a disaster, something he could have made better himself. To this day, I believe, it is one of the movies he does not like to hear mentioned.

Lilith is a movie about sex, about nymphomania, about a rapture so intense it must be a matter of judgement whether it is termed madness or nature. Perhaps no other American movie has addressed this subject so thoroughly, or been so convinced that woman is the ultimate source of sexual power.

The film is taken from a novel by J. R. Salamanca, published in 1961. It will be the last film of writer-director Robert Rossen, the maker of *All the King's Men*, a victim of McCarthyism, lately returned to America to direct *The Hustler*. Rossen is struck by an idea in the book – "that of comparing the person whom people call 'adjusted' to the one called 'maladjusted' in our society. Society considers the person who is outside its norms as sick. Now, my own feeling is that society, itself sick, is only refusing a certain form of unreason."

There speaks a Hollywood radical, possessed of a simple notion of social malaise and looking for a movie vehicle to embody it. McCarthyism feared such intentions, and never saw that the film industry always translated such "ideology" into a personal melodrama. Thus the film *Lilith* is about sex, not madmen; ecstasy, not malfunction.

It may not be exactly the picture Rossen believed he was making – but the elements of myth in the material cannot be prevented from marrying with the medium's urge toward legend. If a beautiful woman plays Lilith, if she is starry, then any view of her society pales in 'her brightness.

The film does change the novel's ending. In both, the protagonist is a young man, Vincent Bruce, who takes up work as a nurse in an asylum for the wealthy. He is a troubled figure, trying to seek out his nature and do good by the world. The asylum where he works has Lilith as a patient, and Vincent is seduced by her. In the novel, Vincent manages finally to break away from her power. He gives up the job. Lilith's parents remove her from the asylum and she is sent to Europe. While there, she drowns, apparently, though the lake in question is too deep for her body to be recovered. Her possibility is eternal. Vincent survives. He restores the relationship with his grandfather and he writes the book, like someone coming back from an encounter with a demon.

This would be a diffuse conclusion for the film, and so Rossen's script has Vincent being increasingly led away from sanity by Lilith's influence. The picture ends with Vincent walking towards the people who have employed him and towards the camera and saying "Help me." It is fearsome, but tidy: the nurse becomes an inmate, but the moment is given life by the terror and intensity with which Beatty delivers the line. For whatever it says, and whatever the character must do, somehow the actor refuses to ask for help.

If only because of their shared water imagery, it is reasonable to think that *Splendor in the Grass* influences Rossen in preparing *Lilith*. The first actor he engages is Beatty to play Vincent, persuaded by the Kazan picture that Beatty can convey a normal young man driven crazy by desire. At this stage, the actor and the director are very close. *Lilith*, after all, is the film that will bring Beatty out of his "nothingness"; and Rossen is an anti-establishment figure, surely recommended by Odets. It is in this mood of friendly collaboration that Beatty suggests Jean Seberg for Lilith.

Several other actresses have been in line for the part – Yvette Mimieux, Samantha Eggar, Diane Cilento, Sarah Miles, and even Natalie Wood, who had gone crazy for *Splendor in the Grass*. Beatty has seen Seberg not just in her first films for Otto Preminger (*Saint Joan* and *Bonjour Tristesse*), but in Jean-Luc Godard's *A Bout de Souffle* and perhaps even in a charming romantic comedy, *L'Amant de Cinq Jours*, in which her hair was long, as opposed to the close-cropped look that had made her famous. Rossen casts Seberg, despite her seeming to have "gone over" to low-budget, French movies. When he makes the announcement to the press, he says "She's got that flawed American-girl quality – sort of like a cheerleader who's cracked up."

Beatty goes with Rossen on the trip to Paris to decide on Seberg: he is being paid three times her fee, even if the woman is bound to be the object of the film's worship. When pre-production begins in April 1963, in New York and in Maryland, where the chief locations are sited, Beatty and Rossen have what Seberg sees as a "fraternal, very intimate" relationship. The three of them visit several mental hospitals, they talk to patients. They work on the script. As they rehearse, and come to the scene where Lilith must say, "You know what is wrong with Lilith? I want to possess all the men in the world," it is Beatty who guesses that that line will work better if she says it in the third person.

The shooting is an agony. Seberg sees the bond between Rossen and Beatty deteriorate from the day filming begins. Rossen is not well. He is suffering from a mysterious illness in which dark spots appear on his skin. He may sense that this is his last film, he may fall under the sway of Lilith and Seberg as shooting starts. I do not mean he sleeps with his actress. But he ravishes her with his camera. No other Rossen picture has anything like *Lilith*'s erotic intensity – and if Rossen smells his own death then this turning of desire into art may be like a way of clinging on to life, a panic that leads to very little coverage of Beatty in the love scenes.

Or perhaps the persistent impression from the film of Beatty scowling, his head lowered or his back to the camera, is because he is so unmanageable, and so reluctant to act. He delays the shooting with doubts and anxieties. There is a famous argument as to whether, early in the film, Vincent should say "I've read *Crime and Punishment* and *The Brothers Karamazov*." Beatty thinks the character never finished *Karamazov*, and should say so. It does sound better that way, but such arguments cloud every scene. Is the actor really more in touch with the material than the director? Can an actor ever have that advantage if a film is to be shot? Or is Beatty aware that it is not "his" picture, and trying – in a mix of cunning and unconscious maneuvering – to drain the picture into his own hunched disquiet?

Has Seberg made it clear that she does not want Beatty as more than a professional colleague? One of Rossen's assistants says, "Warren is a brilliant, charismatic person, and he made sure he got his share of the spotlight. He has the charm of the stalking cat, and he preyed on Jean with all his power as a seducer. But nothing was ever what it seemed to be on the surface. He was busy playing games, manipulating people and situations. For Jean, it was a terrible handful."

There is a fight scene between the two of them in which Lilith has to slap Vincent. Time and again as they try to shoot it, Beatty puts up his arms to ward off the blow – is the character flinching, or is there something in the action that the actor cannot allow? Seberg's arm is battered and bruised. Peter Fonda, in a supporting role, threatens to beat the shit out of Beatty. There are fears of real violence between the two actors. There are stories that Beatty's trailer is vandalised, and that he is asked not to appear at the wrap party. The shooting goes on through the summer of 1963 amid growing arguments and a decline in Rossen's health. When he dies, in 1966, it will be said that he names Beatty as one of his death blows.

It is all the sadder that Beatty, the only one of the three major participants in *Lilith* still alive, seems not to like the film. His performance cannot be separated from the achieved tragedy, no matter how much he was an outcast or a problem to those making the picture. And it takes only a moment to see how fully *Lilith* fits in with the slowly emerging screen persona of Beatty. In *All Fall Down*, there is a conversation between Clinton and Berry-Berry in which the older brother proclaims his hatred of life. Still in awe, Clinton tries to agree, and he asks Berry-Berry, "What do we live for?"

"You mean what's the point of everything?" says Berry-Berry, and he looks away at one of his women: "Well, maybe *that's* the answer. It's the only thing I could ever figure out."

Lilith, the movie, is an exploration of that possibility, the picture that most clearly engages Beatty in something like his own appetite for sexual encounters without the codifying legitimacy of marriage. Yet *Lilith* is an American movie made before the real relaxation of censorship and the work of a director who chooses to romanticise sex with poetic dissolves. The animality of Lilith's desires is not shown; in 1963, I don't think it could be. There was a silly press thrill when it was thought that a semi-nude scene was to be filmed.

But the movies are more erotic if the thing, the ultimate *there*, is not shown, but evoked or gilded in rapture. *Lilith* is a very rare movie in that it understands the force and primacy of sensuality and portrays it thematically as Lilith's urge to have everyone, without condemning her. Vincent is the chief enemy to her desire: he is a therapist, supposed to guide her into normalcy, and a lover who wants her all for himself. He

With Jean Seberg in *Lilith* (Columbia)

cannot endure the ease with which she turns to other men and women. Beatty's rather grim, tight face – sometimes reminiscent here of Elvis Presley, but tight-assed and disapproving – is the embodiment of outraged decency and propriety.

"You dirty bitch," hisses Vincent, finding Lilith with another woman, and Seberg's lovely face flowers in a smile: "I show my love for all of you and you despise me." How many times in life has some such dialogue been played, in reverse, between Beatty and a woman who has had to discover his helpless need for others? Of course, he need not be mad for Vincent to be an irrationally disconcerting part for him to play. The seducer never feels he has been seduced: it is the most complete usurpation of his power. The thought might destroy him.

Perhaps this is reading too much into movies. Perhaps movies are just a job. Perhaps. See *Lilith* and decide. And notice how imprisoned Beatty looks and feels; see what a good job he does for this remarkable film. In particular, there is a scene in which the new therapist talks to Dr Lavrier, the head of the asylum. Vincent is talking about how the work is going. He is hunched. There seems to be a great tension in his body as he struggles to give answers. He is half turned away from Lavrier as they talk about Lilith's charm.

"It's almost like she wants to share this magic little world of hers," he says.

And quietly and gently, Lavrier asks "Do you ever feel like accepting?"

"Yes!" says Vincent. It bursts out, his body nearly falls over across the frame, his face opens, the wall cracks, and he is like a child confessing to a terrible wish. It is one of the best things Warren Beatty will ever do. Perhaps it is great acting; perhaps the final giving of self.

In the film Lavrier then uses the word "rapture" and there is a stricken but uplifted close-up of Vincent repeating the word. In the novel it is Vincent who comes up with the term – "She has a kind of . . . rapture about her which is very compelling. Do you know what I mean? A kind of rapture that perhaps I'm jealous of."

*

It is a bad time for Warren after *Lilith*. The picture does poorly, and the ailing Robert Rossen does not hesitate to tell others the young actor is a trial. We should remember that there are other careers of the early 60s which do not last at the star's level – Fabian, Dean Stockwell, Richard

Beymer, George Hamilton, Terence Stamp, Troy Donahue. There is a chance that Warren too may be a three-year wonder.

He is in a restaurant one day, the story goes, when a letter is delivered to him from the office of Darryl F. Zanuck, the head of Twentieth Century-Fox. The two have never met, but the letter from Zanuck says, in effect, be of good cheer, you are *the* actor of your generation, I can see your career reaching ahead, anything you want to do, or anything you hear of, just bring it to Fox. Something like that, a letter for his dreams.

He is hugely cheered up: here is valuable evidence that he was once a young man. He tells his world about this unexpected endorsement; he looks for projects to take to Fox. The mishap of *Lilith* falls into place.

A few days later he encounters an old friend who remarks on how much more cheerful Warren is. Warren tells the friend about the letter. Oh, you liked that? Did I ever! You wouldn't believe the trouble I had getting the letterhead stationery, admits the friend. (Is this really friendship? remains a question for Plato or Miss Manners.)

This is the story I heard. I don't have the letter. I'm not sure of the friend. But in the story, Warren is aghast. He wonders, what can I do? I've told so many people. Must I explain to everyone that I was fooled, had? He considers; he waits a day or so; and he decides – what the hell, let the story run . . . .

And now here is his biographer, years later, wondering whether or not to believe the legend. I think the story plays, and in Hollywood that is always the ultimate transcending of history.

Body in the pool

Cy Lighthiser moved to the bookcase in the walnut lounge and pressed a switch where Elmore Leonard met Lermontov. There was no thrill of strings, but a section of fiction turned into a smoked window in which it was still possible, from the secret angle, to see the spines of the books. They were engraved in the glass, or a picture printed there. The switch simply rearranged the dots and molecules to provide a way of looking out at the terrace and the pool. D assumed from Cy's openness that nothing of this subterfuge was visible from outside.

The people on the terrace were gathered at the pool: the water cast a blue glow on the women's legs and the men's slacks. D was struck by the chromakey frieze at the pool's lip.

"Is there someone in the water?" said Cy.

D shared the anticipatory stillness of those by the pool. "Should we go out?" he said.

Cy did not move. He was so entertained staying there, waiting to find out.

D could not expunge the loneliness of watching. He wanted to be out there, a part of the wonder or amusement. Then, quite plainly, but from farther away than the pool, Cy and D heard a rumbling, as if something had been irrevocably disturbed. Then one woman at the pool turned. It was Drew, and her face was blind and agonised, staring towards them and crying, but knowing nothing.

"Look at that one," Cy asked.

Drew's distress isolated her. Some pitch of feeling had made her a membrane, helplessly bearing witness.

"Who is that?" Cy wanted to know.

D did not pause to recommend her to the producer. He went out through the kitchen to the terrace. He heard water lapping and the muttering of the people. Doc bumped into him, still looking back over his shoulder but trying to get to the house.

"Where's a phone?" he said.

"What happened?" asked D.

"Someone drowned."

"Was he drunk?" D imagined the man slipping into the water without a sound, opening himself to it.

"I heard he made a dumb guess in the game."

"And for that he drowned himself?"

Doc was flustered, still thinking of how to phone in a crisis. "No one knows," he said.

"It was only a game?" D remonstrated. "Was there money at stake?"

"Probably. But he made a fool of himself."

"Everyone here is already foolish," D burst out.

"You think so?" Doc had given up on the phone now. "Everybody says it's a madhouse here." He hated the cliché. "That's no help. You loathe it, but you're here, aren't you?"

There was nothing D could say. He wished a sweeping force could reach across the hillsides, obliterating the party and his own failure to grasp its sickness.

"Try to see it," said Doc. "Let's say this man was ambitious. He was a designer, I think. He may have been close to making it, and then one slip –"

"What slip?"

"What does it matter? Perhaps he got a title wrong."

"And so he killed himself?"

"Maybe he knows he's lost it. Feels he's sliding down the snake all the way to the bottom."

"A game!" D's smothered fear escaped with the cry.

"There's always some game," said Doc. He made it sound past blame or dispute.

The body was in the pool, face down, scrutinizing the water – a man in pink shirt and yellow pants. Of course, someone was taking photographs. Cy presided. A windowless white limousine came for the corpse; it had a stretcher that reached out, like a tongue. Statements were taken, with the tone of press interviews. There were arguments over the man's name: some said Richard Burger, others Rick Berg. A few claimed Ricky Burr or Rich Blur. People discussed his credits – a horror film and several music videos. There were those who felt he had had brilliance, but others began to see a derivativeness that should not be overvalued.

D searched for Drew. Since leaving the house – expressly to comfort her – he had lost her. More people were leaving, in talk of imminent storms. Some said they had seen lighting in the gaps between the hills. D guessed it was past two in the morning. He felt he could go on forever. A contempt for time and order was dawning in him, and he was not afraid. He saw that this Berg blur might have glanced at the empty pool and seen the electricity of his colors there, knowing he wouldn't be forgotten, going out on a hot shot.

D called cautiously to the pale averted figure on a stone seat by a fig tree. A face on the figure turned, and he hurried down the steps towards Drew. She was not crying now.

"Know what happened?" D asked.

Her mind moved back up to the terrace, to an hour ago. "Oh, that," she recollected, touched by the far incident.

"Doc says the fellow was ruined by some minor mistake in the game."

"It's not a game of minor mistakes." She gazed away, addicted to private knowledge.

He guessed she had taken some other drug. She was so cut off now from help or his presence.

"Go away," said Drew, without interest.

Her heavy head swung round: it looked like death challenging him. "You don't do the game. You think it's enough to say ha-ha, isn't it senseless?"

"Why were you crying then?" This should hold her in his faith.

She couldn't remember.

"At the pool. You turned away. I saw it."

It was as remote as her childhood, out of her reach. "I just did that." She was weary, and doing could be trivial.

"Did it?"

"Everyone was eyeballing the water." She made the face of stupid staring. Then it was her again. "I wanted to fix the memory," she wavered, like someone telling Merv a confidence, "so I made it into a scene." She laughed out loud to see his glum face. "I like acting! It's what I do."

"Well, Cy Lighthiser saw it and seemed impressed."

"He did?" Drew was aroused by this news, but D could not tell whether because of its promise or because it was a cherry on absurd cream. "Cy'll put it in Claudia's next picture, you wait. Claudia and Chuck were very twosome earlier. What do you think of that?"

"What is there to think?"

"Wouldn't you say that in seven or eight shots out of ten Claudia and Chuck could pass for Claudia and Eyes?"

"He has none of Eyes' flair."

"Oh, Eyes," said Drew, as if the name was a curse and flair the cheapest trick.

MICKEY ONE

Mickey One is flash when we first see him, when he goes by a name we will never learn. That name is like an apartment he knows will be staked out, so he never risks going back to it. But if you had to guess at the name, it could be Tony Lombardi or Tommy Terrific. He's a night club comic, and he says he's Polish. But that's an act already, a Polish joke. He's New Jersey Italian, or maybe he's just a smart Harvard kid trying to hide his shyness in this awful act. He *is* a lousy comic. That's the funniest thing in the picture. He could be Rupert Pupkin's father. Arthur Pupkin – got it. Not so much flash as hair oil, sewn-on sequins and silver shining through the mirror. But a pretty kid who might be nice-looking if he wasn't so dumb or if he wore glasses and a masseur could get rid of that little knot of loose flesh above the nose where he holds everything together and tries to pretend he is a cool mother who is never going to be taken.

He is a comedian working in Detroit, at a place called Lapland, owned by Ruby Lapp, a guy with a destroyed face and a capacity for grand speeches that can echo all the way from a chance remark to the tomb's shade.

Something happens one night at Lapland, something so important that we have to know it was the dream of Arthur Pupkin's life, the bit that would make him Terrific so he could tip twenties and sit there with the girl reflected in his dark glasses. In Detroit.

At the start of the movie we get a series of fragments. There is "Mickey" sitting in a steam room, concentrating on wearing his overcoat and a black derby while smoking a cigar: he is all routines. And the four fat old guys in towels are laughing at him – not at the act or the material, but at his sweet thought of being a comedian. One guy gets up and smacks him on the back – like he's an idiot, but a decent idiot – and the actor playing "Mickey" lets his head drop so that the derby rolls down his arm and onto his hand. You have the feeling that the actor probably

212

worked four weeks on the trick and could get it to work cleanly three times out of ten.

Then you see a sports car come out of a highway tunnel with the sign (to downtown Detroit). It's daylight. It stops and the driver, Mickey, looks back at another sports car with a girl in it who might have been second or third in a Miss Breck competition. If it was held in Detroit. He seems to have noticed her in his rear-view mirror. She is played by an actress named Donne Michelle, and the name is the best part about her. But Mickey thinks the girl is sensational, and he waves to her and signals a direction they should both take.

You think he wants her. But in the next fragment it's night and the girl is climbing up on the hood of his car and trying to kiss him through the windscreen. So he turns on the wipers, because he's cool.

You see the girl on a bed from up above, from the ceiling mirror; or maybe the shot is looking up at the mirror. Mickey comes to her. Then they're both in front of his dressing-room mirror, and he has white cream and make-up on his face. But he starts to kiss her, which gets the cream on her face too.

Then Mickey is looking into a dark alley where two men are beating up another, and the girl comes up behind him – she's maybe just been to the bathroom – slips off his jacket and starts to kiss him. He shoots craps in a club. The girl dances. Men are watching: large, ugly faces, thrilled by what they see and what it means. You see the girl on her own, off in some ecstatic, unwinding dance. And then it is later and Mickey comes looking for her and there is nothing but her dress or her wrap on the deserted drum kit.

You might think that this Arthur has been the victim of a montage in the silly yet wonderful American artiness of *Mickey One*. But he *is* a Harvard kid, versed in Kafka and the literature of alienation, and perhaps an assassination buff on the side (who thought "Ruby Lapp – Jack Ruby" when he arrived at Lapland). So he reckons that he messed with a gangster's moll the night before, took her from the gangster, maybe lost her money at the crap table and asked her to put the dice in her panties and to get them *hot*. And now she's gone, and he's in trouble.

He talks to Ruby Lapp – what's that ruined face and its sepulchral eloquence for?

MICKEY: Ruby, what did I do? What do they want? All right, so tell me how they set me up at least. Shooting craps drunk? That's the only thing they could have. How much did they fix I should lose? You can tell me that. Five grand? Ten. Twenty? Tell me! Why? Was it the girl? I've been playing around this time somebody's private stock?

213

She ain't private anymore. Who owns me? Ruby? You know, I really was nuts about that girl. I can't three times a night go out and make jokes on my own grave. I can't! Maybe I can raise the money and pay 'em up. You help me – 20,000 – it ain't the end. Why not?

RUBY: How do you know it's 20,000– I didn't say it? How do you know it's only money?

MICKEY: Why? – shooting craps? It's –

RUBY: You say. How do you know it's not all the other crap games they tore up on you? And the bookie slips? How do you know it's not the car they gave you you smashed up? And the liquor, and the good times and the apartment and the clothes, and Christmas and birthdays and the rehearsal hall?

MICKEY: They were favors!

RUBY: Favors as long as they want them to be favors. How do you know it isn't all the trips they paid for? Or the special material, and the arrangements in music? The dentist. The law suits. The parties. The expenses. 20,000? 20,000's just a fraction. How do you know it's not your whole life you're living?

Mickey One is a Hollywood Kafka job, in black-and-white, handled by a French photographer, made for under $1 million, with Stan Getz's wistful tenor saxophone improvisation drifting across its squalid scene like the last smoke of hopefulness. It is filmed largely in Chicago (the place to which the comic flees after his Detroit disaster), on wasteground, in wretched tenements and on the shabby streets. Like an allegory, it is made with a few very beautiful players (Beatty, Alexandra Stewart as the good girl who helps him, and Hurd Hatfield as Ed Castle, the jittery, organic food aesthete who owns the Xanadu, the big club where Mickey might play) and a surrounding world of the picturesquely ugly, ranging from Franchot Tone's Ruby Lapp through a dwarf, giant ladies and a bum with an S-shaped nose who studies his features in an arcade mirror, standing beside the muddied and messed up Mickey, who is still only a disguise for the magnificent Warren.

It is difficult not to chide *Mickey One*. No matter that it is the collaboration of an actor bristling to show his intelligence and his scorn for Hollywood conventions and of a director, Arthur Penn, who embodies the hope that cultivated New York theater traditions can take over the movies, still it is the kind of pretentious picture that exposes the huge gap in depth between literature and film. In time to come, Beatty will say, "It's not a bad film. It's not a waste of time." But he finds it unduly obscure: "It reaches further than it needs to." This is Hollywood's fear of difficulty or evident strain. "I didn't know what the hell Arthur was trying to do," he says. "I'm not sure that he knew himself."

Mickey One is solemn, spectacular and flashy in its pessimism, and downright juvenile in an optimism it never flinches from spelling out. For Mickey is not just an actor going crazy, he is an Everyman who has the wise and tender reassurance of his girl and the recurring example of a speechless but enthusiastic Oriental who gathers together scrap metal and turns it into Tinguely-like art works entitled "Yes". His work and vivacity have a message, spelled out by the girl – "Courage is Freedom": come on, Mickey, you can go, you can go back to the business. That is the slogan set up as a polar opposite to the moment at which Arthur Pupkin is re-named, at the Rent-a-Man Agency, and assigned to his job in a cafeteria: "Mickey One – Garbage".

His girl, Jenny, tries to coax him back to reason and work, but her therapist talk is always tangled up in his spirals of fear and loathing. The actress, Alexandra Stewart, has the forlorn task of being gentle to Beatty's snarls. Just in the sound of their voices, and in the pattern of "be nice" – "I'm bad", there is a power not really noticed by the film's schematic parable.

MICKEY: 4½ years I travelled up and down the back end of the South – an animal. Tried, two, three times to get in touch with Ruby Lapp, Detroit. Nothin'. Now today they have pressure on me.
JENNY: They know?
MICKEY: I don't know for sure they know who I am or not. Yet. But I haven't got the kind of guts to stick around and find out.
JENNY: Can't you talk to them?
MICKEY: I talk to you. 'Cause you don't talk. Nobody's gonna talk to you.
JENNY: I don't understand. Anything. I mean, hiding from you don't know who. For a crime you're not even sure you committed.
MICKEY: The only thing I know – I'm guilty.
JENNY: Of what?
MICKEY: Sure you don't want a drink?
JENNY: Of what are you guilty?
MICKEY: Not being innocent. What the hell am I – a lawyer?

The stories from the set in Chicago say that Beatty is as surly and unapproachable as Mickey. Actors say they can't hear what he's saying when he talks in scenes; years later it is impossible to know exactly what Mickey says from repeated study of tapes of the sound track. It is said he orders tailor-made "old clothes" for Mickey's underground life, and then loses his temper when they don't fit. That he spends all his time combing his hair to get the right tousled look for a Mickey who sleeps in alleys. That when he tries to pick up female extras they are turned off by his arrogance. He has a stand-in, John Gibson, who says: "I spent about ten weeks with Beatty, and we exchanged about twenty words. The rest of the time he tried to give me orders – 'Get my water!' 'Get my yogurt!' 'Get my orange juice!' After a few days of that, I told ol' buddy Warren to 'Get lost!'" Which is the kind of cocky story Mickey might have told. Is it chance or design, or does Beatty have the power to turn real people into the kind of support his characters need? Or has this always been the way movies would take over the world?

Mickey One is a failure when it opens, as nearly everyone anticipates. If there is an exception, someone who reckons on good reviews, festival garlands and a modest profit, it is Beatty, for this is his first step towards being a producer, someone who says "let us make this," rather than "yes, I will appear in that." *Mickey One* is still, in many respects, half-baked, fatuous and full of that unconscious humor which takes it for granted that a comedian is the ideal figure for a universal story about alienation and madness. Nevertheless, it was made – in defiance as much as creative absorption – and it endures as an attempt at a statement in which underground forces struggle against the deliberate but adolescent concept.

Suppose for a moment that *Mickey One* is a curiously penetrating and oblique portrait of acting. Then, it has no more daring or interesting aspect than that Mickey is a bad comic. But was that the intent or the inadvertent residue of such arty ambitions? The framing of the story seems to turn on a great talent whose paranoia takes him out of circulation. His agent, his girl and Ed Castle all want Mickey to risk the crucial audition at the Xanadu. He is presented as a kind of natural, someone whose great fears cannot quite overcome his urge to get up on stage, take the mike and start talking.

But his act is hackneyed, cynical and mean-spirited. Mickey can never fully give of himself. He snarls at the audience, at the idea of jokes and at the situations and the spotlights he craves. He has a problem about being a performer for which the possible Mob vengeance is only a pretext. The film does not notice, let alone explore this, but it is there in the hunched bearing and delivery of Beatty and in his convoluted sense of his own glamor. For this is a contradiction, a movie about reclusiveness, in which Mickey One, taken up by a kind but not especially alert girl, turns on her, bitter, cruel and liberated, and says, "I'm the king of the silent pictures – I'm hiding out till talkies blow over. Will you let me alone?" And says it as if even the generosity of words hurt his soft, pulpy, ego-blown mouth. There is an anger in Beatty far greater than that in Brando or Dean, for it is closer to the core, and it turns upon a loathing of himself as spectacle, his own visible glory and his role of speaking the big speeches. He is a star wanting to become a black hole.

Reviewers in 1965 say that Beatty plays the role badly. In *The New York Post*, Archer Winston writes: "Beatty gives it the fast-clatter routine which he seems to have learned for the occasion, but it doesn't come out of him with authority. For instance, he's not up to the style of the minor burlesque hall comic who has a bit. He's not in total control of the rest of his character either because that's not his kind of character. It can't fool anyone who believed him in his good ones likes *All Fall Down* and *Splendor in the Grass*. This is all a surface act, surface sweat. It's not inside him because he doesn't understand it."

But suppose the situation is really that of someone not very skilled as an actor, highly ungiving as a presence, chronically averse to becoming a part but addicted to observing his own attempt. *Mickey One* comes into focus if we reappraise it as a picture about self-denying narcissism. Of course, no one has that plan for the film. This is the biographer wanting, wishing the picture had dropped its black-and-white harshness, its Chicago and its stage-like message of courage. If only *Mickey One* had been in color and in L.A. with a performer who was searching for an excuse not to perform, and who had to find a girl and a Mob and woo or bribe them into pretending to be cross with him. For Mickey truly is someone who wants to shape the world to fit his fears. And what is paranoia but the self-willed melodrama of the shy?

There are moments in which its confusions suddenly lift – a slow dissolve in which one image of Mickey/Beatty seems to be watching another walk towards him; or when he closes out one act by playing the piano, grinning like a kid and singing "I'm coming, Virginia"; or that fragment of his act, in shades, tuxedo and cigar smoke (the teenager playing Lucky Luciano), and he chats up the mike: "How do you do, gentlemen, welcome to the Pickle Club. You all remember me, the human tranquiliser. I'm the management's answer to the cold shower," and then adds this line, as if trying it out, "A tidal wave just wiped out all sex in Chicago," tempted by the thought that there could be someone there, but really believing in his own isolation. And then there is the end of the film – at night, on the roof of some building, open to the air and the city skyscrapers, with Mickey sitting at a piano, alone in the spotlight, and the camera craning upwards, swept away by the majesty of this bashfulness that has finally become legendary and no longer needs the daily grind of telling jokes three times a night on its grave, not even at the Xanadu.

Claudia Cannon

Those left at the Lighthiser house had been inspired by witnessing death. The show had had such force – tragedy can be as bracing as three hard sets. Those left felt freed, the story-tellers and not its victim. Cy Lighthiser was exhilarated. He talked of putting a statue by the pool or a gold plaque in its tile floor. He encouraged rumors that the deceased was melancholy, that he had been fatally ill, that the incident was a mishap, inexplicable and marvellous because of that, that it was murder (hadn't everyone wondered?), or that it was the young man's gift to the assembly, a mystery they could always ponder.

"Rick and his splash," said a slender, tanned youth – sixteen or so – said to be a son of Cy by another marriage. His name was Beau, and he was just back from somewhere: his bare feet were stained and scarred. He might have walked across a burning desert. But everything else about him had a high finish, like the radiance of a sword that guarantees its danger and the sword's indifference.

"By the way," Beau whispered to D, "my stepmother wants you." D could tell that Beau liked to exploit whatever lurked in another's shadows.

"I beg your pardon." D was trembling.

The stark face was insolent with wonder. "Do you say that sort of thing all the time? The 'I beg your pardon' and 'What did you say?' Cy will kidnap you from Eyes. It's all talk with Cy – routines, sketches, lines. You'd be his dreamboat. Oh," this over his shoulder, as his example bade D follow him, "and I like the crestfallen look, too." Beau's laugh was like water scuttling from a bath.

D hurried down a corridor in the perfumed slipstream left by the youth.

"Seen her?" asked Beau.

"Only on screen," D was struggling to distinguish 'knowing' and 'seeing' with famous people. "Of course, I know who she is."

"Not even the lady knows that," Beau sighed. "If she ever thought she was catching up with herself she'd take a sleep cure. She has to guard that uneasiness." Then he added, "It's feeding time. You'll see her mummies, you wolf. Don't attack her. And one thing." He suddenly stopped, so D could not avoid bumping him.

"Don't laugh."

"No?"

"Not at her. *With* her is fine. But never at, over, under or about. She'll throw a blue fit."

"I'm glad you told me," said D, though he couldn't recall the last time he had laughed.

"You'll love her."

"I expect to."

"Oh, you're perfect," Beau pinched his cheek. "Tip-toes now, we mustn't alarm the little usurper."

There was a powder-blue ante-room, like an air-lock, and then a door and its jamb both edged in white felt and velcro so that the door would not mar a babe's sleep. The air was warm and it smelled of Johnson & Johnson, milk and shit.

"Highness," whispered Beau, and Claudia Cannon looked up from her Queen Anne nursing chair. Her ivory robe was in folds at her waist, crystalline slime from which the goddess was emerging. The child was attached to one of her prime white bosoms, the left, its small leaf of a hand on the bowl of her right breast. Claudia was looking down at it with brave wariness.

"Have you got it?" she demanded of Beau.

"Of course I've got it, step-mama."

"Fuck you," she murmured, her expression toward the baby never altering. She had not seemed to see D.

"Ma petite soeur," drawled Beau. He stroked the baby's brow with a finger, and emptied a sachet onto a saucer on the side table where Claudia had put baby's gripe water. A rough white cone stood up in the lamplight.

"Voilà."

"You're hateful," she told him.

"I'd only do it for you, Claudia."

"Until you tell it to the *Enquirer*," she replied.

"Never!" cried Beau. "I want enough for a book. I want it to be in libraries and book clubs. You deserve hard covers, an index and pictures." And then Beau, on his knees at the side table, looked across at D. "I'll show you my pictures if you're good, D. Claudia likes me taking her. She says it's massage. No one knows how young she looks. Her ass is still as high as a back pack." And then to Claudia: "You know you shouldn't be sitting."

"Nursing mothers sit," she told him.

"What's that got to do with it? You're just getting off on the brat's soft gums. Admit it. I'll bet you're wet."

"Claudia Cannon is always wet, mousehole." It was proverbial.

"That's a chapter in my book," Beau promised D.

D could not tell how often they had run this conversation. It sounded spiteful and natural, but that could be Ms Cannon's genteel reluctance to get into further unpleasantness in front of strangers. D was still inclined to think she cherished this baby, its small grumpy face being led into affection by her bodily sustenance. D liked to believe mothers were brought closer to abiding calm in nursing. He had loved to watch C feeding their children. He could remember lying in the dark, listening to the lapping, the tiny belches and the sense of being on the edge of a sea of benevolence. The smell of shit came from a diaper, tossed on the carpet. It did not go away.

"Look at her," said Beau. He was sitting on the floor, watching his half-sister like a chess player who sees an intricate check coming.

"I enjoy your envy," said Claudia, slipping a transparent tube from the baby's gown. It was a foot long, bringing the cocaine closer. The glass slanted past the baby's head. D was fascinated by the different beats involved – inhalations by the mother and the placid swallowing of the child's system. The baby's hand reached up for the tube. D saw white grains settling in it when Claudia paused.

"Isn't that good stuff?" Beau asked.

She could not answer. She was gasping. The baby's eyes widened. The mother regained control and peace came back to the baby.

Claudia turned to D. She was revealed, that was the effect, intruded on before she had got the decent mask on her face and screwed it down. "You don't see me at my best," she said to D. It was an apology, but a seduction, too, letting him know she was ready for him to survey greater disarray. Then she looked at her stepson and said, "Out, Beau."

"Ma mère!" he pouted.

"And take that shitty rag with you."

Beau crawled across the floor like a drowsy dog (you could see him amusing his little sister), and sniffed at the diaper. Then he picked up the towelling in his teeth, and went away, dragging it with him.

"Come closer, D," said Claudia Cannon. "I want to whisper."

PROMISE HER

If a handsome man wants to be esteemed for his intelligence, he will become contemptuous of a world whose stories only concern his looks, his attractiveness and his romantic aura. He may then endeavor to insist upon the power of his mind by treating his relationships with women with some extra detachment or humor – just to stress that he is in control of, and superior to, them. He says to himself that if the world sees only a Don Juan, just a lover, then he will play that part with dark glee. He will have them all. Then perhaps some of the women will go away with the story that he was thinking all the time, that however many times his body climaxed and came, the hard on behind the eyes never lost its grip, never diminished.

Of course, it could drive him crazy, this attempt to smother himself with intelligence. There are not many more tortuous or gradual ways of going mad than being supremely intelligent about everything. And it will be especially warping if this man has amounts of kindness or affection that he would like to offer people, but which he learns to guard against because so many of his relationships have a twisted way, sooner or later, of becoming public, and because after a time he notices that there are women coming to him with the frank opportunism of tourists who want a story and a picture to prove they were there. He makes his real there more inaccessible, and provides a false front, the popular veneer of himself, for most of them. And when he fucks them, the popular image is doing the work, and the real one, the true one, is sitting in the dark watching. The man known for his love of women may be a ghost who loathes them by the age of forty and whose fucking does not hide the edge of disdain. Will no-one have the courage to cast him as Bluebeard?

And if he gives interviews, he is badgered with questions, "Will you marry *her*, or her?" or even "Will you ever marry?" He learns how to smile and say, "You know . . . I really don't know," and it is years before he appreciates how true that is, and how the easy satisfaction of every sexual desire is a cover for not knowing. Then intelligence begins to worry, for it cannot convince itself that it is still in control. Suppose this man is in the movies, he takes his dismay to see films and he comes slowly upon this last comfort: that there is an attractiveness, an eroticism and a desire – maybe even a love – in seeing but not being seen. He sees the new movies, and he sees the new hot actresses, and he gets to meet most of them, and his chance with them. But he realises that maybe he felt most about them before he met them. And he has seen some lovers become as bored with him as ever he has been with them. The distance becomes alluring. And if he remembers all he has fucked, he may say to himself it wasn't really always him who did it. It was the other one, it was Beatty. After all, how could *he* have had so many, and not remembered them all? But intelligence begins to see a dilemma in all of this, a riddle: does this almost obligatory infidelity mean that the mind's control is necessarily dark and pessimistic? And compelled by its nature to permit no roots, no family attachments, no children? Must it be a martyr to itself, only at home in a kind of resentful loneliness?

Whatever he says about the films when they are made, Beatty is making pictures in the early 60s that seem to be experiments with self-hatred: a gigolo; a cold, nihilistic exploiter of women; a nurse who sleeps with an insane patient; and a neurotic comic who seems to have wallowed in garbage before appearing on the set. Such parts are a corollary to the way aggrieved journalists squeak at his surliness and his uncooperativeness. But the world, which entails chiefly those journalists, continues to say that he is gorgeous, sexy, beautiful etc. Some of them add, as if to establish that they were there, that he has a charisma, or a glamor, in person that exceeds even the best that the studios can do for him.

He meets Leslie Caron early in 1963 at a Hollywood party at the Bistro given by her agent, Freddie Fields, to boost her recent Oscar nomination for her performance in *The L-Shaped Room*. Caron is six years older than Beatty, and she is in her second marriage, to Peter Hall, the director of the Royal Shakespeare Company in England. She and Hall have two children; she is thirty-two, the star of such Hollywood films as *An American in Paris*, *Lili* and *Gigi*. On stage, she has been directed by Jean Renoir in his own play, *Orvet*, and by Peter Hall in a version of *Gigi*. Of course, she is French, and originally a dancer. She falls for the American actor. "It was quite strong wooing," she says later. "We practically didn't leave each other after that party for the next couple of years."

Peter Hall contents himself with Chicago, Jamaica and Beverly Hills as instances of togetherness established by a private detective when he names Beatty as co-respondent. This is some eighteen months later, in the summer of 1964, as Hall files for divorce, charging his wife's adultery as the grounds. Chicago represents *Mickey One*; Jamaica is for when Caron films *Father Goose* with Cary Grant; Beverly Hills is where they go to when not working, the place to which Caron wants to bring her two children.

The relationship with Caron has some reason to be judged the most serious of Beatty's life: it leads the perfectionist into making two pictures, *Promise Her Anything* and *Kaleidoscope*, that are not just bad, but trivial, foolish and unnecessary beyond the fact that they give him some income while he is in London. That is forced upon him because a London court accedes to Hall's request that the two children should not leave England.

The court hearing to decide the divorce is in February 1965. Beatty is ordered to pay the costs. Shortly thereafter, shooting starts on *Promise Her Anything*. The picture is made in London, but it claims to be set in New York. Caron plays a young widow with a baby son who moves into Greenwich Village. Beatty's character, Harley Rummel, lives upstairs. He wants to make serious films but is for the moment sidetracked into tasteful pornography. It is a romantic comedy, or so its advertisements say. Mr Rummel goes so far as to use the baby in one of his dirty movies, but then the hound redeems himself, saves the infant's life and wins the heart of his mother.

It is the film of an actor with something much more important on his mind, a disaster so great that it can only be explained as not being noticed. Beatty is in love, ready, perhaps eager to have his life changed. He and Caron live together in her house in Montpelier Square, in the most fashionable part of a London going through all the motions of what the media will soon identify as "swinging." This is the first great age of the Beatles. English movies have come to life. London is the center of the world for exciting, cut-price fashions.

One does not have to take the notion of "Swinging London" at face value. Still, it is a more stimulating environment than Beverly Hills. Moreover, the show business circle in London to which Beatty is attached is likely to include writers, painters, musicians, designers and even politicians and restless members of the royal family. The sojourn in London allows Beatty to live more steadily with a woman than he has ever dared since leaving home. He meets and talks to children, as a shy prospective step-father. And he lives in the time and mood of films like

With Leslie Caron, a publicity pose for *Promise Her Anything*
(Warner Brothers)

Losey's *The Servant*, the Beatles films, directed by Dick Lester, Kubrick's *Dr Strangelove*, Jack Clayton's *The Pumpkin Eater*, *What's New, Pussycat?*, Polanski's *Repulsion*, John Schlesinger's *Darling* (with Julie Christie) and Antonioni's *Blow Up*. The films Beatty makes in London are not nearly as interesting, but it is out of the London experience that he comes more fully into his own as both an actor and a producer with a new kind of American film.

The influence of Leslie Caron may be even more important than that of London. She is never just a sexual partner. In the summer of 1965, the usually taciturn Beatty is ready to tell columnist Sheilah Graham that he will marry Caron "whenever she wants . . . when she says 'Now!'." That might be a lie, or part of the subtle gaslighting that says to the woman, you haven't ever asked me, dear . . . oh, you were waiting for me to ask . . . well, I've been asking, haven't you heard? . . . no, of course, I'm not being difficult . . . well, if you say so, let's think about it. But that habitual masquerade doesn't need to woo by way of the press. Everything suggests that in Caron, Beatty finds a woman wise in the ways of show business, intelligent, forthright and creative. Someone he can talk to.

Earlier on, in Jamaica, when Beatty is on the island with her, as incognito as he can manage, he lives quietly in her house and waits for her to come home from the shooting. Night after night they talk, and the chief topic is his career and its troubles. He tries to place himself in the tradition of Brando and Clift. They are taken seriously, he complains. "He was considered just a playboy," Caron says years later. "He had spent too much time wooing women in the public eye. Of course it bothered him that he wasn't taken seriously. We used to talk about it. He was in despair about it."

Beatty has reason to be upset with his status. But if he looks hard at Clift and Brando, he must see larger difficulties in being a movie star. Clift will be dead in 1966; he is nervewracked, dependent on drugs and drink, terrified at the loss of his looks. Brando is increasingly disenchanted with his career. The picture he directed, *One-Eyed Jacks*, has been a failure. He finds little pleasure left in acting. *Last Tango in Paris* and *The Godfather* lie ahead, but he is near the end of his patience as a regularly working actor and utterly perplexed at how to secure more power in the business.

Kaleidoscope is not quite as bad as *Promise Her Anything*, largely because it casts Beatty as a rogue, Barney Lincoln, a playboy who eases his boredom by planning a gambling coup that requires breaking into a playing card factory and marking cards soon to be used in a big casino. This "caper" is couched as another romantic comedy, with Susannah York as his partner. Beatty is no more at ease in comedy than he was before. He does not deliver jokes properly: he seems to feel the silliness in serving up laughs. He even looks humorless, cute or heavy. Here is a real paradox in his nature as an actor: ask him to play comedy and he is forlorn; put him in certain near-tragic situations, and he can deliver an exquisite humor. It is as if he cannot deal with his own image at the speed of slapstick or in a ridiculous light.

But when Lincoln has to be the casual mastermind, when he sits at the gambling table, a little like a Yankee James Bond, then he seems excited by himself and the context. You can believe he often falls asleep thinking of himself in fantasies of power and command, the lone gambler who walks off with a fortune, favoring those who guess he cheated but cannot prove it with a slanting grin in which you see the shark has a diamond set in one of his teeth.

One more film in this line and Beatty might have died of boredom – if he was noticing the films. We have to think he was in love with Leslie Caron, happy to be with her, and to go with her to Paris.

Dive into darkness

Being alone with Claudia Cannon! – except, of course, for her new babe, whose world and library were its mother's warm teat. D was persuaded that the child was not yet spoiled by the pipeline of cocaine that slanted across its feeding like an hypotenuse. And he preferred to let the baby's meek adoration fill his mind. But being alone with Claudia Cannon was like confronting a famous painting. There was a powerful urge to have all the serenity for himself, or deface it irretrievably. But the most poignant feeling was of being with an entity culturally apart. As she turned her grave and lovely head this way and that, without any bidding or eye contact, D appreciated that he was like history for her. She did not look at him when she spoke, but alluded to his possibility.

"So, dear Eyes stood us up, the prick." The words were sharp with animosity, but the light of Claudia Cannon's gaze stroked her baby's brow. D wondered at that brow and its waiting mind being impressed by the mother's saintly glance. It was a pose that might have found its way into Claudia's emotional filing system on some trip to an art museum. She was in her prime now to play the Virgin Mary. Cy was probably planning the Christmas card, and haggling with Helmut Newton on which serpents there might have been close to the manger.

"I'm sure he's upset not to be here." D tried to be diplomatic. How often strangers found themselves excusing or conjecturing a hopeful best in Eyes.

"He didn't call," she carped, but her face steered straight on for baby's bliss. "Mr Hold-the-Phone didn't have the grace to touch-tone us, did he?"

"I believe he is in a retreat." D struggled to be plausible. "Away from a phone."

"He has one implanted in his body." Claudia was smiling now, in a wicked dream. "He's just doing it to show us how small we are, Cy and I, Cy and Me." She had winced at the echo. Claudia had a taste for melody.

She had learned over the years which lines worked for her, and now her mind spun them out as effortlessly as the DNA, or whatever, generated her beauty. With both looks and dialogue, thought had been circumvented. There was just effortless nature being endlessly consistent, a passionate persistence. "I'd like to cut off his royal dick," she said, "and feed it to baby – suitably moulinexed, of course. Let her eat it early, before she has to swallow humiliation with it."

A shudder coursed through D's body at what Claudia had said. She was not looking at him, but she detected the spasm. She was so tuned to alterations in atmosphere or vibration, a nerve to her vicinity. Wasn't there often a scene where the Virgin felt a hand touch her in the crowd? D could not control his seeing of Claudia in the eternity of scenarios.

"Ah, D," she said softly. "You are moved by children."

"I may have eaten something a little off." He wanted to make a joke of it.

"We all have," she promised. "We have all of us here sucked such poison," she was looking away into the depths of ignominy, "and kissed their cancerous asses."

"Please!" yelped D. He had the first heaves of nausea, and this was no time to vomit, not alone with Claudia Cannon.

"Dear D, I meant only that I felt the true parent in you." So saying, her unencumbered right hand reached out into his groin. His rod of parenting had shrunk – exhaustion, the occasion and sheer bewilderment – but Claudia had a discovering touch. And very soon, she had a respectable part of him in her hand. "You're very handsome, very fine," she told him. She knew; she never looked. D did wonder if his dimensions or even a living video image were put up for her, off in the dark, like the lines in a soap opera, when work is too intense for dialogue to be learned. But her eyes did not focus narrowly, as in reading. They communed with the faraway, with absence, her truest lover.

"Wouldn't you like to touch me, D?" she asked. "I'm nearly ready again. What you might call a restored virgin." She simpered; it must be her silly hope to be intact again, always love's fresh fruit. "You would have to be very gentle, slipping in and out. Could you be like a mouse?" She did not wait for his opinion of this. "I think you could. I do think so. Not that I want you to be *un*obtrusive. No, I do want to notice. Astonished even. What say you?" The lilt of regality had carried her close to Quentin Durward or the Round Table. But what chance had D of impinging when Washington had Cary Grant and Eva Marie Saint on his face and never flinched?

228

"Will you tell me stories, D, if I lie in your arms? I am so fearful of the dark, and so restless a sleeper."

D was crushed, "I can seldom think of stories."

"You must have told them to your children," said Claudia. "I can see their rapt faces, imploring you not to stop or go away."

"Ah," sighed D, for he saw the same picture, and it stirred him with guilt and fondness.

"You and I are parents, D. We know. Not like the Eyes of the world, so promiscuous and unestablished. We have children here and there, and we know those tuggings of duty that we can never quite fulfil. We are grown up, that's the difference." D was always staggered at where her speeches carried her.

Her hand had to come away from her loyal swain. The baby was full. Claudia placed the child on her shoulder, and eased a stupefied belch from its little balloon of a body. She sighed with gratification at the effect, and then took the infant to its cradle, plying it with crocheted blankets like lace handkerchiefs.

"There, baby," she said to the powdered air. "Go to sleep, wake up strong and true – and watch the bedbugs don't bite." She tiptoed away from the cradle – it took a couple of minutes – so as to be certain the child was sleeping. Then, as if with her last strength, she drifted to a day bed and sank upon it.

"I'm so drained when I have fed my baby. I feel I have given it my life." There was a sense of true loss.

"Should you rest?" D wondered.

"With you here, foolish? What kind of hostess do you think I am? Come sit beside me." And her hand flapped on the few inches of the day bed not filled by her and that liquid ivory robe, just another version of flesh. Such a hand. D could not take his eyes from its gloss of marble. It was the hand she had held him with.

"You do desire me, don't you?" Her eyes were closed now, in tribute to sleep.

"Well," D began.

"Tell me truly," she ordered. "Is it me you want, or just the star? I cannot bear to be used."

"I'm sure it must be you," said D. He did not add that, while her stardom was unquestioned, he was not himself among her greatest fans. Indeed, he groaned at announcements of her new pictures.

"You would have to be so very careful. I am not fully healed."

D imagined the inner Claudia Cannon beneath the loose robe, with flaps of unknit wound, like sails in the doldrums, and the funk of blood. There might be scars still, white and blue in their new state, skin ready to tear again, so that if he entered her there might be the look of invadedness in her suddenly opened eyes.

"Do it anyway," she said. "You only live once, and when it's done we can trash that rascal Eyes together. Come along, darling, pop it in," and in a trice she had rolled up the yards of silk and swung her legs apart, like a dockyard whore.

"Well," said D, and dived in the darkness.

IN BED

What is Warren Beatty like in bed then? He must wonder himself. We are not supposing from this book someone so monotonously secure or self-adoring that he does not scrutinise the tremblings and the commotions in his ladies (and in himself) like a seismologist on the San Andrea Fault. And it is very much to the book's point that he will have seen himself named – on bathroom walls or in the gossip columns – like a Kilroy or a Casanova, so earnestly imagined, so zealously trumpeted, that he must have recognised how far he stands for the *idea* of sexual splendor. No doubt he has his moments in bed, but can any of them match the thinking in advance or the neo-poetic descriptions? In the end – no matter which end or which way – there is a purely factual, physical aspect to what goes on in bed, so ecstatic in its nature, so brief, so high, that it is bound to move in legend in one of two directions – it will be lied about, or forgotten. There is no surer function in art than its ability to pin down the imagined sexual peak. Movie stars are as sexy as their pictures, and there must come a day when they know the drudgery and thankless labor of actually being in bed with anyone. It testifies to our Warren's sense of ordinariness if he has persevered.

Britt Ekland has this to say, in a book in which she never gives a mealy-mouthed impression of herself in bed:

> "Warren was the most divine lover of all. His libido was as lethal as high octane gas. I had never known such pleasure and passion in my life.
>
> "Warren could handle women as smoothly as operating an elevator. He knew exactly where to locate the top button. One flick and we were on the way."

Where is the man who couldn't stand to have this printed about him? Who can tell the revelation of intimacy from the enhancement of legend? And it is in the nature of this sort of legend that intimacy has been transcended, with the star exploding to fill space.

Ekland's account surpasses the racy gentility of Joan Collins' "four or five times a day". Here is a metaphor that might allude to a history of visiting Warren at the Beverly Wilshire, going up and down for him. Is it a fond tease, saying, remember when we nearly did it in the elevator itself, jammed in a corner, all awkwardness forgotten, romantic effort racing the ponderous rattling climb of the walnut cabinet?

Warren and Britt could not have done it in the Beverly Wilshire elevator: it is only a ten-story building, and the elevator has an operator. But I can never enter the elevator without the thought occurring. When mortals dream about stars, or when one person wonders about another, it is the thought that counts. Which lovers alone in an elevator have not calculated the chances, or considered what would happen if the box halted between floors?

The Ekland metaphor does offer the woman's body as the elevator, with man the dextrous operator, existing in and out of that body as need arises, like an engineer at a power plant. It is a description of the woman's body that seems passive and submissive at first. But it is so extensive, so elemental, as to be more powerful than the man's. (No one finds the little engineer if the power plant melts.) The elevator could have other kids to press its buttons. But what would those boys do if they had no elevator to play with? Warren in Britt's scenario is a master, but a potentially homeless expert, the servant to her existence, merely skilled (and humbled) in the face of authentic power.

In this context of biography – admittedly discursive, playful and speculative – isn't the nature of metaphor the best hope for insight? It is not enough to depict Warren as a womaniser. He is used too. It is likely that from time to time Warren Beatty has received carefully handwritten letters from young women in Arkansas or Zagreb, with snapshots of the writers enclosed, nude pictures even with the girls grinning patiently at the camera, their legs spread to show targets and prizes, or that the letters have said, "Dear Warren, what I would like is for you . . . (all put so bluntly that a romantic skims across the alarming words) . . . And I will be your slave and do anything you ask, and I can go all night, Warren, can you?" Or daunting words to that effect, so that the reader feels exhausted already.

Now imagine, if you will, that I had found ladies ready to describe such scenes with Warren and stand by them. I cannot believe that my publisher would dare to put such words in print. For it is in the true and noble nature of sexual or romantic intimacy that the act occurs in such a way that even the parties wonder what happens. There is no sex without the imagination, and no way of rendering it that does not reach out for fiction.

It may not be necessary always for Warren to do it. He may become more culturally potent with abstinence. The French director Roger Vadim recalls a Malibu party in 1965 when Warren, "surrounded by young actresses, explained that he had become suddenly impotent and would be leaving for India the next day". In those 60s, India is supposed to hold so many answers and rescues. Vadim sees that it is a ruse – "sometimes Warren loves to mystify people". He knows already that an idea can be more magical than its thing. And teasing can merge with the mind's heavenly India or philosophy.

Let us say he thinks such things on the flight to Paris, while dozing through the movie, holding hands with Leslie Caron. I buy the hand-holding; so many women speak of Warren's kindness. And if he's dreamy with sex and flying as their palms grow moist, isn't he growing into Howard Hughes?

Why Paris? Because it is where Caron grew up, ballet-crazy amid Occupation, Resistance and Relief. There is even a chance now that she and Beatty will act together in the movie of *Is Paris Burning?* And because, once before, Caron was the guide to an American in Paris, and now sees a need to broaden the young actor's mind and awareness. There are things she knows he has not heard of, and he probably listens to them quietly until he has learned them.

One has to do with the history of the movies. It goes as follows. The movies were invented simultaneously in France and America, but the word the world uses is American because in the first two decades of the form American commercial power took such charge of the medium and its business. The French made small films for themselves and for those parts of the world prepared to deal with "foreign" films. In France, it was possible for leading writers, painters and musicians to be interested in film and occasionally involved with it. The pictures made there won a reputation for being "adult". The greatest film director in the world, Jean Renoir, was French. Many years later, while he is discussing a venture with Martin Scorsese, Beatty will see a picture of Renoir's *La Règle du Jeu* on Scorsese's wall, and he will say, "That's *Shampoo.*"

Meanwhile, America makes movies for the world, so many of them that in the next four decades film alters the way people regard reality. For we look at things and consider how they compare with the photographs, and when we think of how life's own drama and narrative work, we remember and are influenced by the plot structure and the romantic imagery of movies. The movies made in America are intended as versions of real life, albeit versions made for fiction and entertainment. But as time goes by, so the Hollywood story structures – the genres – become at least as familiar as, and rather more reliable than, the ways of life.

By the late 1950s, the task of broadcasting those genres and their extensive, implicit ideology has been passed on to television. American theatrical movies are therefore stranded, far from life and losing their audience. There are a few pictures which, consciously or not, respond with a wicked, desperate creative energy, as if to make films about this movie ideology. They are absurdist, camp, and the best American films of their time – *Rio Bravo, Psycho, Some Like it Hot, Written on the Wind, Men in War, Touch of Evil* – extraordinary works, full of dark humor, in which the various genres are going cubist and crazy.

This is not much noticed in America at the time. But in France there is a resurgence in adventurous, small films, made now by men younger than movie-makers have ever been. The movement is called the New Wave; its directors are Truffaut, Godard, Chabrol, Rivette, Rohmer, and so on. They love the natural photographed look of life and new, casual actors. Some say their films are very real. But they are, in truth, films about film made by young people who think of themselves as artists and who have grown up in the notion that the cinema is a guiding part of reality.

Why Paris? Because this new attitude has been discovered there and vindicated. Films are about films. It is a more appealing insight than a self-absorbed actor could ever have imagined. And if he loves Leslie Caron very much, as much as he can, it may be because he is deriving from her not just her body, her lessons, her love and herself, but glimpses of a way ahead for himself. Yet this is not a simple discovery, with eyes suddenly widening in delight. No, there is something in Beatty that does not like to be seen discovering; it does suggest he was not as intelligent as he wants to be if there is so vast a novelty, one that requires discovery. So if revelation comes his way, he is cool about it, and learns to grin through clenched teeth and say, "Uh-huh, I see," giving away as little as possible.

*

How is he in bed, if he is so reluctant to be surprised?

This is a story about a party at Marianne Hill's house, some time in

234

the middle 1970s. And Warren Beatty arrives with Michelle Phillips; and an observer sees his act.

First Michelle vanishes into the kitchen and Warren stands there surveying the room. He picks on this woman – not an especially beautiful woman, but sharply dressed. She has come with a man, but Warren comes on over and he just positions himself between them with his back to the man, and after a while the man just goes away.

Warren says, "Don't I know you?" to the woman.

She says no.

Then he starts his whole shy thing. The head down, muttering, not very articulate. He even kicks at the floor with his toe, trying to get it out. And he offers the woman a cigarette.

She says, "No, thank you. I don't smoke."

"Neither do I," says Warren.

So she points out, "You're smoking now."

And he says, "That's only because I'm nervous." And he says, "I'd really like to get to know you better."

She says to him, "Didn't you come with someone?"

"Yeah, Michelle," says Beatty. "Have you seen her?"

"I don't think so," says the woman.

And at that Warren gives up, and he retrieves Michelle Phillips from the kitchen and they leave.

Torn room

"Let me tell you," announced Claudia Cannon, a swan's neck of an arm thrust back for emphasis, and knocking the backboard. "And you may quote me – look at my hand, I'll be bruised."

"Heavens," D called from a more southerly spot on the day bed.

"Anyway," Claudia was looking for the pain to peep through. "Eyes has nothing on you. Rien!"

This news did not swell D's head. It supported his caution with most popular myths. Every cat is gray in the dark was his opinion, plus the likelihood that all wangs waned. There is a law of gravity in such things, like aging and the fading of swish tricks.

"Now let's see what we have on Eyes," Claudia cajoled.

"What do you mean?" asked D in the tented shade of the sheet she had drawn over them.

"All those distant, lordly ways," complained Claudia, "pretending he's different from the rest of us. Ducking my party. Being so stingy with himself. What are our strings if not to be plucked?"

"Indeed," said D, whose own fingers were still tingling from ostinato attention to Claudia's viola.

"He has a debt to the public. Eyes does get a touch solemn. It's a kind of sadness. I have never once seen him at the Lakers, he disdains Superstars and I know for a fact, the producer is an old pal, that Eyes will not do *Donahue*."

"And he would be good with Phil," D surmised. "Two genuine worriers addressing a broad range of issues. And no suckers."

"So right," said Claudia. "And if he is serious about politics, the poor dear, it's the only way to get yourself about."

A little time went by in silence – it can be cut.

"Kiss me, sweetie," she asked, and D dipped his head again into the vanilla blancmange. He felt his renewal stirring, the spent & thinking again of being a ! for her *.

236

"And tell me the story, I wish you would. I can be quite unrestrained next time, you know. I really am a wicked thing. Just tell me what's on your mind. So long as we don't wake baby."

D reminded her of her very recent fluttering, rising and falling like an anesthetist's bladder, her face gorged on excitement, but without so much as a sound.

"Every mother has to learn the muted orgasm," Claudia told him. "And, after all, the great actresses needed no sound. Anyway, you were driving me wild. What else could I do?"

"I guessed as much," he said demurely.

"Weren't you going to tell me the story? Unless you want to come in my face first?"

This target astonished him.

"It is more beneficial than any oils or creams on the market." She liked to sound practical.

The dilemma for D was that he could only be loyal to Eyes and Clear by making love to Claudia. It did distract her from the script. He was still in a blithe state of mindless desire for her, but simple prudence said neither that supply nor his! could last for ever. Moreover, D's view was complicated by his chronic problem: he was already in love with la Cannon. When she sighed and shut her eyes with pleasure it convinced him that she liked him and gave him open house, this very celebrated star. But love needs sleep.

"This script," said Claudia, "I know you shouldn't tell me," she put a tangy finger on his lips. "And you mustn't. But it's daring, isn't it?"

"I think it is." He saw the fate of the future turning in her heady eyes.

"Good work must be," she knew. She smiled shyly and caressed his !; her touch was so cool still.

"Oh my!" D moaned.

"Yes, yours," she allowed, and in a moment she had him like a corkscrew, so anxious to obey her request for hush, but so impelled to give voice, until the sweet relief and he was pouring into her cupped hand. From which she next sipped and then lathered the rest into her breasts until they shone.

"We should be in a film." He was besotted with her. "Our love-making should be shown."

"Oh, really?" she said.

"Without censorship."

"I had a slightly different idea," she confessed.

"Yes?" She was the expert, after all.

"I believe you should direct your script. Only you can understand it. Now, of course, directing is a chore –"

"Oh no," said D, a writer who had no doubt where authorship rested.

"You would have to watch some Eyes or other doing his feeble best to make love to me."

At this moment, D could see worse fates.

"But you would know I was thinking of you."

He tried to imagine exactly how that would be knowable.

"And you could spite him by making sure the camera saw me."

"Just the back of his head, burrowing away," D could picture that unruly mop doing its best.

"I think the true exaltation is female, don't you?"

"How could you guess I wanted to direct?" he asked her.

"We have had . . . knowledge of one another. Secrets travel with that cargo. I felt it. I do feel things." It is the knowledge, isn't it? Not the body, that cocky meringue. So saying, she took his hand and led it to the mouth of her *. The flood was so great, D worried there might be blood there.

"Put your hand in, your whole hand," she urged. There was room for him to feel around the swimming softness, testing the elastic walls of the chamber.

"Mmmmm," she said to him, so simple and quiet, he was smitten to the quick. They both sighed at being there. "Tell me the story," she said.

"Well," began D. But he had to roll to get a firm base on his elbow if he was to keep his whole hand in the honey and tell the story. The manoeuver must have turned his wrist for he saw a tremor of bliss hurry through her eyes, not conventional, not movie-like, but scary and untidy, as if she thought her insides would rip.

"What was that?" she asked. There was fear in her voice. She was asking not D, but the story.

"I had to move a little, my arm was going to sleep."

"Not that." She dismissed the details. She waited but there was nothing. Then, when she had subsided again, the room cracked apart and a rift of earth, air, night, cold and a smoking, wrenching noise came between them and the baby. There was a sucking sound and D's damp hand came free as the naked Claudia scrambled from the bed to the brink of the chasm, looking out across it at the rest of the room and the baby's cradle floating away.

Her scream began, and D saw his script, a white tablet, tumbling into the pit. Now he had only the money.

PARIS

In Paris, with Leslie Caron, Beatty encounters François Truffaut at a party. They have lunch together. This is not their first meeting, for Truffaut has been in Chicago during the shooting of *Mickey One*, visiting his girl friend, Alexandra Stewart. At lunch, Caron and Beatty talk movies and parts. They would like to do something together more worthwhile than *Promise Her Anything*. Truffaut says there is this script that has been offered to me which would be more suitable for you. After all, it is an American story, and Truffaut hardly speaks English.

The script is the work of two young American writers who met at *Esquire*, David Newman and Robert Benton. They do not have a movie credit between them, and their story concerns a pair of outlaws who had a brief fame in Texas and Oklahoma in the early 1930s. Their names are Bonnie Parker and Clyde Barrow. They are both killed by Texas Rangers and assorted deputies on May 23, 1934. Neither of them has reached the age of twenty-five. They have robbed small banks and killed people who got in their way. They are the sort of brutes we go in dread of meeting; unless we meet them in imagination, in which case they are raw energy, recklessness and a kind of exemplary panache – part theirs, part the savagery of gleeful, demented newsprint – ready to assist our fantasies. Their lives seem to have been lived in the American instinct and desperation that fame would be enough, and that it would change all else.

Newman and Benton have sent the script to Truffaut because they have been inspired by his films (especially by *Jules et Jim*), and because they do not think the American business is capable of making, or even understanding, their picture. They have liked the quality of a ménage in *Jules et Jim*, two men and a woman, and the unexpected juxtaposition of laughter and tears in Truffaut's films. They regard this as a lifelike spontaneity not evident in American films, not quite seeing that it is in the influence of montage and scene-making on his scenario, that it is film making the new conditions for the medium.

239

In America, in 1964, Truffaut has met Benton and Newman, and startled them by showing them a French translation he has had made of the script, the better to deal with it. The three men talk about the project, and Truffaut suggests an improvement: "Bonnie writes 'The Poem of Bonnie and Clyde' in a car, then cut to a Texas ranger reading the poem in a newspaper, then cut to Bonnie and Clyde lying on a blanket in the meadow with Clyde reading the poem in the paper." This sequence will be intact in the finished picture, the climax in its notion of star identity as a liberating aphrodisiac.

But Truffaut says he cannot take the script as he is trying to make *Fahrenheit 451* in England. His generosity has been for its own sake. And now, over lunch, he sketches in the story for Beatty, with Caron translating when Truffaut's English lets him down. It is an awesome moment for those sentimentally inclined to believe in luck and drama. For it is the chance of a great American movie in which American ways have been bypassed. And for the lovers looking for material to secure their unofficial marriage, it looks like a blessed fantasy. The press has made Beatty and Caron outlaws already – which they resent and regard as wrongful reports. Let them make their own ballad then and be a team, peppering the hostile world and its media with bullets and grins. Sooner or later, if an American movie is going to work, its stars must believe it tells *their* story. For if the picture frees their desires, then it has a chance of capturing the large audience, too. All sensational American pictures delight in outlawry, whether the shooting up of banks or the soaring above everyday dullness.

Leslie Caron must see herself as Bonnie. She may be leaping ahead of her winning translation with plans for Bonnie Parker's French mother, a woman from New Orleans. Who ever really knows the reliable truth, ze 'ole truth, about such desperadoes? These are lost loves, *n'est-ce pas?* More than that, Caron has been urging Beatty to be his own master, not to play according to the system, but to be another kind of outlaw. Here is a project he can tell himself he found. Of course, its actual authors are in New York, but Beatty can go back to them, woo them with offers, and then let them realise, slowly, how in France he saw the picture afresh, and his seeing it made it his so that now, in a way, they, the writers, have the chance to serve *his* version. Let Warren seduce you – if you want your script made.

Someone who knows Beatty at this time says, "He likes and can get on with every woman, any woman. But every man is a competitor." Moreover, Beatty has been taking on a psychological stance towards older men in which he wants to give them respect, awe, reverence and service. He wants a hero and a leader, but his inner nature is so competitive and so mistrustful of these men that he begins to battle with them until he finds and fixes on a flaw, some small way in which they fail or let him down. And then he judges them, and says, "Oh, yeah, so-and-so . . ." and smiles with superiority.

This has happened with William Inge and Elia Kazan. It is what accounts for the awful breakdown in the relationship with Robert Rossen. When Beatty first knows Clifford Odets in Hollywood, he approaches the worn-out, compromised, alcoholic and neurotic writer, only a few years from death, and wants to talk books and art with him. All Odets wants to do is play gin rummy, and Beatty goes along with this and then remembers with a cool mixture of sorrow and triumph that he's a better player than Odets.

When Beatty meets Arthur Penn in *Mickey One* they are in love with their own closeness and the feeling of having discovered a comrade. Before the shooting, Penn says Beatty must live with him and his family in New York so they can talk all the time. And in the six weeks that follow Beatty finds Penn's faults, his limitations – let us say his human nature – and again feels victory and that old detachment. There are those who will hail *Bonnie and Clyde* as Penn's triumph, his self-expression. So it is in part, but Arthur Penn always knows who is in charge, and he may realise that he is the first leader who has become a follower. It is part of Beatty's gradual realisation that he must take control that he sees the need to hire instead of be hired. He will not say this, but inwardly he thinks he has control of the vital, dynamic, brilliant Penn. He would not hire a true rival.

To be so judgemental, to go so zealously and ruthlessly in search of flaw in order to feel secure seems like immaturity. It is not necessarily conscious behavior, and it does not block out the class or the intelligence of Warren Beatty, or his very good instincts about those who need to be loyal to him. There is a way in which he is using people, but the manner is ambiguous and the goals are often very worthwhile. Moreover, Beatty is always in search of some other figure he can believe in – his eyes have the hopeful smile of a disciple. It is just as real a need as the mechanism that begins to undermine the hero. Occasionally, it finds a perfect model.

A few years later, in 1971, Beatty pursues a young actress after a party. They walk together through the streets of Beverly Hills and he points out houses to her where stars live and he tells her how ten years before, as a newcomer, he had walked the same streets at night and wondered whether he could ever take over one of these houses. The young woman realises he did the tour – not in company, on a bus – but privately, secretly. He is a movie buff, in love with all the old Hollywood history. As if to dramatise what she is thinking, a darkened limousine drives by and enters the grounds of one of the larger houses.

"Do you know what that is?" Beatty asks her. "That's the hearse with Mike Romanoff's body." The death has just occurred, at the age of eighty plus, of the man who said he was related to the Tsar, who had become a restaurateur and a pillar of Hollywood society. As far as such things are ever known for sure it was known he was a fraud. But Hollywood is crazy over frauds, if they get away with it – that's what acting is – and maybe this Romanoff, real name possibly Harry Gerguson, did have a French mother. Romanoff was a young romancer: he seduced women, he advised on movies about old Europe, he told stories, and he became one of the city's first magical hosts. You knew Mike was a bullshitter, but you listened because the city is so superstitious.

And Warren has timed this nocturnal stroll to pay homage to the hearse. What a part Romanoff would be for him, and what a hero, for Romanoff is dead. The flaws are wiped away by his going. You could maybe love yourself as a killer, too, if the killer died in time. To be up there on the screen is to partake of life and death simultaneously, it is to be the most vivid thing in life and absolutely out of touch, the only secure hero. As Warren Beatty finds himself, he is working out the nature and the necessity of being a certain kind of magical ghost, of being more imagined than real.

Doolywohl

It was now only a flap on the edge of wilderness, but the door to what had been Claudia's room before the new ravine struck through it, opened and the weathered face of Doc appeared. He was windswept in the gale left by disruption. There was a look of long-suffering on his face, as if he doubted that any story could proceed without his watching over it. He had the manner of a plumber at a domestic flood.

"You had to do it, didn't you?" he said.

"Do what?" asked D, sheepish but defiant.

"Have your precious earthquake!"

"Well –" D felt caught in the act.

"Not enough to hint at it, keep the reader guessing. You could have had all your metaphors without bringing the damned thing down on us. Everyone gets the point!"

"I know, but –"

"Do you have any idea what it entails?"

D was too mortified to speak. He had been crass.

"This'll need months of effects work. You get those guys in, it's all bureaucracy and things you never see properly until you preview in Seattle, and then you're in the can. You have a decent thing going with actors, you're working up a nice idea, and then it's blown. Your actors are left making faces at blue screens. They go bananas. They lose the picture. And those effects people, they talk a language no one understands. It's giving the picture away for some stupid gotcha. To say nothing of the damage and the lives. I'm disappointed. I thought you could keep it cool."

The gloomy Doc prowled into what was left of the room, stood by the naked Claudia frozen in a scream on the brink, and looked out at the other half of the room, receding, and at all the wasteland in between. It was like a back projection.

"Right here, you've got another million, million two. What else do

243

you have in mind? Jesus," he groaned, "this could be as bad as that thing with Heston and Geneviève Bujold."

"Oh no," D was worried now. "This is simply to get the action out of the city and into the desert."

Doc considered the options. "How about a modest local disaster up on Mulholland? Enough to get your characters driving. But not so we have to show Westwood or downtown coming apart."

"Well," D began.

"You'll thank me."

"I did have a scene coming where they pause in their flight, look back at the city and see the HOLLYWOOD sign start to hop and jump."

"It does?" Doc was interested in spite of himself.

"DOOLYWOHL," D offered. "OLDWHOLYO."

"Well, I can see the charm of that," Doc admitted. "The big shake comes after they've got away?"

"That's what I thought."

"I suppose one good model shot of the sign would get you a lot of mileage."

"Exactly," said D. "And then later we can have radio reports –"

"Cut off in mid-sentence," guessed Doc.

"That's not too much?"

"It never fails. Just silence and the faces of Angelenos wondering. But no effects shit."

"As little as possible."

"It's like having a SWAT team in."

D shuddered sympathetically.

"How many dead?" asked Doc.

D looked at the texture of the goose bumps on Claudia's unwavering shoulder. "Millions, I suppose," he said tentatively.

"Has to be," said Doc.

"I don't know what to say," said D. "The writing gets a momentum of its own."

"Still," said Doc, drawing his fingers through the strands of Claudia's hair, as if he was sorting fossilised time. "There isn't one of them living here doesn't expect it to happen." He looked into the abyss – it stank now of sewage and summer waste. "Or want it."

D said nothing; what could professionals say? It was more important that silence prevailed between them, so that the howling and the din in nature washed up against their resilience. Two tough writers - hardboiled, some said? Or just two wordy fellows, hopelessly susceptible to destruction, hoping their terse dialogue might mask the fear. Talking well is an honorable courage, when the earth's plates are grinding in opposite directions, and a baby is being swept away on the rush of lost ground with the mother at your feet, as fixed and wounded as a Weegee face. But Doc and D did have their saving port at the aghast edge: they could putter about there; time passed through their shifting images, like light through blinds; and they could chat.

"So what do you reckon?" asked Doc.

"I was going to have a panic – nothing fancy – and Clear getting the escape together."

"Yeah, Clear's the one. Who goes?"

"Claudia and Cy," D began to make a list.

"And his scumbag son," added Doc.

"Certainly. And Chuck, and all the entourage that's here."

"They're here still," Doc knew. "They're always last to leave."

"Tusk and Zale?" D asked.

"I saw them running old Perry Mason tapes," said Doc.

"And Drew, of course," D was contrite at not having named her sooner.

"You have a problem there," said Doc.

"Really? I thought just a bitter moment when Drew realises what must have happened with D and Claudia. One piercing close-up and perhaps an acrid remark."

"Oh, it's easy to *show*," said Doc – what a task it was to be a teacher, what a test of faith and dismay. "But then you've got a sweet kid pissed off at you. I mean, that is a good young woman, and she's going to be hurt. That doesn't wear off with one nice close-up. Added to which," Doc nodded down at Claudia, "you've got this bimbo who's going to be Gish-ho on 'Where is my poor babe?'"

"I do see that," said D, ruefully. There was so much to look after.

Doc smiled crookedly, "You know, you have turned into a major ladies' man."

"It just seemed to happen," D protested.

"Oh, it did?" Doc's eyebrows went up like hawks. "That *is* tough."

"Well," D struggled, "let's hope the crisis can cover it all up."

"Where we going?"

D took fresh heart in the plans that had to be made, "I thought a motley caravan of limos and trucks."

"With Clear as traffic cop."

"Making our way out of the city."

"The roads?" Doc had done this sort of thing before.

"Just as you said, this was an early tremor. They – we – make it to safety before the big quake."

Doc nodded, "So you get your local mayhem *and* the grand panorama, the sign doing anagrams?"

"What do you think?"

"I've heard worse." And he had. This was a city used to slapdash disasters. "Do we have enough vehicles?"

"I'm sure."

"You're sure," Doc was nagging now. "You've done a body count? You have to line-produce as well as spin the yarn."

"Well, no –"

"Too busy counting the freckles on Claudia's ass, I suppose? Come on, D, you have obligations. Fuck the star on your own time. So, then, where we going?"

"To the desert, of course."

"Out to see Eyes?" Doc could imagine this for himself.

"Isn't it neat?" D was proud.

"Well, it's about time. But just remember, because you wanted to get D and Eyes together, you razed the greater Los Angeles area." Doc was a pillar of civic integrity.

D fudged. "You said yourself it would come as no surprise."

"No surprise! Philosophically it's right. But don't kid yourself that there isn't going to be a lot of ground-level distress."

"I understand," said D, biting his lip.

"No, you don't," Doc added. "The tenements, over on the other side, where your wife and kiddies live. Where *you* live." Doc's finger struck him in the chest. "That's all coming down like a house of cards. Gas explosions. And no one to fight the fires or go through the rubble listening for cries. That's how bad it is, and you'll be wrapping up this coked-out mother in her mink, calming her down and reminding her of the story so you can juice her again."

"I –" D was loud and brief with protest.

"You would."

"I would. It's true." These creatures were so available, and no one could be in movies without discovering the appeal of power.

A silence resumed between them. But Doc was not sanctimonious, and he knew the rigors of writing. He'd had a heroine once he'd taken to bed and then let the cops shoot her eyes out. A writer was so full of desire but so sure of disappointment.

Doolywohl

"So where in the desert?"

"Well," D had the map in his hand. "I was going out by way of Lancaster and Mojave."

"That's good," said Doc. "You could have planes in the air over Edwards. Planes that can't land because the runways are ruined."

"Oh, I like that," cried D.

"Use it," said Doc.

"And then by way of China Lake and Death Valley and into Nevada." He loved the name, its sound of emptiness with burnt mauves at dusk, the ghost towns and the big breaks.

"Where would you cross the line?" Doc wanted to know – clearly another desert buff.

"At Beatty?" D hazarded.

"Seems reasonable," said Doc. "And then a life in the desert for this weird crew?"

D paused in time. "I don't want to spoil it for you." He knew he had the master hooked.

"OK, OK," grumbled Doc, looking around the room, and getting ready to go. "Just one thing."

"What's that?"

"What about me?" This question was muttered. Doc was too bashful, too squeamish, to make it a plea.

"Why," D laughed out loud. "You come with us."

"Oh, I do?" Doc was asking. "You're sure about that?"

"I can't do it without you." This was said so naturally that D knew it must be true.

Doc was fidgeting at the door. "If you're certain."

"I am!"

Doc nodded, thought to speak, abandoned the project, and then told himself, hell, no, it has to be said.

"Don't say it," said D.

"No?"

"No need."

"OK. It was just that the earthquake bit was . . ."

"Vulgar?"

"Kind of. Promise me something."

"What's that?"

"You don't have a nuclear holocaust lined up for us, do you?"

"Never entered my head."

"That's good. I can't stand that shit. A new life in the desert."

"A new life," repeated D, hoping it could be so, and turning to attend to Claudia. She was beginning to move again and coming back to reclaim her scream.

PARIS – TEXAS

Warren Beatty comes back to New York from Paris. He calls Robert Benton and says he would like to read the script of *Bonnie and Clyde*. This is not a conversation between agents. Half an hour after the call, the movie star himself turns up on Benton's Lexington Avenue doorstep to collect the script. Of course, Benton hands it over, along with his doubts. He and Newman have set out to write a French film; they cannot quite see a movie star as a film-maker; and their script has an important homosexual relationship between Clyde and his gang-member, C.W. Moss. *Can you be gay, Warren?* I'd really like to read the script. *I don't think you're going to like it.* I just want to read it.

Later that day Beatty calls Benton and says he wants to do it. *How much have you read, Warren?* I'm at page thirty-eight. *Wait until you get to sixty-four. That'll curl your hair.* I want to do it.

There is another call a few hours later, and the actor's mind is still made up. Benton cannot talk him out of it – that is the story that will be told years later, as part of the legend of *Bonnie and Clyde*. As if Benton had somehow been put in the negotiating position of trying to deter his only buyer, and as if no one remembered that Beatty got the script for $10,000. So let's suppose that there were also moments like *Well, Warren, that's wonderful that you want to do it. We've always liked your work.* Yeah, it's an interesting script. Not a flawless script. *Well, what is?* Exactly. *Truffaut loved it.* But he's not American. *Well, what exactly is wrong with it?* It needs a lot of work yet, don't you think? *Maybe, but what kind of work?* You mentioned the homosexual thing yourself. *But that's very important to us, and we did warn you.* So maybe we need another writer to look at that afresh. *Where does that leave us, Warren?* Well, you fellows have to see that I'm going to need to put a lot more work and money into this project. There's no way of knowing if it's ever going to get made. *So, $10,000?* I'm taking a hell of a chance.

He is, though on terms by which he can afford to lose. In business, he is like an actor watching his own performance, an actor who is master of the show – just like the pick-up scene in *All Fall Down*. From the outset, Beatty has been drawn to *Bonnie and Clyde* not simply as an actor, but as an impresario and a manager. Morever, just as when acting he has insuperable problems in revealing himself, as a businessman he is at his most naked and least compromised.

When it comes to a director for the picture, Beatty defines the ground by saying he could do it himself. *That's an awful lot for one person to do, Warren.* I know. But Orson Welles did it. *True, but Citizen Kane, you will recall, was not a hit.* Maybe it is asking too much of myself. *It is, you'll feel easier with a director.* Exactly. *Who do you think would be good?* Well, I think I'd like to hear your suggestions. *There's ——.* Oh, I don't think so, he's ——. *True, what about ——?* I heard bad things about him. *Oh. Well, there's Penn, of course. You boys like Arthur? He's damned good at psychological action, and I know he'd kill to do it.* Yeah, he has that feeling for danger. *So you'd like Penn, Warren?* If he's the one you fellows want. If you really think it's him then I'm not going to stand in the way.

In fact, Penn is not certain about doing it straightaway. Other directors are in the running. One of them is Brian G. Hutton, but he is typical of Hollywood sentiment in his reactions. He is looking at the Benton-Newton script one day with a young writer Beatty knows, Robert Towne. Hutton asks, "What do you see in this?" Towne tells him, at length; he loves the original screenplay. But Hutton looks at him as if he is crazy. "Well," he sighs, "I just don't see it. I'm going off to do *Where Eagles Dare*." Hindsight is not kind to this choice, but it shows industry wisdom at that moment.

And so it is Arthur Penn who has the central task of persuading Benton and Newton (and Warren to some degree) that the homosexuality is not right for the film. He tells them it confuses the story, that they don't know enough about it. *I mean, you boys aren't gay, are you?*

The re-writing of the script begins, and as Benton and Newman are offered more and more suggestions, so they are given help. It comes in the form of Robert Towne, then in his early thirties, a man who has written a couple of horror movies for Roger Corman, and some television work as well as a Western, *The Long Ride Home*, from which he removes his name. This is the start of a way of working that Towne will make famous – of having helped out on scripts without official credit. It is called script doctoring, and it is a measure of secret insiderism and unspoken pacts in a city of cliques that rattle like castanets in flamenco. Beatty sees and likes the script of *The Long Ride Home*, and Towne becomes one of his first most abiding disciples. In time, people will say Towne is maybe Beatty's closest friend. Twenty years later, they are just as close.

Towne will be credited on *Bonnie and Clyde*, in the head credits, as "Special Consultant". It is a unique credit, and perhaps the best public rumor anyone in Hollywood has ever had. Benton and Newman get the screenplay credit. But it is Towne who writes some scenes fifty times for Penn, and for Warren. It is Towne who is on location and who sometimes even corrects a line reading. On a good and successful movie there is enough credit for everyone, but there is a battle for it, too. The idea was Benton and Newman's. Much of the detailed craft is Towne's. All three prosper from the film in terms of work, if not money. But it is Beatty who brings them together, and who keeps them all a little uneasy. And it is Beatty who would blame himself if there was one word, glance or frame that he didn't like. And this man with some self-hatred is on the edge of an opportunity to rise above all his own doubts. He is flying, as anyone will when picking and goading talent is his greatest skill.

And now skill must cut through fondness. Leslie Caron says that even as Beatty was reading the script he called her for advice. He wonders if it isn't too much like a Western, a dead genre? No, Caron tells him, it's a new kind of movie. Maybe she even says it's a movie about fame, and about movies – she may be the most intelligent woman Beatty has ever lived with. So, she urges him, buy it for us. And he buys it.

But when she comes back to America, he tells her she's not quite right for Bonnie Parker. "The way he discarded me after I got him to buy *Bonnie and Clyde* was rather ruthless. Anyone who has come close to Warren has shed quite a few feathers. He tends to maul you." Not that Warren can even tell Leslie straightaway who will play the part. It's just that it won't be her.

He has Natalie Wood in mind: she was the kid on the run with James Dean in *Rebel Without a Cause*. But Wood is reluctant to go to Texas for two months with Warren without her psychiatrist. According to her sister Lana, Natalie has tried to kill herself some time in 1966 after a visit from Warren. He is far from her only problem, but he is someone who reminds her of how easily she can be manipulated.

Carol Lynley and Tuesday Weld come close to getting the role of Bonnie. It may only be Weld's pregnancy that keeps her from it. They are not the only names considered. Beatty is one of those Hollywood

people for whom casting is a way of life: he does not just cast and recast pictures in his head; he looks at real situations in terms of "casting". Casting is a power in which the imagination plays with the future, and even puts an ad in the trades saying that any beautiful and interested young woman should be at the door at 8 a.m. and still ready to show her best at 6 p.m.

In thinking about which actress should be the one to bring his Clyde to sexual fulfilment, Beatty thinks of everyone he knows or could dream of knowing. Afterwards, Shirley MacLaine says, yes, he talked to her once or twice: "You know how he is, sitting in the corner of the Beverly Wilshire coffee shop and acting mysterious while he's on the phone. Then he never called again. All that stuff in the cornfields. I guess he couldn't do it with his sister. But come to think of it – maybe he could!"

Casting is wondering who you could do it with. And in time it will become a deliberation that slows the actual making of movies. Faye Dunaway gets the part. So obvious now, so uncertain then.

And casting goes all the way down the line: it picks on Gene Hackman, so good in *Lilith*; on Michael J. Pollard, who played with Beatty in *A Loss of Roses*; it chooses Estelle Parsons and Gene Wilder (for a one-scene part), sure that they have something. It can go from a veteran cameraman, Burnett Guffey, known for mastery of black-and-white, to a young production designer, Dean Tavoularis. It awards costuming to Theadora Van Runkle, a brilliant newcomer, and make-up to Robert Jiras, a good friend from *Mickey One*. It must think about all these areas, for there is to be a new look in this film that springs up at parties within months – it involves clothes, long skirts and hats, as well as make-up. Indeed, when Clyde first meets Bonnie he tells her to make a small alteration in her hair, dropping a cutesy curl for free fall. It does improve her, and it shows us Clyde as a producer of history. Maybe the scene comes from Towne seeing Beatty stroll among actresses adjusting hairstyles here and there, like a sultan becoming a genius. A film is full of details, and Beatty has learned in his movies so far that sometimes people are too tired or too casual or too bad to chase down all the details. He collects them, to prove himself.

Bonnie and Clyde goes on location to Dallas, with a base at the modest North Park Motor Inn. It is never set up as a big picture. This is only three years after the John Kennedy assassination, and people on the crew are impressed by the local aftershock. And so the history of American violence seeps into the picture, where it will become a shocking new beauty. Very quickly, relatives and buddies of the real Bonnie and Clyde come by, with stories of the "hard times" and the understandable outlawry. Robert Towne spends time with Clyde's nephew, who was eleven when the gangster died, and picks up anecdotes about Clyde's skill with cars and the way "he could cut a corner square when he drove".

They are filming here and there, thirty miles to the north of Dallas, at Pilot Point and Ponder, having no difficulty in finding desolate fields that feel like the 30s and drawing very few spectators to their shoot-outs. A routine sets in of filming, with Towne in the Motor Inn re-writing pages for the following day. When the crew comes back in the evening, he has dinner with Arthur Penn, and sometimes Warren, to discuss the work, and then they all go to a theater in downtown Dallas to look at the dailies.

A lot of the time, these are printed in black-and-white to save money. Warners are cutting back on the picture as it proceeds, shaving the budget so that Beatty personally has to make up the difference. As a result, by the end of production, he owns a more substantial share of it than was ever envisaged – let the kid carry the risk, says the studio.

> "Warren was truly a great producer," says Towne. "I remember a scene we had, it's just before the final deaths, and Bonnie is supposed to get some fruit and be eating it with Clyde in the car as they drive towards the ambush. Well, we wanted a peach that would squirt and squish on the big screen.
>
> "The day before shooting, Warren asked the property master if it was going to be all right with the peach.
>
> "'I don't have them,' the guy said, and Warren's face went white.
>
> "'They're not in season,' the guy said. 'I got apples.'
>
> "'Somewhere in the world they're in season,' said Warren. 'In South America or North Pakistan. I want peaches tomorrow.'
>
> "Well, in the end, we couldn't wait for peaches. We got a pear and we injected it with water with a syringe. But I never forgot Warren's response and the feeling that it was a detail that was going to be on the screen a long time. And Bonnie and Clyde _were_ peaches, not apples. Warren said, 'It's hard to argue, but you've got to keep doing it.'"

He does his best to keep everyone content. Faye Dunaway is not the least eccentric of actresses, and she has to worry that her co-star – not quite thirty – is running the show. But Warren gets on with her as well as anyone in Texas does. Estelle Parsons will later praise his care and consideration. You have to be the producer every person needs – confidant, confessor, fan, bully, tease, buddy, and amateur juice-maker for stand-in pears. There is a moment when Towne has to go back to Los Angeles for a few days, and Beatty – grinning – goes down on his knees to beg him not to, because he knows that Towne is going anyway, but will treasure the grace of the act. And Towne comes back to Texas early.

He is having to argue his case all the time. Warners regard Warren as a famous young actor whose films lose money. There have been seven before *Bonnie and Clyde,* and no one says that any except *Splendor in the Grass* made money. And since Warners distributed that, and three others, they're ready to dispute even that claim. *Kid, the people don't like you. You're very bright, but sometimes that frightens the public.* The pictures have been bad. *You chose them.* Yeah, but I was working for others. Now I'm working for me. I will never make a failure when I'm working for me. *Until you start to second-guess yourself, baby!*

The stories all have Beatty on his knees to Jack Warner saying let me do it, let me cut it my way. Joe Hyams, a long-time Warners man, says he was *there*: he saw Warren *kiss* Jack's feet, begging to have the picture in better theaters than the marketing people had booked. Those lips? Those shining shoes? Perhaps. There is not an office on show at Warners, with grooves in the carpet where this supplication occurs. You can imagine Beatty on his knees, with Warner grinning, *Whatever next?*, and Warren grinning back – it's all camp in such offices, actors trying to upstage one another. You can picture the kid on his knees, asking. You really think I should do it, Jack? Little me? The shy thing, head down, hair tousled. Not all the stories add that Beatty's deal and his buying in on Warners' fear and bewilderment have got him up to forty per cent of the profits.

Getaway

It was a scene of mythic significance: the escape from a civilization in cataclysm for a wilderness as empty and hypothetical as a billiard table. They had all anticipated it, uncertain whether dread or energy would carry them through. They had bags packed, lists of things they could not do without. And when they foresaw the terror of the metropolis, they were as sure of passing through it as Crusoes, taking dry flints, bean seeds and Rock and Roll's Greatest Hits to their private shore. For heartfelt frontier people had thought ahead and picked out a little desert refuge, somewhere off the map.

Cy Lighthiser had typed inventories of the things to go and a truck in his garage with camping materials, sterile water, cases of dried tomatoes, board games and worry beads. Clear, whose practice it often was to go out to the desert to consult, had a company camper and a stock of safari clothing, guns, Fontella Bass tapes and iron rations. So many show people, having been so long homeless, or unattached, are constitutionally suited to such a departure.

So Cy was sweeping up his collection of bound screenplays while kicking his best Persian cushions into a basket with the aplomb of Pele or Puskas. Even D had the wisdom to rake the surface of Claudia Cannon's vanity into a wastepaper bin, while imprisoning the lady in yards of Indonesian silk. (He found no mink.) Sooner or later she would want her make-up, but for now it was all "My baby! Oh Lord, the child", as grating as Blanche in *Bonnie and Clyde*, until D hit her once, speculatively, in the jaw, the golden scallop, and was touched to see her sag in silence.

"Guessing her weight?" asked Drew, coming upon D, his arms full of the vermilion-wrapped Claudia. Only her dainty feet and head protruded from the silk, with a smudge of blue on her chin.

"I am rescuing her," D answered his former amour. He had meant to be firm about the strife in his feeling. But when he saw Drew's woeful

256

look, his heart lurched again. He was ready to toss the dire Claudia after the babe. That girl had been hurt by his wandering eye. How she must care for him. Hadn't she warned him to have nothing to do with any of them? Was there a surer sign of virtue?

"Where's Claudia's kid?" she asked.

"She was carried off by the landslide."

"We'll look for her on the way down," said Drew.

"She may be lost forever," D pointed out. He was anxious to get on. You had to keep the line going forward.

"Don't say that!" Drew's eyes fell on the absent, set face of the mother. "She doesn't get off that easy." D thought he saw a flicker in Claudia's eyelids. He was shocked by Drew's severity, until he saw the strength of necessity in her face. She had never been more beautiful. She made Claudia look effete. He was so thrilled he wanted her there, on the dangerous spot. She felt it, too. For she smiled and told him he was still her D. "Do you think we're going to die?" she asked.

"Perhaps," he agreed.

"Then we may have to kill," she told him, and he nodded.

The crisis was enough to make D act and change his mind without regret. He was ready for death or murder; it was like being in a fire without burning. All ordinariness had fallen away. He felt like someone in a story, not simply willing to kill, but pledged to the implacable destiny of plot.

The strange convoy made off into the night. But one car, a Mercedes, would not start. It blocked the way, so Chuck, driving a Lincoln, rammed it repeatedly, the celadon metal becoming as crumpled as a dress tossed on the floor. They all roared encouragement, and at last he barged the soft sedan off the road. Those whose car it had been looked back with loathing. "Shoot it!" someone cried to the night. It was Beau. There was a pause and then shots, and in an instant the wreck exploded in a gasp of orange heat, putrid with gasoline. The assembly bathed in the heat, their bared faces amber and delirious.

D was in the camper with Drew and Clear. Chuck was driving and Claudia was still stretched out where D had put her along a bench seat. Her body bounced helplessly as Chuck surged into every bend, braking to save them. The vehicle groaned and bucked from his driving, and Chuck laughed out loud, fighting the bastard of a road and shouting at those ahead to go faster. D wanted to go up to him and poleaxe the idiot. But the camper was riding such a stormy drive, and who but Chuck could handle it? So D held on and felt the jarring in his head.

257

This jagged immediacy broke in on Claudia's rest. D was crouched at her side, ready to apologise.

"Miss Cannon," he began.

"I dreamed of you," she held his wrist.

"I had to strike you."

"Is that what you did?" Her eyes widened.

"We beat a very hasty retreat."

"Did we?" said Claudia. She sat up, and her silk sheath could not hide her nakedness. "Oh my," she murmured. "Gentlemen, forgive me. I appear to have come out au naturel."

Drew spoke to her from the other side of the jolting camper: "Claudia," she said, "we've lost your daughter."

"Claudia?" she echoed, wan and fitful. "Who is she?"

"That's you, mama," said Drew. "Your baby went sliding down the hillside in the earthquake."

"I really don't remember," said Claudia. "I had a child?"

"Oh Jesus," Drew realised, "the amnesia bit."

"Was she pretty?" Claudia had to know.

"We'll find her, of course," D told her.

"Oh no," she wearied. "I don't expect so. These hills are so wild and so many. And there are such fearsome people around. We will have to wait for the ransom demands." Her voice was piteous but firm, a victim with a hold on her pathos.

"Why did you hit me?" she asked D.

"Well, I –"

"I know." She put a hand on his. "It was to protect me from the loss. You are my knight. And what a puncher, too, that I should lose all recollection."

And so on, down the twisty hillside, into a city more asleep than dreaming. Drew and D sat side by side. Claudia drew closer to Clear and began to think aloud with him.

"Do you know," she said, "that I have a lost child? A poor babe taken by the sudden violence of the land. Of course, I shall search for her, no matter how long it takes. It will become like a legend. People will ask one another whether they have ever seen the mother whose child was lost. And the woman will go on and on, roaming everywhere, hardly aging, her spirit is so taut and ardent in this quest. Do you like it?"

ESQUIRE PIECE

Just before *Bonnie and Clyde* opens, in its August 1967 issue, *Esquire* publishes a profile on Beatty, written by Rex Reed. It is somewhere between a report of the actor's life and an attempt on it. But it qualifies for its chapter here because it is also an event in the life, a moment which helps the subject discover his own *mysterioso*.

The article is still entertaining and expressive. More than just good reportage, it helps define a new relationship between "adventurous," "creative," "gonzo" journalism and the few remaining giants of the movie business, increasingly cut adrift from the studio protection and the pre-prepared publicity kit. Reed's article may not be the first "new" movie profile, but it does become a model for others. Which means that it influences the movie people getting ready to be interviewed, as well as the writers sent out to capture them.

There is a history to this development worth sketching in. In the past, American movies have been promoted by studio publicity departments. Stars have made tours of personal appearance, photo occasions and the passing on of homilies, lies and good cheer to every shorthand reporter in the room. In the great age of stardom, an engaging but quite false glare is broadcast on the human nature of these stars. There is a general tendency in the media in the 60s to look deeper and to discover the crass and dishonest roots of heroism and glamor.

In film writing, its first great example is the series of articles Lillian Ross writes for the *New Yorker* on the making of *The Red Badge of Courage*, published as a book in 1952, called *Picture*. The innovation in these pieces is that if a writer simply sits in on the meetings that make up the process of American film-making then the recall will be hilarious, startling and fascinating because picture people only reveal their stupidity, vulgarity and duplicity when they open their mouths. And they cannot help but open their mouths, because they are all of them actors at heart.

The business is appalled by *Picture*, but it can temper neither its way of talking nor its occasional weakness for letting itself be overheard. In 1968, Twentieth Century-Fox will let John Gregory Dunne's retentive ears onto the premises and the devastating result is *The Studio*. Of course, ears are not enough. Nobody on *The Red Badge of Courage* noticed Lillian Ross writing it all down – perhaps she just learned the timing and the rhythm and then recreated it later. By the 1960s, small tape recorders are giving us every grunt and delay. Hollywood narcissism finds a fresh form – the sentence that goes on for ever without achieving form or period.

As the power of the studios declines, so their promotional machinery falters. The big actors, and especially those determined to be masters of their fate, take on publicity agents or agencies. When a film opens, the studio has to deal with these agents, who may put out the word, "Warren's not doing press," or some such. Partly out of fear of their own inarticulacy, and partly because the new power gives them something to control, actors begin to flinch from promotion. It leads to a bizarre anomaly, that of people striving to become movie actors and then refusing any further prostitution of themselves in selling their pictures. Warren Beatty is a patron saint to this reticence, and the Rex Reed interview will stand as a warning test case to all those beauties afraid of getting trashed.

Still, such profiles as Reed's do not happen by accident. A magazine editor, and its writers, are eager for good material. They assume that the public is most (or only) concerned with a star as one of their films opens. But it is often the publicity agent who initiates such pieces and arranges the key meeting with the star. Beatty has as his agent Pat Newcomb, who came of age in the business by being one of Marilyn Monroe's closer confidantes. These agents can be very powerful figures, prevailing upon their clients and even instructing them how to behave. In other cases, they are not much more than the star's answering service. For it is a part of Beatty's developing nature and influence in the business that public image is too important to be trusted to others. It may be more central than the film. It may be more vital than the person.

Reed's article is entitled "Will the Real Warren Beatty Please Shut Up." This may or may not be Reed's choice – but for the star, and his peers, it is testament to the attitude of the press, begging their time and talk and then slapping them publicly in the face.

The article is in some ways a meditation on such pieces with an undertone of disdain in the writing and an ambivalence in the subject.

We are left to decide whether that is instinctive or calculated, or whether it is Beatty's own shyness and vanity being professionalised and brought almost to the point of myth by his own realisation that the process can be teased.

Why should a man, much less a star, not adopt elusiveness as his own style when the article opens with U.C.L.A. students not knowing who Beatty is, confusing him with Tab Hunter and generally contributing towards a New York writer's sense of how silly California is, and how flimsy its products must be? After that, Reed does a round-up of rumors (in the new way of outflanking libel lawyers) as a build-up for the article's high concept:

"Back in New York, I had skipped the public and asked Those Who Know, and from them I learned that Warren was a draft dodger, a Communist, that he had two illegitimate children living in London, that he had been arrested three times by the Los Angeles vice squad, that he was a sadist who loved to invite ten girls to his hotel room at one time and not show up, that he wore black leather pants and carried a whip when he was not working, and that 'at least fifty women were seduced by him' as one man swore. Above all I learned that Those Who Know knew everything but the truth.

"The Truth – as I came to find out – is that nobody knows very much at all about Warren Beatty, including Warren himself."

Now, Truth or even truth may be a little heavy a label for this insight. But I am not averse to it: there is something essentially Warren in his screen depths of perplexity, of language spilling into a hole of stricken silence. But it is more interesting still to see this dumbfoundedness as one more actor's trick, as a caption for closing off the question of who he is – so that even he need not puzzle any longer.

The interview complains about Beatty being hard to pin down. We get a feeling of the bored Reed trapped in his hotel in Los Angeles waiting for the call. And then Warners press agent, Guy McElwaine, gives Reed his shtick, drives him in circles, says Warren's hard to get and why doesn't he do Nancy Sinatra instead?

At last Beatty is discovered in his office, "a tiny pink room at the end of an empty corridor in a tiny pink stucco building that looked like a temporary wartime army hut for training-center personnel." Reed is still in the mindset that finds it hard to believe in pink. Reed describes Beatty's staring look, his "rather slow and cumbersome" way of speaking. He fixes on "the desperation to be liked, approved of, the fear (the greatest terror of his life, to be exact) of being considered unintelligent. At least four or five times during our talks, he would turn to me defiantly and say, as if in self-assurance, 'I *am* intelligent; I *know* I am intelligent.'"

My own research and wonderings would not dispute the gist of Reed's point. But his accusation, his superiority, is misplaced: wanting to be intelligent is not inconsistent with the thing itself. It is only Hollywood that defies intelligence. And Reed gives not nearly enough credit to what his recorder has Beatty saying: a stunning litany of accuracy that should have terminated the project there and then in *Esquire*'s mind and offered the life and work of Beatty up to some rather more adventurous writing:

> "There is, as far as I can see, no reason to do a story on me. Most of what I have to say you couldn't print anyway. [Such magazines do nag their writers to get scandalous revelations that their lawyers then forbid them to use.] Most movie stars are not interesting, so to sell papers and magazines in the fading publications field a writer has to end up writing his ass off to make somebody look more interesting than he really is, right? What this all boils down to is publicity because somebody's got some movie to sell, right? What do I need with publicity? You want to see me driving up and down the Sunset Strip in my car picking up girls, right? Well, you don't think I'd be stupid enough to let you see *that* side of me, do you?"

This may not qualify as intelligence in those circles where intelligence is adjudicated. But it's smart. It rattles off like a big speech. And it manages to blind even the sour Reed to the fact that no one – not even Jack Warner – was keener to promote the pants off *Bonnie and Clyde* than Warren Beatty.

A few years later, while travelling for George McGovern, Beatty is interviewed by two young reporters for The *Daily Cardinal*, the newspaper of the University of Wisconsin at Madison. They ask him about Rex Reed and the *Esquire* interview:

> "I don't know what to say about a person like that. You would have to address yourself to the symptoms of American journalism and what allows that kind of sickness to sustain itself.
>
> "This was a guy who said he thought I was the best actor of my generation and that he'd seen these films of mine over and over again. He tried to get me to pose for a picture with thirty girls. I thought that was insane. Why would I do a thing like that? I only spent an hour talking to him – certainly an hour of a mistake. He made up the article largely out of things out of columns. He had me involved with women I'd never met in all sorts of incidents that never took place. I would say the whole thing may come out of some homosexual anxiety.

"As I remember Rex Reed sat there for that hour . . . the only word I can think of is 'dewy-eyed'. I remember having a feeling of sympathy for him and trying very hard to answer seriously the questions he asked.

"I think the man is contemptible, dishonest, and a very hostile creature."

The *Cardinal* boys may be hopping in their chairs with excitement at getting such candor. "Do you mind if we print that?" they ask.

And there in Madison, in 1971, Warren Beatty has one of his great moments when life allows him to utter a movie line:

"What do you think I said it for?" he asks.

Night man

Driving through the great city at night, with as much circumspection as a glittery caravanserai could muster, none of them missed the destruction poised in the air. They looked on every glass tower as a shower of splinters still held in place by the need for dignity. They saw the loops and strands of freeway ramps like curls about to fall on a barber's floor. And if they saw night people in doorways, wrapped in *The Times* or plastic bags, they felt the soft centers waiting for the collapse of rubble.

"Can't we warn any of them?" Drew whispered. "Not even D's wife and children?"

"No cigar," said Clear.

So they drove on, with the hiss of wheels and Claudia's developing story. She was muttering to herself and feeding from a giant jar of peanuts, the small dry pellets churning with her scenario: "I'm the most wretched woman alive. I had a child, a newborn child . . ."

It needed work on the dialogue, a montage of changing scenery, some soaring score to reach to the edge of eternity, and Claudia could lose a few pounds – but such things were easy enough to manage. D had to admit he was touched by the concept. He could see it working. Nothing so constituted the nature of an actress as her readiness to serve us all in metaphor. Claudia had no steady reality. Even being with her, locked in some of the sweatier Sutra holds, D felt she came and went. Her nature was always ready to slip "out there" into story, to pose on the horizon of imagination, to belong to everyone.

They had reached the eastern edge of the city when they pulled into the forecourt of a filling station. They must have every drop of gas for the desert trek. Clear was having spare cans filled and taking a collection of credit cards to pay for it all when it was appreciated that the station was untended.

"No one here?" Clear asked of a man filling up his car, a pale black in a faded orange suit.

264

"We're here, man. I know we're here."

"I meant the operatives, the officials."

"Night man's in there," the black man nodded towards the office.

"He's not working?" Clear asked.

"He's not breathing." The black took the nozzle from his tank, careful not to spill a drop. "This a freebie night."

D moved towards the office. The door could not close because the body of another black was there, lying in its own blood. The man's hand had sought to write something in the blood before he died. There was a scrawl, or a shape: it might have been a name, or the outline of a face, all the man could do to express rage or his disappearing self.

"See that market over there," Chuck was saying. "There's a pick-up backed in a window and guys loading it." Chuck edged closer to Clear. "What you say we freshen up on supplies?"

"You don't think we should escape now?" asked Clear.

"We're nearly out of the city. The fault doesn't reach this far. This is almost the edge of your desert."

"Who knows who's over there?" said Clear doubtfully.

"We can take guns," Chuck answered him. "It's wide open. Whatta you say, Cy?"

Lighthiser had joined them; he was brisk and cheery, like one enjoying the outing. "Let's take them," he said. "Six, seven of us go over there with Uzis, who's gonna get in our way?"

"It's against the law." Drew's warning came from inside the camper.

"It's the early hours in east LA," said Chuck, "and there's an act of God coming."

"Who says?" Drew challenged him.

"Everyone says," Chuck told her. He was talking to a kid. "You too stoned to see the hole in the ground on Mulholland?"

"I've seen holes there before."

"On what you do, you've seen Aladdin's caves."

"Well," said Drew, "if you're going, get me a box of Tampax for the desert."

"In the desert!" Chuck was shouting and shaking. There was an excitement in him too great to fit into words. "In the desert, you bleed." It was as if Chuck knew he would be vindicated there. All around him, D felt the mood for the crisis. People wanted their babies lost, the gas stations open so that you had to drive in over bodies as well as the rubber lines that rang a bell in the office. And all of them wanted to go shopping in the market with the limits off. D could imagine himself grabbing up armfuls of oranges, laughing with glee. All those dayglo fruits, and all of them dry as cobwebs in the desert in a week. The supplies would only scratch the desert's surface. What they would always need there would be the liberty to take anything and shoot any face that got in their way.

"Let's go," said D, picking up a rifle, the first he had ever touched. It leaped up to meet him, and the oiled black metal told him, "I'm your lover, fellow."

BONNIE AND CLYDE

When you think about *Bonnie and Clyde* now, you see their last car on the country road, stopped to help a friend, then peppered by bullets that come back at the gorgeous creatures like an explosion put in reverse. It is a shooting picture, from the target practice with the hanging tire that rebukes the Depression, through the motor court ambushes to the last stake-out. Too many bullets to count, but enough to inaugurate the new movie lyricism of bodies ripped, pecked, chafed and urged into abandon by lead.

This is the crucial American movie about love and death, lit up by fresh-air faces that have been burning underground for years, too much in the dark to admit, yes, we're in love with death, let's fuck death. But *Bonnie and Clyde* surpasses its early, easy claim that violence is aphrodisiac (Bonnie stroking Clyde's casually offered, groin-crossing gun) and reaches the far more dangerous idea that death brings glory and identity. If you want to know what the film is about, think how thoroughly Bonnie and Clyde have given up the ghost for sex-crazed American immortality.

There are enough bullets to constitute the film's musical score. What can be counted are the references to identity and fame and the instances of naming. When Bonnie and Clyde meet, and his hard-on limp threatens to steal into her airless West Dallas stew of heat, boredom and unused skin, they stroll down the art director's street of 1931, falling into a ritual of spot-on small talk in which she vamps and drawls and he tells her just exactly who she is – the sexiest insight.

She asks him what armed robbery is like and puts her hand on his bashful barrel. He lurches into the store and comes out clutching cash, like weeds he has pulled up. Then it's off and away in her car – one of the great lovers' meetings in movie history, and proof that this picture must be watched as closely as the fine points in a movie deal contract. And as they tear off, happy at knowing they've found a way to die, they introduce themselves, just as smartass droll as actors who foresee the fun of fucking each other in the roles they are playing.

After that, the picture never stops the naming process. There are over thirty blatant namings. I do not mean the natural occasions in conversation; I mean a heightened, boastful stream of namings – enough to suggest that America has a greater dread of anonymity than of poverty.

The characters are introduced flamboyantly. Thereafter, they chew over one another's full names, as if they suspected they were bogus – "Well, Mister C. W. Moss" and so on, full of leers and goosings. When the dispossessed farmer and his black come upon the target practice, and get a shot at their own old windows, Clyde is like Jack Benny in the lush, delayed timing that introduces Bonnie and himself and adds, "We rob banks", trying to get the ex-farmer's vote. He has a self-destructive glamor that wants to give death and the cops a chance.

It's not long before Beatty's shy, muttered "This is a stick up" (which he has to repeat, shouting, before he gets respect) has turned into a smooth, matinée act in which the gang strolls onto a bank set, and Clyde allows himself to drawl, "Good afternoon, this is the Barrow gang," half expecting a round of applause. Bonnie and Clyde want to be known; they are sublimely committed to this openness, so misguided in real outlaws. But they are not as crass as brother Buck, who pushes his ugly mug in front of a policeman so he won't forget Buck Barrow. Bonnie and Clyde do not want to be vulgar; they want the billing and streamlining of stars.

The plot of this very skillful movie turns on identity. The Texas Ranger who pursues Bonnie and Clyde is not just their nemesis, but their servant, lured into dealing out death by the cunning that has compromised his reputation. When Frank Hamer comes upon them, off the road, the gang consider killing him. But Bonnie's poetic genius elects to have Hamer photographed with them so the gang can send the pictures to the papers making a stooge of the Ranger. The ploy is carried filmically by the avidity of Faye Dunaway's face and by Bonnie's urge to French-kiss Hamer's frosty mustache. The real guile in the photo session enlists Hamer's implacable need to get them. Of course, this is not spelled out directly. You can believe, some of the time, that Bonnie and Clyde do have a notion to grow old and plain and settle down.

Hamer's posse kills Buck and captures his distraught widow. Blanche is so intriguing – the gang member whose polite living-death style is something the gang are desperate to escape. Blanche is blind, in a cell, when Hamer creeps in to question her. "Blanche Barrow" he roars in her ear – the naming never stops, and is always more than is necessary. He coaxes a whole name out of her, the one gang name he didn't know, "C. W. Moss", and the lip-smacking bravura of the film has Blanche's whining coming out of Hamer's sullied mouth.

The Ranger finds Moss's family home – where the wounded Bonnie and Clyde are hiding out. He draws C.W.'s father into a death plot on the grounds that C.W. can be spared – not officially named yet as a gangster, he can get off lightly in return for the father's act of betrayal. And so the summer afternoon roadside is arranged, and our lovers drive towards it with all the aplomb of movie stars who have so given themselves away they've brought the slowest and most stupid of posses down on them. They want it, and they are ready.

"Everyone" now knows how *Bonnie and Clyde* met death: in their passing they became fixed forever, like Lincoln, John Kennedy, James Dean, Billy the Kid and the man in the Weegee photograph, poised in mid-air, saved from hitting the certain sidewalk. But the real Bonnie and Clyde died . . . how? The answer is lost along with their blunt, rural faces and the strained clutter of their teeth. But in the picture they are the best-looking couple in the world, actors togged up with rare enterprise, yarning away in smart Texas accents, and shameless about their bright teeth and the strange cult of being movie stars. Thus, to the parable of fame, *Bonnie and Clyde* adds the metaphor of performance.

The first day in West Dallas, Clyde is like a kid with a snappy impersonation of a Hollywood producer. So it's lucky Bonnie is at her upstairs window naked with a window steamed up enough to let Clyde *know*, without getting the scissors out. And Bonnie *knows* opportunity has knocked. She has gone to the window and called out, "Hey, boy! What you doing with my Mommie's car?" And Clyde has looked up with a grin so savage she yells, "Wait there!", so she can throw on a flimsy dress and leap down the stairs after him. She comes in a lovely rush, the camera looking up her flying skirts, so quickly done you do not *know* if you saw it or not. But you know why she's hurrying. This early Bonnie is untapped orgasm in need of a showman.

They walk. She puts on a brittle act which Mr Producer cracks by asking her, "What do you do – a movie star? A lady mechanic? A maid?" before letting her have the answer he's known all along, "A waitress?", uttered with Beatty's most intimate, withering disapproval. As if to say, if you think I could trouble with a waitress, think again. It's like not doing television interviews.

As they drive away from Clyde's demo hold-up, Bonnie just wants to get fucked. She can't wait for him to stop the car. This is the ingénue naivety that thinks Hollywood is just getting laid. The producer has to educate his new actress. She begins to think he doesn't like sex, or that he can't even do it: "Your advertising is just dandy. Folks would never guess you don't have a thing to sell." At which Warren grins – it's maybe more of a sucking smile – and goes into a heartfelt scene in which the famed lover asks the world to look past mere sex to its drive for something more ineffable:

> CLYDE: All right, all right, if all you want's a stud service, you get on back to West Dallas
> and you stay there the rest of your life. You're worth more than that, a lot more than
> that, and you know it, and that's why you came along with me. You could find a lover
> boy on every damn corner of town, and it don't matter a damn to him whether you're
> waiting on table or picking cotton. But it does make a damn to me.
> BONNIE: Why?
> CLYDE: Why? What do you mean why? Because you're different, that's why. You know
> why you're like me? You want different things. You want something better than
> being a waitress. You and me travelling together, we could cut a path clear across this
> state, and Kansas! and Missouri! and Oklahoma! And everybody'd know about it.
> You listen to me, Miss Bonnie Parker, how would you like to go walking into the
> dining room of the Dolphin Hotel in Dallas, wearing a nice silk dress? And have
> everybody wait on you? Do you like that? Does that seem like a lot to you? That seem
> enough to you? You've got a right to that!
> BONNIE: Hey! When did you figure all that out?
> CLYDE: Minute I saw you.
> BONNIE: Why?
> CLYDE: Well, you may be the best damn girl in Texas.

This seduction is audacious because it has been launched on Clyde's sexual failure. That may be traumatic impotence, if one wants to live with the idea that the gun brings sexual liberation to Clyde. It is much more interesting to see how far fame is his key aphrodisiac. For Bonnie will "free" Clyde from his reluctance by writing a poem about him and sending it to the newspapers. What makes the movie so lastingly fascinating is the glimpse we get of a great seducer setting himself the hardest task, of withholding his most celebrated force and asking us to see that reputation, the mystery of being known, is what most compels him. It is the producer's film, the imprint of his views about the world and himself.

The scheme could be arid and merely clever without its filmic embodiment. The credit for this can be shared among many. But, amid all the death and violence, see the beauty in the movie. Beatty had never been so giving on the screen, so ready to laugh and smile, so little addicted to hiding. You can hear what he says, because Clyde enjoys talk. Further, despite the very active intelligence in a smart actor who is also producing, Beatty does begin to reveal his potential for being less bright than he might like. Clyde is a kind of wizard: C.W. says no one can catch him. But he has limits in awareness, and Beatty lets the movie see them.

He shows fear sometimes, a dumb swagger and a slowness on the uptake. He even fidgets when driving because he needs to take a leak. He has no larger design than having a good time for the moment. Asked how he might live his life afresh he has nothing more than a new strategy for taking banks. He is Buck's brother, caught in the same stupor of easy-going perplexity when the question arises, well, apart from having a good time, what shall we do next? There is a country-boy stoicism and sweetness in the way he says he chopped off two toes to get off work detail in prison and then got paroled a week later, free but limping. "Ain't life grand?" he chuckles in a sudden ravishing close-up.

But Clyde is less perceptive than Bonnie. He does discover her, he does have the vision that alters her life and the eye to know she should get rid of her cute kiss curl. Clyde runs the gang and overrules Bonnie on new members and cutting Blanche in on the take. But it is Bonnie who sees the future, tells Clyde's story and gracefully conducts her man towards death.

It is Bonnie who feels fatality in their beauty. She turns to ice on hearing that the man they have picked up in the reverse car chase is an undertaker. She sees that all their going is getting nowhere, with no way they can come to rest, close to their kin. There is no ordinary life. The future is all Dolphin Hotel, self-announcement and taking the risk (a kind of Hollywood).

The poem Bonnie sends to the newspapers is as slick and shallow as film. But it is what the characters want. "You told my story," Clyde exults – this is his rapture, and Beatty's too, the acting is so open. "You told my whole story, right there. One time I told you I'd make you somebody. That's what you done for me." They make love on the picnic grass, with the pages of the poem blowing in the wind.

It is a transforming passion, but more discreet than the earlier scene in which Bonnie was ready to fellate Clyde and he rolled away in despair. But there is an afterglow in which she tells him, "You did just perfect," and the self-reflexive layering of the movie is laid bare as Warren says, "I did, didn't I? I really did."

But love isn't perfect or memorable enough. The real love scene is the finale when bodies separated in space twist, roll and sigh from the fire of ardor. The death scene is the climax, and it is graced and consented in by the rapid exchange of knowing close-ups as they look and see what is coming. Naming is no longer necessary. Death is greeted as something as rare as ecstasy because of the great outlawry. Being famous has been shown as the most certain way to beauty. The only way.

24-hour market

It was a 24-hour supermarket, but someone had backed a small truck through the plate-glass front. There were nuggets of glass strewn underfoot and squashed shopping carts beneath the wheels of the truck. This outrage excited the gang moving liquor, frozen chickens and quivers of baguettes into the truck. But other shoppers were still going in and out of the regular doors, determined not to notice. D saw no bodies around, nor any other damage. The lights were on, and muzak was falling on the merchandise like snow. Robbery went on smoothly, beside the calm, digestive measure of shopping. People picked over porterhouse steaks and waited patiently to get at the special offers on swordfish and sunchokes.

"What's the plan?" Chuck wanted to know.

Clear shook his head. "I was always a hopeless shopper."

"Shopping's a great way to meet women," Doc suggested. "You run your cart accidentally into theirs. It gets a conversation going. The market's like an old matinée."

Chuck was tapping the barrel of his gun on Doc's shopping cart. "You're right," said Doc, sheepishly. "It's just that I look at a market and I picture chance meetings at the coffee grinder."

"It's charming," said Clear.

"And it sucks," said Chuck.

"Then it's a good thing we have you here, too," said the diplomatic Clear.

Meanwhile, Claudia had accosted a large black woman pushing a cart full of groceries and small children to the car park.

"Have *you* seen my baby?" Claudia asked the woman.

"Ain't seen no baby."

"Mama," said one of her kids.

"I lost my child, my only child."

"Where you do that?"

"Oh," said Claudia, "up in the hills."

"Why you lookin' here, then?"

"Gravity, my good woman, the cradle was moving downhill in the landslide."

"No slide here, lady," said the black woman. "We got a toxic cloud last year."

Chuck was assigning the men. D was to get meats. Doc was told to collect liquor and beer. Clear was sent after pasta, rice, grains and pulses. Then, unwilling to yield to his weakness for potato chips, Chuck wandered towards fresh produce, sentimental about desert scurvy.

He came to a range of melons, green with rough hides. Chuck felt one, and it was soft – wouldn't last as far as Nevada. He slammed the fruit on the floor. It burst. Juice and seeds ran out on the polished floor.

"Hey man, easy," called out a black, who was packing a crate with oranges. "Folks can slip on that, break their legs."

"That's right," said his friend, who was juggling mint-colored apples from a bin to his cart.

Chuck looked at the two blacks, sensing threat.

"What's it to you?" he asked.

"We don't want our grandmother breaking her hips. Old folks get a bad hip it's misery for the family."

The elan of these blacks curdled Chuck. They were doing a song and dance with the robbery. They weren't true low-lifes, but trained dudes, maybe some FBI blacks ready to arrest him. He looked up and saw the video camera eating them all, stirring slowly from side to side. That was the plan. Get the evidence, make the snatch. Fucking spooks. He took his rifle and splattered the camera with fire.

"What you doing?" reasoned one of the blacks. "We can't be on no TV now."

"Real gun, man?" the juggler wanted to know. The camera was still dripping its splinters on the ground.

"You didn't see?" Chuck was sulky.

"I saw." The smile had gone now. "What you going to do? Going to shoot us, too? Want us to be the baddies? We hide behind the dried fruit, ambush you, you come on like Chuck Norris? We throw up our arms, jump in the air, shout, 'Wow, I's dead'? You like that?"

"I'll take your oranges," said Chuck.

"Plenty more, man."

"I like yours," said Chuck. "I like that asshole way you packed them."

"They're for my granny. She got a C deficiency."

"Get yourself some more."

"I don't think so."

So Chuck took them out. One waft of fire wrapped them in falling blood. They were weeping on the floor, their blue-brown hands trying to stop the wounds. The muzak did not pause, but the aisle emptied of people. Chuck took one of the crates of oranges and sauntered on, adding Idaho potatoes, heads of broccoli and bundles of carrots to his cart.

In another part of the market, D heard the chattering noise. He thought it was a cash register gone berserk with figures. He had seen that before. There was a girl near him, in the market's pink uniform, restocking the cold meats. She was lovely in her sharp-eyed way. He thought of Rosanna Arquette.

"What was *that*?" the girl said, eager to gossip.

"Firing?" D speculated.

"You think?"

"The market seems to have been abandoned by the staff," D added in an off-hand way, letting her draw her own conclusions.

"Rats!" she was stranded, dumped on.

This girl was so piquant, with a nose like a pickle and a mouth as emblematic as the heart on a Valentine. Her eyes slipped around her face when she looked at anything. It gave an erotic sense of surface instability. How one stumbled on untrained beauties in the most unlikely neighborhoods. California! She had noticed his admiration.

"You want to make it?" she asked him. Being watched aroused her.

"Here?"

"Uh-huh." She was acting the hoodlum, daring him with a dead-eyed leer.

"You do that with customers?"

"Well, you look like you're going somewhere," she was examining his cart. "With two hundred cans of beef stew. You can tell the guys with plans." She was a little dry comic, on her honor not to laugh at the jokes.

"Actually," said D, "we have a trip ahead."

"I love trips." The girl took off her pink cap and shook free brown hair that had streaks of green and red under the lights.

"What's your name?" asked D.

She put on an innocent face, as if she hadn't heard of names.

"You look like Rosanna Arquette?" But she did not respond; she let her eyes roll. "*Baby, It's You?*" he added.

"I know," she pouted. "And it's you, and it's all it is. So why don't we?"

"Well," said good old D, resigned to his sway as a sex object. The girl was already down, shivering on the floor – the uniform had a free, skating slipperiness – and he could see the glint of her sex. He could not shut out the label picture on all the stewed beef cans.

"Oh," the girl shook, and "Oh, I love you, I love you," in time to the drive of his body with hers. Her breasts spilled like Dutch cheeses on the ground, smelling of custard, walnuts and ripe strawberry.

"I'm not going to ever let *you* go," she said. "We'll make it in all the wild places – in photo-booths, in banks. If they have banks still."

D might have slept. But there was no time. His head on the floor watched the wheels of shopping carts pass by. They churned and squealed. He started to get up and perhaps peril hardened him anew, for as he stood she came with him, impaled and as cheery as a kid on a ride.

"Wow!" she cried, and he saw the soaring face of his child mate.

"You can come too," promised D. "Wherever we're going."

"My name's Look," she told him. When he watched the slide in her vivid face it seemed he had always known this.

LIFE OF DRAGONFLIES

It is never enough to make a picture. You must secure the image and the reputation of the picture, too. You are exhausted, physically and emotionally, when you deliver your final cut to the studio. And you will have had to protect that final cut and speak out against all worries on a cut, a transition, a scene, a shot over which you may yourself have had enough doubt to occupy nine nights in a row. So you are tired from the exercise of fine judgment and by testing and re-testing your own response to inner rhythms. It may be the trimming and the fretting over the transcendence in the close-up and the "ain't life grand". Your tiredness may have reached the point of craziness that *knows* if that flicker of all the feelings thirty years have gathered is you, then the film will be all right. You may be so tired you are impotent and lucky to have a woman who lets you alone and hopes for you. It could be as close as you ever come to marrying.

Why not? You will never be more tender, going deeper and deeper in the folds of your film. You may discover that you love the form, that you could work in it like this forever. Except that you know you would die of the tiredness. Indeed, you are shocked at how much you have extended yourself, afraid of the passion you have seen and maybe a touch too fond of yourself, of your own looks and health, to risk it. But you are at your best, and you know it is good, just as you vowed that no one else would ever be blamed by you for this film. That is not hard, if you do not naturally trust others. But paranoia, too, yields to fatigue, and you may never have felt so warmly for others before, or seen the silliness in mistrust more clearly.

But this best does not equip you for what is to come, immediately. Prints will be made from the cut, and someone has to check the quality of those prints before they reach theaters. The laboratory does it; the studio does it. It would be so sweet when so tired to trust them. You learn you cannot. The decision is taken at the studio on when and where to

278

open your film. The advertising campaign is designed. Posters and trailers are made. You have been in the business seven years and these are matters that you left to others, that you never understood and never much believed in. You told yourself a picture took care of itself: if it worked, the audience bought it; if not, well . . . Tiredness would so like to hang on to that principle. Then you see a terrible ad, and you know you must not trust the studio publicity people. Then you discover that they will open your picture on the 13th of August. You knew they meant to destroy you.

Beatty has fought for the power to make *Bonnie and Clyde* his way, even fending off Jack Warner's exasperation on seeing the rushes. But there is a debt incurred in such a victory. It is that Jack now calls it "Warren's picture" and smiles a little sadly when the subject comes up. Those forty-five years' seniority have to find their moment and their advantage, and they come in the chance to be patronizing. The studio machine feels that and knows, even if Jack does not quite know it, that the studio head will bear up nobly if *Bonnie and Clyde* is a failure. A kid has to learn, after all. So we'll open it in the middle of August, at the end of the summer, but before the important fall pictures. And we'll open it in New York City, in the summer of 1967, let's see how those people back east like this weird shoot-'em-up. It may never make its way into words, but there is an attitude about – this picture will be limited.

Bonnie and Clyde opens in New York City in two theaters, the Forum and the Murray Hill, and nowhere else. The reviews are, at best, mixed. Judith Crist in *Vogue* and Hollis Alpert in the *Saturday Review* are impressed. But *Variety* sees only inconsistency and incongruity. In *The New York Times*, Bosley Crowther calls it "a cheap piece of baldfaced slapstick comedy that treats the hideous depredation of that sleazy, moronic pair as though they were as full of fun and frolic as the jazz-age cut-ups in *Thoroughly Modern Millie*" (another film of the moment, and a hit). In *Newsweek*, Joseph Morgenstern is equally offended by the clash of "the most gruesome carnage since Verdun . . . accompanied by some of the most gleeful offscreen fiddling since Grand Ole Opry . . . For those who find killing less than hilarious, the effect is also stomach-turning." He calls the picture "a squalid shoot-'em for the moron trade."

And in *Time* magazine, in an issue with a cover story "Inside the Viet Cong", there is the same horror at such jaunty violence: "Both Producer Beatty and Director Arthur Penn have elected to tell their tale of bullets and blood in a strange and purposeless mingling of fact and claptrap that teeters uncannily on the brink of burlesque. Like Bonnie and Clyde themselves, the film rides off in all directions and ends up full of holes."

There is one review of the picture that is both favorable and discerning, and it comes from Penelope Gilliatt in *The New Yorker*. She alone grasps how far the picture is concerned with fame and with reflecting on the process of film itself. She says it "is about two real thieves of the early thirties who behaved as if they thought of themselves as film stars in a movie . . . The film shows them holding up grocery stores and banks as if the two of them were box office draws who were bound to survive because of their audience pull . . . *Bonnie and Clyde* could look like a celebration of gangster glamor only to a man with a head full of wood shavings. These two visibly have the life expectancy of dragonflies: their sense of power and of unending gang fun is delusion, and to see them duping themselves is as harrowing as the spectacle of most other hoaxes. Their motive isn't gain but an urge to be theatrically remembered . . . The picture often makes you think of Lee Harvey Oswald."

Something happens in theaters that seems to bear out Ms. Gilliatt's insight. *Bonnie and Clyde* does $59,000 in its first week at two theaters. And then, in the second week, the gross goes up to $70,000. There is no way of knowing why or how – no matter how hard you work at carrying your film to the public, or how much experience you have of the business, there is a mysterious chemistry. Very quickly, a controversy arises over the violence, fuelled by repeated attacks from Bosley Crowther, never a Beatty admirer and now seemingly furious.

Of course, the violence is very real and very fake – at the same time. Some critics and moral guardsmen are outraged that attractive people are being violent and that the film rushes them away from hold-ups and murders on merry banjo music. But audiences may see how boldly the film is exploring the absurdity of violence, and the absurdist potential of film in which "reality" and fantasy work off one another. This is but a few years after the death of John Kennedy and Lee Harvey Oswald, and in a time increasingly faced by newsreel coverage of Vietnam. There are many appalled at violence, and there are some who see how far it has become a show, a reality that cannot be regained for the larger public. Real people are becoming mythic – that is what Beatty has done to those allegedly real, dog-faced desperadoes, Mr Barrow and Miss Parker. There is already an unvoiced urging – awful but compelling – in which fame is overpowering ethics and decency. And *Bonnie and Clyde* has this very enduring sub-text to the later 60s, it hates and fears authority and system.

There is also an uncommon reversal by *Newsweek* and Joseph Morgenstern. A week after his first review, he speaks again, calling his original notice "grossly unfair and regrettably inaccurate". He has seen the film a second time, with a large audience, "enjoying itself almost to the point of rapture". He may also have had a call from the producer: the telephone is not to be wasted, and if no critic will respond to bullying, still few critics are averse to flattery or to some such hesitant prattle as "I respect what you say . . . and I really value you saying the film was 'interesting', and I wish if you had the time you'd look at it again".

Morgenstern's second thoughts are not really much more intelligent that his first, but he has made a great effort, and done something that critics usually avoid: he has looked again, and he has risked the company of a large audience of "innocent" moviegoers. Now he realises that the film "knows perfectly well what to make of its violence, and makes a cogent statement with it – that violence is not necessarily perpetuated by shambling cavemen or quivering psychopaths but may also be the casual, easy experience of only slightly aberrated citizens, of jes' folks."

In its third week in Manhattan, the take is up to $74,000. By that time, the film has played two weeks at a single theater in Los Angeles, the Vogue, and takes $28,000 and $29,000. In week four, it does $69,000 in New York (the first decline) and $22,000 in Los Angeles. The following week, these declines continue, but the movie adds Cleveland to its market and picks up $30,000 there. Detroit and Chicago are added in the sixth week, and in Chicago it gets good reviews and $42,000. By its seventh week, it is the third most successful film in the country, running behind *To Sir, With Love* and *Thoroughly Modern Millie*. By week eight it is in major cities across the country, still taking $39,000 in New York, doing $40,000 in Kansas City and $18,000 at the Charles in Boston, despite local interest in the World Series.

Beatty studies the figures and uses them in his assaults on Warner Brothers. He travels widely, angling himself into local promotions. He notices the early rage for the picture in London and uses the lessons there to challenge American cities where the film is doing less well. He knows that it is doing less well than was possible. He makes himself a pest to Warners, who are taken aback by its good opening. When he should be pleased, he's asking for more. He earns dislike as well as respect for his persistence. He is told, what a pity, if only we'd known earlier, because you can never get over the first release of a movie. He starts agitating for re-release, and in the moment of fiercest bargaining he trades back a part of his ownership so that Warners will re-open, with a new campaign. This comes early in 1968, after *Bonnie and Clyde* is nominated for ten Oscars.

By then, it is an unmistakable phenomenon, and in this second, wider distribution it secures its full success, amounting to net rentals in its first year of at least $30 million. For that second release, the general audience comes out, the country kids most like the real Bonnie and Clyde, older people initially alarmed at the talk of violence but now wooed by prestige. In short, a working version of everyone, at last aware that *Bonnie and Clyde* is as much of its time as the Beatles – hard and soft, a kind of charming rape that we all like and deserve.

For its December 8, 1967, issue, *Time* has thoroughly rewritten its past. It has a cover story, "The New Cinema: Violence . . . Sex . . . Art . . .", with a silkscreen collage by Robert Rauschenberg devoted to *Bonnie and Clyde*. It reassesses its earlier review for comparing the real and the fictitious Bonnie and Clyde – "a totally irrelevant exercise". And it claims, in Stefan Kanfer's story, that America is now ready to handle complex movies and deal with them as it would with . . . art! The New Wave has reached Hollywood and Warren Beatty is its boss. The Earl Scruggs record of *Foggy Mountain Breakdown* is a hit. Chic young women look like Faye Dunaway's Bonnie.

A Californian film critic comes to New York, fired from *McCall's* and unhappy at the *New Republic*. It is Pauline Kael, who writes a 9,000-word essay on the film for the *New Yorker* in October. It is a stimulating piece of work, and it helps get Ms Kael on the staff of the *New Yorker* even if it does not match the briefer insights in Penelope Gilliatt's first review. But it is an event, a little like Bonnie's poem in the papers, and it surely tells Beatty's story in a way he likes.

Among other things, Kael remarks that Beatty is for the first time less burdened by his limits as an actor. She goes to the heart of American film-making in seeing how power and success are the greatest stimulants:

> ". . . in a number of roles Beatty, probably because he doesn't have the technique to make the most of his lines in the least possible time, has depended too much on intuitive non-acting – holding the screen for too long as he acted out self-preoccupied characters in a lifelike, boringly self-conscious way. He has a gift for slyness, though, as he showed in *The Roman Spring of Mrs Stone*, and in most of his films he could hold the screen – maybe because there seemed to be something going on in his mind, some

kind of calculation. There was something smart about him – something shrewdly private in those squeezed-up non-actor's eyes – that didn't fit the clean-cut juvenile roles. Beatty was the producer of *Bonnie and Clyde*, responsible for keeping the company on schedule, and he has been quoted as saying, 'There's not a scene that we have done that we couldn't do better by taking another day.' This is the hell of the expensive way of making movies, but it probably helps explain why Beatty is more intense than he has been before and why he has picked up his pace. His business sense may have improved his timing."

*

He also learns how extensive the business is, how many things there are to worry over. Time and again, people are touched and impressed by the dogged way this star comes off the screen with persistent questions about why his image there is not quite clear or his voice not loud enough. It is a way of learning humor.

He goes with *Bonnie and Clyde* to London for its opening there, and he attends the critics' screening at the Warner Theatre in Leicester Square. It is a large place, and he is struck by how modest the sound is, especially that of gunfire. In making the picture, he has drawn upon years of viewing and remembering, and he has always liked the emotional force of the gunfire in George Stevens' Western, *Shane*, made in 1953. He has talked to Stevens about the innovative techniques used on that film, and with his own sound man, Francis Stahl, he has played with different ways of recording shots so that they "jump out at you", moving the viewer with a mixture of fear and arousal.

But in London, the shots sound tame. "So I ran up to the projectionist, and I walked into the booth, and he was a little surprised to see me, because I was in the movie. He didn't know I'd produced it. And he said, 'You're the producer of this picture?' And I said, 'Yeah.' And he said, 'Well, I've really helped you out in the sound here. I've made a chart, and I turn it up here and down here, and so on. It's the worst mixed picture . . . I haven't had a picture so badly mixed since *Shane*.'"

Check-out

"What's happening?" asked Cy Lighthiser, over his shoulder. He was at the check-out, reading an *Enquirer* story on how Lee Majors had lost 21 pounds in seven days and was about to make astonishing career headway.

"Hey," said Cy. He looked twice at D's companion. "Take-away Rosanna Arquette?"

D put his arm around the young woman – her identity could so easily get out of his control.

"Looks like Rosanna," said Cy. He was examining her, as if she were an antique of controversial provenance, holding back his bid.

"That's right?" said Look. She let her head loll to one side, as if it was so boring it was a scream, and she showed Cy the ball of gum in her mouth.

"You could go on shows," he reckoned.

"This is Look," D explained. "Can't you see it?"

"Sensational!" cried Cy. And Look grinned so Cy added, "Right!" with feeling, and the shelf-filler about to be hoisted from humble circumstances writhed up to Cy in bashful twitter so that he picked her gum as cinnamon. "You're a quiet riot," he told her, Lee Majors' redemption forgotten.

"Yeah?" she asked. It was a movie moment.

"What was that racket back there?" Cy nodded towards the far reaches of the market.

"Backfire?" D surmised.

"Backfire, back story – what's the diff?" Cy was studying the shelves and their divisions, brooding on the sugar and cake mix aisle. "Kids, I have just had a hell of an idea. You can tell your grandchildren you were here when I had it."

"Fantastic," giggled Look.

284

Check-out

"Can't tell you now," said Cy. "Wait till we're on our way." Then a doubt crossed his mind and he looked at D. "She's coming?"

Look said, "I guess so," her olive oval eyes swinging from one man to the other, trying to assess the originating force in the going. Then she winked at Cy, "D swept me off my feet, you know."

"Do I?" said Cy. "He's a musketeer."

There should be some musical flourish as this crew of adventurers and frauds put their all together in limousines and campers to make it away to the desert. Chuck comes backing into the camper, his leveled Uzi holding off the several blacks whose pals he had wasted. The bounty was brought in and loaded, with Clear at his best in the arrangements. They were at the point of being off, when a gaunt black woman came up to Claudia, led by Beau, carrying a bundle of rags.

"Oh, sweetheart," called Beau. "A moment."

"What is it?" cried Claudia to the air. She was not quite focusing, but speaking to the fates and the darkness outside her gathered light.

"You the one los' the chile?" asked the woman.

"I am, I am —"

"Got one here," said the woman.

"It's at least a possible," whispered Beau.

"How could this woman find my child?" wailed the mother.

"Claudia, you never know. What you have lost, someone else must find." Beau pulled back the shabby wrappings to disclose a baby.

"It's white," said the black woman.

"I don't know," Claudia complained. "How can I know?"

Cy came up to offer his opinion. He tried to remember – babies do look alike. Then he shrugged and told his wife in a bargaining way, "What you got to lose?"

"Claudia dear," said Beau. "You could be a universal mother, like Ingrid in that Chinese orphan picture." D saw him slip a twenty into the old blanket in which the black woman had wrapped the baby. The child had already been inserted in a more suitable shawl.

"You all be well in Christ," said the black woman and hobbled away.

"What a fine soul," sighed Beau.

"It's not your step sister." D was ready to be indignant.

"How should I know?" protested Beau. "It surely wasn't the old crone's, was it? You want Claudia doing her woeful Crawford bit forever?"

"And this gives your lawyers a better chance at the inheritance."

"You're cynical, baby," said Beau, with the utmost fastidiousness.

As they bundled themselves and their provisions into the vehicles, Drew came up beside D, as silent and mournful as an assassin.

"Picking up more women?"

"I bumped into her."

"You're a disgrace."

"If I am —"

"If?" She was proud of him, no matter the hurt.

"Look will be useful to us," said D, on the spot. "She has experience storing foodstuffs."

"Look?" Drew glanced swiftly at her rival. "Looks like Debra Winger. That's what she looks."

"Others think Rosanna Arquette," said D.

Drew scowled. "No way. No comparison." She was bitter a moment. "Rosanna could have played me. You know, if they'd done me."

"You should play yourself," said D.

"Too late. They're used to me. 'Old Drew' they say. They like me. They understand my position. But I'm gone. Best chance I had was for some hot-shot writer," she glared at him, "to write a script about me. Then Arquette would have been made for it."

"I do see it," D admitted, hoping to make her see that he had eyes for her *and* the Arquette look.

"You horny goof," she was smiling at him. "Why don't you get out?"

"Not again."

"We could get out together. You can do what you want with me. You know that, don't you?

"Well, yes, I —"

"But it bores you? Let me tell you, you'll wish you'd settled for being bored." She looked at him again, struck by something new.

"What is it?" The worry came so quick.

"You're getting better looking," said Drew. "I swear you are."

AS GOOD AS IT GETS

It is as good as it gets. It may be all he can imagine ever wanting, without straining or altering himself. He is so high, he sees other people around using drugs and he laughs like a happy kid wondering why they need them, when you can do success. But it may never be better for him, and he is young enough to have ample time for discovering. He has been famous before, and no one has had difficulty thinking the worst or the best of him romantically. He did stand for a breathtaking limit – call it cool or callous. But the face was that of a tight-minded, spoiled kid. Now everyone has to admit a different kind of emergence, a Beatty they had not seen or understood. It is heaven if you think you have been misunderstood, but it is the first moment in which the intelligence, the watchfulness, or just the smarts he prizes, may falter, and may even be seduced by what people think of him.

He has a hit that runs counter to one of Hollywood's great warnings – that a picture never transforms itself commercially once it has opened. So he can wear the magical exception lightly, and know that everyone in the business knows it was his extraordinary persistence and accuracy – his being right – that lifted *Bonnie and Clyde* into new life. There will be a great deal of money coming to him over the years. And he feels so good about it all that he may even look forward to keeping such an eye on the numbers that he is never cheated. Once upon a time at a party, Beatty knows, Jack Warner had cornered John Wayne, who had been avoiding the studio head. What is it, Duke? Warner asked. And the Duke shuffled and reddened, too angry but too proud to say out loud that he thinks Warners were cheating him. But the Duke spat it out, and Jack Warner grinned and said, "Duke, I know, but that would have happened anyway, and we're your friends!" Warren could always ask Warner to stop embarrassing him if he thinks the studio is cooking the books.

Beatty has accountants and lawyers who actually urge him to spend more or invest more. This book is not going to get access to Warren's

David Hockney, *Chair and Shirt*, 1972

Swimming pool, as seen from the old wing of the Beverly Wilshire Hotel; now
the site of the new wing (Beverly Wilshire Hotel)

financial records. We have to guess. And I'd guess that over the years he has paid rather more tax than he might have done, because he never takes quickly to advice or investments (no matter he pays for the advice) and never realises that their is sense in spending money that will otherwise go in taxes. Not that he's being stupid. It's just that he may not trust anyone to be as clever as possible, and just that he is not naturally daring, generous or free with money. And when he signs the IRS check, he tells himself it is being responsible and public-spirited; it is a hint to himself that he takes the good of the country seriously.

Of course, he spends money, but never at a rate that will put his reserves at risk. He stays at the best hotels, he wears good clothes, he eats at expensive restaurants, and he travels a lot. He has whatever he wants – cars, places to live, clothes sometimes. But the business is himself. He never seems to think of owning the things that appeal to so many young successes in the business – boats, planes, palaces, islands, studios and even the business. He has never yet sought to make or distribute a picture with his own money. In 1967, he looks like the new man in Hollywood, and he can be cold and insolent to the stalwarts of the old system, scorning their stupidity, but he is not averse to the system, he will never go near partnership with any of the other young geniuses who come into film after *Bonnie and Clyde*.

He does not buy a house; he prefers what is always a modest arrangement at the Beverly Wilshire. Indeed, success may make him feel vindicated in *leaving* home, in enjoying his detachment. He relaxes a little: everyone says he is more open, and more amusing. And he has Julie Christie as his new princess, as if to prove he is moving on and attuned to now.

It is in 1968 – which is easily recollected as a terrible time, because of assassinations, Vietnam and Chicago. But it is a moment in which people feel as internally alive as they do close to death, and *Bonnie and Clyde* is often cited as an instance of this. One of the appealing undertones of the 60s – and a source of the age's subsequent betrayal – is the sense of thrill. For that exquisite, dangerous momentariness will pass, and there will be more disappointment left after it than true change.

But in 1968, Warren Beatty can feel he has risen above the silly system of pictures, that he is closer to the heartbeat of the country than movie people have been before. And it will still be a while before other people in the business think of him as part of the bullshit, and a while longer still before he realises that.

He is so happy that he may not notice how far the tiredness has reduced him to doing very little. But his body and his soul will pick up on this rhythm of doing everything and then nothing. And the most intriguing and mysterious part of that habit, and the part that beckons undying reticence and shyness, is nothing. What now proves his success is, for days on end, for a year if he wills it, he can do nothing. It does make all the contorted, fussy and aggrandising forms of something seem foolish. He has always been an actor of pauses, of hesitation. And if *Bonnie and Clyde* made him quicker, then the peace that comes when it is over may make the attraction of a much larger pause all the greater. It is like being dead, yet still alert to your own funeral: watching the show and imagining you are its director.

Julie Christie is the perfect mate for happiness, she is so fully given to experience and lack of cant. He has encountered her while he was with Leslie Caron in London: he may explain to Leslie, wide-eyed, that it's very difficult being in London in their particular circle, and *not* meeting glorious young women. Caron will only see how ready he is to be met, however strenuously he is campaigning for the wisdom of marriage to her. And Christie is not just physically gorgeous: she is the promise of a new kind of wild, uninhibited actress who sees the sham of movie-making and will not be deterred from addressing the issue of how to be a decent person.

Christie has had a small, striking part in John Schlesinger's *Billy Liar* in 1963. Two years later, she has won the Oscar for the same director in *Darling*, about a young woman who proves her own moral ruin as a success in pictures. Immediately, she is winning some of the best female roles around: Lara in *Dr Zhivago* and the two women in Truffaut's *Fahrenheit 451*. She lives in London with an art teacher: they are devoted, she tells the press he is the only man for her, as if she wanted this to be so, wanted to convince him and her, and felt the pressure of her fame. In 1967, she opens in *Far from the Madding Crowd*.

It is not really Beatty who takes her away from the art teacher – her destiny cannot escape moving out. Caron says it is simply Warren's weakness for Oscar nominees. We might see the relationship as part of his continuing attraction to women who are not American, and who may help him see the narrowness and naivety of his country. But Christie is appealing because her need for liberty is more demanding than Warren's, because she surprised him by volunteering for freedom he is shy to spell out. And he must guess, quickly, that he is never going to find a better screen partner. The event is buried in the future still, but in hindsight, in 1975, he may realise that there never was another actress as likely, as happy, to risk her prestige, her respectability, by saying out loud, "I'd like to suck his cock", the line from *Shampoo* that flusters Beatty a good deal more than it does Christie.

In 1967, when she is making *Petulia* in San Francisco, Warren is up and down the Pacific coast to see her. He does follow her, and arrange his busy schedule to see her as much as possible. Christie comes to Los Angeles for the 1968 Academy Awards. Warren does not win anything personally. *In the Heat of the Night* is reckoned to be the best picture, Rod Steiger is best actor in the same picture and Katharine Hepburn best actress for *Guess Who's Coming to Dinner?* Hollywood is still at the stage of being impressed by its own ponderous racial liberalism. *Bonnie and Clyde* wins for photography, and Estelle Parsons as best supporting actress. Which is as much as to say Hollywood is still perplexed by the picture. But at Oscar time, the movie is riding very high and Warren smiles away the loss – he must feel his best chances are ahead, and cannot foresee the hard night he has to come at the Oscars.

Christie stays on with him at the Beverly Wilshire: there will be a similar gap in productivity in both their careers. They must be very much in love for Julie Christie to be content to live so long in Warren's suite, the Escondido, at the Wilshire, a very good hotel wedged between a Boulevard that is really a highway and blocks of composed suburbia. There is nowhere to walk to – no parks, no lanes, no secret places – and nothing to do once one knows the several bars, restaurants and the bookstore at the hotel. Every time you come or go you have to let your car be parked by the valet. It is not easy to storm out after a row if the car is not waiting, but must be retrieved by the polite Mexican kids.

The suite at the Wilshire is modest – Elvis Presley had used it as a rehearsal room when he stayed at the hotel – two rooms and a bathroom, with a balcony, many mirrors and the untidiness of someone who says he knows where everything is – books, scripts, magazines, contracts, correspondence. There is another room in the hotel where his secretary works, but he keeps the things he wants to read or refer to in the suite. And after *Bonnie and Clyde* he is being sent everything – not just scripts, but the galleys of any novel anyone hopes could be filmed. He does his best to look at them, even if he starts to employ readers. It is a strange dilemma, so duty-bound to literature and so conscientious about hard work, suspecting a masterpiece in the pile if he can find it, but knowing he could probably pick up any book, say "This?", and get it done. Every month or so, someone throws out the old and the stale. He is a publisher's clearing house, not a man with a library.

There are room service trays buried in paper in the suite. There is a large bed, the telephones and the mirrors, and the weights he works out with. Over the two and a half decades of his career, no one has seen Beatty out of condition or overweight. Yet he does not jog on Rodeo, Wilshire and Charleville; and he is not seen on courts or at the gym. He does his exercises upstairs, on the carpet and in the mirror or on the balcony. It is as if his perfection had to seem casual, or as if the ex-jock was reluctant to show strain in public. He may even wonder whether he should murmur to one or another of the would-be interviewers that he gets his best exercise in bed, or trust them to deduce it? This is a joke Warren's father sometimes tells – a man of no greater fame than having two top stars for children. Proud and overwhelmed at the same time: "I did my greatest work in bed." What sort of man would be content with that?

Because of Julie Christie he is often in London, and he becomes closer friends with Roman Polanski, who is also there. They have had an acquaintance since the Pole's first feature film, *Knife in the Water*, caused such a stir in Europe and America. Fox had an idea to remake the story, in 1964, with Burton and Taylor as the couple and Beatty as the interloper who separates them. In London, Beatty meets Polanski at parties given by Victor Lownes, an executive with the Playboy organisation. Polanski asks Beatty if he would play the husband, the devil's agent, in his forthcoming picture, *Rosemary's Baby*. But, "He procrastinated, as usual, and finally rejected the role as not important enough. Warren's parting shot was, 'Hey, can I play Rosemary?'" John Cassavetes will get the husband's part.

And again, Beatty is in London, in August 1969, when Polanski's wife, Sharon Tate, and others, are murdered at the director's house on Cielo Drive in the canyons beneath Mulholland. Beatty, Lownes, Richard Sylbert and others do what they can to look after Polanski. Beatty is one of the close group that flies with him, back from London to Los Angeles, to confront the horror. He is one of those who takes turns to keep the Pole company, maintaining "a stream of improbable stories, mostly relating to his hyperactive sex life" which Polanski supposes are meant to make him laugh.

Beatty and Polanski have tastes in common: beautiful women, movies in which violence plays a part, and the roving life of show business celebrities. But put the two side-by-side, and one must see how circumspect and middle-class Beatty is in comparison. Yet this is not the only time he will be fascinated by those who live much closer than he to

293

danger. Why should he not be curious about what disaster does, as well as friendly with Polanski?

When Polanski thinks of working again, he sees Beatty as his natural actor. He wants to make a film of the book *Papillon*, about escape from Devil's Island. He approaches Warren – "Like Papillon, he could con anyone into anything" – and Beatty is enthusiastic. Polanski goes to Paris to raise money for the venture, and a few days later Warren follows. They are supposed to discuss the script. But several nights pass with nothing but "parties, discos, and girls."

Recognising Beatty's characteristic delay, Polanski tells him it is time to work. "You're absolutely right," grins Warren, "we've had our fun." But perhaps he is still set on therapy for Roman. There is another night of partying and in his hang-over Polanski is frustrated.

He goes to London for a break and gets a call there from Warren, who seems now to have read the script. He refers to one scene that it calls for: "I'm not going to appear bare-ass. It's a hang-up I have. What did you say the budget was?" Polanski reads this as refusal. They part and the project drifts on, to another director and to Steve McQueen in the lead.

There are other parts to be turned down, of course; that is steady employment now. He does not do *Laughter in the Dark*, from Nabokov's novel, and he will not play Michael Corleone in *The Godfather*. The first has a tinge of gayness to it, he thinks, and as for the second, he has had his shot at being Italian. Suppose he and Christie laugh together at the foolishness of contrasting accents and foreigners for all those absurd scripts. This is the late 1960s, when acting can seem like an escape from the richness of life's responsibilities. It is in a state of laughter and happiness, of a power that could do anything or nothing, that he agrees to act in *The Only Game in Town*.

This picture comes from a play by Frank Gilroy that failed on Broadway: it is about an aging showgirl and a gambler who meet in Las Vegas and fall in love. Tammy Grimes and Barry Nelson play the leads on stage. When it is all done with, and the $7 million loss is clear, no one can recall why this film was made, except in the search for success. It is a vehicle for Elizabeth Taylor that will reunite her with George Stevens, who directed her in *A Place in The Sun* and *Giant*; and it is a property full of the worldly sadness stars think becomes them. It also promises to be an easy film to make, for it is essentially a play for two characters.

Yet it turns out a kind of monster. Originally, Frank Sinatra is cast as the gambler, Joe Grady, but he withdraws when the start is held up by Ms Taylor's hysterectomy. And so Beatty takes the part at the eleventh hour: some say for $750,000 , some for $1.2 million. The movie is to be made in Paris, despite location research in Las Vegas, because Taylor wants to be close to Richard Burton, who is making *Staircase* in the same city. And so much of the aura of Nevada is brought in to the Paris studio – craps tables and gambling apparatus have to be flown in and a vast Vegas perspective is built, of hotel towers and mountains beyond, to be seen through the windows of the story.

The shooting begins in October 1968, and it will last over 100 days, with time in Los Angeles at Fox and even a few days on location in Las Vegas. Despite two stars so potent and prominent, the film is not released until March 1970, which is a sign that some people have been asking, "What are we going to do with it?" It does not work; it takes maybe $3 million towards its cost of $10 million.

There is a story about its making that may help explain this. The first day on the set in Paris, Warren strolls over to where Elizabeth is sitting. What follows is like a parody of his seductive routine to those who have observed it. He studies the actress, never losing a polite but slightly bewildered smile. She knows she is being looked at, and she rises to the scrutiny and its challenge. She has heard of him. She's only seven years older than he is, and she has noticed his taste for brunettes and English origins. But she is engaged in one of the world's most celebrated romances, with Richard Burton. They may recall the earlier prospect of Polanski's *Knife in the Water*, and its hint of Warren's power. Will Warren test her out himself, will he make her decide whether she has to turn him down and have his failure show? Does he work out in public view?

So he prowls around her and then he laughs out loud, but to himself. "What is it?" she asks. He has aroused her curiosity. He has started by making her ask – to show what he might do. "Oh, nothing," he says. "It's nothing." And he walks away.

The following day there is still no explanation. So Taylor goes to him, and asks again, "Why did you laugh, Warren?" He has the timing to wait here, long enough for both of them to see the world press howling with another coup for Liz, to see the lunacy and the indignity. Then he says, "I laughed because nobody can be that beautiful." It is a sweet and voluminous line, and it tells her from the start that she is not quite real, not even possible, not simply or definitely there. She is her image, and he is just a mortal.

The film they make preserves this odd, close-company distance. *The Only Game in Town* is not a movie about people. In the script, they are

295

With Elizabeth Taylor in *The Only Game in Town* (Twentieth Century-Fox)

both failures, downcast and flaky; but in the casting they have become inexplicably disconsolate gods. The picture is about two actors considering what they are doing. That puts it more in Beatty's vein than in Taylor's. When the script says they are in bed and in love, he looks wary – of her emotional power, or of her recovery from illness. He wants to edge away. For he has elected to play his role as a fake watching impossibility, mocking the lines, the character and the gigolo-stooge way he gets to play the piano for her. "Give me a kiss," he asks her. "Why should I?" she says. And he answers, "Because I'm a winner, and winners are irresistible." But there is something in his stance and distance that knows he cannot risk himself, and it feels camp or contrived when he has to be a helpless gambler. Self-control is the cool, dark place where he is hiding. Years later, Beatty will note he has played gamblers three times (here, in *Kaleidoscope* and in *McCabe and Mrs Miller*), but never actually gambled himself. This is a curious omission when it would be so easy for so wealthy a researcher to play seriously one night, or one week-end, or . . . Is it a thrill he fears? Or does he say everything is a gamble, every word, meeting or kiss?

As for Taylor, her great emotional need is warned off. Perhaps she wants a more reckless lover. The picture is a failure and a curiosity, often touching and funny, and filled with Warren's elegant, charming promise of himself that finds he is making the picture, absent-mindedly, when he thought he had refused it. "It was like telling a joke underwater," he remarks afterwards, dismissing failure.

The writer, Frank Gilroy, meets briefly with Beatty in Paris, after he has written the script. But when Warren is cast, George Stevens asks Gilroy to go to Beatty's Paris hotel for an evening and read the entire script to him. Read it into his record.

Much later, Gilroy sits down to look at a rough cut with Stevens. "It became very apparent the movie was a disaster. I had been ready to make notes. It was beyond that. Warren was the best thing in it. He was working hard and well. But other things had gone hopelessly wrong. And it proved to be Stevens' last film, and the last film of producer Fred Kohlmar too. I think it was sunk when they went to Paris. Maybe if they could have gone to Vegas and made it very real for $1.98. And yet it had meant a lot to Stevens. Something in the story moved him very much."

And George Stevens will be one of the few directors Beatty refers to when he thinks of the best – an instinctive and emotional man, but a controlled, careful director, sometimes a little academic. He has a way of arriving at very strong scenes and then filming them studiously from every camera angle he can think of. George Stevens makes several very successful films; he is a respected liberal and a heartfelt American; he likes order and decency, and he believes in the outsider getting his chance in the system. But he never quite proves himself as a film artist. And he is not far from Beatty's model for directing, a very significant influence on *Reds*.

Terrific note

"I feel strong on how we stand," announced Cy Lighthiser as the camper made its way through gray-dawning suburbs. "Not solid, but positive." None of the traffic lights was working now, and Clear – who had head position in the convoy – edged across intersections, looking for movement in the dingy streets. "Of course," Cy conceded, "things could be better."

"Right," snapped Drew. "I could have a part and someone to trust. You could have your baby, and we might be hopeful about next week."

"I never have five cents for next week," said Cy. "I take 'em day by day."

Drew regarded him as if it was that attitude that had let things get out of hand. "What about you?" she turned on D. He had known there would come this lunge in her attention. He would have to suffer for his Look.

"It might be worse?" he suggested carefully. "We're getting out of the city."

"And you like to have the story moved on, get some momentum going, the smell of wild flowers and gunpowder on the hot air – kind of thing?"

"Well, I've not been out of the city before. I'm curious to see a desert."

Drew was shut out by this innocence. It sounded docile but mad. She looked at him askance, in case he had been teasing. But all she saw were his eyes set on whatever he imagined desert to be.

"I've seen films about the desert," he added. "*Zabriskie Point* –"

"That's very desert," said Drew.

"And a lot of Peckinpah," said D.

"Oh well," she breathed, waving her hand, dismissing more talk with benediction. "I was the only woman I know went with him he didn't turn on."

"He was very rough with Claudia," Cy commented.

Drew was grinning as she remembered: "He put you in the position of defending him, and he had that wicked look because he knew you wanted to say how terrible he was."

"I wrote a picture for him once," said Doc. "He was going to do it. We just couldn't get the right actress."

"What was that?" Cy wanted to know.

"About a woman with a false eye and a wooden leg. And she was bald. Only, she's also very sexy and attractive. But most men don't see it at first. So she becomes a contract killer. Sam was high on it."

"I would have done that," said Drew.

"There was this great ending when she finally gets the guy she's wanted. And he decides he's in love with her. He realises she's sensational looking –"

"I can see it," Drew was carried away.

"And they're in bed, and he screws her all he can. And then it's a while later, and he's still in her, and she says, 'You stay here. I'm going to cook us some eggs.' And she gets up and goes to the kitchen. And he's lying there, half-asleep, but very slowly he realises she's left the part of her he's in in the bed."

Drew was laughing out loud at the end of the story. And Look was laughing too, but that didn't deter Drew. The two women were guessing they might get along.

"How would Sam have done that?" asked Cy.

"Done it?" Doc never smiled.

"The bit of her he was still in."

"Well," said Doc, "I told you. We couldn't get the actress."

"Sam said actresses weren't worth patience," said Drew proudly.

"I like his deserts," said D, after a pause.

And then Cy, a while later, put it to Doc, "You made that up?"

"The story? Sure. I'm a writer."

"I mean you made it up that Sam was going to do it? You couldn't *do* that."

"He could have done it, Cy."

"A woman who comes apart?" Cy was outraged. Claudia had bred in him an ideal of feminine completeness.

"Just a woman who's lived hard," said Doc. "One day, we'll all be parts."

"One bright day I'll have Eyes' dick," snorted Cy. "What'll he do then?"

"Oh, he'll go back to the magic wand," said Clear from the driver's seat.

The camper shook with laughter; the unevenness of the unmaintained streets was lost in merriment. It is natural in any company in awe of someone or some thing, or travelling toward it from afar in a spirit of reverence, that there should be a momentary need to laugh at the person or the object. For there must be a humor in greatness if it is not to soar into absurdity or tyranny. Gods should have the wit to reckon on this and deal tenderly with prayers that cannot be met, responding with a courteous rejection slip. A paranoid in Eyes – if such a creature existed – could have felt threatened by the laughter and sent a drunken truck to smash them. But our Eyes would have known the laughter was normal.

D realised they were going to pass close to his home. Here were trashy corners and foul alleys he knew, desolate sites where he walked the children on hot afternoons. Without drawing attention to it, at the proper turning he stared down the long gray chute towards his building. It was there still, not stirring. Perhaps all his children were asleep, their small snores freshening the damp on their pillows. What bliss to look at the surrender of their sprawled heads, to be so tired that rest came in like a tide.

The wheels screeched: D imagined a streak of cat squeezed beneath them, a bloody fur skid on the blacktop.

But Clear called out cheerfully, "D, we could easily look in on your family. Aren't they hereabouts?"

"Well –" he struggled to dissemble.

"Oh, treats," cried Beau. "Let's see D's place."

D felt hot shame pouring from his face. "There's really no need," he said.

But Drew wouldn't have it. "No need to tell your wife you're going?" He wished she wouldn't say it, but there was an unfailing kindness in her saying it for his sake. It was only in persistent ties that ethics had any chance, stretching to encompass dilemmas that the solitary could always regard as fate's ill-will.

"Down there," D admitted. Clear worked at the steering wheel and brought the unwieldy caravan around behind him, as cumbersome as a python turning a corner while it swallowed a donkey.

"Maybe your wife could lay on breakfast?" said Cy. "Pancakes perhaps?"

"We couldn't impose on her," said Clear. "And there's a breakfast stop planned in the desert."

"We shouldn't be late then," urged Cy.

"A quick call," said Clear. "I won't even turn off the engine." D caught his reassuring smile in the mirror (the sweet pacts people put together), but he wondered if Clear was fearful of never starting again.

"Here, I think," said Clear, coming to a halt outside the mottled charcoal front of a block. Amid blocks so similar, there was nothing to make this building stand out. Of course, Clear knew it; he probably had specifications.

"I'll hurry in, then," muttered D.

"I'm coming," said Drew. And Look would not let him go either. So D, it seemed, had to say hallo-and-goodbye to his official loved ones with two new goodies, both a little the glossier for recent loving. How many times in one day would D have to do it? He did stagger as he stepped down from the vehicle, but Drew and Look were there with hands in his armpits, like angels lifting an amazed soul into heaven.

They went up the echoing stone staircases, stepping over the garbage, and came to D's floor, wintry and fishy.

"This is so like my building," said Look.

Drew was ready to talk about her Westwood duplex and parents in the Valley. But how could she touch this pitiless, unpromising world? It made her more impressed by D's politeness – he might have turned out a killer.

The door to the unit was open.

"They're up?" asked Drew. No doubt the poor had to be.

But D was surprised. Had C been up all night, trying to find some authorities? Had she had to deal with the odious Scrug? He shuddered. What had he left them to?

He went in, and his girlfriends surged in behind him, hushed but blatantly curious, like kids examining a party spread.

There was no one in the unit. All the beds were made.

"Gone back to mother, maybe," said Drew.

"There is no mother," D explained. "Nothing like that." He saw that his scripts were gone, too, along with his dictionaries and favorite reference books. As far as he could tell, very few clothes had been taken in the departure, but all his vital papers were missing.

"They could be at an all-night entertainment center," Look offered.

The suggestion horrified D. Could his influence die so quickly?

The plainness of the unit was sinking in on Drew, leaving a sadness she could not express. Yet Look was discovering a blackened stove on a broken floor like those in her home. Drew felt her distance from it all, and she half-supposed that D and this Look were made for each other – if the world must always stay as it was. Then she rallied. "Well, sweetheart," she said to D. "We know they'll be all right. And we should be moving on."

D wanted to get away, but he felt the urge to stay, too, to wait for their return, to be here as if nothing had happened or ever would.

"You've started to go, D," said Drew. "I expect your wife knows."

That would explain their unaccountable absence. It was the sign he was looking for, the bleak response to his own desperate measure.

"I'll leave a note," said D.

"Oh yeah, a note would be terrific," Look agreed.

And so D wrote this – "I got back early in the morning. Found you all out. I am off to the desert, to see Eyes. Hope the earthquake has not troubled you. Such tumultuous times. Take care of yourselves. Who knows what will happen to us all? My love, D" – and left the page on the table with an empty milk bottle on top of it. Then he reconsidered and replaced the milk bottle with the white case of money he had been carrying. He was pleased to be rid of it, and he felt freer now for whatever was to come.

With Julie Christie in *McCabe and Mrs Miller* (Warner Brothers)

McCABE AND MISS CHRISTIE

Warren loves Julie – are there enough conifers in the British Columbian forests for them to carve out their feelings? But if you're filming there you don't want every tree in sight branded with their heart-and-arrows. No, if you're making a movie with an actor and an actress who are in love, better to have their days spent somewhat apart and their screen roles not always, all the time, in kissing scenes and bedroom sprawls. They have enough of that in their honey evenings together; imaginative creatures that actors are, they may even be close to having enough of it altogether, with Warren discovering the problem of dialling directly in the north-west wilderness. It is perfection for the picture, and the lovers, if the script thwarts them, if it makes them partners beset by misunderstanding and mettlesomeness. That way, they look at one another as they might have done when they first met – and it is the looking that film wants, no more. The medium is so callous to those whose looks it sucks on – it is a lesson in modern coldness.

McCabe and Mrs Miller thrives. It is a Robert Altman picture, made a couple of years after the career-making hit of his *M.A.S.H.* And let us note that that picture – and then its influence on modern television – might not have been possible without the example of *Bonnie and Clyde*. For *M.A.S.H.* works on the same stew of apparent opposites: a field hospital in the Korean war where the blood and ruin of the operating table exists a foot and a half beneath banter from a 1930s comedy. It works, and the sleepy public learns another lesson – that in the pits of horror and death it is possible to make jokes. Indeed, the survivors may be distinguished by the intriguing harmony of their poker faces and their jazzy lines. Early in *M.A.S.H.*, at least, there are moments of life that have somehow crept on to the screen, so adult, so startling, the medium may be changing: it is probably nearing its end. Altman is one of the best directors America will ever have, and it is Beatty's good fortune that – in love with Christie – he waltzes into the director's demanding arms.

As if someone has felt the true meaning of *Bonnie and Clyde*, or something in the air is climatically leaned upon by it, *McCabe and Mrs Miller* is a gentle mockery of identity and reputation. It is as if, in four years (the space of a college education, after all), wisdom has settled in so that it can see, whereas the blaze of meaning in one film is valid and fun, a decent man a few years later has to move on, has to be subject to more doubt and to the altogether larger feeling for things that knows in art (as opposed to sensation) identity is always mistaken.

And so we have John Q. McCabe (the Q is never filled out by the picture, allowing us to play with thoughts of Quentin, Query or even Quilty – or is McCabe a true modernist, and is the Q just Q, not Q., standing for something, but like the O in David O Selznick, a beat for rhythm, meaning nothing?). He comes plodding into Presbyterian Church some time around 1900, looking as good as Warren Beatty ever will. He wears a fur coat, black shirts, a bushy beard and flowing dark hair, mysteriously shampooed all the time, the whole set off by a crisp black derby, just as hard, curly and detachable as the frosty little sayings that McCabe pops out to ward off conversation or investigation of himself.

They are, "You know how to square a circle? You shove a four by four up a mule's ass" or "If a frog had wings he wouldn't bump his ass so much, you follow me?" McCabe does look like a dandy on this woebegone frontier; he is taken for a very lethal and distinguished gunslinger; and he begins to deport himself like a business genius, a gambler, an impresario and the manager of the few whores who do not have access to his shampoo. But he is worried about his ass, and quite properly so, for he is one of the great idiots of fiction. Let us be clear: Q is the best role Warren Beatty has yet taken.

There then arrives in Presbyterian Church Mrs Miller, an English (I would guess south London) madam who has a team of girls that includes Shelley Duvall. She moves in on the town and on the truly frail brain of John McCabe. He watches her eat a zesty meal (his own stomach settles for raw eggs in whiskey), and while she scoffs that and sniffs his "cheap Jockey Club cologne", she devours him in a snatched glance and tells him, "You think small, because you're afraid to think big."

So she gives him a deal: his money, her girls and know-how. She'll pay back the investment, and then they'll go 50–50. But they are partners only, and if, say, John Q comes knocking on Mrs Miller's door for solace, why he has to drop his grubby dollars in her pink, heart-shaped box, along with all the others. When the caution and the timidity and the business pride of McCabe watches the brisk dexterity with which he is taken over, the pain and wonder in Warren's eyes – the sheer perplexity of guardedness taken out of itself – is a thing of beauty. His watching, listening face, and its efforts to mask amazement, will never be finer. You notice, within the beard, those big soft lips, like tenderness hoping to be mistaken for a tough cat. Whereas Julie Christie's mouth is made to wolf oysters as big and soft as men.

The business flourishes. In its gloomy days and mole-like mining spirit, Presbyterian Church grows a little happier. McCabe is cock of the walk, and only Mrs Miller yearns for something else, and looks for it in opium. Then bigger business comes to find them, to swallow them. Mrs Miller knows, of course: we realise that, eater as she is, she has been chewed over in her time. She knows the name of the larger company, Harrison & Shaughnessy, and she knows they are not to be temporised with. But McCabe has never heard of them. Where has he been? Maybe in his room alone, working up his cryptic jokes ("You boys know about the frog that got ate up by the eagle?")?

He makes jokes about the messengers' names and their offers. They are decent enough men, troubled that this innocent does not understand the offer is one he cannot refuse. They do not wish him dead; they no doubt have a case in their set minds that big business getting bigger is good for the world, and they regard outsiders and losers as unhappy, unwholesome creatures who should be pleased to be asked in out of the cold.

But McCabe struts as well as a gimpy man can – he does not quite seem to have all his toes either – and says, not nearly enough, even if he was inclined to sell. Mrs Miller despairs of his stupidity. She sees death settling on him, ignoring the fur coat. And he is not quite so unaware that he doesn't respect her instincts. But when he looks for those agents again, to renegotiate, they are gone. There isn't a second chance. And when McCabe seeks out a magnificently inane lawyer (out of Mark Twain) the client is baffled by the fulsome picture of the example that is to be made of the case. McCabe sees slowly that he may end up a martyr for liberty.

His idiocy would not be as dramatically fine if it was merely dumb. In her otherwise exciting writing on the picture, Pauline Kael makes the mistake of saying McCabe is "too simple" for Mrs Miller. Whereas, I think he is a very complex character, as rich in interest as anyone anxious to be deemed smart and whose shyness does not have the muscle that knows how to ask or apologise, and who is not cunning enough to get out of a fix because he is afflicted with a quite disastrous sense of nobility and honor. McCabe is a beautiful man in much more than looks or ironic contrast – he can act bold and tough, he deals in whores and so forth, and he does not say he *hasn't* killed people. His shyness is a part of his kindness and his helplessness; but it gets him into trouble because it is mistaken for swagger. He is chronically beset by virtue and integrity, this would-be operator. That is the stubborn impediment to his intelligence. He is so romantic, his snarls are a bluff waiting to be called. His caution dreads this exposure, and makes him more hidden, more laconic . . . until fatalism descends on him as a final, cold peace. As with all great movie roles, the credit belongs to many: to Edmund Naughton for the novel, *McCabe*; to Altman and Brian McKay for the script; and to the actor for providing such a living example and some of his own lines. For being there.

And he has timed his getting there exactly. The picture has not been easy to set up. The screenwriter, Brian McKay, recalls long, deteriorating struggles with nervous backers. Whereupon, Warren arrives from Europe with Julie Christie. He asks what's wrong, and McKay says the picture could be dead. At which, Warren flashes a grin and says, "No problem" – it is a grin that already has McCabe's silver-plugged tooth. Warren has been getting in character, and it makes him cocky. He admits it:

> "I like to play schmucks. Cocky schmucks. Guys who think they know it all but don't. It's been the story of my life to think I knew what I was talking about and later find that I didn't . . . McCabe made me laugh all during the movie."

A similar pattern of comeuppance affects McCabe in his relationship with Mrs Miller. She does not try to save him from his mess; she is too Tooting to think of rosy rescues. And she knows he can never change, anyway – that much insight is possible for characters, and sometimes Julie Christie looks hurt, as if she had caught sight of his lovely limits and a solitariness too great to be talked about in the evenings. McCabe is so tested by Mrs Miller that, when he is alone, he talks to himself about her. He is the only person he can ever come close to trusting, and it is part of his honor that he is inarticulate at this moment. It may be the best speech Beatty will ever have in a film, energy and jazzy talk beating up against the things that are beyond him:

> "Making me feel like I'm making a fool out of myself. Now we'll see who the fool is. Sons of bitches! Never did it in this goddam town. God! I hate it when

those bastards put their hands on you. I'll tell you, sometimes . . . sometimes when I'm taking a look at you, I just keep looking and alooking, and if I don't feel your little body up against me so much, I think I'm gonna bust. I keep trying to tell you, a lot of different ways – just one time if you can be sweet without so many around, I think I could . . . Well, I'll tell you something, I've got poetry in me. I *do*, I got poetry in me, but I ain't going to put it down on paper. I ain't no educated man. I've got sense enough not to try. Can't never say nothing to you. If you just *one time* let me run the show, I'd . . . Just freezing my soul, that's what you're doing. Freezing my soul. Well, shit, enjoy yourself, girl, just go ahead and have a time with it. It's just my luck, going with the one woman who's ever been something to me ain't nothing but a whore. But what the hell – I never was a percentage man. I suppose a whore's the only kind of woman I'd know."

Beatty and Christie live with a few friends in a cottage at Horseshoe Bay on Howe Sound in Vancouver during the shooting. It is a kind of wintry idyll in which she says he eats like a baboon, they stick pictures on the windows to deter gulls from flying at the glass headlong and killing themselves, and – when Christie has an eye ailment – Warren calls not the eye specialist of the world, but the ex-ophthalmologist of the picture business, Jules Stein of MCA. If it is cold at night they have McCabe's fur coat and their love. But on screen, love is so much more moving if the lovers' feelings remain as yearning, like the wish to be intelligent. But such hopes are vulnerable to life's ordinary failures and the realisation that there is a poetry which cannot be sent to the newspapers, which will never come out – because it is a man's death getting ready to spring at him.

The movie is well received, when it opens in June 1971, but too odd, too dark, too druggy for wide enjoyment. But it is the best thing Beatty has done; perhaps the best he will ever do. It is all the more intriguing because of the way he has understood McCabe, and perhaps himself. The film is made because of Warren (he has ten per cent of the gross instead of salary), because he is "interested" in Altman and inclined to give the film life with his name and presence. He therefore imagines he is in charge, and Altman has sometimes to tease this attitude along. Beatty does make suggestions, and surely some of them are blessed with his private pact with McCabe. Altman grabs good first takes from the impulsive Christie, and lets Beatty's performance build more slowly. Warren likes to keep going for takes; this is doubt and caution being creative, waiting and unwinding as he works. It is when Beatty acts well that you can see how fearful he is of himself; you can wonder how far inertia and delay are just guards against the fear. So intent on what is happening to him, the actor may not see that it is someone else's film, and that he is just a part of the greatness. He may not notice that the greatness has eaten him, like an eagle swallowing a frog.

Some years later, Gore Vidal remarks on how he meets Beatty at a party. Vidal says how much he has liked *McCabe and Mrs Miller*. Beatty asks Vidal to write him a picture. Did Altman write *McCabe?* Vidal asks. "Well, actually," says Warren, "but I did most of it." Whereupon Vidal replies, "If you can write that well you don't need me." And Warren sighs, "Oh, well . . ."

Why not? "Well –" or even "Well" are decent responses to the world's fury and cleverness, as D's progress makes plain. And don't imagine that an honest, outsmarted well-sayer isn't capable when the time comes of going out in the snow, or some other desert, and dispatching his three killers, wrapped in the silence of the muffled ground and a morning that has forgotten him.

Breakfast place

They drove into the desert and the rising sun; they were laughing because they could see nothing ahead in the rosy glare. The road was a silver line vanishing in the blood and the roar of the sun that effaced the faint edge of the pewter hills. By the time they got into the hills – to that "there" where the sun was tipping out its bucket of light – it would be higher and they might pass beneath it. So they drove on into the primitive condition, and if the road curved, or if there were obstacles in the light, no one would be to blame. Even Clear found himself driving at 110 miles per hour, and hardly moving on the steady plain of sun-washed gravel and mescal-clear plants. So he had time to count ants and dewdrops on the diamond-white stalks.

D took it all in – the mountains, with stains of white and mauve in the dung color, mineral bitters in the rock; he thought he saw jack-rabbits, dawn foxes and the slither of a snake by the roadside, but he knew maybe none of them had been there, except in his eager eyes; he might see the dead, too, those who had perished walking across the crinkled desert, maddened by thirst; or the Paiute, who knew which cactus flesh to score and how to suck its cold juice. He revelled in the distance and the deadpan availability of space. It was a world abandoned, but waiting for new life. He could imagine himself riding across the parched ground on a sure horse, with water, a gun, beef jerky and his favorite books, a survivor ready to make a start again with history and civilisation. In the desert, every man can believe he is the first and the last, and be unafraid.

". . . like a screen," Drew was saying. "Makes your head race."

"Oh yes," he agreed, in love with it, and with her for being his companion. He could believe that he and Drew in the desert might start a new family, even if the disaster had taken away everyone else. They would live in an abandoned stone house with the only well in the area. They would have an orange tree and a walnut tree. And they would study the colors and have children. It would be a castaway life, and they would give the world its new chance. D would cherish the insects and the lizards, and learn to live with snakes so they were at peace with him and the rattlers were attentive at twilight when he read Dickens to his family. Or made up more CD if the books were lost.

"People go quite mad in the desert," Drew said, out of the blue.

"Will that happen to us?" D asked.

She didn't answer. She was more fearful than he had realised.

"Eyes will be there," he sought to encourage her.

"Or he's disappeared," she said.

"Why would he? He lives here now."

"In the desert? Big movie star just goes away to the desert?"

D felt like the spokesman for this man he had not met. "He is personally reticent, a little withdrawn. He likes to hide, prefers to peep out. He attains a unique status which he wants to preserve. So he moves away from the picture city. He goes off into wilderness. It is quite practical, yet very romantic."

"And insane," said Drew.

"Well," said D, "a little. It's hard without a little."

"The Eyes I know," Drew told him, "he liked room service and limousines, and lots of telephones. I bet he's been in the city all the time, at the heart of things."

"But Clear arranged this, and —"

"Clear doesn't always know. And Clear's on payroll."

"I imagine so."

"But Eyes doesn't pay regularly. He doesn't like to be taken for granted. So sometimes Clear is short. What would he do then?"

"Talk to Eyes." It seemed natural.

"But Clear knows Eyes wouldn't like that. He'd be embarrassed. Richies get so edgy. So Clear calls his laywer, and his lawyer talks to Eyes' lawyer, and then a messenger brings a check. And Clear and Eyes, they never have to mention it."

D thought about this eccentric discretion. "Well," he decided, "that kind of man could be holed up in the back end of a desert somewhere."

They were still on the western rim of the desert when they stopped at a small diner for the breakfast Clear had been recommending. It was getting on for eight, and they were the only customers, but the old-timer and his Indian helper had them sit at the counter and served them eggs, hot cakes, muffins, bacon, hash browns, coffee and orange juice. It was as if everything was provided for, this extensive fresh breakfast, this trading post, all set down and waiting for them.

"Much business here?" asked Cy.

The old-timer scratched his head to consider. "No sir, not exactly," he decided.

"Rocket-fuel OJ," said Look. You could see the C shining on her eyes.

"Thank you, miss. It's the fresh-squeezed does it."

Look grinned some more – it was as if she was being squeezed.

"How many breakfasts would you do in a week?" Cy wanted to know.

"In a week?" the old man took his time.

"Yeah," said Cy, wiping up wet yolk with a wedge of pancake.

"That'd be hard to say."

"In a month, maybe," said Doc, trying to help.

"Ah," the old face moved ahead, figuring. "Well, we do a breakfast most months."

Cy looked at the length of polished mahogany counter, every red-topped stool taken, with not one spare or one of them required to stand. "You stay in business for that?"

"We're a breakfast place," said the old-timer.

And the new desert pioneers murmured in consent as their knives and forks worked away over the thick plain plates gray with use.

"What a character!" said Cy to D and Drew later, as they were walking outside in the morning warmth, waiting for the one restroom the post possessed. There was a blush of violet and amber where the wild flowers grew in the desert.

"You really swallow this heavenly breakfast place," asked Drew, "and your grizzled old-timer cracking eggs and jokes?"

"Well –"

"Pretty convenient," she said in her off-hand, nagging way. "And pretty damn good-looking."

"We were in there," Cy begged her to consider.

"Like a set, wouldn't you say?" Drew would not be caught.

Cy shrugged. "It was what I'd hoped for."

"And there it was – in the desert – just what you wanted."

"Did she have grass in her hot cakes?" Cy asked D.

"Shit," said Drew. "Don't you think it's a pretty wonderful mirage?"

"Mirage?"

"We are in the desert!" Drew shouted at him. "On location!"

She walked away. It was her turn with the bathroom; she was already musing on whether it would be there or she would have to be inventive with the bare ground.

"Wasn't there a *Star Trek* like that?" Cy said to D. "Some planet they reached and it was anything they wanted it to be?"

"People go crazy in the desert." D passed on the wisdom.

"If you can find the people," said Cy. "You know the trouble with deserts?"

D didn't answer. You never had to, and the serenity of the desert was seeping into him.

"No water," said Cy. "No rivers. No status quo."

"Right," said D. And the people talk like signposts, which is disconcerting if you don't believe you're lost.

THE MOST IMPORTANT
MORAL FORCE IN . . .

He has been thinking about his country, and its management; and he is not sure that he might not have to become involved, for he has a taste for running things and he can feel the beguiling solitude there might be in being in charge of everything. "The American presidency is the most important moral force in the world," he says in 1972. There it is, the true transcendent voice of the screen – stirring, quotable piffle. It is a line, from the book of lines that can make thought archaic and unnecessary, just as existence may one day be subsumed in photo-opportunity.

In modern America, actors and politicians are rivals for the high, clear, intoxicating air. They watch one another with the same sort of bleak humor and respect we might imagine in opposed nuclear missiles. Few top politicians can do without acting now; and few stars do not feel the urge to run, or the chance to advise America in their pictures. Only a few back off:

> "I don't do those things," says one, in 1972. "I don't believe anyone cares what I have to say. Something funny happens to actors. As soon as people know you, you have some kind of power. As soon as people want to see you, you begin to think you really have something to say.
>
> "I think actors are suckers for politics. You've just begun to see what's going to happen. Ronald Reagan is only the beginning."

That is Robert Redford, in 1972.

But Warren is presidential timber, and a tree that feels the wind blowing that way. He has the equipment. He has such a memory, and he thinks so thoroughly ahead that he has nearly escaped the present. As Tommy Thompson says of him, in 1968, referring to his physical mobility, but foreseeing ubiquity: "He is seldom here or there in a definite place, as most of us are – he is simply 'somewhere.'"

This is a condition of modern leadership, an ability to be in the air. You can be motivated to seek the presidency by so many things –

316

ambition and martyrdom, calculation or altruism – but not least by the worry that no one else can be trusted with the job, so that your pervasiveness must count. "Do I have to do everything myself?" says one voice inside the head; and its friend answers, philosophically, "If you want something done, get a busy man to do it."

This chapter spans chronology. There are urges in a life that are always going on, driving the person forward, even if nothing appears to happen pertaining to these goals in a day, a week, or a year. Being president is vital; doing the job, a bonus. And Warren is an image in the mind – just like a modern leader – even if unseen. In the spring of 1986, anyone would recognise Warren Beatty as an actor, yet he has not acted for five years – in a film. But he has mastered acting without films, or parts. More than any of his contemporaries, he has set up an extreme imbalance between the wanting, wondering and thinking about doing a thing, and the thing itself. It is what makes him unequalled as a desiring spirit: film after film has the essential Beatty shot, of his face straining toward something, of beauteous desire kept alive. Women are overwhelmed by this look; it is what makes Warren unique for them, and tender despite the way he may eventually dislodge or ignore them. Indeed, the expression does not disappear, because so often he arranges events so that he is left, alone and still embalmed in desire's oil. It is the wishing in the eyes, and not everyone realises that the point of focus is beyond the level of immediate companions. He is looking out there.

And the presidency is not just out there, but the thereness of there. And as he comes to the time of life when people are presidents he has to decide whether the object of ambition or the steady state of desire matters most.

Moreover, he lives in a country and a time when intensity of desire in politics is honored and searched for because it is cleaner than the hash and muddle of the system. Of course, if any leader thrives on just that charisma, he will be chided for it and for the shallowness it is presumed to conceal. This is a nod to the old, lost order, like blaming stars for being fabrications when we feast upon their imaginative appeal. It is an American way of seeing that prefers to overlook the solid detail of party program and the onerous, depleting routine of political life, and see instead the supreme force and direction of the country in one man.

The language of American politics has required charm, amiability and mystery in leaders – to such an extent that it has become possible to see the system depending on nothing else. That is a fallacy: Washington is a city of detail, intricacy, meetings and monstrous labor in which passions are brutalised in winning half an inch there and revised wording here. But the nation's view of itself is that leadership must be finer than the dense, killing battle among clerks, lawyers and lobbyists. And so presidents have to shame the detail: we dread a tired leader, and we rejected early traces of it in Mondale. Nothing so establishes Ronald Reagan in this mood as much as the well-furnished legend that he does not over-work, or let the tangle in issues betray his clarity; that he may sometimes catnap in cabinet meetings. This is taken as a measure of his resilience, his nearness to us, his freedom from political compromise, his imaginative energy and his still active desire – for only those hoping to dream would sleep. And Reagan may have learned the value of a few zzzs in his movie days, when actors strove to keep moral force shining until the day's last close-up.

And we are not astonished if, on waking, this leader talks to microphones (they will always have more of him and his husky intimacy than other people get) about the Budget Committee that may be getting ready to propose a tax increase. His steadfast refusal on such cuts is already a glowing instance of desire overcoming reality or mathematics. And as he chuckles and ponders over what the Budget Committee may do (with lowered head and inward gaze), he tells the mikes, well, let them just try it – "Make my day!" He is like a seer who has quoted one of the holy lines, a second-rate actor still paying homage to stars as lofty and Whitney-like as Clint Eastwood. Some groan at the vulgarisation of political discourse, but the public has voted for this instinct for immediate identification. They can face not understanding all the problems, all the minutiae, if they know how the chief's fancy works. And the line refers not simply to Eastwood's refusal to be bought or used (God save it!), but to the ardor in all movie star eyes, the believing in being believed.

So, if the time comes, it can be recalled in Beatty's "literature" that his first childhood wish was to be President, until at seven he wanted to be Governor of Georgia, and only at eight an actor. This was before Jimmy Carter had used that governorship as a stepping-stone. It can be said that Warren is president of his high-school class, that he is a child of teachers, a young man who makes himself a millionaire. He can point to liberal sentiments, none so pronounced that it would detract from his practical ability. Above all, he is known. Every statistical survey reports that Americans vote for those they have heard of the most, and the best. Any decision on Beatty's part, to run or not, would turn on how he feels that word "best" is measured in the public mind.

He has already worked hard, if cautiously, in the machinery of the Democratic Party. Since 1968, he has participated seriously in every election but that of 1980, which coincides with the making of *Reds*. In 1968, he campaigns for Robert Kennedy. So did many show business figures: it is not hard for them to make easy gestures – to sign a petition, to buy a couple of plates at a fund-raising dinner, to let their names be used and to appear at a few events. This is routine endorsement, unlikely to impress real politicians any more than it does the electorate. Getting Hollywood celebrities lined up is a way of convincing yourself you are doing the basics if you are a candidate. There is a risk, though, in being associated too closely with such figures just because the public takes for granted their self-interest and their irrepressible urge for attention.

What marks Beatty's political campaigning is its developing personal reticence, the movement away from being a public speaker or a photographed presence. What impresses Pierre Salinger in 1968 is that "Warren was a 'guts' worker, not a movie star. He read every speech Bob had ever made in the Senate, and when he talked to hostile kids on college campuses, he won them over as skilfully as Bob himself did." The second Kennedy assassination only adds to Beatty's feelings about violence. He works on John Glenn's Emergency Gun Controls Committee, and in *The Parallax View* his character has a line, "Every time you turned around someone was killing off one of the best men in the country," that is plaintive and arresting. As he says it, the face is full of the longing for something better. For desire always focuses dramatically on its obstacles. And election day, 1968, is the day on which the action of *Shampoo* takes place. Not that that film is overtly political. Still, there is a pressing uneasiness in the possibility of some affinity between George Roundy's destiny and America's. It suggests that Beatty was an early sceptic of many of the libertarian dreams of the 1960s.

But it is in 1972 that he commits himself to political work, for a candidate defeated in one of the most famous of landslides. That man, George McGovern, says, "He took a year out of his life to do it. He traveled around the country making speeches, debating issues, interpreting me to the public, and he personally was responsible for raising more than a million dollars."

The core of Beatty's work in 1972 is to organise a series of star concerts. Gary Hart, McGovern's campaign manager, says that Beatty "invented the political concert" at which major performers would give their time and their act to boost the campaign funds. The concerts take place in Los Angeles, Cleveland, San Francisco, Lincoln, Nebraska, and

At Candlestick Park, San Francisco, July 6 1968

Madison Square Garden, New York. At Los Angeles, Carole King comes out of a temporary retirement to appear with James Taylor and Barbra Streisand. 18,700 attend and $320,000 is raised. At Cleveland, the audience is 14,000 for Joni Mitchell, Paul Simon and James Taylor.

Beatty prevails upon these stars to perform and directs the stage shows as well as the political themes they embody. It is the first time he has directed. At Madison Square Garden, he uses the slogan "McGovern Can Bring Us Together Again" for a concert that reunites famous teams: Simon and Garfunkel, Mike Nichols and Elaine May, Peter, Paul and Mary. Dionne Warwick shows up, but her former partner, Burt Bacharach, cannot make it. There are always some stars who let him down. At the Garden, there is a plan to have stars work as ushers. Some do, Goldie Hawn for one, but Beatty has to employ some of the arena's regular workers. The New York concert brings in 19,500 people and estimates of $450,000.

Warren Beatty is seen at these concerts, but not too much. He has learned to be wary of having himself seen. On July 6, 1968, weeks after the shooting of Robert Kennedy, he goes with Julie Christie to Candlestick Park and before the game between the San Francisco Giants and the St Louis Cardinals he stands at home plate and speaks to the crowd. "A sound and reasonable gun control law will only help curb violence in our society," he says. "Now is the time to act, and Americans should wire or write their Congressmen to approve a law that will impose reason and good sense on possession of firearms."

He is booed; he can hardly be heard. The 28,233 crowd wants Juan Marichal and Bob Gibson. Do they recall how recently Faye Dunaway stroked Warren's pistol and spent a movie teaching him it was flesh? That evening, Warren and Julie hit the Cow Palace with a similar speech before the Sonny Liston-Henry Clark fight. Beatty is asked about his attitude to real and movie violence: "I see no conflict. The movie simply tried to show a historical situation as it was . . . To my mind, the movies that are most dangerous are those that show violence but show it as not being dangerous – the type where all the shooting goes on but nobody gets hurt."

He is badly received again in 1971 at the University of Wisconsin. Such experiences prompt him into devising a role for himself as organiser, no matter that he enjoys talking about politics. Why is he booed? Is it just a few drunks or rowdies setting off an easily swayed crowd? Beatty has learned how to command and direct waves of cheering at McGovern rallies. (He may not know it yet, but this is a training undergone by John Reed at political pageants more than fifty years earlier.)

Would any star be booed at home plate, if he delayed the game? Henry Fonda? Paul Newman? Gregory Peck? Marlon Brando? Clint Eastwood? Is there an American crowd brave enough to taunt Clint? Or is there something in Beatty's reputation, even in 1968, that has stored up resentment or mistrust in the public? Do the people detect his innate guardedness, the veiled watching that is weighing his effect? Does he think it's sultry to keep his shades on? Is that why the crowd turns on him? Great lovers do not easily possess the vast, vague affection of the people. They don't seem to need it. They smell of private satisfactions, the privileged fruits of beauty.

Beatty supports his candidate. He says McGovern "has a greater degree of foresight than anyone I know. He is eight to ten years ahead of everyone else in what he perceives the truth to be, and if we can't deal with the truth then what the hell are we doing?" There is a whiff here of the political novice who wants to run by throwing out all the old, stale ways of the game. And in the campaign of 1972, he often sounds like an evangelist: "Before Florida and Wisconsin, people would ask 'Does he [McGovern] have a chance?' I'd say, 'What difference does it make? Do you want to be for someone who has a chance, or someone you think is right?'"

But when foresight fails to persuade voters, he blames McGovern for losing, and even for extracting such effort and dedication from himself in a losing cause. "The most desperate feeling in the world," he says, "is to hope people will vote for you." Yet, in a campaign how can a genuine candidate keep himself from some moments when he looks weary, ignorant, spiteful, petty, inadequate and wrong to those closest to him? The supporters must understand the ordinariness and live with it; this is how lovers negotiate marriage. The uncompromisingly idealistic may have to ignore or shun day-to-day politics because of its spectacle of drabness. And what self-control would it take in a candidate to go through that schedule and ordeal and never look petty or mistaken? People in show business have remarked on Beatty's frustrated search for heroes, and on his remorseless need to prove himself superior to those who might be models. McGovern too falls short, and shows how anyone "right" can still fail. There is very little about politics that is artistic.

Still on the edge of politics, Warren can sound easily hurt and child-like as he runs from one tough "line" to another: he is Butch Cassidy in, "I even tried to rope in Marlon, but he's so far out politically, he thinks the elections are a lot of bullshit"; he is Michael Corleone in, "You need organisation in politics, and I'm a good organiser. McGovern needed visibility, and he needed money, and we supplied him with both." But he is himself, spot on, in:

> "You drop everything to work for a guy who was *zero* a year ago and immediately you're doing it for publicity. These Washington writers feel guilty because they want to make it with Raquel Welch, so they take it out on us. I could have made $1.5 million this year, but I felt it was important to spend the time working for McGovern."

Beatty works as hard in 1984 for Gary Hart. It is not that he gives up or shelves movie considerations this time. He can never do that entirely. Film associates get used to him being interrupted by political phone calls. They wonder if anyone can control so many diverse things, or whether Beatty can be as earnest as he says he is about their picture project when he is apparently promising the time not just to a candidate but to the president that candidate wishes to become. Does Beatty know he has another loser in Hart? Does he count on it, or is he organising his life so that time is filled and nothing is ever done?

He does not appear in public for Gary Hart. The political concert has largely died away by 1984. But he is closer to the center of the campaign. For in 1972 there are times when Beatty may out-argue Hart, the manager, on how McGovern should be presented. Hart is never as much of a hero. He is the man who has Beatty's advice, and it is sometimes fiercer, quicker and more ruthless than Hart's nature. People who see them together in private situations say that Hart is in awe of Beatty, ready to be directed by him. They say Beatty is not always willing to be impressed by Hart. Beatty helps shape the campaign, the speeches and the issues. As late as the party convention, in San Francisco, he is in attendance as an official delegate, and he has written the drafts of speeches for Hart if he wins or loses. No one else in San Francisco believes Hart can win, but Beatty works on two speeches. He has come close to making a winner out of Hart. For Mondale's defeat by Reagan is always more likely than Hart's. In person, and by phone, Beatty is never out of Hart's decision-making process, and never as exhausted as Hart. He is defining a role for himself as power-broker, and he works decently for Mondale when he has the nomination, to ensure that the Party is not offended.

He would be 51 in 1988, 63 in the year 2000 and still only 71 (the age at which Reagan had his first year as president) in 2008. What will the country want then, and what will government entail? Suppose that by

The icon and the candidate: Clint Eastwood in *Pale Rider*, and in Carmel, California, running for mayor (Warner Brothers; Ben Lyon and *Monterey Peninsula Herald*)

1990, Beatty has made two more substantial movies – in the sense that they make him a great deal of money, and bring him prestige. Suppose he could somehow find a role that earned him our love? Suppose then that he ran for office in California – the Senate, the governorship? Then by 2000 he might be at least as plausible a candidate as Ronald Reagan ever was.

But there are liabilities. Crowds boo him, and the public regards him at best with coolness and an amused envy. His life has already accumulated love affairs that any opponent could present in a scandalous light. He would have to defend himself in public, be open to bitter, unfair, unreasonable questioning, whereas he has always preferred not to explain or justify, not even to speak much or appear. Any political campaign exposes the candidate to tedium, fatigue and triviality in a way he might not be able to stomach. He has always made use of secrecy in his life, whereas a major political figure must go in terror of being discovered and must master or own that generosity, a sheer openness of spirit and disposition that can let itself be seen and pictured and smile through the years with warmth and vitality. It is a look that too much intelligence can kill.

He may be too thoughtful, too restless, too private a sensibility to run for office, and too easily bored to ensure administration. Buck Henry has said, " 'Easygoing' is not a quality he has. You know how presidents age in office? If Beatty was president, either he would be dead after the first year or the country would be dead, because his attention to detail is maniacal."

And, of course, we hope that presidents are constitutionally opposed to death, whether theirs or America's.

*

Is it the closeness to politics, or just the irresistible force of flirtation that makes him say it?

This is 1974, and he is being interviewed by Joan Dew for *Redbook*. It has to be near the end of their time together, the thing she has been wondering whether to ask.

"What do you have anxieties about?" It may be the quietest thing on her recorder.

He pauses; she believes he is groping for a reply.

"I don't usually like to reveal those," he tells her.

Nothing can stop her now: the lines are carrying her into her dream movie. *She* is talking to *him*. "Why not?" It's loud now. "It would make you more human." Maybe *she* is the rescue she imagines.

This is when he says it. It has to be straight to the camera, as clearly the end as Tuesday Weld saying "Why not?" in *Play It As It Lays*. It is the line of a self-observing campaigner perhaps, breathtakingly dreadful.

"But I have no need to seem more human."

It is a line like handing someone a rattlesnake, until you see the harm the snake must have done while the person waited to hand it away. Waited years, perhaps.

Desert stop

"Perhaps here," said Clear. He spoke calmly, preferring to leave no eyelash of query in the seared sheen of the late afternoon. He was lost, but he knew the need for assurance in uneasy times, and his kindness wanted them to regard it as a group decision.

"Couple of hours to sunset still," complained Chuck.

"Why not stop and enjoy this light?" said Beau.

Look settled it. She lounged out of the camper and discovered that her hums, her giggles and any snatch of song came back at her, small and clear, from the ruffled wall of mountain nearby, its umber holding up in the blue smokiness of time of day.

This mountain was not deniable, yet it looked like creased silk dropped down from the sky. In the desert, the density of reality flattens into theory. And the clarity of light and the belated reach of every scratching sound is hallucinatory. D did feel he could walk up to the mountain and stroke its surface, yet he understood it was miles away. He could imagine he was the figure in a diagram in a physics book. He could see them being an exemplary society here. He noticed he had a hard on – an unaccountable rising, like something you find when waking from a dream – and so he promenaded for a spell into the emptiness until it woke and diminished.

"Taking a leak?" he heard Chuck's call. There was impatience in it, a first rip of panic. "Got to get that organised. Define our foul territory."

"Oh, really?" D sang back at him, noticing that he might not be suited to such rules. "Where should I go then?"

"Back of those mesquite trees?" guessed Chuck after lengthy deliberation. "You see a sidewinder, piss in its eye." D heard Chuck snort with mirth. "Don't miss, now, or it'll freshen up your pecker."

D examined every poised dead twig, every twist of gray leaf, every agonised stem, for glistening scales that might move if he unzipped. But his cock felt happy in the sun: it had always been the one tanned part of his body, the colour of Lena Horne, he thought. He let his gentle arc reach out to the desert and the sunset; it sparkled above its tracer shadow on the dune. What could it matter? He saw a Kodak packet in the mesquite, blanched but recognisable.

They were somewhere in the northern end of Death Valley, where it comes up to the Nevada border. Their tinny noise of camp-making seemed fake and craven in the bed of silence. It was easy to believe they were not fully there, that the "there" was a vast fossil spectacle and they were people at a museum observing it. Though supplied with atmospheric heat, their "there" was a sheltered dome in the immensity. The stillness had already impressed D, as if a kind of nothingness that had always waited inside him was growing in the fantastic sun. The heat was beyond sweat or discomfort, he was already thinking of himself as mere air in it, his body discarded and dry as a snake's skin.

"A particularly desolate area," murmured Doc. "Known for its absence."

"Apparently," said D. He heard it.

"I was out here several years ago on a Foreign Legion pic," Doc was telling him. "Scotty's Castle must be somewhere out there. Then, beyond that, it's the Last Chance range. Fifty miles or so and not one soul or construction."

"Could we go there?" D felt the urge.

Doc weighed it: "With enough water we might."

"The empty quarter," said D.

"Eureka Valley, Slate Ridge, Deep Spring Lake. Nothing else. A hole on the map the size of an apple."

"And Eyes might have a place up there, a stronghold?"

"It's what he'd like us to think," said Doc. "But what kind of stronghold could you muster up there? How are you going to bring the strength in? Without it being noticed?"

"He might reside in a simple hut."

"Or a ghost town. Might have been mining hereabouts once. Or people who tried some prospecting."

The dusk drew in rapidly and the temperature fell away with a silent scream in which they heard the wind at the bottom of a saucepan. The vehicles made a circle. There was a scrappy mesquite fire, bitter in the air and burning too quickly in the night breeze. They tossed cardboard boxes on the fire; their panels floated on the hot air before sinking and melting.

Chuck was gloomy. "We can't go on like this."

"What do we do, great scout?" said Drew.

Chuck stared into the disappearing fire. "I hope that damn Eyes shows up."

"Don't doubt it," said Clear. "We should try to sleep."

"Anyone care to cuddle with me?" they heard Look's voice in the dark. "Just for practicality purposes."

"Sure," said someone in the dark, a voice no one quite recognised. But they were too enclosed in worry and too cold to wonder at it.

And Chuck helped them all to sleep with, "Don't we have to stretch something round the camp to keep off snakes?" They hesitated in the doubt. "I thought we did," he added wistfully.

"That's the moat," said Doc. "I did it."

"Right," said D. "We took a dip in it."

"Sure," said Doc. "Being in the desert is a holiday."

In the morning, no one had slept better than Look. "I had terrific dreams," she told them, "like fresh French fries." There was a honeymoon glow to her that surprised their faded faces.

"What a kid!" Cy laughed. "I'm in love with her."

And after their uncooked breakfast, and the decision to stay where they were for the day, Cy Lighthiser asked D and Doc to accompany him on a walk – to explore, he said, a direction that looked promising. They walked for a mile during which no landmark came closer, but the broken surface of the ground exhausted them.

"Let's sit," said Cy, pointing to a group of boulders. And so the three of them had a conference out there in Death Valley.

"What I have been thinking," said Cy, "is that our Eyes seems less and less likely to make a picture, and even less likely to say, no, he won't make a picture."

"At his age, a false move could be fatal," said Doc.

"Hysterical," said Cy, without warmth. "How are you guys on Chuck?"

"Low," they said together. They had always hoped someone would ask.

"Strictly visually," said Cy.

"He is like Eyes," said D. "I have a shock whenever I look at him."

"Correction," said Cy. "A lot like Eyes was. Which is better. Because who knows how he looks now?"

"You do wonder," D offered.

"When flesh goes, it rushes," Cy assured them. "Jayne Mansfield went in one summer." He still regretted that.

"So?" Doc could see it coming.

330

Cy looked from D to Doc, and back again. "Suppose Chuck makes the picture."

"What picture?"

"D's script," said Cy, amazed it took so long to get a breakthrough concept across. "It needs a polish – we've got Doc. We go with Chuck as the guy who shoots the president – Chuck is stranger than Eyes, anyway. And I like this Look for the actress."

"You'd bill Chuck as Eyes?" asked Doc.

"Why not? We can make it work. The guy shouldn't talk too much, right," Cy looked at D. "I like a silent assassin. We photograph Chuck OK, we can get a brooding quality. It'll be in the desert a lot of it, narrow eyes, heavy tan, wild hair, funky. I get excited talking about it."

"And Eyes?" asked Doc.

"We make a good enough box office, my guess is he doesn't say a word. He goes with it – sees the joke, Or," Cy had just thought of this, "he lies low, waiting to see if it's a conspiracy."

"What about Claudia?" Doc remembered. "She isn't going to be the actress?"

"I know, I know. I get to be the traitor. But I tell you, and it's heartache saying it, Claudia is bouncing her marbles on a hard floor. In which case she isn't going to look good."

"Maybe old D could write in another part," Doc was grinning in his foxy way. "I'd polish it, of course."

"Well," said D, cautiously.

"You could?" asked Cy. "The Eyes part could have a very sexy let's-say-forty therapist? A lot of ways that could be better for Claudia. She's still good at the rueful wisdom thing. Jeanne Moreauish. Our best chance with Chuck, I'd say, is steamy scenes." He looked at D directly, as one asks a mechanic what time this afternoon it'll be ready. "Can he fuck the aunt?"

"Tell me, Cy," said Doc. "Does this constitute an offer, this little chat?"

"Listen," said Cy, "we're a long way from where we can do reliable business. I haven't got a secretary out here, not even a copying machine. I just wanted to pitch the idea. You two don't like it – I'm an idiot. Tell me. I'll think again."

"I did take money," said D, "and sign a contract."

"Kid," said Cy, "this is the desert, and for all we know it's the end of the world. New rules. The survivor adapts the quickest."

"That's what Chuck says," said Doc.

"But he seems depressed," D pointed out.

"He's not swimming in the moat," said Doc, and D nodded.

"What is this moat?" asked Cy, scratching at a bite on his arm.

"Moat's at the castle," said D. "Where else?"

The sun cranked higher and their new life in the desert wilted in its gaze. Drew and Look lay beneath the camper in its oily shade, listening to the vehicle stretch in the sun.

"Anything happen to you last night?" asked Look.

"Not a thing."

"I thought you and D were an item?"

"He's a married man." Creak, crack. "What about you?"

Look sounded dreamy. "I thought I got off on the most sensational fuck last night."

"You thought?"

"I must have had a fever."

Some distance away, Clear was consulting with Zale and Tusk.

"Nothing on the radio," said Zale.

"What does that mean?" Clear wanted to know.

"That civilisation as we grasp it is kaput?" suggested Tusk. "That the quake took out LA and everything else?"

"It could be temporary," said Clear.

"You want the radio to put out a bulletin saying no, this is really the end?"

"That would help," admitted Clear.

"He has a point," said Zale to Tusk. "If we knew for sure that the Constitution was in suspension, so to speak, then there are powers we could assume."

"Like what?" asked Tusk.

"Like we could pick a leader and write out rules. Define sexual liberties and shoot enemies."

"What would Eyes do?" Clear wondered aloud.

"Where is he?" asked Tusk. "I have documents waiting for his signature."

"Documents, my friend," Clear lamented.

"Don't knock documents," Tusk told him.

And in the afternoon, when they had been there nearly a day, Doc said to D, "Maybe we should go look for Scotty's Castle."

"Do you know which way?"

Doc nodded up the valley.

"How far?"

"Probably too far, but I'm getting blue here."

"Listening to Cy's ideas?"

"That was a good story he had."

"You think we should do it?"

"No, not that. But I've been thinking about it as a story about a guy who takes over some star or tycoon who is not immediately present."

"Like Hughes and Clifford Irving?"

"Perhaps," said Doc; he was searching still. "Could make a nice role for Eyes."

"A fake who might be real?" D saw it in an instant.

"Right," said Doc. "Someone who gets hired to impersonate a lost millionaire because he looks like him —"

"And then wonders if he might not be him," D was excited again.

"You could have a scene," said Doc, "where he discovers that the guy's old shoes fit him."

"Or his spectacles," said D.

"Oh," groaned Doc. "That's lovely."

And the two of them, at twilight, slipped out of the camp with only a plastic bottle of spring water, a box of wheat thins and this new idea.

PARALLAX VIEW

The Parallax View aches with a loneliness and mistrust that the film cannot release or escape. It is, on the surface, a paranoid thriller about American politics in which a vagrant reporter discovers and then opposes a mysterious corporate force that assassinates promising presidential candidates. The film is not "about" Lee Harvey Oswald and the Kennedy killing, as those who make it are at pains to protest. Yet it would not have been imagined or made without that event or the ferment of unease that follows the hurry of the Warren Commission to explain what it is that happens in Dallas on November 22, 1963. The picture opens only six weeks before the resignation of Richard Nixon, yet it does poorly at the box office, no matter that it is frightening, well-acted and "spooky" in the way of greater successes and similar pictures made by its director, Alan J. Pakula, *Klute* and *All the President's Men*.

In Seattle, at a reception high up on the Space Needle, a Senator Carroll is shot and killed. The movie's flurry of murder shows us two men with guns, one of whom falls from the Needle moments after the assassination. The investigative commission says this man was the killer, and that he acted alone. A few years later, Lee Carter (Paula Prentiss), a television reporter present at the killing seeks out Joe Frady, a newspaper reporter of far lower status. Indeed, just prior to the killing, we have seen Frady attempt to gain entry to the reception by saying he is "with" Lee Carter. But she pauses, looks him in the eye, and denies it. We guess that some time before they have had an affair, and that she feels he let her down. And now, when she comes looking for him, Frady is with a much younger girl; her visit seems to have interrupted their love-making. Frady grins to himself at the bad luck of the world. The sullen girl trails away.

Lee tells Frady that witnesses to the Carroll killing have themselves been murdered. He says only a few have died, and they just died; there's no conspiracy. But she brings news of a death he hasn't heard of; and then a little later she dies herself. Frady is not in good standing with his own editor, Edgar Rintels (Hume Cronyn) – he has had a drinking problem, apparently dealt with, but he has still to "curb your talent for creative irresponsibility". He is a loner and a reckless journalist who employs stunts to find his material.

Frady begins to investigate on his own, and as he finds more deaths and the existence of the Parallax Corporation, which seems to be hiring misfits and preparing them as assassins, so Rintels backs his campaign. Frady is nearly killed himself in the death of Austin Tucker, Senator Carroll's campaign manager, and when he returns from that mission he tells Rintels, "Print my obituary – I'm dead." He goes undercover, takes on a new identity and poses as an outcast to penetrate Parallax. He lives in a room in a rooming house, cooking ineptly on a hot plate. He is accepted by Parallax. But only because the Corporation is on to him. They kill Rintels. And then in a second major shooting, that of a Senator Hammond, they manage to frame Frady as the killer. The film ends on a freeze frame, as Frady runs from the area where the killing occurred, into a blast of gunfire. Another tribunal intones the verdict that Frady killed Hammond, that he was a lone agent.

Warren Beatty is Joe Frady. *The Parallax View* is not his production and yet it is known that he involves himself a good deal in the rewriting of the script, and that he has serious if constructive arguments with Alan Pakula over the film. It is also the first picture he makes after his experience on the McGovern campaign of 1972. Which makes it more significant that the movie has a dread of politics, power and the vulnerability of its America being manipulated. And while this fault can only be located in the film, it is plain that Beatty's presence as an actor is serving to pull the film in opposite directions, first to raise and then to deny a fascinating potential which leaves *The Parallax View* the most substantial failure in which he has yet been involved.

This is still in his time of supreme beauty. There is a close-up in the scene where Lee Carter discovers Frady with the sulky teenager, his face washed in morning light, with just a spoiled puff in his cheeks and a tired smile on his face, of confession turning into pride, that is among the most ravishing he will ever allow the camera. But the picture gives him no relationships, and after the death of Lee Carter there is not another grown woman in sight. The loveliness is stranded by the story, but it cannot quite sustain the proposition of Frady's dark solitude, his lack of success, and the picture is goaded into doing something about this anomaly. It has to admit to the angel's aura.

Thus, on one of his early investigations, Frady goes into a bar in a country town in the north-west. The sheriff and his deputy are sitting there telling stories. Two waitresses are with them, and both of them are instantly attracted by Frady. One of them, Gail, goes up to him at the bar.

"What can I fix you?" she asks him.

"I –"

"How about a martini?" she jumps in on a Beatty hesitation, eager to occupy his inner spaces. "You know what they say about martinis? They say that martini is like a woman's breast." She curls up inside, to draw him into the punch line. "One ain't enough and three is too many."

She chuckles and he tells her, dryly, that it is an amazing joke and he settles for a glass of milk.

At this point, the deputy comes up to the bar, looking to dispose of this glorious male stranger.

"Can I buy you a drink, miss?"

Frady sighs: he, too, has seen this movie scene too many times before. The bar is nothing but folklore, the place where anecdote occurs.

A big young guy, the deputy plugs on: "You know, for a moment I thought you were a man. But you aren't, are you?"

"No, I'm a, I'm a girl," Frady answers quietly.

"Why don't you go right over there and tell those people that, real loud?"

The deputy puts his hand on Frady's arm, and Beatty says, "Don't touch me unless you love me."

There is then a complicated, fancy fight: it is, really, the only extended physical struggle Beatty has ever had in his films, and he is not easy in it, no matter that he wins. Nor, later, does he seem convinced, fluent or eloquent when he has to run to jump on a truck to make an escape. His clothes seem tight, his spirit tighter. As an actor, he would always rather sit still, listen and talk a little, using his bland milk to mask a daring sexual speculation. No one can doubt he is fit; he was a footballer in college. But he appears reluctant to show strain, and he has none of the natural joy in prowess that marks Wayne, Gable, Cagney or so many other male stars. Sometimes he seems too shy even to move; as still as a watcher, his power is in his recessiveness.

The fight is one of several scenes in *The Parallax View* meant to provide action, but going nowhere and only serving to build up Frady as a conventional hero when the actor cast in the part has urges to take it elsewhere. There is this ponderous fist-fight, a battle to survive in a river, a car chase, and so on. There is, later, an elaborate sequence on a

In *The Parallax View* (Paramount)

plane where Frady realises there is a bomb aboard and wonders how to alert the crew without drawing attention to himself. Only there is the action properly addressed to Beatty's fastidious character as an actor: for he is trapped; he has to be casual and unobtrusive. There is even a moment in which he writes a soaped message on the restroom mirror, opens the door to find another customer waiting outside, goes in again and wipes away all trace of the message, that shivers with the weird neurosis that does not want to be seen or caught in a bathroom. It is a glimpse of a Frady we do not get enough of, as playful and paranoid as the lovely, visionary line: "Don't touch me unless you love me".

It is not that we are seeing a homosexual here, but a chameleon, someone who has grasped the encyclopedic range in acting and is therefore within touching distance of playing a person who is disintegrating. *The Parallax View* sets Frady up as a failure, and then has him masquerade as a psychopathic outsider. But it never challenges us, or Beatty, with that prospect. Quite simply, the film says he is pretending to get into Parallax; that he is by then so provably robust that we trust him and are "with" him. But the picture is cold, grim and distant, in awe of its own series of plots. We do not feel for Frady. Beatty's own inability to give of himself, to come out with the energy to win our love, has defeated the simple purpose of suspense or melodrama. We neither care about his loss, nor believe that the world of the film can be saved. *The Parallax View* is a totalitarian theorem that serenely proves itself, killing people and shutting out hope, amiability or untidiness. It is high on its own cool, sinister air. It is surely made by decent, liberal people, but it has the dead calm and elegance of fascist design.

The picture cries out for less of its irrelevant, unfelt action, and more of Frady's neglected intricacy. We need to examine his recklessness: there should be a threat of craziness in it. And we need more than the hint Lee Carter throws off in "As long as you were there", when Frady chides her suspiciousness, "You were always scared a guy might come up and attack you in bed." And it forsakes the richest ambiguity to have Frady seek advice on how to answer Parallax questions in order to qualify. There might have been a different film, a film always circling around Frady's inner life, his alienation from others and his absorption in a sheltering, reassuring imagination in which he *knows* already how to respond to the remarks we see on the Parallax personality inventory, because the shy eyes, looking out, discover themselves there:

"I am often frightened when I wake up in the middle of the night.

338

I am at my best in large groups.
Sometimes strange men follow me.
I have never vomited blood.
I would like to be an actor.
I can't understand why I have been so irritable and touchy.
Someone is out to get me.
My father would hate me if I got into trouble with the law.
I like to win when I play games.
I never liked school.
I want people to remember me when I'm gone.
I have never cried.
My friends always end up double-crossing me."

If we feel that person there is no need for the questionnaire or for the academic explanation that it is meant to draw out anger, repression, frustration and violence. Suppose, instead, that we have a fired reporter working on his own, living alone, masquerading as a personality type he is so close to being that he may pick up the rifle, unaware.

That would be like *Taxi Driver*, in that it would be a movie about a man of a certain kind of warped goodness driven to kill, for love and to be remembered when he is gone. It would be claustrophobic, dangerous, disturbing; it would endanger Warren Beatty's image, and it would be a commercial failure. But *The Parallax View* did not do well, anyway.

And if we saw, from within, the subterranean life of this Frady, then the movie would not need its very provocative but absolutely digressive sequence in which Frady has to watch a short film of potent images during which his responses are measured. It is the questionnaire made more vivid: key words like ME, LOVE, HOME, FATHER, MOTHER, COUNTRY, GOD, ENEMY, HAPPINESS in a montage of familiar pictures – a happy couple, children, old age, babies, mother and child, fatherhood, a still from *Shane*, baseball player, idyllic home, apple pie, cornfields, Thanksgiving, Statue of Liberty, Mount Rushmore, Lincoln, a church, Hitler, Mao Tse-tung, Castro, whiskey, red meat, and so on.

These are the clichés of Americana, a storyboard for Lee Harvey Oswald – and for Kennedy, too – and the variable ingredients of political advertising. Again, Beatty did not make the picture, or compose this sequence. But he lent himself to it, and to the overall Hollywood vision of politics as a popular spectacle directed by malign, faceless men whose desire it is to have control and to manipulate a gullible public.

We are not told what Parallax is for, though the suggestion is that it is of the Right. It could be the Left, or it could be a movement interested in power for power's sake. The picture of America arrived at by the movie is of a country propelled by imagery, largely unaware of small but crucial criminal sections that actually determine events. As such, it is so devoid of hope that it cannot find people who live or show any sign of optimism, independence or departure from this set pattern. It is politically despairing, but actually drawn to the mechanics of control that may be bringing America closer to totalitarianism. The two senators who are killed are resplendent but hollow creatures – TV figments (one is Jim Davis, soon to be in *Dallas*) who repeat homilies or are cut down in the rehearsal for their "spontaneous" triumph. It is bad enough that they are assassinated; but it is worse perhaps that they have not deserved to be elected. There is a way in which they are dead already. And that slackness gives silent support to the sinister effectiveness of Parallax. If these stooge candidates do not merit office, it makes them more deserving of the bullet.

Melodrama is so paranoid: suspense movies have plots into which every detail should fit. There is no life outside the dread, and no rationalism brave enough to overcome its power. And there is a polarity in the spiral of paranoia in which to be heroic you must be either President or the killer. Nothing else works. If America has had all its ordinariness stifled by cliché, then it is less a country and a people eager to be guided than communicative controls that wait to be possessed.

*

If *The Parallax View* disappoints, it is worth touching on some problems in its making. Director-producer Alan J. Pakula knows that he has to start shooting without a "ready" script. More work needs to be done. But Beatty has and insists on a pay-or-play deal, so shooting has to commence. As it goes along, the actor contributes many good ideas to the picture. But there is a control, a shape, never possible if it is not there early enough. Pakula has to impose some of the shape in the editing room, and so the mysteriousness of the film is compounded by the pressures of production.

Pakula is exasperated with Warren. When the film opens modestly, the star calls the producer, nagging him about its numbers. Eventually, Pakula has to tell Beatty that if he's concerned he should get out and do publicity for the picture. If not, then Pakula would rather not have his relentless calls.

But charm does not accept defeat. A few years later, Pakula has a sure hit, *All the President's Men*, and there is a party for its opening. When the director arrives, Warren is there, lounging in the doorway, shy and grinning, aloof but appealing. "So who do you like the most," he asks, "Redford, Hoffman or me?" And, as Pakula acknowledges, hard feelings dissolve with that smile.

But if *Parallax* had more of this mixture?

Scotty's Castle

They had kept up a steady pace through the night in the kind of unspoken agreement they treasured. And whose mind does not sometimes sway to treasure in the desert?

They did not walk at one another's side, but took turns in single file, leading and following. Five steps apart, the one behind could see the silver puffs of dust at the other's feet, disappearing in the moonlight. Their feet crunched on the cold shale and grit of the desert floor. If D closed his eyes he could imagine they were polar journeyers packing down the snow. He assumed they had fallen into a rhythm of walking, unaware, in one another's footprints, indifferent to the cold compress of their sweat. One night like this can be the perpetual bond for a significant friendship. Whatever minor professional rivalries there may have been before between D and Doc, whatever irritation in the latter at the former's rawness, they were by dawn like the last brothers on Earth.

They sat down in the first twinges of light as the sun loomed up again, the Valley's old dragon. This was the moment to be breakfasting, in air like an English Spring. They could smell the renewal amid all the mustiness of the desert. Miles away, like a parenthesis, a hawk cruised in the air, planning a quadratic equation. They saw their first snake, a fluid fucking diagonal, a muscle of Ss, making it's speedy way across the ground to hiding. It came close to them. Its oval eye went past like a non-stop train, a blind eye. And the two men felt suddenly sure that snakes did not think about men.

"We should find the Castle today," said D.

"If I'm not a buffoon," Doc reminded him.

"I have every confidence."

"I appreciate that," said Doc, snapping a wheat thin in two to prolong breakfast's glow.

They rested twenty minutes; it was already warm and pink when they started again. D was sure that if they went another full day in such heat and found nothing they would die. But he was not concerned about it.

The water slopped against the sides of the plastic bottle. It was a third down already. Neither of them said anything about estimates or limits. It was taken for granted they were going on. Realising that self-destruction was in prospect, D wondered about Drew's warnings of madness. But when he looked at Doc's face he saw only the calm eyes of one without worry. He hoped to hell he would not have to be so stupid as to ruin this bond by remarking on it.

Then Doc said, "This is the life," looking at the bland distance; it was nothing to do with them; they were like men admiring the fine brushwork in an Old Master. The desert was a classic, a fundament of their culture, a climate that would wear away their tragedies as it smoothed stones and snakes.

"You tell the first story," said D. It was so apparent that they would keep talk going as they made their way.

"I like Scotty's story," Doc told him.

"The man who built the Castle?" said D.

"Didn't build it," Doc explained. "There's the beauty of it. Walter Scott, that was his name; he was born in the 1870s in Kentucky."

"He was not a Westerner?"

"Only by inclination," Doc was smiling as he paced along, seeing the shape of the story. It was like watching a young creature take its first steps. "He worked for a time with Buffalo Bill's Wild West Show."

"He was a cowboy?" D wondered.

"I doubt it. The advertising and promotion part of the business."

"Which is what that business is," D added.

"Exactly. Which is fine. Anyway, some time early in this century, Scotty comes out to Death Valley and goes in for prospecting. I don't believe he ever found so much as a lost ring. But, because promotion was his calling, his character, he was good at having it thought that he had found gold."

D chuckled. So fearfully honest himself – dull, nearly, some say – he was warmed by the thought of an inventive fraud.

"He said he had a mine here in the Valley," Doc continued. "He said it was one hell of a mine, and he got some people to put up a little money. He told 'em he required it for equipment – which was encouraging."

"Then what did he do?"

"I'm telling you. Then he'd go to some town and spend that money, spend it in a showy way. So what did people think?"

"That he's rich. He must have struck gold!"

"And then they were lining up to give him more money!"

343

Road scene, Death Valley

D clapped his hands. "And there was nothing at the heart of it all!"

"Nothing but Scotty's native inventiveness," said Doc. "And then there was this rich man, Albert Johnson. He came West to convalesce after some serious illness. But what made him better was Scotty's company."

"Scotty told him tall tales," D surmised.

"He couldn't look at his breakfast without building it into a romance. And Albert, I suspect, was a dry stick. But he constructed this house in the Valley. The Castle. Where we're going, I hope."

"Scotty's Castle?"

"Except that Albert paid for it. But Scotty –"

"Said it was his," guessed D.

"Yes, sir," said Doc. "And they were grand friends. I don't mind telling you now," he added, "that I have always reckoned Scotty as a role for Eyes – whimsical, a charmer, a yarner, a tease, a will of the wisp, but an American. It was after I mentioned the project to Eyes himself that he got this hankering to live in the desert. He's a deadly researcher, you see."

"Know what you could do?" D was looking ahead. "You could have Eyes play Albert, too."

344

Doc went on another five steps before he stopped and turned. "In the same picture?"

D had to come to a halt. Doc's gaze was so demanding. "Right. Two roles."

Doc looked up at the blue sky, battered and beaten, without a cloud. "Jesus," he said. "That's it. That's singin' in the rain."

"The rogue and the recluse," said D.

Doc was grinning all over his face, "The story-teller and the sickly rich man."

"Don't you like it?" asked D.

"I'm having an orgasm over it. And no split-screen nonsense."

"Certainly not," D assured him.

"Just the two men watching one another in the cutting."

"So Eyes could do it comfortably."

"He'd be in his element. Always able to consider himself in another role."

"It's a fine plan."

"Well, it's yours," Doc told him.

"But I couldn't do it without you."

Doc considered this. "Have to do it together, then."

And each smiled at his portion of the far sandy distance, pretending to wince in the glare. The desert has these facilities. Though it may be a barbaric environment, still it can polish old souls.

Towards noon, without premonition or indication, they came round an outcrop and found before them a dell, a glade in the desert valley, a tidy flourish of trees surrounding a castle – there was no question in D's mind – so flagrantly designed that it had parts in diverse styles, the medieval fortress and the Spanish hacienda, the courtyard and the battlements. It looked an ingenious gathering of castellated sets where adventure serials might be shot. D looked to see if there was even the eagle of the old Republic perched on a turret.

"Not quite how I recall it," said Doc.

"Is there a choice of castles in Death Valley?" D asked him.

Doc was judging. "No, there's the wishing well."

He pointed at a low stone wall in the courtyard with a wooden arch. The timid fountain was dribbling out a little water. As they came closer they saw coins in the pool, shimmering, a little larger and cleaner than life.

The castle was abandoned. The café and the ticket office were closed, but the notice saying the Castle was open to visitors every day had not begun to fade. Looking through the windows of the gift shop, between the credit card decals, D could see souvenirs lined up on the shelves with the packets of film, the dark glasses and the candy.

"Door to the house is open," he heard Doc's call across the courtyard. There was excitement in his voice. The mood and its echo made it easy to appreciate the beguiling vacation place the castle might have been once. D went up to the door and saw a Packard saloon, 30s vintage, silent and dusty in the covered shade. He entered the house, on red tiles, with beams above and heavy Spanish furniture, in leather and brocade, where ranchers could rest up with the blinds down. There were leather curtains and small waterfalls to cool the air. Death Valley was 125 degrees in summer. The castle would not have been worth a nickel without its siesta mercy, a place where buddies could doze, with lemonade and an unread book on their laps.

The two men made their way about the house, marvelling here and there – at the pipe organ upstairs, at the thick yellow and green chinaware in the dining room and the plates with curled lips (for serving, said Johnson; from the heat, Scotty answered). They could hear the slow measure of such old repartee, lugubrious jokes and the amazed laugh of a rich man who had eluded death. They saw the white shirts, the sombreros and the row of red ties in the wardrobe in Scotty's room.

"What a country," murmured Doc, "when a man can wear red ties and be set up for life."

There was fresh food in the kitchen, with wine in the refrigerator. All the power was working. Whatever stroke had afflicted the land, Scotty's Castle had its own generator – there was an engine within the fake part of the castle – and it was still in touch with whatever source it had, the snow in the Sierras, the heat in the ground, or the spirit of two friends braving out the furnace days.

D and Doc fed a little and then they found a bedroom each and succumbed to the great force of the afternoon. They rested. They promised to meet again at dinner: they had no plans beyond that and a pink salmon in the icebox waiting for them, as firm and piquant as an untold story. And there were lemons they had found to squeeze on it as it broiled.

The room that D took himself to had a canopy bed. He was cautious, letting himself down on the coverlet; he thought it might be a museum bed, with only chips of styrofoam beneath the embroidered cover. But he felt a different kind of substance, and when he drew back the heavy drape material he found an unmade bed – tousled sheets, one sock and a pair of women's panties, pale chocolate in colour. The pillows were crushed from recent heads and there was a smear of lipstick on one of them. Moreover, D could feel a good-natured wildness in the bed that bespoke a college co-ed's room rather than this antique place of companionship. There was a sneaky whiff of sex, and when D lay down, he saw, close to his face, a coarse black hair in the shape of a comma.

He studied the beams in the ceiling, and the stucco walls. He let his gaze slip from one portrait to another, framed black-and-white photographs of women early in the century, in white, buttoned up at the neck, their hair bound in on itself like turbans. These must be beloveds of Johnson and Scotty, women still tense at having their pictures taken, or warding off Scotty's relentless comedies.

D's tired head lolled for a moment so that he saw, on the table beside the bed, a pair of spectacles with fine steel rims. They were not folded, but put down as taken from the head. He could see the lower moons of bi-focals, and then he was slowly impressed that in the upper, inner quarters of the lenses, there were still the fine, pinhead bubbles of perspiration, as if these glasses had been very lately worn, out in the sun, and only just set down by someone who had come in for a merited snooze. The glasses were as fresh (and every bit as up-to-date) as the salmon in the kitchen.

At which unnerving realisation, D heard steps in the corridor outside, the light flicker of a barefoot child – at most a slender young woman – making her way in familiar premises. The person was singing, "I Can't Give You Anything But Love"; the voice could have been a girl's or a woman's. D sat up. The breezy intrusion was coming his way. The door's ajar widened and a rippling young thing came in. She stopped in mid-stride, on the brink of singing "Baby", seeing a stranger in the bed.

"V!" cried D, a little less the finder than found.

"It's Virginia, now, Dad," she said, as if somehow the bed he was struggling on explained the enrichment.

SHAMPOO

In the early 1970s, he has been entertaining more and more ventures. As well as *McCabe and Mrs Miller* and *The Parallax View*, he has made a picture called simply *$*, written and directed by Richard Brooks, with Goldie Hawn as his co-star. It is another "caper" film, opening at Christmas 1971, in which he plays Joe Collins, a supposed security expert who becomes the thief of safe deposit boxes in Hamburg. Hawn plays Dawn Divine, a hooker who was once a showgirl in Las Vegas. There is a suspenseful scene in a bank vault, and a prolonged chase across ice. It is light and forgettable, a picture remarkable in this composed and brooding career for having been made at all. Gary Arnold, in the *Washington Post*, calls it sour, disorganised and dismally facetious. Beatty, he says, remains cute, "but is wasting his and our time (when he read the screenplay, didn't it occur to him that it was *Kaleidoscope* all over again, only worse?)."

He ponders many other proposals – to be in *Ryan's Daughter*, for David Lean, but in which part? – the Christopher Jones role, the young officer and lover, or Robert Mitchum's, the sad husband? He is at that in-between age. He does not make *The Adventurers*; a Yugoslav actor, Bekim Fehmiu, takes the part that Beatty probably never considers seriously. He declines to play the man Marlon Brando will be in *Last Tango in Paris* – and here we cannot fail to notice, hypothetically, the more dangerous commitment of which Brando is capable on screen, the depth and pain of his voice and the nakedness of self-revelation. Beatty in *Last Tango* could hardly sustain the defenselessness of its bare, empty apartment affair without names. He could not live up to its desperation. He is never a man that Francis Bacon would paint – David Hockney perhaps?

And he thinks about and rejects four roles that will become the body of Robert Redford's screen career – *Butch Cassidy and the Sundance Kid*, *The Sting*, *The Way We Were* and *The Great Gatsby*. On *The Sundance Kid*, he says he "didn't feel much like getting on a horse and riding around". But he has been interested earlier, when Polanski is in sight as a director and Elvis Presley is to be Sundance to his Butch. It is Presley, apparently, who rejects this opportunity. *The Sting* never impresses Beatty; the man in *The Way We Were* strikes him as apathetic; as for *Gatsby*, he delays, he asks to renegotiate, and the project lumbers on, leaving Beatty with this communiqué: "As an artist it wasn't something I felt I needed to do at this time." But, in fact, at another time, he has thought of producing *Gatsby* and having the producer, Robert Evans, as his Jay. Beatty may be the one actor in town who feels the charm of that role, but sees what a handsome nothing it is.

One can see Beatty in all these Redford roles: he could be the wary eyes in Sundance, watching the jazzy smoke rings of Paul Newman's talk; he could be the con man in *The Sting* who might be about to double cross the picture; he would inhabit the brittle Hollywood success in *The Way We Were* and the disappointment of promise that lacks stamina or the strength to face difficulty; as for Gatsby, he is a character who anticipates the narcissistic hollowness of just about every young Hollywood sensation.

He is entering other ideas and situations, just as enticing, but more immediate. In 1970, in London, at a dinner for Polanski, "Warren's gaze descended on" Britt Ekland. She has need of a new affair to detach herself from Patrick, Lord Lichfield; and she falls in love with Warren. They make love in her bed-sitter, and fall asleep exhausted.

She has to travel to Los Angeles: she has been invited to appear on Dean Martin's television show. He follows her: that is to say, Warren follows her, not Dean, follows her to Los Angeles. "I missed you a hell of a lot, Britt," it is said he says. They live in his suite at the Beverly Wilshire, sunbathing naked on the terrace, with Warren going inside occasionally to make a call. He worries that Julie Christie will find out; he tells Britt he is worrying about this. "But I guess that's one of the gambles we're gonna have to take."

They go to see a pornographic movie; they sit in its dark unnoticed. Afterwards, Britt says she was bored by it: "I will never make a porno film unless it's for real and only with you," she tells him. He laughs and says maybe they should bring in a camera crew to film their activities in the penthouse.

There are other names mentioned – Maya Plisetskaya, once a ballerina with the Bolshoi and twelve years older than Warren; Brooke Hayward, the daughter of Margaret Sullavan and briefly the wife of Dennis Hopper; Joni Mitchell, Liv Ullmann, Carly Simon – does she write

"You're So Vain" about him? It is the point of the song, its great rejoinder, that he is left wondering. And Lana Wood, Natalie's sister, becomes briefly his lover when he lets her live at his Wilshire suite when she is broke and down on her luck. "Warrén is a passionate and inventive lover," she writes, "a curator of women. . . . Whatever his motives were, Warren helped to restore me, gave me shelter and some of my self-esteem back and for that I remain grateful."

His romancing has become not just a topic in the press, but a climatic constant for America that can be alluded to at any time without explanation. It is proverbial, which must make the real thing that much more elusive. It is like wondering what "they" think in Peoria, or when the first snows will fall in New England. Outlandish names and prospects are put next to Beatty's name – Princess Margaret, Jacqueline Onassis. One would not be caught off guard by a picture of Warren with Mother Teresa and a nudging caption that says, "Yes, she's human too!" For this legendary Warren could melt ice and eroticise all women just by looking at them, even if he was without his glasses at that moment. His seductiveness is helpless; it is a force of public need and faith that requires so little action from him, and which so lends itself to his caution and his indolence, that just a sigh could seem to suggest a touching. He has become a wind on open fantasies – there may be women sure he secretly ravished them when all he did was look at them once across a table or brush their cheek with a goodbye kiss in a crowded salon. "And he never even said hallo."

And he entertains a movie about this infinite capacity, a talent and a suggestiveness that are almost indistinguishable from the nature of film itself. For hasn't Warren Beatty's looking at women from the screen (without ever seeing them) become almost the same as contemplating them at a party, the image a little blurred perhaps because it is all in passing and he *is* short-sighted? One promise in his love is that he wants you to come very close so that he can really see you; he manages to make seeing seem a function of the whole skin, not just the eyes.

This film begins very soon after *Bonnie and Clyde*. Beatty rents a London house on South Audley Street, and Robert Towne is his guest there. They talk of a script that Towne might write for Warren, instead of one to re-write. A few years earlier, Towne has written an episode for the television show *Breaking Point*, "So Many Pretty Girls, So Little Time", which is about the dilemma of a womaniser. At the Chichester Festival Theatre in England, Towne and Beatty see a revival of the Wycherly play, *The Country Wife*, starring Maggie Smith as a woman seduced by a rake named Horner who deflects her husband's suspicions by pretending to be homosexual. These influences gather in a script Towne writes about a Beverly Hills hairdresser who has many women in his life. Its first working title is *Hair*, but between 1967 and 1975 that is taken by another venture.

The first script is 220 pages: it has two large female parts, but Beatty says he wants only one. According to Towne: "He was very angry about it, and I was very angry about his being angry about it, because I thought the script was really pretty terrific. For a period of about six months we hardly spoke, and the project was put aside for several years. It was like two brothers quarreling. I don't know anybody who's a bigger prick, but there's no one I love or admire more."

The project languishes, and then suddenly comes to life again, in 1974. Towne moves into the Beverly Wilshire with director Hal Ashby for an eight-day blitz. He discovers that, in the meantime, Beatty has himself written another draft of the script. Eventually, the two men share the writing credit and the stand in a trial when a woman says that the picture has plagiarised her 29-page treatment, *Women Plus*, which she has sent to Columbia in 1971. Moreover, the jury finds for her, until the judge throws out the verdict and is sustained by the California Supreme Court. The picture is *Shampoo*: it is Beatty's second production and, when it is released by Columbia, it will be a huge hit, with $22 million in rentals on its first release.

Shampoo covers a little more than a day in the life of George Roundy, the star of a hairdressing salon, who is trying to open his own business. He lives with Jill (Goldie Hawn), but in the time the movie covers he betrays her with a client Felicia (Lee Grant), with Felicia's daughter (Carrie Fisher) and with Felicia's husband's mistress, Jackie (Julie Christie). There is a moment when George seeks to reassure Jackie's lover, Lester (Jack Warden), by acting fey that is the single reference to *The Country Wife*. It comes when George has just done Jackie's hair for an Election Day party (this is November 4, 1968), and so transformed her that they make love, only to be interrupted by Lester. And Lester is straightforward enough to believe that women are not drawn to gays, and that strong men like himself need not feel threatened by them.

The film might more boldly have made George bisexual, or at least erotically appealing to everyone. That aside, its great insight is to see how far the Beverly Hills hairdresser is a servant who may have more power, knowledge and intimacy than lovers or tycoons. For he conjures appearance: when George softens and enhances Jackie for the party, when he lifts her out of weary, common attractiveness into beauty, it is the greatest gift that movies or LA know. It is the generosity that could seduce anyone there – the accurate understanding of how they might be beautiful. There is a story told that one day Natalie Wood sees Leslie Caron at a party at the time of the Caron–Beatty affair. Isn't Leslie looking unusually lovely? people say. Warren, Wood replies, as if Caron has made herself look better for him, or as if he has willed and summoned it, been the mirror in which she reappraises herself. And surely Natalie has felt the same light lift her face, and seen her own radiance in the mirror. This is not just cosmetics; it is only grace that makes people feel better about themselves.

Body servants in Los Angeles are a priesthood: they know the stars and the star-lorn yearning in others, and they may have the power to make the person anew as well as the opportunity to hear their confessions. Such intimate attention to the flesh may easily prompt sotto voce revelations; the artist is only a few inches away from the ear and the mouth. There is a scene in *The Roman Spring of Mrs Stone* where Beatty's Paolo reveals himself to his barber. It is a clue that the best insight into Beatty might come, not from his women, but from Robert Jiras, his valued make-up man on several pictures.

Shampoo is a lucid moral disaster, with resemblances to comedy of confusion: it is funny, and it is bathed in the painless light of southern California and the downy glow of bodies better cared for than any in human history. But it is always on the edge of melancholy, as if it knew the horror of aging and decay. Its ambiguity grows out of the very level way in which so many characters are seen. No one is rejected, or seen as without faults. Lester is foolish and vulgar, but he is kindly and open-minded. Felicia is rapacious and selfish, but she believes in lust. Jill is superficial and Jackie opportunistic, yet the film steers away from condemning them. It regards such frailties as everyday things. Like a Jean Renoir picture, it never loses sight of the sound reasons we all have for what we do. But the picture does finally sink into George's pity. For while it is a comedy, still its central character has no humor about what he does. He is a philanderer – yet somehow he is hiding from his own promiscuity, saying it is only liberty. He wants to think well of himself; he longs for some Roundy of his own who will make him morally lovely and unimpeachable.

The election night party is a fiasco. George's betrayals all come to the surface when, at the dinner table, the tipsy but discerning Jackie tells the world she would like to suck George's cock. (Yet isn't even that what *he* would like, no matter that he has the performing instinct to look embarrassed by the confession?) Late at night, George is seen fucking Jackie – Beatty's bare ass on top of Julie Christie in the gloom. He loses everyone, and he rushes here and there, having to run and look stupid again, in the strobe light of a very Bel Air 60s party, Don Juan out of breath.

Next morning, he has his last scene with Jill. She has gone off at the party with another man who offers her a new life. She comes back to the apartment she has been sharing with George. It is a scene that, in script and preparation, Beatty must know is not just his big moment in the picture, but *his* scene. In rendering it for the page, a book must admit failure. It is not just that we are without the droop of Beatty's head and his chronic physical efforts to withdraw from the scene and its place, to fade out, as it were. It is that, as well as speaking he makes sounds. They are the moans and primal creakings of misery, of inarticulateness, of having to be honest when he is a poseur, of the knowledge that in words he will start lying again, not speaking but wooing, so eager to be liked he does not know what he thinks. The sounds are the edges of his voice; they come from behind his nose. They are very moving. They are the sounds that must have seduced a mother once, let alone adult lovers. They are beyond words, they are the naked creature. They amount to extraordinary performance, and yet they are a nakedness that cringes from being seen. They are the scream of someone too shy or proud to ask for help. They are called "noises" here.

JILL: I don't want to fight, George.
GEORGE: I don't want to fight, either. Look, er, I'm sorry. (This is said with boyish vigor, the shallow wish to be simple and direct, to look everyone in the eye, and to get the scene over with quickly.)
JILL: Bullshit.
GEORGE: *noise* Why didn't he come in?
JILL: Because I didn't want him to.
GEORGE: Well, I hope he doesn't mind me being here. (Be sorry for him.) Did you get a job out of it, at least? (And if you're not sorry, he'll jab you.)
JILL: I'd like you to leave now. And take this with you. (*She throws a small piece of female jewelry on the floor. He picks it up.*)
GEORGE: Where'd that come from?
JILL: Who knows? I'm sure you don't. But if it'll help any, I found it in your bed. Obviously there were others. Weren't there?
GEORGE: Obviously.
JILL: How many?
GEORGE: What do you want to know for? (A fending off that is also seductive: don't you want to know?)

In *Shampoo* (Columbia)

JILL: Because I want to know. (She has to leave him: She will always think the way his mind works.)

GEORGE: What difference does it make?

JILL: Because . . . I don't want girls looking at me and knowing, and me not knowing. No, it'll help me, really. It'll help me if you tell me. (Yet the film is not essentially concerned for Jill.)

GEORGE: How?

JILL: Because I'll know that you've lied to me all along, and I'll know that you're incapable of love.

GEORGE: *sighs* If it'll do any good. I, I just, you know, like, I, I . . . You really want to know?

JILL: Yes.

GEORGE: *sighs* There were a couple . . . I mean there *noises, sighs* Let's face it, I mean, that's what I do. *noises* That's why I went to beauty school. I mean, they were always there and I keep, I just, I – I – I *noise* You know, I, I, I don't know what I'm apologising for. *sighs* I go into that shop and they're so great looking, you know. And I, I'm doing their hair, and they feel great, and they smell great. Or I could be out on the street, you know, and I could just stop at a stop light, or go into an elevator, or, I . . . there's a beautiful girl. I, I, I don't know . . . I mean, that's it. I, it makes my day. Makes me feel like I'm gonna live forever. And, as far as I'm concerned, with what I'd like to have done at this point in my life, I know I should have accomplished more. But I've got no regrets. I mean, gee, because . . . I mean. *noises* Aaagh! *sighs* Maybe that means I don't love 'em. Maybe it means I don't love you. I don't know. Nobody's going to tell me I don't like 'em very much.

It is a riveting scene, but one better for a biography than for the film. For, in truth, it says what we have already gathered about George, and it takes away from *Shampoo* being about a group of liars, connivers and appealing fakes. It takes away from the place, the light and the froth of the title to have one character on the analyst's table, and so available for pity. There seems to me in the speech and its uncanny playing to be the instinct that the fault is not the speaker's, but a condition that has made him the victim. He is drawing the dilemma into himself, making it private, after we have seen his shortcomings clearly in a social sense. But if he can inhale it – there, behind the nose – it becomes his burden, not his failure.

Shampoo is a very good film, and very rare from Hollywood in that it is more about Los Angeles than it is a reworking of habitual movie genres. It is the second film to exhibit a brilliant, bold, self-obsessed producer; and it shows how in American film the producer can be the artist. Yet *Shampoo* might end more challengingly if it had a vision other than the producer's, or one that could be colder in looking at him. It might end more challengingly if the forlorn George was cheered up by the film's most frightening character, the Carrie Fisher part, in a blunt, unadorned, unalleviated scene of sexual excess, a home movie of them getting it on, with her sucking George's ankle and Warren's faraway face watching, nearly deserted.

V

His daughter's coming in so casually and happily had altered the room; it had shifted from being a composed monument, normally open to the public's hushed, "don't touch" inspection, to a motel cabin. V, Virginia, inched open the top drawer in a chest D had taken for solidity – time cast as walnut – and retrieved a packet of gum.

"Well," she said, perching her small self on the end of the bed and slipping an oblong wafer in her mouth.

"Virginia?" he wanted to be sure.

"I know," she groaned. "Eyes says it makes him think of England."

"He . . . he christened you?"

It was the first time his daughter had assessed the process. "He said he couldn't keep track of me in his head as V."

"I didn't know you were friends."

"Oh, yeah. You see, Dad, he thought that might upset you."

"How long have you, er, known him?"

"Don't *do* that," she grinned. "Since you were doing that script. He thought you'd feel uncomfortable if you were possibly writing it for Eyes and I."

"Eyes and me," D told her, and a flush of thunder swept across Virginia's face.

"Right, right," she dismissed it. "Anyway." Her eyes rolled at voices ranting in her head over dads' silliness.

"And you were telling him about the script? Reading scenes?"

She shrugged, "I thought you'd be pleased. Think how many scriptwriters wouldn't mind having their kid in the sack with Eyes."

"You are intimate with him?"

"He's not a pervert, you know."

"And you are – "

"Nineteen," she piped in, "in case you've forgotten."

"I've not forgotten," said D. How swiftly relatives could put one askew. "I remember quite clearly."

"Oh," she pondered. "I thought, you know, you'd been busy."

D smiled modestly at this understatement. "I have been through a lot," he admitted. "I am lucky even to be here." He wanted to say she was fortunate to have him still.

"You were with *them*, though," said Virginia.

"With them?"

"Clear and the gang." Then Virginia grinned, and D could see the ball of gum, rosy and salacious in her mouth. "And that Drew et cetera . . ." And as he made to speak, she dropped in one more "et cetera" and let the gum expand in front of her mouth, like a kiss in a nuclear blast. It popped and the tension faded.

"Anyway, Dad," she was conciliatory. "I think that's nice for you. My old Dad."

D didn't know how to respond. He could see a long line of lies ahead of him that might end in tyranny or running a movie company.

"I was stupid," he said.

"Listen," she told him.

"Yes?"

"What?"

"I was to listen?"

"Yeah? Oh, yeah. Well . . ." The chewing seemed to be what was interrupting thought in his daughter's head. But D saw that it was really the old thing, the difficulty of thoughts. Virginia gave it up. "Just be nice," she said.

"Is that your motto?"

"It sure is." Virginia nodded soberly, as if hand-on-heart issues were involved here. "I mean, you have to be loving."

"That's what Eyes says?"

"I'll tell you, Dad," she wriggled further forward, giving up her lotus position, levering on the cheeks of her bottom so that the old bed squeaked. "He is a very tender guy."

"I'm glad to hear that."

"Actors, you know," she explained. "They really see into people."

Especially those in the mirror, he was inclined to say, but he was learning to wait out the homilies of the young. She might surprise him. Sooner or later, everyone did. He had not dreamed she could be so calm or stoical, so far ahead of any possibility he had thought of for her. No, it was always D being caught unsuspecting. He was the idiot of the piece.

"You don't have any knicks there, do you?" she nodded at the bed.

"Chocolate colored?"

"Right. Eyes got 'em at Victoria's Secret." Her voice fluttered at the memory and D waited for insights into the fitting. But none came, so he fished behind him for the scrap of rumpled silk. How close he had come to sniffing their worn odor when he was alone.

Virginia took them, jumped off the bed and shimmied into them, drawing them up under her Navajo skirt.

"You gotta wear them," she passed it on. "Because of the snakes."

"Ah," said the father, relieved that he had made his peace with those reptiles. "Are there many in the desert?"

Virginia thought about it. "How many would many be?"

He shrugged. "Enough for you to take precautions."

"Oh, yeah. Enough for that. You see, Dad, what you have to face is there's no back-up now."

"No?"

"You get a snake bite there's no hospital, no flying doctor with the serum. It's curtains. Eyes says this is year zero."

"Aha," said D, recognising the political potential of a good caption. "Yes, that does clarify one's thinking."

"Does it ever. And you really have to carry a gun, whatever your feelings on the subject."

"To shoot a snake?" That tiny eye and the head not much larger. Slithering past. It would take genius.

"Uhn-uhn," she told him. "Survivalists."

"What are they?"

"People who live in the desert in new communities. They've been here since long ago, long before the disaster."

"Survivalists," he repeated the name.

"They're killers," she told him. "Shoot first. Don't ever get talking to them. They are so crazy you can't reason with them."

"You have a gun?" D asked her.

"Sure. It's outside in the basket on my cycle."

"You don't live here then?"

"No, this is Eyes' weekend place. He has the real base north. I rode over. It's great biking in the desert, and what it does for your body."

"I can see," D conceded with pride and true enjoyment for her innocent firmness.

"You gotta try it."

"It's a long time since I've cycled."

"In the desert it's a cinch."

"So," said D. "Eyes is to the north."

359

"Toxic Flat. The seat of government."

"He must be very busy?"

"Well," she considered, "no, there's not a lot to do. I thought he might even be here."

"These spectacles," D pointed to the table.

"Yep, that's him. He's gone off. Maybe he heard you and it frightened him away."

"I don't think I would frighten anyone."

"Oh, he's very timid." Her gum was losing its flavour, and she was looking for somewhere polite to dump it. "He broods. It's a load, you know."

"The seat of government?" D supposed.

His daughter looked at him. "Yeah, that too, I suppose." Then she made up her mind. "Listen, can you keep a secret?"

"Did I ever say anything about my time in espionage?"

Virginia's jaw stopped. Her eyes widened. "Fuck, no! That's aces."

"You begin to comprehend the nature of my secrecy."

"I'll say! What did you do?"

"How can I say more?"

"Oh," she was dashed, but respectful. "That's all gone now, I suppose, in the disaster. No structure."

"It'll be back."

"You think so?"

"Don't you imagine we are prepared for things like disaster?"

"You'd have to be, I suppose. God." It was sinking in, like evening watering in a bed of roses. Then she whispered, "How truly thrilling." D wished it could be true as well, but he took his small pleasures when he could.

"What secret?" he reminded her.

"Well," it was lovely for D to see his child having to organise a story: he knew no higher measure of civilisation. Was it really disaster if the instinct grew back to describe it?

"Well," she tried again. "You know Eyes has a reputation."

"He is a celebrated movie star."

"I know, but a rep, too."

"Romantically?"

"As a lover supremo. Well, some time ago he got a letter from the Smithsonian asking if they could have his . . ."

"Yes?"

His daughter blushed. He wished he had a picture of her, or could

V

freeze her embarrassed heat and all the room and have it forever. "His splendid member," she said. "The scepter of his authority."

"They wanted that?" D had imagined the nose, but Virginia's eyes were looking sharply down and sideways, like a man in a skit about urinals.

"Look, they've got Archie Bunker's chair and Kareem's goggles. Julia Child's apple pie dish. Trademarks. Americana."

"Still," said D.

"He felt honored. He said it would be the first part of him established in Washington."

"They wanted it now?"

"Of course not, stupid." Virginia sighed that fathers could be so crass. "When the time comes – if it does. But they wanted to do the measurements and so on, so they'd have a nice satin case for it. Well, he had a deal going at that time and he couldn't go. If you leave LA they think you're bored."

"So?"

"So he FedEx'd it."

"It comes off?"

"You would be amazed what it does."

"So must the ladies be."

"You bet!"

D thought about the most delicate phrasing of his next question. "He's everything he's said to be?"

"It's like TV, I tell you."

"Ah," D's imagination raced. "And it comes off?"

"He's so far ahead of his time," said Virginia. "It's another entire level of consciousness. You see, Dad, most of you guys are just over-attached to your things."

"I know I am," D said, to be agreeable.

"Right. So he sent it."

"Don't say it got lost." D tried to remember the insurable limits on Federal Express.

"Worse."

"Damaged!"

She spoke very slowly and clearly: it was the punch line. "He thinks they sent back the wrong one."

"It doesn't fit?" D couldn't help but wonder whose Eyes might have acquired.

"As far as I'm concerned," said Virginia, "it's as pretty as ever, and no

361

one I've talked to can detect a difference you could put your finger on."

"There's a group? A club?"

"Yeah, it's nice. Like a society. We talk on the phone."

"And does it perform . . . in the way it did?"

"Wondrous," said Virginia, full of honest admiration for older people.

"Still," D could see it, "he's suspicious."

"He is and he isn't. Sometimes he's sure it's his, but then other days he starts to wonder if it's a practical joke. It's occurred to him it could be bugged."

"He must need a great deal of reassurance."

"Well, men do, you know. No offense, Dad."

"Of course not. I feel proud that you can . . . cope with such rare problems."

"We all of us have to grow up fast now. That's the thing."

"True," D thought, "yet there's still a slower process that should be allowed to persevere."

"Yeah?" Virginia took the gum from her mouth and stuck it on her left elbow. "Seen Mom?"

"Not since – when was it? She wasn't at home when I called by."

"She's here. Up north. She's doing real well."

"That's wonderful. How did she get here?"

"Eyes arranged it."

"I am even further in his debt."

"Oh," she dismissed it awkwardly, for the young are so fearful of having done well. "What do you think is going to happen?"

"I really don't know. I expect we'll all be together again soon."

"I mean with the world." She made him feel dull and commonplace.

"Ah yes, the world. Well," he hoped to be broad in his view. "I daresay we can make a life in the desert."

"I suppose so," said Virginia. "But can we make movies? You gotta have the population base for real pictures. Otherwise they end up private art things."

D was saved from having to contemplate the future of the media by questioning calls from the courtyard. He left the room and bumped into a drowsy Doc in the hall.

"My daughter Virginia," he said.

"No kidding? How are you, Virginia?"

"I'm great, thanks."

And so into the sunlight where they found Drew and Look counting the coins in the wishing well.

V

"Hi," said Drew. "Know what we did? We followed your tracks. It works. You have any water?"

"We were going to drink this pool," said Look.

"How about a salmon dinner?" Doc suggested.

"Here?" Drew was amazed.

"With all the trimmings," D added.

"That's Eyes's salmon, you know," Virginia pointed out.

"This is my daughter," D explained.

"I'd have known," said Drew. "Same foxy look." And D was so happy to feel Virginia's slender arm slip into his. "Eyes would want us to have the salmon," she had made up her mind.

"Oh, that Eyes," said slypuss Drew, reading the whole picture there in the dazzle. Who says we need crowds or the dark for the picture show?

A PATTERN EVOLVING

As he grows older, he begins to seem youthful. But he has no children to play with. And as he puts more of his time and energy into money, business and calculation, so he explores a screen image that is impulsive and open, a man of good, rather innocent intentions, an inept idealist with never the time, or coolness, to get everything in order. His face stretches, to accommodate widening eyes; it is as if he is talking a lot to the young, and inhaling their naivety.

There is a flutter after *Shampoo*, the wake of his sexual prestige in which, the media assume, millions of women bob like corks. It is the start of an automatic reference to him that the press can make. But it comes from a picture of Beatty's own doing, in which he tempts the belief that the character on screen *is* the actor. At the same time, he cannot endure or dispense with this legend of Don Juan.

Not long after the film opens, he agrees to appear at a forum at a high school in New York where the subject is to be the treatment of women in films. Molly Haskell, the critic, is leading the forum. She is the author of a book on the treatment of women in film, *From Reverence to Rape*; she is also a native of Richmond, Virginia. She recalls that, as she is introducing the panelists, he leans over and polishes his spectacles on the tail of her jacket. This is done so everyone can see.

It irritates the audience, already prepared to be critical of Beatty. Yet he charms them by a policy of direct attack – yes, he says, he knows their view that Hollywood does bad scripts, but he sees the scripts that ordinary people submit and they are worse by far. He beguiles the audience, and at the end of the forum women flock round him. Next day, he telephones Haskell to apologise, in case his gesture with his glasses was misunderstood. She says she thinks she got the message.

*

"There does seem to be a pattern evolving," he says in March 1975, in

364

Boston to promote *Shampoo* and receive the Harvard Hasty Pudding Award. "It's very hard for me to play a guy who is a Superman. It just embarrasses me. I think it's funny. I guess I prefer to play men who are very stuffed-up, like a blowfish. I don't do it consciously but, it's funny, because, if I looked back on things that I've done, especially things that I've written, they are similar people. The guy in *McCabe*, for example was so full of b.s. and puffed-up that, when he gets into a situation where the heavy starts negotiating him down, he goes down, down, down. The guy is very timid. I mean, it would be very hard for me to play *High Noon*."

He has another film that opens in May 1975, *The Fortune*, to date the last picture in which he has simply acted. No one will understand why it is a failure, for it has two of the most attractive stars of the 1970s, Beatty and Jack Nicholson, playing inefficient confidence tricksters who do all they can to dispose of a young heiress. The partnership seems natural and fitting, for the two are friends and admirers, and there is the same streak of fatalistic, sardonic intelligence in the two of them as they partake of the same limelight. It is part of their modern hipness that they can suggest the attention is faintly ridiculous. This is the sort of wry kinship dictators must feel as they regard one another across oceans and purges.

Jack and Warren have been introduced by Jules Feiffer, somewhere in the area of Vancouver, when *Carnal Knowledge* is on location only a few miles away from *McCabe and Mrs Miller*. As the two actors approach one another, Nicholson, grinning and acting up, looks up at a Beatty who is five or six inches taller than he is, whistles, and says, "Now, *that's* what a movie star's supposed to look like." Feiffer witnesses instant mutual infatuation: Beatty is not averse to being teased, and Nicholson likes a tall straight man. A Chief to prowl around. Of course, the infatuation is etched with rivalry, as if each man knows and is saying to himself, "Well now, look here, this is the other good guy, and it's a damn good thing I think I'm going to like him, because otherwise I might have to kill him, and that could be a situation inclined to lead to my own death." They are both very keen to be natural fellows; but they cannot help but talk to one another in a script that their heads have been working out in advance. They are two bums who will try to be a little shabbier than the other; and they are skyscrapers hobnobbing as best they can.

The Fortune is written for them by Adrien Joyce. They are Nicky and Oscar – Nicky an aging dude with such combed back, greased down hair, and such a tidy, stuck-on mustache that, for the first time, Beatty looks

In *The Fortune* (Columbia)

Howard Hughes in 1947

like Howard Hughes; and Oscar, an untidy little scruffbag of a man, with a bald dome and wings of electric hair. Nicky has married the heiress (Stockard Channing) to get her money, and Oscar is suspicious. As the story develops, they become a ménage à trois, the men regularly confounded in their efforts to kill the woman and inherit from her.

The film is directed by Mike Nichols; it has a pleasing, cute air of the 1920s. The dialogue is pointed, and Beatty has been encouraged to rattle out such lines as "This is purely a love proposition between her and I, kiddo." Stockard Channing gives an engaging, funny performance, but a first fault may lie in her casting. For we do not feel that she has a sexual power over either man, or that she is capable of a craziness that overawes them. Until shortly before production, Beatty has been seeing and reading a young improvisational comedienne, Robin Menken. There might have been a restless queen bee center of sensuality and imperious unpredictability with her in the picture, a kind of danger.

As it is, Beatty allows Nicholson to steal our attention, or has to watch it happening, helplessly. Next to Jack, he looks suspicious, tense and almost constipated. The one rogue is loveable, and the other is outside our attention. In labelled comedy, Nicholson is so much surer of himself than Beatty, and the script or the actor does not seem quite ready enough to let Nicky be a properly vain idiot. Beatty does not have a free part of himself loose enough to put beside Nicholson's lazy, randy mercury. So he becomes clumsy fingers trying to pick it up. He often looks like a stooge, and the film allows him none of those pauses or those occasions for hurt noises in which he can become a center for pathos.

Jack and Warren also have Michelle Phillips in common. After her divorce from John Phillips and the break-up of the singing group the Mamas and the Papas, and after a short marriage to Dennis Hopper, Phillips lives with Nicholson for a time in the early 70s. She moves on from that to a relationship with Beatty sufficient to persuade him to inhabit the Mulholland Drive house he has owned for a few years but never really owned up to or taken possession of. He lives there with Michelle and her young daughter, China, and there is again talk that he may marry. He sometimes drives China to school. But he keeps his suite at the Beverly Wilshire, and if he sometimes confesses his awareness of growing older and feeling more sedate, no one close to him ever knows what other contacts have been cut off, or which flower in the dark. He will build himself a house on Mulholland Drive, but if a girl supposes this is an urge to settle he can murmur that he must, because the Beverly Wilshire addition has given other guests a view of his balcony.

In the audience, with Michelle Phillips, at the 1975 Hasty Pudding Man of the Year Award (Associated Press)

How do such uneasy associations end? Warren is not in the habit of sitting women down and telling them that he is bored or depressed with them, that their laughs or their bodies have run their course for him, that stagnation is taking away his larger optimism with life and making him disagreeable, that he is seeing someone else so this is over. He is too kind for that, or too afraid, for it is not simply kindness to let the tedious party notice the fresh excitement that some novel party has aroused in endless Warren.

"The truth is," he says, "that whenever a relationship has ended, the decision has never been mine; it's always been the other person's." We could deduce from that that Julie Christie has come to her own wilful decision that it is time for her to move on, that she has found someone else – that Warren is left, just as George, in a purely technical sense, is "left" at the end of *Shampoo*. But suppose that Christie was driven to that end out of self-protection, from so many hints of other affairs and out of eventual fury at the delicate manipulativeness that wants always to see itself in the right, and not unkind?

The fury may not always last. Many of the associations never quite end, so much as drift. When old girl friends pass through town, then old habits pass through Warren: it flatters them and helps him sustain the thought that he was not brutal. Friendship is a fine and extensive thing, but it can be a veil to the ugly shifts in life that leave us older and wounded. Friendship can be another word for unchallenged promiscuity, a synonym even for disloyalty.

There are some hurt. A few years after the relationship with Michelle Phillips ends, she speaks out: "He feels that marriage isn't a happy, productive way of life. He prefers not to be involved. He prefers shallow, meaningless relationships – he thinks they're healthier, or at least the only kind he can have."

He would hardly accept that portrait in quite such cold lucidity. Yet he is aware of the rootlessness, fascinated by it and horrified: he sees George Roundy's sickness but he cannot spoil the guy's glamor. He has to argue this out in his own head – can a woman fuck him and still feel decent? Can he be Warren and survive the mirror?

He decides he is not suited to marriage and its ties. But he has such high, vague ambitions to be significant in America – and how can a president, say, seem, rootless? The manipulative mind sorts through the problem and begins to conceive of a notion of "maturity" that is free but committed to reason, liberalism and purpose. He spells it out sometimes, and it is as close as he comes to sounding stupid or crazy:

"One way to describe maturity is to say it could be the capacity to postpone gratification. And when someone with my particular history has not been asked to postpone certain gratification – and I'm not speaking just of sexual gratification – it's impossible not to sense that you might be cheated out of maturity. And I try not to get cheated out of that."

*

Women hover in the air, like projects; and like projects, they can be given wings with the telephone. Beatty is especially occupied with the thought that he might act in *Hardcore*. This is a screenplay by Paul Schrader, the author of *Taxi Driver*, about a Michigan businessman, a strict Calvinist, whose teenage daughter goes missing on a Church trip to California and who becomes an actress in pornographic movies.

Some time later in 1975, Beatty announces his interest in playing this role. He talks of directing the picture himself, or of hiring Arthur Penn. Schrader has himself been set to direct originally, but he defers to the wishes of so big a star in what is regarded as a difficult picture. He rewrites the script for Warren. According to Schrader, Beatty

"wanted the daughter to be a wife because he didn't feel he was the appropriate age to be a father – which is a very typical actor's fantasy. I went on one of those Warren Beatty shifts – it was two hours a day every day for a month. He was living in the Beverly Wilshire. I did not find it a very rewarding experience, though it was a very educational one. He set in motion a series of changes which, ultimately, to my mind, destroyed the script. A softening."

What Schrader discovers in Beatty is the prolonged, gradual, diffident, unyielding assertion of power:

"He will always win. If you have a particular disagreement with him, let's say on an artistic issue, you can sit and convince him for two hours and he will walk away from it and then one week later he will bring up the issue and you will convince him again. And this can go on for years. You get worn down. In the end you never really convince him. You help him to find what he has already decided. And he apparently derives great energy from this. Other people walk out of the room exhausted, and he walks out energised."

The softening of the script is not without benefits. Beatty, finally, will back off (in order to make his film about Howard Hughes, he says at the time), and Schrader resumes as director with George C. Scott playing the central role and with the woman being made a daughter again. But

Schrader keeps at least one scene from his days with Warren, a scene he allows that Beatty wrote and which mirrors his subtle ways of getting what he wants. It involves Jake Van Dorn talking to his designer about a display:

> JAKE: Hmm. This all the display space you could get?
> MARY: I tried to get more, but this is the limit. The De Vries line has the same area.
> JAKE: What do you think of that shade of blue, Mary?
> MARY: I like it, Mr Van Dorn.
> JAKE: Don't you think it's a little . . . bright?
> MARY: Not really. But if you want me to tone it down?
> JAKE: I wouldn't hire a display designer if I didn't trust her taste. Maybe we could bring more of that shade in. Perhaps a panel?
> MARY: No, that would be much too overpowering.
> JAKE: Overpowering – that's the word I was looking for.
> MARY: Mr Van Dorn, I've worked on this color scheme for weeks. I think it's just right.
> JAKE: What do you call that shade?
> MARY: Pavonine. It's the same shade as the fabric.
> JAKE: Hmm-hmm. You still going with that fellow, that teacher over in Grand Valley?
> MARY: Sam?
> JAKE: Yeah. Nice guy. You don't want to lose him. Maybe we could take it *down* a little bit, it's such a –
> MARY: Overpowering?
> JAKE: Yeah.
> MARY: OK, Mr Van Dorn, I think we could knock that pattern in blue a bit.
> JAKE: Are you sure it's all right?
> MARY: Yes, I think it'll look better.
> JAKE: If you say so.

At least six months after Beatty has dropped out of *Hardcore*, Paul Schrader is at a party, talking to an actress. She says she is being considered for a part in a picture he has written; it is called *Hardcore*. Just a few days before, she has run into Beatty in the lobby of the Beverly Hills Hotel and he has asked her to read for the role of the woman – daughter, wife, whatever. "And apparently he read her," says Schrader, "whatever that entails. He discussed the role with her at length. To some degree you say it's just the machinations of Don Juan, but on another level it's a man who is a compulsive caster. And, if she had been totally right, maybe Warren would have picked up the phone and come back on *Hardcore*!"

Some years later, Beatty will be talking to another director with a project Beatty considers producing – when he is ready. The director says he risks losing actors and crew because of delays, but Beatty tells him, "I know what everybody's doing, and you're not going to lose anyone you wouldn't mind losing." This is a mind so full of reports, information and gossip, so much in control, so disposed to casting and arranging, that it may think it *is* the picture business. But there is a risk – that the game of casting takes over, and lets speculation dispel action.

He says, in 1976, that he will begin to make a movie about Howard Hughes. "I've been working on it for years," he discloses. "It seemed that the urgency of the project made the Schrader picture a more secondary priority." At the same time, he says it would be premature to suppose he is also about to re-make the 1941 picture, *Here Comes Mr Jordan*, about a boxer sent too soon to Heaven and allowed to return to life. "If you make that part of your story," he tells the *Los Angeles Times*, "you could be vastly incorrect." And he says he is thinking a lot about Hughes, about where he is and what a man of that stature is like, reclusive, in the desert somewhere or on the top floor of a luxury hotel, having a hand in the great affairs of the world, or simply existing, as an imagination.

Then, on April 5, 1976, Howard Hughes is reported dead, in the air, an hour out of Acapulco on the way to a hospital in Houston, a ninety-three-pound legend. One of his aides says that in the complex and scarcely plausible state of Hughes' business empire perhaps the mogul has had to die to establish that he was ever once legally alive.

Night desert

Not to disparage the salmon dinner they composed at Scotty's Castle, much less the deadpan amiability of Doc, or the entertaining conclave of whispering, spirit and conspiracy among Drew, Virginia and Look, still D had a hankering to be off, away for a while, in the capacious desert. He was moved by the prospect of its solitude and unobserved rites of mastery.

"Don't worry. We can be alone soon," Drew drawled as she passed his carved teak chair with salad. He must have been staring into his thoughts, gloomy with concentration.

Then Look asked him if he'd show her the house, at which Virginia recommended the organ, upstairs, and all of them fell about laughing. But they were soon dozing off the assault of their rich meal. There had been chocolate decadence waiting at the back of the ice-box, so heavy the wire shelf sagged beneath it.

When D awoke, there was no one to be seen. It was night yet it was warm with the day's heat gathered in the timbers and a scent of eucalyptus through the house. He went back to the bedroom where he had had his first rest, not sure why, until he found the note that Virginia had left him:

> "I had to get back. I've taken Eyes' glasses. Look out for yourself with all these hot babes, Dad. Joking. Seeyasoon. V. I mean, Virginia."

The last stroke of the V soared like a tick. D was reminded of the note he had left in the city apartment, and he pictured it there still, unseen, paling as the crisis set in, relic of an earlier life and discarded cares.

In another bedroom, he found Doc and Look naked and sleeping on a bed, their arms tangled, their bodies turned to face each other. Doc was a stringy old athlete, and Look was like a ripe persimmon beside him. D did not breathe in the doorway, and he heard the tranquil creaking of their two minds in sleep. Doc made a sound and moved one leg: Look responded with a soporific moan, an opening in the air to accept his noise,

374

and her hip rolled in time with his, as if the two bodies were oiled by the sounds. It was like finding gorillas asleep in the jungle and realising that every snuffle was true to their existence. The sleeping brains were steaming fecund earth. The tiny amendments to silence soaked into the ground so that the two people might wake, not needing to speak, but amazed and refreshed by the complicity. D was happy for Doc and Look, and he saw nobility in his erection between them, standing like a guard dog.

D ventured out of the house into the courtyard. It was as hot as day-for-night; there were shadows on the ground, and none of the chill of other nights. It was like a night that Doc and Look might be dreaming, pumping it alive with their long, slow snores. He looked up and he saw Drew standing on top of a rocky outcrop. She waved to him; slivers of light ran down the tautness of her body.

"Climb up," she said. There was no need to shout.

He found a way, feeling the warmth baked into the stones and the smoothness of the surfaces. Drew was sitting on a broad slab, a table rock; and though it was night, she was sunbathing, her head tipped back to let her neck turn golden. She moved to kiss him and he smelled the lemon juice and herbs at her mouth, tarragon and thyme, as well as the nutty convection from the rock and her nakedness. She moved like a dolphin across the rock. He was driftwood beside her, a plaything in the waves, but he shut his eyes and found that she was water now and that he could ride along in her swell. Pressed against him, her fragrance spurted: there was chocolate on her breath, and a virulent fish in her armpits, the confidence she was a siren. She moved on him expertly and she was smiling above his pleasure – the smile was their moonlight – coaxing and timing it, like a mother powdering a child with affection after its bath. If only he could take such moments for what they were. But wherever he was, he looked further ahead, with dread or desire, and now he saw past Drew's bouncing immediacy and the artful love in what she did here, now, to a time of being bored, to guilt, horror and death, and to needing someone else, anyone, just to move on and stay alive.

"Frightened?" she asked. He could not stand the way she saw into his plans for thought.

"I'm the singer," said D. "Not much good at the song." It sounded like a quotation, but he didn't know where it had come from, or even what it meant.

She was just as perplexed, but more daunted. She backed away and sat up. "Do you think I'm beautiful?" she asked him suspiciously.

"Of course." He didn't see how she could worry over that.

She sounded bitter, or resentful. "We all want the beauty for ourselves." She had a stance; he had noticed it and loved it many times – of being erect and lonely, set in an empty space. It was desire filling the view of a single full shot. There were times when it filled his mind, like a picture on the wall. But the poise escaped her now, and Drew was left behind, shakier, like someone nearly struck in an accident.

"Movie people," she despaired. "Two or three parts every year for twenty years, maybe. Looking the same, but slipping along. Such a lot of lovely pretending, and never being tied to any dull you. But those rovers get scared too, sooner or later, and in the end they beg, 'Don't leave me.' Such leavers!"

"They sing to stop the quiet," said D.

She pulled on the large T-shirt she had brought with her. It was her nightshirt, the souvenir of some picture she had been on, a tube of white cotton emblazoned with a title, dripping in dead flames, some forgotten sensation.

They followed the ridge that circled Scotty's Castle and took a spur sloping down to the plain. Moonlight had brushed it clear of debris or coiled serpents. They were walking on a crushed velour, and they could see their footprints appearing soundlessly, with the raindrop circles of their toes.

"You think the air here is poisoned?" Drew asked him.

"The best I've known," he told her.

"That's not suspicious?"

"It's the lack of contamination," he said, but he wondered where the lemony hints and the salmon pink in her sex went in the night. Had they been the first womanly smells in this stretch of the dry desert?

"Or poison from the tests," Drew imagined. "In Nevada there are pieces of land sixty miles by sixty where you can't go."

D thought of Virginia cycling across them, leaving one closed zip of track to perplex the snakes.

She had a story: "Howard Hughes was in Nevada once, and very fearful for his well-being. He had given up sandwiches because where the bread met the mayo seemed a certain place for infection. Every item of his food came separately: the bread, the ham, the Swiss and his mustard."

"He liked mustard?"

"Adored it. All in airtight cellophane packets. And he had stopped seeing his business associates. He regarded friends as a source of tainting. He spoke to his people endlessly but on a phone that did not touch his skin. And he wore only new clothes that had been fumigated and kept in a vacuum. As far as he could, he existed in neutral – in air so clean it was barely air, in a life so sparse it was nearly coma."

"Yes?" D held his breath, trying not to blow away the gossamer Hughes.

"And then one day his chief physician called him and said, 'Oh, by the way, Howard, did you ever consider that sex and money are major contagion carriers?' There was a stricken silence. The doctor wondered if Howard was mortified, or might have passed out in panic. But then Howard coughed and said, 'Well, we all die – send in the next one.'"

They kept walking. D did not remark on the story, or question its likelihood. But Drew knew he was revolving in its spin. He could no more resist stories than some people can leave a last dry-roasted peanut in the jar. And if some stories were tall, D only felt more upright because of them.

"Going to write for Eyes?" she asked.

"It would mean security," he answered.

Drew laughed. "Whatever it brings you, it won't be that."

There must have been a look of innocence on D's face. It never goes – stupidity locks it in long after youth's shine wears off.

She was elaborating: "There was a writer once Eyes hired, a good enough writer. This was when I was in favor. There was such a time. But this writer and I had a little thing going, you see. Maybe it wasn't for any more reason than so Eyes could feel betrayed. And one night we were at the writer's cottage in Malibu. It was warm, and the beach doors were open. You could hear the waves. We were making love, very quietly and peacefully, when I saw the look on his face. The worst look I ever saw. He was staring over my shoulder. Know what? Eyes was screwing me from behind at the same time, so soft, so slinky, I hadn't noticed. And Eyes looked over my shoulder at the writer – they had a rhythm going, and I was just the space in the middle – and he said, 'Hi kid, how are my pages coming?'"

"You never felt Eyes entering you?"

She shook her head. "Try that on a girl's sensitivity."

They may have been a mile from the Castle. It is hard to be sure how far you are going when you talk. But they heard three shots, heavy as doors slamming, and then a woman's scream from the same direction. There was horror in the scream, a hopelessness that made them sure a mile was too far away to be of any avail or mercy. Then a second scream, years sadder than the first, full of woe and revulsion, as if some pain had eaten into the worm's rot of the scream itself. There was only one cure to that scream, and it was deafness.

"We have to go back," said Drew, and he answered yes, he knew, he had known that all along.

HEAVEN CAN WAIT

He is forty when he makes *Heaven Can Wait*, too young yet for the grim but ravaged face of Hughes. And this is a picture that one might use to pass the time while waiting for others that are weightier and which will test stamina to the limit. Of the films Beatty has made for himself, it is the least necessary and the most easily forgotten. Yet it will be his greatest financial hit and it is so slight and so frivolous on the one hand, and so momentous on the other, that it may mark a moment at which he wonders if he can get away with anything.

But suppose he can never be simply cocksure or cold-blooded. Suppose that in the misty, cloud-cuckoo muddle of *Heaven Can Wait* there is or was something that intrigues and moves Warren Beatty. Well, it is a picture about being dead and alive at the same time; about being forty but pretending to be the Los Angeles Rams' quarterback in the Superbowl, while also looking back on life from the sterile but perfect vantage of a white Heaven; and, not least, it is the first movie in which strenuous, nearly depleting efforts seem to have been made by Warren to deny, evade or transcend his real age. It has the kind of tender soft focus that in the 30s and 40s was used to reassure still lovely but cracking actresses.

Joe Pendleton, a health freak football player, is killed in a traffic accident just before the big game. On his way to Heaven, he establishes with his Escort (Buck Henry) and the Archangel Mr Jordan (James Mason) that he has been rounded up too early. It is an error in Heaven's book-keeping. They hurry Joe's soul back to LA, but his old body has already gone up in smoke. So they let him be Leo Farnsworth, instead, a millionaire lately murdered by his wife and secretary. It is akin to acting, which is the enclosure of an imagined spirit in an old body.

The story is framed as farce, and clumsy farce at that, but is that plot simply as contrived and absurd as farce is presumed to be? Or should we consider whether Warren Beatty is not unusually tickled by the notion of a spirit and a mind that can escape its own body and then find itself stranded? The film does not grasp or develop the possibility, but there could be an extraordinary comedy here about a man who has managed to escape materiality, who talks to God (Beatty had wanted Cary Grant for that role, the locus classicus of his lounge suit acting) and has only occasional nostalgic twinges about doing something real and having a body for others to touch and . . . Suppose it was about a man able to watch and wander unseen through the life he had just left, pleased to find everyone waiting. I am guessing – but one has to do something with the disarray of *Heaven Can Wait*; and I am so fond of Warren I would rather think the best of his ventures. Let us just say there is a prospect worthy of *our* Warren here – a sublime film which, three or four times, peeps through all the busy untidiness of the picture that made a medium-sized fortune.

He has bought the movie rights to the original play from old Jed Harris. The play is *Here Comes Mr Jordan*, by Harry Segall. It has been filmed in 1941, with Robert Montgomery in the lead. The rights have come into the possession of Harris, seventy-five in 1975, sick, bitter, dying, once the greatest stage director in New York and one of the most feared and disliked men in the world. By the 1970s, Harris is forgotten, living in Los Angeles, a peculiar torture to the once famous, smoking himself to death. Beatty pays him $25,000 for the rights to *Here Comes Mr Jordan*, money for cigarettes and a hotel while Harris is "wasting time waiting to die".

Beatty hires Elaine May to write the script, and then becomes her collaborator. The script never seems to bear May's caustic charge, the instinct for danger and giving public affront evident in *Such Good Friends*, *A New Leaf*, *The Heartbreak Kid* and *Mikey and Nicky*. Elaine May is a regular in Beatty's telephone fold, an obsessively private woman whom he likes to hire and encourage, despite her reputation for dark and difficult films. One other associate says she is the sort of "smart, funny, cynical urban person he likes to have around".

Beatty talks to Peter Bogdanovich about directing *Heaven Can Wait*: after all, it is meant as a recreation of classic Hollywood, such as Bogdanovich has managed in *What's Up, Doc?* and *Paper Moon*. Bogdanovich is willing. But as they talk, Warren says, of course, he could direct it himself. The debate goes on many months, at the end of which Bogdanovich announces, "Warren, I'd like to dance with you, but I'm going to have to leave."

It has turned out so that he *has* to direct himself; the other person has walked out. But he is wary of being over-extended and he enlists Buck

Henry as a co-director. What does this mean? Henry never quite knows. He says of Warren, "He likes to work under pressure, and if it's not there he'll create it. He's a demonic producer . . . he fills every minute. Nothing deters him, nothing stops him. He barely sleeps and he likes to do as much as possible himself." Perhaps a co-director does lay off some of the pressure. He is also another opinion on the set, and another entertaining companion.

This is the first time Beatty has lodged one of his productions at Paramount. He likes it there. He gets on well with Charles Bluhdorn, the chairman of Gulf & Western, and with Barry Diller, the chairman of Paramount. He also gets the best deal he has ever had there, and secures exceptional power in the promotion of his film. I do not know the figures on the deal, but its outline shows the power Beatty has: first, Paramount pays for the production – Beatty does not use his own money; he gets a significant fee for his work – say, $3–4 million; and he gets a portion of the profits. Beatty is not alone in enjoying such a deal. Half a dozen other stars command similar terms. But he is unique in being a producer who does not let anyone outside his circle interfere in the film, in its conception or production, and now as little as possible in the marketing too. Yet he abides by the old Hollywood scheme of studios taking the risk. He is notably not like George Lucas and Francis Coppola, who seek to rid themselves of the old system and who put their own money in their projects, thus ensuring much more of the gain, and the loss. For Coppola it brings ruin, but for Lucas it is the means to wealth and power such as Beatty cannot approach. His business instincts stay conservative, faithful to Hollywood.

Heaven Can Wait opens in June 1978. It has a famous poster of Warren, legs crossed, head bowed, wearing a track suit and angel's wings. Indeed, it may be the wings that are keeping him upright. In the summer of *Grease* (a far bigger hit), *Heaven Can Wait* is material for a rather older audience in search of romance. There are laughs in the picture (mostly from Dyan Cannon and Charles Grodin), a great deal of undisciplined good nature, and much wishful thinking about true love surpassing death and other ecological threats. At the end of the picture, there are poignant looks between Warren and Julie Christie – as if they were both gazing at advertisements – which makes the public sentimental for a relationship that no longer functions in life. And in Beatty's millionaire masquerade there is a puppy-like naivety in which anyone can imagine they would handle being rich too without ever having to become more or less than decent and kind. (It has a sophomoric bounce, an unawareness of difficulty's existence, that is like the elixir than keeps Reagan young.)

In Beatty's own performance there is a blur of wide-eyed hurry and self-consious eccentricity that seems like the wish to be charming. But the picture never pricks the bubble. It obviously works in 1978, but it is such a departure from his earlier watchfulness, and it is the chief reason why he seems to be becoming younger on the screen. Something is asking us to see, and trying to make himself believe in, an earnest, idealistic, likeable Mr Beatty. He has seen a possible public image, and he strains after it. But short sight has left him in a fuzz. He is desperately trying to come out into the open. But the more he appears, the more lightweight he seems.

The picture earns $47.5 million in rentals in its first release. It is his third production in a row to be a big hit. He has never been richer, or attached himself to so minor a project. *Heaven* has several Oscar nominations, but no significant awards. Oscar night in 1979, in the company of Diane Keaton, brings him not much more than the test of his sister's wide-eyed jokes from the stage.

Warren and Shirley have at least two things in common – a place in the highest rank of American show business, and parents who are neither young nor especially well. They have something else to share, of course: a sibling they do not fully understand, who vexes and provokes them as naturally as he (or she) commands their love. This is not too uncommon. Few siblings close to the age of fifty still dream of absolute harmony. They get along as best they can, pleased (if they reflect) that their tiffs and silences do not get on television.

Warren has reason to regret that Shirley goes on about him so much. Over the years, she has talked about him to reporters, weighing the mischief and the fun, while he has said very little in public except that he doesn't talk about his sister. She has referred to him during her stage show and wondered at the number of women who have had him. On Oscar night, 1979, her jokes might not have been offered, except that he is sitting there in the audience and on camera. His smile that night says a good deal about family life, his ability to put on humor, and how long he has known her.

There may have been anger after that night, and no one could say she has not earned it. In her most recent book, *Dancing in the Light*, she says she respects his wish that she should not discuss his life. After all, he does not analyse her views on reincarnation in print; he appears to act as if it was natural and proper that she has her life and career, apart from him.

He is so reticent that you begin to appreciate how far her jokes, her jabs, have shown her need to win his interest and approval. He was her first audience, and maybe her toughest.

That said, she has been doing not much more than tease a tease. For anyone very fond of Warren and as experienced as Shirley in keeping up with him, there must be a great urge to puncture that immaculate, superior male grin and to let the world realise that Mr Wonderful has his common, shabby, inglorious moments, too – that it is all a grand act. There is a way in which Shirley serves as the wife Warren has not risked – adoring, enduring, but reckless with wondering whether his gravity has to be taken *so* seriously.

In both of them, there is an urge to surprise the other. On the occasion of the 1984 Academy Awards, Warren prepares a very complex gift for Shirley. It is something he has devised and fashioned personally, in several parts that reflect on his sister's life. He has it delivered to her just as she gets in the car to be driven to the ceremony where she will win an Oscar for *Terms of Endearment*.

*

In *The New Yorker*, in 1978, Pauline Kael says of *Heaven Can Wait*:

> "There isn't a whisper of personal obsession in the moviemaking. The film has no desire but to please, and that's its only compulsiveness; it's so timed and pleated and smoothed that it's sliding right off the screen. This little smudge of a movie makes one laugh a few times, but it doesn't represent moviemaking – it's pifflemaking. Warren Beatty moves through it looking fleecy and dazed, murmuring his lines in a dissociated, muffled manner. The film has to be soft-focused and elided – a series of light double takes – because if Beatty raised his voice or expressed anything more than a pacific nature, the genteel, wafer-thin whimsy would crumble."

So he hires her – as if to prove he is more than she fears. She has been the most noted and eloquent film critic in America for ten years. Ever since *Bonnie and Clyde*, she has followed and been impressed by his work – until this. But she is close to sixty and as worried over money as she is still ambitious for some complete, wild glory in film-making. And so she goes to Los Angeles, to an office on the Paramount lot, to work for Beatty, developing projects and ideas and perhaps, one day, coming to be a producer. One day, at nearly sixty? There are obvious reasons why this deal is dangerous: she is old for the change, she does not drive and she is likely to be flayed by the world of writing and criticism that she is now

383

compromising and deserting. He may never really listen to her, or share her lust for danger. There may be a part of him that seeks to prove her wrong – or ordinary. But there is a headstrong romantic in Kael: it is what makes her sense of movies so eager and sensual. And he cannot lose his respect for intelligence.

There is an immediate project for Ms Kael. In 1977, James Toback directs his first film, *Fingers*. He has previously written *The Gambler*. *Fingers* is a commercial failure, yet it cost only $1 million. It is one of the most startling American debuts, expressing Toback's overwrought feelings for art and crime, for sensitivity and violence. The picture gets a few good reviews, one of them from Kael, who has known Toback a little in New York.

For his next film, Toback has written *Love and Money*, about a man who falls for the wife of a South American silver baron, and takes her away from him. Toback wants Beatty to play the hero. The script is bought by Columbia, but when the top management there changes after the David Begelman scandal, the picture goes into turnaround. Toback telephones Warren Beatty, who asks him to send the script to the Beverly Wilshire.

But Toback knows the suite there is crammed with old scripts, many of which are not read. He tells Beatty, "I've got to read it to you."

"I know how to read," says Beatty. "Besides, I wouldn't let Sergei Eisenstein read me a script.

Toback has a long history as a gambler. "Oh well," he says. "We can't do it."

The next day Beatty calls back and asks to see *Fingers*. It is screened for him and Ali McGraw. It is a very frightening film, visceral and passionate in its disregard of caution. After seeing it, Beatty walks around the screening room in agitation. "How did you get him to *do* that?" he asks Toback about the actor in *Fingers*, Harvey Keitel. Does he think that Toback might unlock his own final security? From the start, something in Toback intrigues and perplexes Beatty and maybe leaves him a little ashamed of his safety.

He meets Toback for dinner at the Four Oaks restaurant on Beverly Glen. Toback reads the script while Beatty feeds. It is in the primitive nature of survival that you cannot eat with someone else not eating without feeling his inferior. Beatty buys the script, and says he will produce it. He may act in it, too.

Then Beatty puts Toback with Kael to refine and develop the screenplay. They work together for a couple of months: she wants substantial changes in the script, but he will accept only a few. In the end, Beatty sides with the man and the film-maker in these disputes. But they are settled by the advance of *Reds*, by the termination of the arrangement with Kael and by Lorimar coming in to take over *Love and Money*.

Kael returns eventually to New York and the *New Yorker* where she works again as the film critic, more secure perhaps but less important in her authority and less potent as a writer. Soon she is cruelly attacked by Renata Adler in the *New York Review of Books*. *Love and Money* is made, with Ray Sharkey in the role meant for Beatty, and Klaus Kinski as the tycoon – the part that would have suited Warren better. The film is hugely inferior to *Fingers* and gets only a three-week run in New York. Warren is making *Reds*.

It all feels like a short story, about vanity, false hopes and hustling in Hollywood. And so it is. But it also concerns three fascinating people, full of creative energy and the urge to manipulate others. Perhaps Beatty has hopes of being not just a producer, but a patron, and hope for the future, a leader in the industry. Perhaps he puts two alarming people in a room together to see if they will destroy themselves. At the least, don't write the incident off as a whim or a wrong turning. Warren doesn't make mistakes. This play is as full of thwarted potential as *Heaven Can Wait*, a man harboring a strange, young hope.

There is another possibility that comes his way. In 1979, at the urging of his friend Henry Jaglom, Orson Welles writes an original script, *The Big Brass Ring*. It is about a senator in his forties, a Vietnam veteran, who runs for president, and a much older man, once an adviser to Franklin Roosevelt. The senator takes on this older man as his chief council and adviser in the presidential bid. And the old man falls in love with the senator, without ever disclosing what he feels.

Welles has known Beatty a little; they dine occasionally. And Welles thinks that perhaps he and Warren might play the two parts in *The Big Brass Ring*. It could be a significant return to American movies for Welles as a director. The script is offered to Beatty and he says he will do it if he can be the producer and if he has the power of final cut. If you think that Welles is the greatest film director America has had, this is a humbling proposal, even a humiliation. Welles refuses. Who knows how valuable a picture is lost here, or how tender and stirring a screen meeting?

Dog

Wavering with drink, but with his deadly suave act unimpaired, the man Dog was taking D on a tour of the Castle. Despite the heat, Dog wore a coat as heavy as carpet, with a fur collar. Wherever he ambled, he carried a ponderous rifle – D thought it might be a buffalo gun, its spear-long, tasseled gravity accounting for the absence of that creature. But Dog did not hold the gun with shooting in his mind. He cradled it, so that it resembled a rod of office.

"Now, of course," Dog explained, "I am in charge, and I believe I am safe in regarding myself as a gentleman."

"Yes?" said D.

"But . . . I do drink immoderately, as the day wears on. Immoderately," he repeated, for the word was his test of sobriety. "And the others are beasts, you see?"

D had guessed it from the wolfish jaw and the pink pit-bull eyes.

"It's just that I wouldn't want to instill any false confidence. I don't want you coming whining to me later."

Dog retrieved a pint flask of spirits from a poacher's pocket in his coat and took an extensive swallow. The hot air became more pressured. "We should bury that slut," he supposed, his wild head stretching in her direction, but impeded by the fur collar and an old crick in his neck.

"Look," said D.

"Be a horrid stink if we don't."

It must have been eleven in the morning, and there were three dead already in the steadfast courtyard of Scotty's Castle, where even the killers, weighed on by perils, looked wistfully at the wishing well.

Look was on her way to dying when D and Drew returned to the castle at dawn. Dog then had been sitting on the stone wall to the well, keeping a serene sideways cover on the weeping Doc, while Breed (an associate of Dog's) was beating up Look. It was like beating a lace handkerchief for dust.

Dog and Breed in *McCabe and Mrs Miller* (Warner Brothers)

"I say, easy on," Dog was murmuring, and then, "Good Lord", to see such absurd violence in his associate. "She's a nice-looking girl," Dog remonstrated. "Not the sort of thing we're likely to find every day in the desert."

"Too pleased with herself," said Breed, and Dog sighed at Doc to indicate that benevolence could only go so far.

"Stop him!" howled Doc.

Breed did falter. When he had no strength left to hit Look, he scratched and gouged at her. And so she fell in the courtyard, and had been left there. She was bloody and broken, but in the space of two hours, without anyone noticing, she had moved a few feet, her body snailing its way on the ground.

"She wants the shade," Drew realised.

"What could I do?" Doc implored them. "I was asleep, and she tried to protect me."

They had stood by and watched the beating, directed by Dog's archaic gun and the lean hatefulness of Breed, a gaunt man in a poncho. "He's unpredictability itself," Dog had warned them, "a lost soul." Dog was sentimental about those born of two races, and he admired the way Breed had adapted to being unloved.

The morning passed: boredom and the enormous terror of expecting to be murdered co-existing like the heat and Dog's fur coat. There was something, D knew now, that permitted ugly power – it was a readiness in the humble to be ordered. It was like sitting beneath an amazingly frightening film in which no torture was spared, hoping it will end but obedient in the dark. There had always been a slavery implicit in watching movies.

"Is there anything we can do?" Drew whispered.

"You think so? What is there? I really don't see a thing we can do," D rattled off answers.

"Don't look so serious," she told him.

"Oh stop," begged D. He was crying, he noticed. Her hand went to his face to lift away the tears.

"I'd suggest," said Dog, "you didn't do that, little lady. Breed here is touchy."

"I'll do what I choose," Drew told Dog.

"Ah well," chuckled Dog, and left it there for the moment, not at all surprised to see D flinching from his lover's courage.

After noon, a troop of prisoners came into the courtyard, led by a single guard, Kid, a white-haired youth. There was Clear, Cy, Claudia,

Dog

Beau, Tusk, Zale, Chuck (have we forgotten anyone?), except that Zale was dead already, shot, and being carried by Cy and Tusk.

"Had to make an example, old boy?" Dog asked the Kid.

"He's a lawyer." Kid still resented the foul luck in meeting one.

"Bravo," said Dog. "Any others?"

"What others?"

"They invariably move in pairs," Dog explained.

"I am a lawyer," Clear volunteered.

"Really?" said Dog. He moved his long rifle a little, and its roar enveloped the courtyard. Tusk was knocked over by the blast, and then they saw he was in pieces on the ground. The gun had been loaded with coins. "I hate them sagging and bumping in my pocket," said Dog. And the amused Kid pried a quarter from Tusk's ribs and tossed it in the wishing well.

"What did you wish for, sonny?" Dog called.

Kid turned to those left. His gray teeth grinned at Drew. "For her," he said, as if it was obvious.

A lunch was made from the kitchen, and it was apparent that only Dog, Breed and Kid were partaking. "Provisions in the desert are so scarce," Dog apologised.

Clear was loyal to his role of spokesman. "We also need to eat," he said.

Dog did not answer, and it was not clear whether this was because he was eating or because he had no answer.

"One has to feed one's prisoners," said Clear.

Now Dog laughed: "What utter rot! Do you think in the great crises of history – in war or revolution – people feed the prisoners and give them magazines to read? Sir," said Dog, "they off them. All modern ingenuity has been given over to the ways of offing them."

A little later, cooking slowly in the sun, Drew asked Clear, "So what do they do with us if we don't do anything?" No one had dared answer. The prisoners gazed away from their plight, like late riders on the subway trying to erase freaks and junkies.

"What *are* we waiting for?" Clear attempted in the middle of the afternoon.

"Well," drawled Dog, "we understand there is another survival group hereabouts – some fancy picture star. They come here to carouse."

As he drank more, Dog expounded on the philosophy of survivalism, its poetry – the raw desert ordeal and a new way of life, the good of the community, the inspiration in stamping out danger, and the sublime fact of enemies.

"I was in bitter mid-life," said Dog. "Had this bistro in Malibu. Stupid place for stupid people. Smiling on their whims. But here!" He stood up and reached for the air. "I feel like Douglas Fairbanks. Senior," he added.

The shade of evening wiped the courtyard. Kid turned on Drew. "No," D whispered, asking his eyes not to notice.

He saw the amber light penetrating from the west. It honeyed all her hairs. He thought how ridiculous that it should be beautiful.

"Don't worry, my sweet," Drew told him. And then, out of breath or pleading, "Go away."

Must we say what happened? There should be a pause for looking away from the gaping screen and its placid rendering of such things. Description makes the writer and the reader more subject to dread. It went on and when it was over Drew was silent, cast down. Her great eagerness was gone and it was night. She was slumped next to D in the makeshift compound where the prisoners were tethered. Her blood shone like grease on an engine.

D did not know if she was asleep, dead or lost to talk. For hours he thought what to say to her. But he lacked the words. The desert had brought them to silence. Three days and they were savage and mute.

Then, quietly crazy, listening to what he might say, he thought he heard a whisper.

"Who's that?" he heard himself say. He wondered if Kid was back for more, more vicious in the dark.

"Who dya think at long last, kid?"

"Don't," D implored. "Not irony."

"What sort of welcome is that?" The voice was chipper and bantering, like a stand-up comic who had died over and over again, but would not go away.

"Who are you?" asked D. The husky voice was reviving him. He had to listen for its elusiveness.

"I have to spell it out?"

"Who?" D was at his limit.

"Tell you what," the voice was ready for another tack. "A man of many parts. Some missing maybe."

"Yes?" said D. "You're – "

"Hey, kiddo, be discreet, por favor. Did you hear the one about the man on a walking tour?"

"This is a joke?" D could not believe in such an approach.

"You be the judge. Anyway, this guy is out in wild country and the weather is looking bad. He comes to an isolated inn. He goes inside. It's warm and snug, and the landlord says, 'You're in luck, sir. We've just the one room left. Now, sit down by the fire, and warm yourself, and I'll bring you a supper. Will beef and oyster pie suffice?'"

"This is a long story?" asked D.

"At its best it is," the voice told him, a little vexed.

"We all of us here need to be rescued," said D. "This lady is close to death."

"I know that," said the voice. "I can very well see that." There was a pause as looking might have been going on. Yet in the dark, perhaps only touching could tell. "Anyway, the man is eating his supper, and the big storm breaks. He is on the coffee and brandy when the inn door opens and another traveler is nearly blown in by the gale, soaked and unsteady on his feet. Well, the first man watches the second man talking to the landlord. And, after a while and a few concerned glances, the landlord comes over and says, 'Sir, we have a little difficulty.'"

"This is Drew," said D. "Remember her?"

"I know," said the voice patiently. "Don't sound so serious."

"I let her down," said D.

"You did?"

"I wasn't good enough for her. But I took the bit I wanted."

The voice waited. It was not unkind. "You don't have to tell me. We've all done that. So the landlord says, 'This other gentleman needs a room, and we have only one. Yours. However, the bed in the room is very commodious. I wonder if, under these exceptional circumstances, you would be prepared to share. Of course, I'd make no charge.'

"What can the man say? He doesn't want to be uncooperative. He says, no problem. And the second man comes over and thanks him, and he seems a decent fellow. He has some of the same supper and they play a little dominoes together. And after a while, and another round of brandies – all on the house – they decide they'll go on up to bed."

"Can you get us out of here?" D asked. If he had to endure the story, he wanted certain assurances.

"Well, I tell you, I'm really not sure," admitted the voice. "That answer your question? Anyway, the two men get to the bedroom and the second man sits down on the bed and he unscrews his legs. Just like that. The first man is amazed. And the second man sees this and says, 'Oh, please don't be alarmed. I had a serious accident a few years ago.

Actually, I live alone now, so I can't often do this, but since you're here I wonder if you'd help me take my arms off? They're chafing tonight; it must be the damp.'

"And the first man says, 'Your arms too?'

"The second man nods and says, 'It was a terrible and unusual accident. The doctors agreed I was fortunate to survive.' So the first man helps him take off his arms, and there's just the trunk of the guy in bed. Looks like a piece of ginger.

"Well, they chat a little about hobbies and so on, and then they go off to sleep."

"Please!" hissed D.

"What is it?" asked the voice, hurt now. "You don't like the story?"

"I'm desperate."

"Well, of course you are. I was telling you the story to take your mind off it. Can't you make the effort to see that?"

"I suppose," grumbled D.

"Right. Well, in the middle of the night, the first man wakes up suddenly, and he can't place what it is that woke him. But the second man, he's awake too. And he says, 'Don't worry. A bird has flown in the window and it can't find its way out.' This is pitch dark, you understand?"

"Yes," sighed D.

"So the second man says, 'I have a way with wild creatures. Just screw my legs back on, if you will. I don't think I'll require the arms.'"

There came a great groan from Drew, as if she just realised she had heard this story before.

"The first man gets out of bed and, in the dark, as best he can, he has to put the second man's legs back on. This is not the simplest thing in the world. All the while the bird is flying around in panic, its wings beating."

"I think she's dead," said D.

"Yeah, she is," the voice agreed. "She was dead when I got here."

"She sighed."

"That was her body settling." There was silence. "She was a bit of terrific, wasn't she?"

"Better than we deserved," said D.

There was a silence, as if the voice was judging whether or not to say, "Don't be solemn", and decided against it.

"What happened then?" asked D. "In the story."

"Well, the second man sits up on the edge of the bed and he makes strange noises, sort of muttering, cooing sounds from inside his head. And the bird is slowly soothed or charmed by the sounds. It flies around less. And finally it lands on the second man's head. He was nearly bald, by the way."

"Yes," said D.

"And the second man gets up on his legs and, very slowly, so as not to disturb the trembling bird, he walks over to the open window."

"There was a storm," D remembered.

"It died away before they retired."

"Oh, well, OK, I suppose."

"And the man gets to the window and he leans his body forward so that his head and the bird are in fresh air. And he says very quietly to the bird. 'Away you go.' And the bird flew off with his head."

LIVING WITH REED

It is not easy making films. Nor is it pleasant. Anyone doing it looks forward to it being over. It is regularly perplexing to hear the remarks of lay friends who are sure it is delightful. But something about the enterprise smacks of hell – I do not mean just the exhaustion, the clash of boredom and sudden, savage crises, the aura of helpless, predestined waste and structural corruption, the ferment of egos all needing intimacy, reassurance and orders. Nor even the realisation at this or that stage that the film may not be worth making. No, the hardest thing of all to digest, if you are the film-maker, is the persistent sensation that the ordeal has become so ruinous, so toxic, you are prepared to sacrifice your precious intention, just to get the damn thing done. So you lose faith in yourself, just as you find ample evidence to dislike everyone else on the picture. You acquire the instincts and the capacity for vengeance, because you have felt so wretched. But if you once believed in such things as unique and precious intentions, you become disappointed most of all in film. You see that you are not as good as you wanted to be, but you discover something worse, that the very medium lacks the depth or faith you wanted. You feel you are on a train going in the wrong direction, and the effort it has all taken appears madness. Ironically, you end up rich and famous, as well as a natural murderer like Salieri.

Of course, you cannot stop the train, or get off, not if this is a large American picture, because there is a weight of money and contracts that cannot stop. You are not allowed to abandon the idea, and if, as the work proceeds, you see ways of changing it – because you have finally found the subject, as writers often discover what they should be doing in the act of writing – still, it is too late. A film is made according to its plan. Alter that along the way and you usually destroy the picture. You would need to begin again, as a painter might quickly paint over a deadlocked canvas, happy to have seen what the painting really is. In a film, you cannot paint over the first $15 million, or crumple it and toss it at the wastepaper bin until you get the throw right. You may have to drag your way on, just to finish it, knowing it is wrong and resenting it all the more because the strain is killing your joy and mugging your youth.

Warren decides to make *Reds,* and although it is a venture he has been nursing for longer than most people realise, when he decides to proceed with this huge picture there is something impulsive about it, like people who have lived all their lives in social discontent who realise one day in their early forties that this particular protest has gone a little further than others and that some arrangement of chance and history have made it such a cusp that something is astir which, by tomorrow maybe, will be called a revolution, and by the day after the hinge of epochs or the end of the world.

He has been intrigued by the life of John Reed, the Harvard boy, the writer, the impresario of political pageants, the middle-class red who went to Russia in 1917, who wrote *Ten Days That Shook the World* and was dead in 1920 at the age of thirty-three. He has himself been at the Widener Library at Harvard to study the many boxes of John Reed papers. He has hired research students, brilliant, pretty kids, who pore over the early history of the American Left and carry the digests to him in the Beverly Wilshire penthouse – blondes in suntops with small books on syndicalism and accounts of mining conditions in 1915. For years, being so rich, he is working on radicalism undercover.

As early as 1972, he films an interview with Manny Kamrov, a New York left-winger. He hears the first, vague words of tumbling memory. He sees an elderly face struggling to separate what was from the wishing. He realises how pleased the neglected old are to be talked to; they could talk for ever, especially those who claim they have nothing to say. This first interview will not appear in *Reds*: it does not have the visual style of the eventual witness scenes, but it is a beginning in which he discovers the need to decide how these scenes should look and how they might constitute a chorus. In 1976, he hires English playwright Trevor Griffiths to write a script for the project.

Griffiths is in America to attend Mike Nichols' wedding. He shares a car and a lot of talk with Warren from New York to Connecticut. A week later, Warren calls and asks what Griffiths knows about Reed. What do you want to know? the writer replies. "I don't want to know anything," says Beatty. "I've been looking at the guy's life for the last ten years." They talk for eight months on the trans-Atlantic phone – "He was finding out whether I could help him," says Griffiths. The script is commissioned and written; it is called *Comrades*.

Beatty reads the script, and considers. It is evidently huge, and not yet what Beatty wants. But he decides to show it in this form to begin to secure support. He sends it to Barry Diller at Paramount, who says he likes it and would want to make it. But it is so large and costly a venture that Charles Bluhdorn, the head of Gulf & Western, must give his approval too. Diller arranges a New York appointment with Bluhdorn for Beatty, and adds that the script should be a lot shorter by the time of that meeting.

And so, with only days to do it in, Beatty, Elaine May and a few others make a cutting circle. But in the time available they achieve only a mess, not a properly revised screenplay. Still, the working breakfast at the Carlyle Hotel cannot be denied. Beatty takes a copy of the script for *Heaven Can Wait* and puts it between *Reds* covers – his title. He can pat it and point to it, and it will look modest and manageable. He'll say, "I know you don't have time to *read* this, Charlie." Elaine May arranges to be demurely at another table in the Carlyle restaurant. If Bluhdorn does begin to examine the script, she will faint or have hysterics, or perhaps hurl scrambled eggs around the room. Can this be so? Is it real, or part of a comedy they think of making late one night? Paramount decides to go with *Reds*.

In time, Warren will ask Elaine May and Robert Towne – at least – to work on scenes for him. He will be reworking parts of the screenplay as the shooting takes place. He will tell actors on the day what they are to say. He will shape scenes at the moment of making them. Only Diane Keaton and Jack Nicholson among the other actors even have a script. Supporting actors, like Edward Herrmann, never see one. This is to allow improvements to be made at the last possible instant; it is to keep the huge enterprise "intimate" and secret; it also has the effect of dramatising Beatty's command and it lets the filmmaker delay making up his mind.

During the writing process, Coral Browne, the English actress, happens to stay with Lillian Hellman in New York. Late in the evening, when Ms Browne has retired, she hears someone come in the front door and go quietly upstairs to Lillian's bedroom, leaving much later. This happens on those nights when Hellman has ordained that they will not go out to dinner. Browne is so curious that on the next such night she lies in wait, manages to open the front door herself and finds a surprised Warren Beatty. "Oh yes," confirms a friend, "they sit upstairs drinking, and talking about radicals in the old days."

In March 1979, before he and she attend the Oscars ceremony, sitting so close to the TV cameras that they must smile patiently when Shirley

MacLaine wonders out loud about Warren's sexiness, Warren and Diane Keaton go with production designer Richard Sylbert to look for locations in Russia. Would the Soviets let *Reds*, or *Comrades*, be made in Leningrad? Would the shrewd Beatty really let them let him in? The Russians ask to see the script, and Warren declines. Alas, they say, the picture cannot therefore be shot in Russia. And so the makers settle on Helsinki for the revolutionary street scenes. After all, the same architect, long ago, had worked on the civic buildings in both Helsinki and St Petersburg.

Beatty is with Diane Keaton now. This does substantiate the observation of Leslie Caron that Warren is drawn to Oscar-winners – for Keaton wins for 1977 in *Annie Hall*. Equally, Beatty may see in Keaton not just the realisation of his sense of Louise Bryant, John Reed's wife, but the living woman. And Keaton is very far from just the best available actress for this central role: she is a shy but assertive woman, a good photographer (someone with her own work) who will display a cool ironic sensibility, in *Reservations* (a study of hotel lobbies) and *Still Life*, her droll collection of old Hollywood production stills. No other Beatty film contains so large or troubling a portrait of a woman, or is so concerned with sexual politics. And Diane Keaton deserves great credit for that, not simply as a performer but as a generating influence, the voice and independence Beatty hears the most. *Reds* has remarkable quarrels between Reed and Louise. It is not simply a film of seductions and betrayals, like *Shampoo*. It rages with the texture of everyday failure and company. A woman argues with Beatty on screen, silencing him again and again, and the tiredness in his face is not acting, but his age and the ordinary, unhideable dimming of romanticism.

The shooting takes place between August 1979 and July 1980 – there are some 240 days of actual filming, in Helsinki, in Spain (standing in for the Baku region of Russia), in New York, Washington and Los Angeles, but mostly in England. Some interiors are filmed at the Twickenham Studios, but the Reeds' Croton-on-Hudson house is found in Kent; Camber Sands, in Lincolnshire, is the location for the Provincetown beach scenes. There is also shooting in the Manchester area. In all, about 130 hours of film will be exposed, involving immense industry of costuming and art direction, large crowds, authentic period trains and cars – this is all the detail of film-making that the small army amasses and which the leader must check and approve.

There are key figures on the shoot – the Italian director of photography, Vittorio Storaro, Richard Sylbert, Shirley Russell, who does the costumes, the production manager Nigel Wooll and the assistant director, Simon Relph, and the associate producer, David MacLeod. But Beatty must be in charge of everything, and his is the mind that shapes the way the picture comes into being.

Sylbert, who has worked with Beatty on *Splendor in the Grass, Lilith, Bonnie and Clyde, Shampoo* and *The Fortune*, is impressed at his tact as director: "He's got an amazing brain, but he doesn't show off. He never says, 'Look at me directing.' He doesn't do phony stuff. He does story. He is never off on story. And while it was a big picture, a lot of the time it was really intimate and we were making it with only four or five people. And, you know, all the time we were learning – you couldn't figure out how to do this picture unless you just started doing it."

When the production goes to Spain, at Guadix, near Granada, Beatty lives in a small house with no hot water with Jerzy Kosinski, the novelist he has asked to play the Bolshevik leader, Zinoviev. For Kosinski, making a movie is rather a lark, something he will do just once, a kind of holiday. But he becomes fascinated by Beatty's deliberate, if not fanatical, absorption in detail and hardship, even at the cost of his health: "For me, as a novelist, I am living in a revolution. But I am also living with this pathetic American. I'm back into my past, like Zinoviev – hot days, cold nights. I'm enjoying it. But I'm living with John Reed, who is doing this ridiculous thing, and I'm annoyed by it. I'm very cynical. To me it's all a game. To him, it's an idea."

One day they are shooting in Seville, in 110 degree heat, a crowd scene with Reed addressing the throng. Warren has what is called the flu, or some collection of illnesses and fatigue that are asking him to stop and be sorry for himself. The Spanish extras are discontented. Storaro's crew begin to put the camera on a podium. Warren is discussing the scene with Kosinski when he breaks away, alarmed, because the podium may not take all the weight. He asks for the contractor for his opinion, but it is the Feast of Corpus Christi. A search goes on and the man is found. He looks and he says, why yes, of course, the podium must be made stronger. "You have to worry about such details yourself?" Kosinski asks in wonder. "Do you let anyone else check your manuscript?" Warren replies.

As the strengthening work goes on, Beatty speaks to the extras. He tells them the story of the film, of John Reed's life, and of the great issues it entailed. All of this has to be done through translation. It is a long speech, because Beatty wants the extras' upturned, listening faces to feel understanding and emotion, no matter that they are 1980s

Spaniards pretending to be Russians in 1920. The extras follow the stirring, but halting outline of socialism, and in the lunch break they come to Beatty with the case that in view of the noble principles of this picture they are really convinced they should be paid $90 a day each instead of $70. The deal is re-made and the scene is shot in the undiminished sunlight.

It all gets done – much more than all, in that only a fortieth of what is shot will be in the finished picture. The budget rises. And this is feared by Paramount, the company that will distribute the film and its largest source of financing. Barry Diller has been anxious at the speed with which shooting began and at the lack of pre-production. It is true that the availability of actors determined the starting date. While originally budgeted at $20 million, *Reds* soon takes on a size that will eclipse that figure. Diller grows angry and refuses to talk to Beatty because he feels that Paramount have been used, kept in the dark. The two men make up by the end of 1979 and resume talking and arguing. Yet, years later, Diller will admit that in long discussions with Beatty you realise later that you have given in, that you agreed, and yet you are not really much wiser about what he thinks. Somehow, he makes you explain yourself to him, as if you were anxious for him to like you.

What does the picture cost? The estimates range from $32.5 million to nearly $60 million. As the years go by, even the official estimate climbs to over $40 million. There is discretion in this, the deliberate downplaying of some costs, and the calculated inflation of others. It is also very hard to determine exactly what it costs. The picture has been a source of expense for years – the research, the script, Warren's time and his running costs. And now it is being made its deal is amazingly convoluted. Paramount are not the makers of the film. The copyright is with Barclay's Mercantile Industrial Finance Ltd, a British banking arrangement set up for this picture. But there is no readier subject for rumor, nor any greater need for imprecision, than spending a lot of money.

There is a lull in the second half of 1980, a rest, during which the editing begins, while Beatty and Storaro film the witnesses. They need a camera, a light and a black cloth, a microphone and a recorder, as well as the eagerness of all the veterans. There are thirty-two witnesses in the pictures, but many more are shot and some of the interviews are as long as two hours.

The editing is carried out at premises on West 54th Street in New York, with a crew headed by Dede Allen and Craig McKay. Beatty sometimes sleeps in the cutting room and tries out new solutions overnight. By the end of the summer, the picture is complete, at 199 minutes. It has been aimed at an early December release. In September, a long trailer – 4½ minutes – starts to play in theaters. The poster is planned – of the Reeds embracing in their last reunion. Not all of these things are exactly Beatty's ordering. He has had final cut on the film, and he ensures by contract and maneuver a major say in promotion. In the fall, he shows *Reds* to Paramount: Charles Bluhdorn and Barry Diller, and then Frank Mancuso and Gordon Weaver, the heads of distribution and marketing. When the picture gets an R rating, Beatty attends the appeal personally. He will not moderate the language or his lovemaking scenes, but he claims the picture merits a PG rating so that American school children may see this chapter of their history. He wins the appeal.

But there are murmurs against the film. Frank Mancuso fears the nation-wide response to its political radicalism and urges that the film be sold as a love story. Independently, Warren commissions political pollster Patrick Caddell (an acquaintance from Democrat campaigns) to survey advance attitudes to *Reds*. Caddell reports that the more people learn about the material of *Reds* the more intrigued they are to see it. But Beatty cannot prevail on Paramount to follow this line. He has a right of veto, but that is not the same as insisting that they accept his wishes. Paramount clings to the romance, but the disappointed Warren will consent to nothing more lyrical in imagery than the eventual poster. The result is a ruinous compromise, a poster in which the stars seem determined to hide.

Too many people in the Paramount organisation do not even see the film in the build-up. For those who do, of course, it is too late to take any action except the drastic. At exhibitors' screenings there are voices raised that had always been anticipated – that the picture will not play comfortably in rural and conservative areas; that it is too long.

Such feelings crystalise in the regret that Beatty is doing so little personally to promote the film. He does no interviews for it. The poster, it is argued, is perversely secretive or recessive – no one knows the woman is Diane Keaton, and the man has half his face buried in her shoulder. The trailer is confusing; it seems pretentious to some people. Out of fatigue and frustration with Paramount, Warren does not speak up for the film. If he ever thinks of what happened with *Bonnie and Clyde*, he may see that it is a young man's game.

Yet, his reticence is also the culmination of an old instinct. For years, he has believed films should speak for themselves, that art is denied or obscured if it needs to be explained. And he thinks that *Reds* is a great film. Those close to him stress his exhaustion and mention the fear that his own mixed reputation could hurt the marketing. He is attacked for doing so little by Rona Barrett. Yet he feels he has done so much.

The film will be a commercial failure, and of a kind that suggests no other promotion would have made a crucial difference. Still, the reticence here is curious. For it shies away at the last minute from an obvious duty, rich with material and potential. Think what might have been done to make a television documentary out of the witnesses, in which Beatty himself talked about the picture and American history. This is the kind of thing he says in spring 1982 when he accepts the Oscar for direction. But late in 1981 he is silent and withdrawn, as if to say love me without my wooing.

The huge effort to be seen and the final wish to be invisible are not out of character. They have been the odd pattern in all his acting, and maybe in much of his life. As Robert Towne has put it:

"I feel that Warren always has to be tougher than he thinks. He presents a peculiar problem as an actor because he is a man who is deeply embarrassed by acting . . . when you write scenes together, as Warren and I did in *Shampoo*, you've got to say, 'Look, you've got to be tough with yourself here, and not be afraid of yourself.'"

It is an odd life for such a man to have chosen, and *Reds* is probably the largest film ever made about hesitancy and shyness.

Lost parrot

Not long after dawn, when his loss had sunk in, Chuck shouted at D across their small prison yard, "You let her die!" D never answered, so Chuck turned to anyone else who would listen, "I knew not to trust him. He was never one of us."

"He seemed so nice," regretted Claudia Cannon, sure she knew him from somewhere.

"Let's not dispute among ourselves," urged Cy. "It hurts our chances."

"On our chances," Doc said to Chuck, "what would be your advice? You're hired for manliness, aren't you?"

"What does that mean?" Chuck was wary.

"Do we wait to die?"

"You think you're funny?" sneered Chuck. There was something abject in his eyes, lest the initiative, the lead, be dumped on him.

"I'm serious," said Doc. "What should we do?"

By the time Dog, Kid and Breed came out of the Castle for their morning promenade, Chuck had given much thought to this. And he made his stand by waiting until the three survivalists were close before getting up and kicking D swiftly in the side of the head, with a whoop of triumph to be sure it was noticed.

"I say, I say," Dog called out, his voice a flugelhorn in the morning air.

"He let her die," jeered Chuck, nodding at Drew's corpse, still propped against D.

"Rats," hissed Kid, who had only dragged himself out of bed at the absent-minded thought of more sport.

"That *is* careless," Dog pouted.

"It certainly is," said the panting Chuck. He was jumping up and down in panic.

"But, of course," Dog began.

"Yes, yes?" Chuck wanted to know.

"It's irrelevant."

Lost parrot

Chuck was drained of energy by this attitude. He was like a bull now, sullen and backed up, opposed to having so many barbs inserted in his hide, too stupid to foresee the fishbone of a sword that would find a way between his ribs, however many thrusts it took.

"Pardon me," said a fresh voice, but one that D had heard lately. The voice spoke in a modest, off-handed way, no heavier than the sneaker tread that had brought its owner into the courtyard unheard.

"Good Lord," said Dog, assessing the slim figure in startling white shirt and slacks, burnished but unarmed. "Where did you spring from?"

"Have you seen my parrot?" asked the newcomer.

"Your what?" Dog was not sure whether to laugh.

"My parrot. I lost it yesterday."

"Did you, by Jove?"

"Green and gold, with a blue splash on its head. Is she dead?" The man in white had halted by Drew. He kneeled down beside her, and did what he could to calm her shocked hair. "What a pretty girl," he murmured to D.

"She is," D answered. "A very lovely face."

"A noble head," the visitor agreed.

"You know, I don't believe we have seen one parrot," Dog began, to break the spell.

"I did," said Doc. "I saw a parrot. Earlier. Big brute."

"There," said the man in white. "You see."

"It was red and blue," Doc added.

"Must have found a friend," said the man in white.

"What is this parrot stuff?" Kid asked Dog.

"Shut up," Dog told his junior, the pest, and to the man in white he said, "We're not the least interested in your bloody parrot."

"No? Well," the man in white reflected, "I imagine not – not if you're making a movie."

"Say again?" asked Dog.

"I get it," grinned the man in white. "You're keeping a low profile."

"A movie?" Dog wouldn't let go.

"That coat. Costume?"

Dog simpered. "More regalia, if you know what I mean."

"Uh-huh," the man in white was smiling through his narrowed, sceptical eyes. "So what's Eyes doing? I heard he didn't work much these days."

"Eyes?"

"Eyes the Star," said the man in white.

At which, Doc grimaced, "For God's sake!"

And D chimed in, "Now you've done it," with much fatalistic shaking of what was still a bruised head.

Dog was bewildered, but quick on the uptake. He could not fail to see how the respectful, sidelong and rather demure glances of this new fellow, and of D and Doc, were all directed at the one they called Chuck. Dog looked again. He wished he had his spectacles, but in a disaster there are things mislaid and survivors must soldier on. He took three grand strides towards Chuck. Could it be? Eyes hadn't worked since – when was it? Chuck's head drooped. By God, yes, it could be.

"You sly fox," said Dog to himself. And then, sticking out a large hand, "Mr Eyes, sir, an honor."

"Shake his hand," the man in white advised Chuck. "You can't pull that star thing in the desert where we're all men together."

"I'll say not," said Dog.

Chuck looked at the man in white. "What is this?" he said.

"It's your turn, kiddo," said the man in white.

"Mr Eyes deserves his privacy," protested Doc.

"Silence, cur!" said Dog.

Kid rammed Doc in the stomach with his booted foot. Doc collapsed and retched on the dry ground.

"You really didn't know?" the man in white asked Dog.

"Know? Why, sir, who ever knows in this life? I had a strong feeling. But one keeps an inborn reticence towards the great stars. They go their way."

"I suppose so," said the man in white. "And we go ours."

"Oh, assuredly. I'm grateful to you for the hint. Of course, it's been the word that he did live hereabouts."

"I heard that too."

"May I ask, sir, what you do?"

"Well," began the man in white, "I'm really something of a harmless old hermit. Had a shack, over in Marietta, but a family of jack rabbits moved in, so I drifted on, you know?"

"Yes, indeed," said Dog. "The great treasure of solitude."

"Exactly so," said the man in white. He was peering through the mounting glare of the day.

"What is it?" asked Dog.

"Well," said the man in white confidentially. "I lost my eye glasses years ago, but I could have sworn that was Claudia Cannon and Cy Lighthiser."

"The famous actress?" said Dog. "And her producer hubbie chappie?"

"The same," said the man in white. "You've got yourself a production here, I'd say."

"You would?"

"Oh, I would. I can even understand the fur coat."

"Yes?"

"It makes you a very big man in the desert."

"Ah!"

"To have Eyes and Claudia, and Cy to line-produce for you – "

"But equipment? Wouldn't we – ?"

"Bound to turn up," said the man in white. "With a deal like this in the palm of your hand," and he patted the buffalo gun, hot in the sun, "everything falls into place."

"A picture?" Dog surmised.

"And if you're short on stock, well, just remember that in Russia after the revolution they made pictures without film."

"Did they?"

"Just pretended, for the practice. Ran empty cameras."

"Cunning buggers."

The man in white considered. "I'd say you had a hit."

"Really?"

"There's not going to be much in the theaters."

"Are there theaters still?" asked Dog, recalling the devastation.

"Are we standing here?" asked the man in white.

"Definitely."

"It was night last night? Then we had morning?"

"The same as ever."

"An orange is still round?"

"I haven't seen one today, but – "

"Then there'll be theaters. By the time you're in post-production the clamor will build."

"This is exciting," said Dog. "I've always wanted to make movies."

"And you'll have Claudia Cannon as your property," the man in white did what he could to nudge Dog in the voluminous coat.

"Sir, I am a gentleman," said Dog.

"Don't think she won't be charmed by a gentleman."

"You think so?"

"Well," said the man in white, pausing, letting the momentum of their talk ebb away, "I'd imagine so. That's what I heard about the picture business. Lot of burying to do here."

Dog looked around. "Things mount up."

"Let me do it," said the man in white. "I know the best places to dig. I'll take these three to do the work." He indicated Doc, Clear and D, the three of them nodding like toy hounds on the back window ledge of family auto trips.

"They're poor material," Dog assured him.

"I can see," said the man in white. "We'll go off and find some bare spot in the desert."

"Back for lunch?" asked Dog.

"Well," said the man in white, looking up at the sun and estimating the labor. "Say high tea."

"That's the ticket," said Dog. "We'll have a roast."

"Oh, careful now," demurred the man in white. "I can't keep up with you showbiz jokesters."

Dog roared with laughter. He realised that he was happier than he had ever been.

And so the burial party fell in, and as they made their way out into the emptiness D was allowed to carry the still springy body of Drew. The man in white walked beside him, and they went along all together, too fond of the dead to speak, but quite sure a fine burial could be made.

REDS

As Richard Sylbert remembers it, *Reds* was sometimes made with only a handful of people present. But on other occasions there is a dead weight of a thousand expecting to be told what to do, resentful of indecision, a silent mass that prompts the nervous producer to recount the history of world revolution. And if you wish to rouse that mass to help you, to be alive and eager for the movie, you cannot very well complete your story by saying that John Reed died with less faith in the revolution or in Russia than he had ever had, overwhelmed and disappointed by ponderous size. You have to ignore that, and do all you can to smother the mood of dismay intrinsic to the story. You know you may kill yourself straining to lift up a proper dying fall and make a big finish of it. If you are Russian, and a Bolshevik, you bury Reed in the Kremlin, so that you can make sure the regret is kept out of sight.

Reds gets bigger as it is made: how can this not be the case? The total footage of exposed film mounts. The budget of the production goes up. The expectations and the anxieties at Paramount build so that more and more of the actor's time is spent in reassurance, no matter that he has to play a man running out of conviction and of the sense that he and history are one. For as the film expands so its maker discovers that his true subject is slight – nothing less than a love affair – and that the tone of his film is all to do with loss, failure and forgetting. If you are in the desert, it is like believing that the wind blows the sand into natural monuments, into epic achievements, only to realise that all the time the wind has been dispersing the sand.

No one as intelligent as Warren Beatty, or with a mind so open to doing so many things, can make *Reds* without some thought to its political consequences in his career. He does take the film and show it to America's President, Ronald Reagan, who says it's fine, but he wishes it had a happier ending. (There is all the market research Paramount needs, and the model of Reagan's success: he knows what America will buy.) *Reds* will be regarded as a picture about politics, and plainly its maker will be recognised for his interest in power. The Left will be touched by his generosity to their views. But the Left in America scarcely exists. There is much more danger, of course, that the main body of the country will be alarmed by undue compassion for reds and their doings. The picture does all it can to disarm that hostility. It says clearly that Russian revolution could not work in America; and it goes on to show that the revolution betrayed itself in Russia, too. What remains is nothing more threatening than the notion that hardship and suffering should be avoided; that the workers deserve fair wages and representation; that tyranny is odious and free love problematic.

No one in America has the heart or the nerve to dispute such views. Barry Diller, at Paramount, complains, "Not one media person, no liberal writer, has pointed out that this big American corporation supported a film that deals with a story that had been buried, a story never told, the absolutely hidden story of the IWW, the American Socialist Party, the American Communist Party. Not one has said, Gulf & Western may be rat bastards but at least they did that."

But this is not remarked upon because the film is so inoffensive and because shelves of dry books *have* told the story. It is a movie executive's fancy that nothing exists except the material of films; and perhaps a film-maker can fall for the same humbug. In fact, the "buried" story of *Reds* comes across as one that has been given up, gradually and naturally, over time. It is not a political picture. But like a few other American movies it makes vague but strident claims for itself. Gulf & Western deserve no credit for civic duty or courage. They have merely broadcast the limited, cautious political thinking of the film-maker, and been contractually confined by his confusions.

Reds, as the picture's terse press book puts it, "is the passionate love story of John Reed (Warren Beatty) and Louise Bryant (Diane Keaton), a couple whose love survived their conflicts over professional ambitions, personal goals and political ideals." Read that again, and then remember the inadvertent outburst of Zinoviev in the film, that truly politicised people do not have "personal goals". Not a word of that press book would be as it is without Warren Beatty's approval. The picture makes several large gestures towards history and accuracy. It has all the resources of well-funded art direction bent on making us believe we are seeing the years from 1915 to 1920. When Louise Bryant arrives in New York, a spanking old omnibus is so cleverly placed in the frame, shutting out more recent buildings, so that we can see the Flatiron Building as she would have seen it. Helsinki was chosen to be St Petersburg because it had mustard-colored buildings that looked like the real thing. There is a montage sequence in which still photographs of Lincoln Steffens, Margaret Sanger and so on are cut in with shots of Jack Nicholson as Eugene O'Neill and Edward Herrmann as Max Eastman. Above all, the thirty-two witnesses testify to the picture's interest in history and its fascination with myth and the turmoil of opinions.

But for *Reds* to be the 199-minute entertainment it wants to be, with two parts and an intermission, history has also been brutalised. The sentimental backbone of the film's second half is the separation of John Reed and Louise Bryant, the efforts she makes under great stress to cross the Atlantic, to trudge across the snowy wastes of northern Europe to find him, only to fail. All of this builds to the reunion – a very strong scene on the screen, despite every memory of other train station meetings – in Moscow, as the drained Reed returns from Baku on a shattered train. They embrace on the platform, and he begs her, "Please don't leave me." It is the moment of the picture's poster: in its vitality and its imagery it is as old-fashioned as pictures from the late 1930s. Like the closing of the first half, it reminds us of *Gone With the Wind*, the embodiment of Hollywood's faith that historical events rise to the occasion of exceptional human romance.

Louise Bryant did not make that thwarted trip in search of her husband. They did not miss one another, and wonder what was happening. She did go to Moscow in 1920 and was there on his return from the south, and for his death days later. It does not diminish the affection and love they felt, but Louise Bryant in America was having an affair with the painter Andrew Dasburg, just as Reed was dallying with a young Russian woman. The film omits these liaisons, though Dasburg is one of the witnesses and Beatty himself had an early inclination of playing John Reed when he met that Russian woman, probably during the trip taken with Natalie Wood.

The retriever of American history and the tactful companion to garrulous witnesses, as well as the endorser of a Reed who hated to be cut or misrepresented, is also a Hollywood picture-packager ready to go with whatever works on the screen. For without this looming obstacle to the romance, the agony of lovers reaching out for each other, the second half of *Reds* has no glue or character. There is little question but that the picture wallows in the detailed account of infighting on the American Left. For many, it founders. Not just hard to follow, and harder to sympathise with, it sinks into the pettiness and provincialism of dead and acrimonious meetings, and offers an inadvertent explanation of the failure of American radicalism. It is earnest of Beatty to pursue the tangle, but no part of the desire to make an epic romance. Still, in narrative terms, it is the pretext for Reed's second trip to Russia. The final twenty minutes of the picture seem hardly possible without some build-up and so we have tedious accuracy and flagrant fabrication to get us to the big finish.

But if there were no second half?. . . . Then there would be a modest romance, culminating almost by chance in the excitement of October 1917, and a superb portrait of turbulent love. For the first part of *Reds* is the best thing Warren Beatty has done yet, entirely faithful to period but alive with 1980's feeling for what film can do and for how a man and a woman should behave together. Beneath the rhetoric of international socialism, the first part of *Reds* is a crisp, challenging and very moving essay on sexual politics in which we see two people alike in so many things that they live together, but perplexed in that they both need to be the center of attention.

The film's subtlety has Reed wanting to back out of that central light while Louise squirms to get into it. Reed is a speaker, a writer, a known personality, a charismatic hero. Without ever meaning to, he over-shadows Louise's life and her efforts to become a writer and to be noticed for herself. In his company, she meets editors, writers and the best of Greenwich Village; but because she is just his girl she meets humiliation and failure that would be spared if she were on her own. They have idylls as a couple, but dissent and rows are their eventual mode. They stare at each other, seeing the pain of this ceaseless aggravation. They are fine and right lovers, but they may worry one another to death.

This relationship is set against the 1916 context of free love and suffragism, and the 1980 perspective of women's liberation. But the love story is timeless, too: it is just two people in love and argument. It could be the story of any ambitious people, of an actor and an actress endeavoring to make a marriage as well as their careers. Diane Keaton has never looked or acted better. She is the more arresting because we begin to suspect that this Louise Bryant is not an especially good writer, not a talent that destiny insists on putting on show. She is only a woman trying to write, caught up in the absolute solitude of that need, horrified by her own ego, but unable to still it or find any satisfaction.

We have seen other actresses work well with Beatty on screen (even if against his grain) – Natalie Wood, Jean Seberg, Faye Dunaway, Julie Christie – the chemistry of fiction igniting, whatever the real-life pitch of feeling. But nothing equals the complexity between Beatty and Keaton in *Reds*. In comparison, her Annie Hall is a flip kid, a surface skimmed for liveliness and flopped on the screen. Annie Hall is ordinary but magical – like most Hollywood heroines. Louise Bryant is of a different order: she is a very difficult human being, grappling with her difficulty and utterly without the advantage of magic or the peaceful cul-de-sac of being widely liked. She is only fit to be loved, and quite impossible. She is so good a character that the normal trappings of film fantasy burn off in her light. You do not get horny over her; but you tremble at the prospect of her company.

And Warren has made her the heart of his film. She is the rock, and Reed is the water, the volatility, that eddies around her. It is said in the movie that he was a great journalist. Henry Miller adds that he was just a busy-body whose political conscience came from empty-headedness or the need to suppress his deeper problems. *Ten Days That Shook the World* is mentioned, but not quoted. If you read it, you will find liveliness and interminable dullness. Reed was lucky: he found a "there" in its crucial moment. His book's success stems much more from that than from intrinsic virtues. It is now a nearly unreadable "literary event", just as Reed is more a curiosity than a lasting hero or achiever.

Beatty's Reed is a man striving to stay young, to be regarded as an energetic idealist, to affect the world while edging away from the center of vanity. He has a face that seems to live on light, twitching at it, flexing in and out from it, like an amoeba. There is an early scene, at a dinner table, when he and Louise look at one another and enjoy a flirting discourse, more glances than words, that must be the best available text on Warren Beatty's seductiveness. For while the face is clearly aging, its hope is growing younger.

It is Beatty's most energetic and beseeching performance, and the closest he has come to naked pain and comfortable sincerity. Yet he pales beside Nicholson's O'Neill just because Jack is by nature a movie actor, a gorgeous fake. He commands the picture effortlessly, peering between his curling brows and his kiss-me moustache. He is as strong and relaxed as Gable or Bogart. But Warren is still fidgeting to watch himself, doubting and growing querulous with himself at the advisability of the whole pretence. How can you pretend to be sincere? his wracked eyes ask. He is playing a man whose presence and immediacy are talked about by others, but who is really embarked on designing history, directing the show. He has the frantic, thin vitality of a flame about to go out. The face is twisted, trying to watch itself: at last, the seductiveness has reached its proper task, to convince the man himself, to woo him and have him like himself.

I think he fails, and fails in such as way that he will never try as hard again. For the wish to be Reed, to be an artist and a politician, to be as fully "there" as Jack, is critically offset by the witnesses, pale, shaking humanity, and the film's stroke of genius.

This John Reed cannot be Rhett Butler or even Clyde Barrow because he is only a phantom remembered by others and recollected in so many contradictory ways that he is not a something but a question mark. The film as a whole, but the first half most actively, is given shape by the witnesses. They allow a fragmented structure, and they give us the constant stream of doubt and speculation that undermines the romantic monolith of the scenes. The witnesses rip the old-fashioned movie apart. They subject it to real, untidy life, and they constitute a pathos much greater than that of John and Louise.

For *Reds* becomes a film about old age, wayward memory, about being wrong – for everyone is wrong, that is how we are ourselves. The witnesses are white faces, proud of their ruin, eager still for attention and the very polite Mr Beatty to talk to. They are exposed on the slab of history, achingly lovely and distressed, decay and vibrance on the edge of expiration – several of them had died before the film opened. Together they say: we do not know, history is just the books, the slogans of the victors, and the stories, but do not trust it, for humans cannot comprehend what has happened to them. They tell stories. They think for most of the time that they lived life and were masters of their stories. But life only passed through them, like a wind, so slowly they did not notice it, so quickly it killed them. And at the end you feel the emptiness coming.

Toxic Flat

"What I had in mind," said Eyes. He was speaking slowly, like a far-sighted planner who could not always remember the point at hand. He was also stepping in loose tumbling sand, with Tusk draped across his shoulder. The four of them had walked for hours under Eyes' silent leadership. Clear wore the corpse of Zale like a collar. Doc was ruminating on how Look was his Cordelia, and D would not be parted from Drew's physical remains.

"We're building a golf course up there, up at Toxic," Eyes added, "and I pictured it how we might bury these four around the seventeenth green. It's bare still, without features. Maybe we could put the two ladies like hillocks on one edge of the green, and the lawyers on the other. We could call that hole the Devil and the Deep Blue Sea."

"With the green in between?" asked Clear, who was likely to get the supervisory role.

Eyes nodded wearily. He had just so much stamina for the detail. After that, he liked to settle to the sunsets, the quiet and the beauty of desolation.

"They would be the mounds for sand traps?" D wanted to know.

"Wouldn't you say?" said Eyes.

"Sand traps in the desert?"

"Kid, this is golf we're talking about here."

D nodded. "We'll have to bury them deep," he said.

"We want those little hills," Eyes pointed out. "Like the Scottish seaside links."

"There's a risk," D foresaw, "of the wind exposing the bodies."

"Ah," Eyes had it now. "Yeah, that wind can go like a bitch." He trudged on for another three minutes, and then he reasoned, "Can't we strike a balance?" His hands fluttered; he wanted to be rid of the issue.

"That'll do it," said Clear, cheering up to see how progress might be made in the desert.

"Think we can?" Doc asked D.

"I daresay," D told them. Even if he had to repair the erosion every day, putting the vanished grains of sand back in their proper places, a myriad silica mosaic on Drew's head, a soft shoulder for her to lie under, while dimpled balls could lift and drop on the no doubt astroturf green. He would honor her and replenish her tomb.

And so the sad but resilient cortège walked into Toxic Flat at dusk, ignoring the skull-and-crossbones signs along the way warning of the most hideous and irreversible damage done to the air, the land, and – if there was any – the water, not to mention human tissue, and making it clear that no known insurance plan would cover any idiot who went a step further.

"So long as the other people around here can read," Eyes surmised, "we'll be safe. But I wouldn't wonder if we didn't have to get a reading program going one day. Enlightenment is the watchdog of stability." His brow was pursed at the prospect – it was evident that the leader was looking far ahead for all of them. His pinched eyes were a little less here than there. "D," Eyes had decided, "I bet your good wife would be outstanding at that. It's something to see her teaching the little ones now, planting the salad vegetables, that kind of thing," he finished vaguely.

There was this tenuous produce patch in Toxic Flat, the golf course (still in its infancy), a small eating place, a number of shacks, the long, low manila experimental building and Eyes' place. It wasn't Bel Air, but it was another start, and you'd be surprised to realise how far Bel Air was just bald fields in 1900. There were a few paths defining Toxic Flat, marked out by rocks carefully gathered from the desert and graded for color so that any eye looking at the line saw the sweet, smooth fade of development.

As they arrived, Virginia looked up from one of the greens. There was a "17" on the plastic orange flag stuck in the hole. She was sweeping the green with a stiff broom.

"Hi," she called out. "Eyes, we have got to do something with this green. It's flatter than Faye Dunaway."

"I know, honey," said Eyes, putting Tusk down. "Got ourselves some mounding material here."

"What? Oh, yuk," said Virginia. "That's gruesome. Hi, Dad. Those poor guys."

"They can become their own memorial," Clear explained.

"I suppose," said Virginia. Then she recognised what D was holding, and her face fell in. "Oh, Dad, it's not . . ." They consoled each other as best they could and put the four bodies by the green to wait for the morning's work.

"I'll stay with them," said D.

"Yeah?" said Eyes. "With the jackals, and so on?"

"I'll bring you a blanket, Dad," said Virginia. "And a bowl of chili. Chili OK?"

Time passed at Toxic Flat. D buried the bodies. At first he thought of them as lumps of feelings, there, in the ground, but little by little he saw Drew turning into the sands, fleeting and indeterminate, everywhere.

Doc and Clear were already in story conferences, with fresh yellow legal pads and sharpened pencils. D found lengths of heavy cable which he used to hold the bodies and then he built the mounds up with old tarpaulins and carefully graded the sand to make the hills. He saw a woman watching him work, standing a way away with a headscarf and a tanned face. She did not wave, but she seemed to believe in what he was doing.

"That's a real job you've done," said Eyes a few days later. He had come strolling by with Doc and a very elderly man, tall but stooped and with lugubrious strings of ashen hair hanging from his head. "Tell you what," said Eyes, "we'd better make you our construction man."

"He's good on dialogue, too," Doc added, and Eyes came to one of his dry, lovely but decidedly desert-paced bursts of laughter.

"Who's the old fellow?" D asked Doc when Eyes and the old man had sauntered on in their evening perambulation, the two of them using sand wedges as walking sticks.

"That's Howard," said Doc.

"Didn't he die? In a plane, in '76."

"Slipped away," Doc smiled. "I worked on that one, a pretty thing."

"Still alive?"

"Shot a ninety-five the week before we arrived."

"How did he 'slip away'?"

"Some out-of-the-way landing strip near Laredo. Another body waiting. The usual. The plane never turned off its engine. Howard had been looking to get out for a while."

"And he's been here ever since?"

"Healthy spot. Good air. Eyes has been looking after him. They're pretty close. Howard doesn't really talk to anyone but Eyes. But he's a nice old guy. Snickers if you tell him a good story and, every now and then, he'll just hover around one of Eyes' ladies."

"He was always prone to flight," said D.

D spent more nights out at the seventeenth, to be sure the hillocks persisted. The wind came up and it changed the shapes of the mounds, but their idea remained and D could always repair the form with his hands in the morning, pushing it backwards and forwards until he wondered if he really remembered its first form. He grew used to the slow life of Toxic Flat in which the emptiness was kept lively by the thought that Eyes might appear.

"Are we going to make pictures?" D asked Clear.

"Ah," said Clear. "The great enterprise. You should talk to Eyes. Better still, wait for him to raise the subject."

The days passed, and D found work on other parts of the golf course. It was not much more than a sketch of a course on the barren surface: There were years of work ahead. He might make a dogleg on the eleventh by encouraging the outcrop of mesquite; and there were rattlers in the swale on the fifth that could become a very testing natural hazard. He began to dream of water on the course, as pioneers and pirates in LA must once have looked to the Owens River, blue pools to keep the fairways honest. He often saw the same woman watching him, and he had worked out who it was. But no one wanted to hurry him.

"You know, D," Eyes told him, "one day we could have a Desert Classic here."

"If such things ever come again," said D.

"They will. They say LA's getting back in shape."

"Movies soon?" asked D. He had time on his solitary days to scheme out story after story.

"Maybe," said Eyes, stretching. "A new kind of movie."

"Ah," D sighed. That old promise.

"You see," said Eyes, "this desert air is all very well, but it's hell on the skin. I can't say I'm your ingénue any longer. More like Slim Pickens."

"Well," said D.

"Don't be kind."

"It's fine to be rugged, too," D pointed out.

"It is, isn't it? Anyway, I think George is going to have it licked soon."

"George?"

"You haven't met him? He's a mole, that one, He's in the experimental building all day long, with his gizmos. Sleeps there, too."

"What is he doing?"

Eyes looked at D and grinned once. "Well, old fellow," he began, "you won't shout this around?"

416

D had not shouted for so long. He smiled the thought away.

"George has this computer set-up. Generations of them. It comes out of animation and effects."

"Yes?" said D.

"Now, I'm not technical, but he thinks he's going to be able to program it, one day, soon, not far off, with all the old movies of any actor you like – some Walter Brennan or Wallace Beery, you know – "

"Yes?"

"And turn out new movies they never made."

"Walking and talking?" said D.

"An infinite archive. No actor need ever work again. You can program your plots, conversations and costumes, however you like. Just generate fresh likenesses till the end of time."

"But the stories?"

"You and Doc can plug 'em in, long as you like. And that Virginia of yours. She has a cute story mind, I can tell you."

"And you?" asked D.

"I can play golf," Eyes told him. "And I can be thirty-four for ever."

"A new life," D was enthralled.

"Not the half of it," said Eyes. "I can do appearances."

"How do you mean?"

"Once George has knocked the rough edges off the holograms, I could launch battleships, speak to both Houses of Congress, go on tours of Europe." He hesitated, for he was shy about the climax: "You see, I could be on TV, just walking around waving."

"And never have to leave the Flat," D saw it all.

Eyes was not exactly a young man anymore, but it was more doubt that had ravaged him than mere physical decline. D could see his determined, hopeful eyes still scanning the future, trying to project order there.

"I have to have some rest," Eyes told D suddenly, as if taking him into his confidence.

"Yes," said D.

"But how can you rest," Eyes explained, "if you see it all coming apart?"

"Will there be a world, you wonder, to take care of one's immortality?"

"God, yes!" said Eyes vehemently. He was close to tears.

"Well," said D. "I'll keep working on the golf course."

"Right," Eyes agreed. "That's the sine qua non."

417

"We might go on for ever," D proposed, his fancy trying to coax Drew's hologram to dance.

"Well," admitted Eyes, "George hasn't given up on that, either."

And so it happened that D earned his way into the settlement and the house where the tanned woman lived with all the children. She worked the land and instructed the young, her own and others springing up in the community. She seemed never to tire or soften with affection, yet everything she did was for others. And she got into the habit of giving D his dinners.

One evening, D was sitting outside the woman's hut. He had just eaten a stewed bean dish. He was thinking of a musical in which Eyes might play an amnesiac who discovers he has healing powers. It was still only a germ. On the golf course, Eyes and Howard were playing. They had dragged George out to caddy for them.

C set a pack of cards on the home-made table that was jammed into the sand. "You play hearts?"

"I think I remember," said D.

"I expect I can help you," C replied.

"Ah," he said.

She dealt. The cards were old and clammy, like slices of ham. There was the face of some pretty, nervous woman on the backs. Why was she afraid? D began to sort out his hand, the sorting remembering for him. He looked at the seventeenth green. He could see the smudge by the raised green that had been Drew, a bump in time. Eyes, Howard and George were standing there, looking down at their feet and at balls D could not see. They moved, they shifted, they turned. It was like a dance, the three men trying to vanish.

"Do you have the two of clubs?" asked C.

And D was pleased to see he did.

THESE DAYS

How does he know, late in 1981 and thereafter, whether he is simply tired in ways that cannot be repaired, afflicted by unequivocal failure, or untouchable? There is a wishful theory in show business that there are a very few people above and beyond the greedy reach of all common forms of mishap or failure. Such people rise above their own failures; they may not even need to work; they have so thorough and so richly alleged a pervasiveness that provable existence may even impair their aura. They have a there of their own, a special place, where the gods and luck live, and where "Fame! – I'm gonna live forever", is the lying muzak. Warren has to wonder whether or not he is there.

He fights long and hard in his own head to deny the disappointment of *Reds*. Industry analysts come to regard it as an example of marketing mistakes: the poster, the follow-up ads so dense with quotation that they are hurried over, the uncertainty that opens in 389 theaters and adds another 276 before Christmas (missing both the eminence of a début in just a few cities, with the picture building slowly, and the power of 1,000 screens), and the absence of Beatty himself. In April 1982, the annual round-up of grosses in *Film Comment* anticipates rentals between $25 and $30 million – "no disaster, but certainly a commercial failure". That is before the film fails to win the Oscar for best picture, or for best actor or actress. The award for direction is its one concession, and that does not affect the box office. A year later, the next round-up reports that *Reds* took in only $21 million – half of what it cost? – when surely it needed $100 million to be securely in profit.

Beatty never permits himself to be caught in a situation where he has to discuss this failure; perhaps he does not even admit it to himself. After all, the film is also a great success – there are many warm reviews, he is taken seriously, he is named best director. Beyond all that, *Reds* does contain some of his best work, so searching and so final that the true source of weariness may be less the time *Reds* took to make than its material and its dismay with both fame and accomplishment. Very soon

420

after *Reds*, he is offered an exciting project, and his quick answer speaks to special depths of depletion: "It's like I've been all night in the whorehouse, and I stagger out in the morning and I see Marilyn Monroe waiting."

Six months after the opening of *Reds*, Warren enlists Mike Mahern, a young man who has made a reputation in distributing exploitation pictures. He asks Mahern to research a way of re-releasing *Reds*, something that has never succeeded for so large a picture. Mahern discovers that the ideal Beatty audience is female, twenty-five and over, and upscale. He proposes a promotion that centers on John Reed as a man who set out to affect history, and Louise Bryant as the liberated woman who went with him. He senses that the film might always have been sold best on the issue of how does a smart, modern, independent woman fuck Warren Beatty and still keep her integrity? Of course, this is a question that interests Warren, too. Mahern devises a campaign and tests it, but the response is grim. *Reds* is now too well-known and too thoroughly written off to have a second chance. Mahern recommends against spending any more of Paramount's money.

But when the picture opens in Japan in 1982, Beatty goes with it. He spends several days with a few selected journalists and he speaks at a press conference for 200 members of the media. And when the picture is released on video cassette, the opening credits name the witnesses, who went unidentified in the first release. But nothing has yet been done with all the witness footage. The real body of history that Beatty recorded is waiting somewhere.

There are signs of him moving on. In the summer of 1982, he spends time with the lawyers who guard Howard Hughes' name, acquiring the rights to the life. He has himself written a first draft script for that project, and apparently it deals with Hughes' public years, with his time in movies and aircraft manufacture, before the great withdrawal. But when asked, Why Hughes?, Beatty's answer addresses the reasons for Hughes's retreat: "It has to do with becoming a victim of your own accumulated power," he says. Paul Schrader remarks that, of course, Warren's own life and career have far more in common with Howard Hughes than with John Reed. "And if he ever delves that subject," says Schrader, "it could be a truly great role for him. But in order to truly delve it, he would have to put himself in the hands of someone who could objectively observe his performance. And I don't think he is psychologically able to let someone else have that power over him. So that's why the Hughes thing persists, and in some way he knows it will be a great statement for him. And he knows that he can't do it. But on the other hand he knows that he can't let anybody else do it."

Other possibilities come and go as he tells himself he will "rest" and wait by merely hiring out as an actor. There is a picture Robert Towne wants to make, *Tequila Sunrise*, about old friends who meet again as a cop and a drug dealer. But Towne's career falters a little with his first direction, *Personal Best*, and with the disputes between him and his producer on that film, David Geffen. Then Towne writes another script, *Mermaid*, for producer Ray Stark. Arthur Penn will direct; Beatty will star. He will be paid $5 million for acting in a love story between a middle-aged man and a young sea creature. But it does not happen. There is a Dick Tracy project, with Beatty starring as the comic-book hero and Walter Hill directing. But it does not happen either. It is said that Beatty is becoming slower and more obsessively dedicated to negotiating his deals. Some others reckon it is a game, that he does not really want to work.

There is another Orson Welles venture in a Hollywood where the great man has managed nothing since *The Big Brass Ring*. He wants now to make a movie of *The Cradle Will Rock*, a play he mounted with the Mercury Theater in 1937. He approaches Beatty for introductions he needs in securing funding. The two men lunch at Ma Maison, a favorite haunt of Welles. Welles brings the script to the meal, and Beatty asks to see it at the lunch table. He begins to read it, and does not stop. It takes him three hours to read the script. In the meantime, the restaurant empties and closes. But the two men are left undisturbed. Then Beatty launches into a two-hour talk – about the script, the changes it requires, the need for further clarification. It is another humiliation for Welles.

It may be noticed that the picture business is changing. In the late 70s and the early 80s, the business gives up many old ghosts and attends instead to what kids want to see. The great empire of George Lucas and Steven Spielberg takes over, and that is the quality end of a product that reaches down to *Porky's*, and then lower. There are hosts of moviegoers who do not quite know who Warren Beatty is any longer. The very young did not bother with *Reds*, and they do not respond quickly to shy, middle-aged men. Legend can sleep a season now and awake to something close to anonymity.

Then there is the political campaign of 1984, a task that honestly beckons him, yet still an escape that he can convince himself he is bound to make. And he is on the telephone to Gary Hart day after day, and he attends parties and fund-raisers. He is a more important member of

Hart's campaign than the press realises. He is in San Francisco for the Democratic Convention, hobnobbing with George Lucas. At that time, he goes out with CBS television reporter Diane Sawyer. They go to see a movie, *Top Secret*, one night and play video games in the theater lobby. There he goes again, gossips murmur, escorting a new, bright young woman. But suppose now that the woman is the activator and that, on her way to *60 Minutes*, Sawyer is taking the opportunity to get acquainted with someone who might one day make an interesting, nostalgic segment on the Sunday show, puzzled witness to his own life?

On the evening of Monday, September 10, 1984, the Toronto Film Festival pays tribute to Warren Beatty – which is to say, they get him to attend and sit still for an hour or so. Roger Ebert and Gene Siskel are to host the tribute, interviewing Beatty on stage. But he is unwilling to contemplate many questions in advance, or even to confer with his future hosts. The arrangements are all being made through David MacLeod, his Canadian cousin.

But he does turn up, and for close to two hours clips of Beatty's films chosen by Warren (not by the festival) are interspersed with the appearance of guests who speak briefly about Beatty. The guests are Arthur Penn, Jack Nicholson, Robert Towne and Jerzy Kosinski.

Then Beatty appears, to be interviewed by Siskel and Ebert. They are tucked and pumped into tuxedoes, but Warren is more casual in a loose white suit. At the outset, he says, "When one has become a familiar face, it endows one with responsibilities to respond to questions. It's one of the things you have to go along with when you become a performer or a household word or a sex symbol." He can sometimes sound like someone or something heading slowly away from the known world.

Yet he is soon questioning Siskel and Ebert, to divert time and attention from himself. He teases them. He has always possessed a humor too elusive for the movies of his era. He mentions but does not read a speech he says he has written on the plane to Toronto, "The Crisis in Progressive Film-making and American Liberalism". Did he fly in from Sydney, or only LA? Reports say that his "charm and unaffected manner drew repeated bursts of applause". What cunning it is when celebrity himself can shape such occasions so that he looks like the only ordinary fellow in sight, an unsullied shaft of natural light amid all the flashbulbs.

So he has shown himself to the public, and given nothing away. He may have a little more reason to persuade himself that he is open and human. Yet the tribute is remarkable for the extent to which he has been not just its modest, nearly reluctant subject, but its producer. As Jack Nicholson confides at one moment in Toronto, indulging his grinning wickedness, "I don't usually tell stories about Warren – because you're not trained to . . ."

There are many women mentioned now, but no one who seems to grip his attention. He sees Jessica Savitch, another television commentator, but she is killed in an accident. The French press assert that he will marry actress Isabelle Adjani, but it does not happen. He is seen with models Dayle Haddon, Carol Alt and the Israeli Sippi Levine. (He is interested in Israel: he visits the country and talks to people at *The New Republic*.) He has Margaux Hemingway around sometimes at his house, and at the Toronto Film Festival tribute Diane Keaton is still there, but silent in the body of the audience, not on stage talking about, or to, him.

He begins to be a commonly mentioned personage in stories about other people – and these are often people of far less talent or distinction, no matter that he had the policy in public relations of never appearing or working with anyone beneath his level.

He has red letter days, but not always his. One is May 21, 1977 – Jerry Hall will never forget that date. She is the Texas model on her way to marrying Mick Jagger. And in the Memoirs she writes early in life, she recalls that day because at a New York restaurant she sits between Mick and Warren. "They were both being pretty keen. I'm sitting there and Warren starts to chat and then Mick leans over to talk and then he gets mad and says to Warren, 'She's with me,' because he had arrived first. And Warren looks at me and I say, 'I'm not with anyone. I'm engaged [to Bryan Ferry]. I just happen to be at this dinner.' And then Mick says, 'Now, Warren, listen, man . . .' and drags him off. And he takes him over to the telephone booth and starts calling up models, trying to fix Warren up with someone else." How long does this take? And what is the most profound definition of the word "model"?

Is this loneliness beginning, the life of John McCabe pressing through the seductive smile? He mixes more with the younger set in pictures, with actors like Timothy Hutton, Vincent Spano and Steve Bauer who seem to regard him as a model of success. He seems ready to give advice about this wicked, duplicitous world. Diane Lane is interviewed by *Interview*. Do you know Warren Beatty? she is asked. "Sure," she answers, "How can you not?" This is surely a testament to fame, yet it makes him sound like blue cheese dressing or the IRS. Lane says she "got some counselling from him". She met him with Spano and Steven

Porcaro, and Warren calls her afterwards and she says she is really uptight about a lot of things. And he says, "If you're going to talk to anyone please talk to me, you know I'm experienced."

How seldom a man really feels that about himself – perhaps it is still a part he is trying on. Lane feels secure about him – "I needed the comforting knowledge that I didn't have anything to worry about from him." But she does not "go out" with Warren: "I don't like being part of a harem."

But for every such instance of Warren with a night on his hands, there is a story that testifies to his authority still. Dominick Dunne is writing a profile on Diane Keaton for *Vanity Fair*. He gathers indirectly that he should not raise the matter of Warren with Diane. It is over, but there are regrets and confusions that remain. Dunne gets on well with Keaton, they talk a lot. And then one day, not long afterwards, Dunne is at a table at a hotel when Warren comes by like a waiter and says he hears that Dunne's been having very good talks with Keaton. But is there anything more fatiguing than to appear occasionally in public with that offhand mastery? How sweet to go away.

He is still – is he not? – a movie star and a filmmaker about to announce his next venture. He entertains many unlikely ideas. He talks to Wayne Wang, the Chinese-American director who has made *Chan is Missing* for $22,000. Warren admires the picture and its ingenuity. Moreover, Wang has a new script, written by Henry Bean, that intrigues Warren. But it worries him, too, because it is about a man who beats women. It is called *Who You Know*, and it is a reworking of *In a Lonely Place*, the Nicholas Ray picture in which Humphrey Bogart plays an embittered screenwriter suspected of murder. Beatty is drawn to the hostility in *Who You Know*, but he wonders if it could be there still, without the violence. Suppose the man drank or gambled? But Wang is determined to make more small, independent films, and Beatty insists that the medium needs big pictures. So they part company, with respect for one another.

As the election hopes of 1984 fade away, he moves back to pictures with what seems like fresh vigor and determination. He starts to develop several possibilities. There is the book *Edie*, a documentary about Edie Sedgwick, co-authored by George Plimpton, who has played a small part in *Reds*. Warren wonders if *Edie* could make a movie for the young actress Molly Ringwald. He is also sponsoring a script written by Elaine May, a vehicle perhaps for himself and Dustin Hoffman. There is renewed talk of *Dick Tracy*. That lapsed project comes back to life with

Diane Keaton (David Appleby, Paramount)

Isabelle Adjani (Twentieth Century-Fox)

Beatty as star and producer, and perhaps with Martin Scorsese as its director.

And he is talking to James Toback again. He hires Toback to write a screenplay on the life of Bugsy Siegel, who walked out into the desert of Nevada and said let's make Las Vegas here. He is also ready, he says, to produce another Toback script, *The Pick-Up Artist*, which Toback wants to direct. He debates with Toback as to whether Timothy Hutton or Robert De Niro is most suited to the central part. He says he is going to set the picture up at a studio; he says this for months, during which Toback has no money. Toback asks when? And Warren says it won't be so long now.

In December 1984, Warren talks to Martin Scorsese about *Dick Tracy*: a picture with musical numbers, a lot of color, a good guy and bad guys, a big picture but fun. As they talk, Scorsese likes Warren more and more. They swap stories, and not a great deal gets done. The script – still problematic – is not reached in their pleasant evenings together. "The trouble is," says Warren, "you ask me a question and sometimes it takes me three days to think out the answer."

Of course, both men have other things on their mind. Beatty has his projects, while Scorsese is thinking about how to finance *The Last Temptation of Christ*, and about getting married again. But sometimes they do get to the Tracy script and Scorsese is impressed with Beatty's ideas on it. They do some research on cities with the proper 1930s look.

But gradually, Scorsese realises several things – that *Dick Tracy* can hardly help itself from becoming a bigger picture, not just $20 million, but at that point where budgets can magically double; he sees that Beatty does not yet have a firm studio deal on it, or even the urgent wish to proceed; and he is losing interest himself. Perhaps it has all been a chance for the two men to get to know one another.

They do haggle out a form of a deal, with final cut being a vexed issue. It ends up as "joint" final cut, with the last decision going to Scorsese in the event of an impasse. He signs the deal, but Warren never gets around to signing it. And so Scorsese marries, for the fourth time, and goes off to Italy on his honeymoon.

He has not mentioned this possibility to Warren. But Warren finds him at a hotel in Venice and calls him. "Well," he says, and pauses darkly. "Congratulations." "Yeah," says Scorsese. They agree to move on to other things.

When he's in Los Angeles, Warren lives at his house, now, on Mulholland Drive, just east of Benedict Canyon, built to his own design on a manufactured knoll, behind a ring of trees. It is modern, with white walls, wood floors and expanses of curved window. It has its own gym and a theater; it has a cook and a secretary. The walls are bare, there are no pictures. A visitor says, "It's a house where you know there's nothing to look at but whose house it is."

On the night of July 1, 1985, in an LA heatwave of over 100° F by day, he sits outside by the pool, oblivious to the temperature or the insects in the air. He has a speech that he is rewriting and rehearsing for a group of associates. It gets to be three in the morning, but he does not flag or settle for the current version of the speech. One of the friends goes back to his hotel, but an hour later Warren calls him to read the latest state of the speech.

The next day, July 2, he takes the speech to San Francisco, where he is to deliver it at a fundraiser on behalf of California Supreme Court Chief Justice Rose Bird, who is threatened by a forthcoming confirmation election. This event takes place at the Fairmont Hotel in front of 1200 people; it will raise $250,000 to help Rose Bird fight the campaign to oust her. The hotel ballroom is decorated with bunting and banners that proclaim "A rose for judicial independence".

For Beatty, this is unaccustomed in that it has the prominence not just of appearance, but of a featured address. It will be seen as a move; it is evidently a matter over which he has taken trouble. Anyone esteeming his shrewdness, therefore, might assume that the occasion has been carefully selected and that Warren and Rose are old friends likely to benefit one another.

Rose Bird is anxious to eliminate any hint that they are more than friends. It emerges that she and Warren have never met before. Beatty's speech is grand, far-reaching and dramatic. Everyone agrees that he has given it in fine style: "Those who are demanding 'Defeat Rose Bird', are the direct descendants of Joe McCarthy, the John Birch Society and the far Right that in the 1950s demanded the impeachment of Earl Warren. . . . Where we see constitutional rights, they see only demons."

The lady herself – seen as in a very delicate position in the polls, and not universally approved of by liberals or lawyers – says, "I think it's a little unfair to have a person who introduces you be better looking than you are." She glances at her keynote speaker. "I think how nice Mother Nature was to put such a nice mind on such a nice body. I hope you'll forgive me, Mr Beatty, for that sexist comment." Warren has to smile, whereas any of his movies would know how to squash such a remark.

If mixed impulses are any indication, this campaign is swaying from side to side. Beatty goes back to Los Angeles euphoric: he recalls a standing ovation and being interrupted three times by applause. He remembers that influential figures talked to him afterwards and said, well, if he was interested in running against Alan Cranston. . . . It was a move, and there was support. Now he has only to decide whether he has made the move or not.

The *San Francisco Chronicle* decides that the campaign got off to an "irresponsible and intemperate start". Beatty's speech is criticised as "outrageous, unfair and erroneous . . . It says little for Beatty's understanding of the democratic process and he can be excused only on grounds of vocation; the words were put in his mouth by others."

He moves arbitrarily and swiftly. He is everywhere – at the house on Mulholland, in LA hotels, at the Carlyle or the Ritz Carlton in New York. There are maybe a dozen projects to which he is attached; or there is only really Hughes. He is in Israel, in London, in Paris, in north Africa, in Deauville. He is on the phone, on the way, in the next room. So many places that he is seldom here, and always there.

Then he holds a press conference, but it concerns an old picture and his decision that it will not be seen on television. Arbitration has supported Beatty's claim that Paramount cannot sell *Reds* to ABC for network presentation if ABC elects to cut the picture for reasons of time. This has been a long drawn-out case, the continuation of a thirty-year struggle between film directors and television (first fought by George Stevens over *A Place in the Sun*). Beatty has had final cut on *Reds*, the contractual right to establish its length and form. Paramount has always dreaded 199 minutes, for it allows only one show every evening. Network television can cut a film on the grounds of standards and practices (for reasons of language, violence or sexual explicitness), but not for length. ABC wants to cut about ten minutes from *Reds* so that they can fit the movie into an evening schedule and finish by 11 p.m. in time for local news. Beatty will not budge and so the deal is off: ABC will not now pay Paramount the agreed $6.5 million for the rights.

Beatty describes this as a triumph of principle, and so it is in its belated way. But it is also madness when the movie can be seen intact on cassette and when it was always too long. As for Paramount – with Charles Bluhdorn dead and Barry Diller moved away to Twentieth Century-Fox what can they be thinking? Who else again would give Warren such a thorough final cut? And how would he work without it? Is his world moving towards stalemate, and is the principle here also an unconscious way of making work less likely?

Beatty gives a rare interview on this topic, he is so concerned about it. But the man emerging from the interview is more like a film-maker ready to give up the onerous business if it insists on being so small-minded. There is an air of retreat that the interview seems designed to illustrate.

He complains about seeing *Bonnie and Clyde* on television: "'I knew every cut and every gunshot and I knew they were there for a reason,' said Beatty, sipping a diet soda on ice in a suite at New York's Ritz Carlton hotel. 'And then they were gone.'"

It is not that he really believes he can change the world; there is rather more sense of an urge to slip away from it: "'At a certain point, you feel a little silly about trying to retain nine minutes of a film. But then you remember when you were at a location trying to get something right. To think that this goes down the tube because someone in some town insists that the local news must start at 11 p.m. – it's bad enough it has to be interrupted by someone selling Roto-Rooter.

"'It all comes back to the same question.' He asks, 'Do we want to make an art form out of the movies, or do we want to just say they're made for distraction? What are we spending our time doing this for? Acting and directing movies are hard enough for me anyway. You feel foolish enough when you are trying to keep a 95,000-ton soufflé from falling, so we have to go through some rituals in order to keep our dignity in this work.'"

After several months of being on hold, *The Pick-Up Artist* moves forward. Beatty calls Toback out to Los Angeles, and every day for two weeks, from about six in the evening to three in the morning, they work on the script together at Beatty's house. They take it line by line, with Beatty always probing with what Toback calls "a good cruel sense of whether it plays". The script is improved commercially, and given an upbeat ending. It remains dark and funny, but it is more conventional and less dangerous than it was when only Toback's vision. Beatty sets the film up at Fox, and it is a script that could make a successful picture, about a young man's chronic appetite for women.

The casting changes. Timothy Hutton has been pencilled in for $1 million, but then Hutton elects to direct a Steven Spielberg *Amazing Stories* for television, and Beatty takes advantage of this to look elsewhere. Vincent Spano is now favored, and there is a chance of the film starting in September 1985, with Spano and Rebecca de Mornay. But then de Mornay says she will be in Sam Shepard's new play in the fall. Toback is very anxious to start quickly; there have been so many

431

delays. But Beatty queries his impatience as being bad for the film. They consider Diane Lane and Jodie Foster, but judge neither will work well on screen with Spano.

Then Warren says, put it off until the spring of 1986. Do it then for sure, with Vincent Spano and Rebecca de Mornay. Then, as an after-thought, he suggests Toback keep looking at other people. You never know what you'll see. By the spring, he adds, he'll be able to look in on the shooting. He says there are people in the business telling him hair-raising stories about Toback. He lets the director gather that Beatty has been urged to watch him closely. Yet the virtue and character of Toback as a film-maker is his recklessness – it is as if Beatty is finding himself as the tamer to this frightening friend.

By the end of September 1985, Beatty is to depart for Morocco, there to make the film that Elaine May has written. It has a working title, *Ishtar*; it is a comedy about two stranded musical comedy men. The cast is Beatty, Dustin Hoffman and Isabelle Adjani, with May directing. The project has survived several pre-production worries – that Morocco is too close to the terroristic Middle East for the safety of stars; that the picture could prove too costly with two stars set for at least $6 million each; that Hoffman is more interested in other ventures; that he and Warren may engage in a destructive contest as to which is the greater perfectionist. Moreover, Columbia (putting up the money) flinches at an early budget of $30 million and talks it down to nearer $25 million, with Warren and Dustin required to put up some cash themselves. After all, a light romantic comedy having to take in $70 million, with a feeling of the *Road* pictures or *The Fortune*, may not be surefire. You have to wonder if this is another 95,000-ton soufflé.

As Warren is about to leave for the desert, Toback is still trying to tie down a cast for *The Pick-Up Artist*. It has now moved on, and centers on Steve Guttenberg and Rosanna Arquette.

*

This chapter could go on for ever, or for as long as it takes. This chapter is just keeping up with the present, mounting up as the days go by.

He returns from Morocco, and there is a holiday break, in January 1986, before filming of *Ishtar* resumes at the Astoria Studio. There are so many things to fill the pause. He has a little physical therapy for an injury from North Africa. He is being pressed to make a decision on whether or not, again, he will do *Dick Tracy*. He agrees to make a personal presentation on behalf of the Russian poet Yevgeny Yev-tushenko's film, *Kindergarden*, in New York. The PEN conference takes place in that city and he is at a dinner party in a Central Park West apartment that includes E. L. Doctorow, some South American writers and Rosario Murillo, First Lady of Nicaragua, who has two young men with her who have to be carrying (if not, why are they there?). The talk is of Gary Hart and Edward Kennedy, of censorship and revolution, the beef and the wine, and Warren says shyly, like a faded T-shirt, "Well, of course, I'm the man who made *Reds.*"

His mind may be somewhere else. He has had the first sixty pages of Toback's Bugsy Siegel script. They are remarkable pages — full of delirious talk, murder and sexual insolence. But only sixty pages.

A few days later they meet, to read the two new prospects for *The Pick-Up Artist* (99 per cent sure to start in April) — Robert Downey and Wendy Gazelle. After the reading, Beatty asks Toback:

"Where's the rest of my script?"

"Another forty pages by the weekend."

"What are you doing with it?"

"I could use some more of my expenses money."

"Tell you what, I'll dial the first digit of the Fox number, and for every ten new pages you deliver I'll dial another digit."

"You like it then?"

"It's very interesting."

"By the way, you know I'd really like to direct it myself. Now I know you like it."

"Uh-huh."

"What does that mean?"

"Finish the script. Then we'll talk about directors."

"Tell me I'll direct it, and that'll help me finish it."

"You know something? When you do *Pick-Up Artist*, you should not have sex at all. You should be totally abstinent from the start of pre-production."

"You're telling me that?"

"The film will be better if you never come."

"You're telling me that?"

"On *Bonnie and Clyde*, I never fucked once. It was important."

*

Ishtar finishes shooting on time, on March 16 1986. That leaves eight months for post-production if it is to make its appointed Thanksgiving opening. *The Pick-Up Artist* begins shooting on May 19. Susie Amos has been ready for the female lead until, four weeks before shooting, Toback is told that the part is re-cast. It will be Molly Ringwald. And Toback agrees, for, as he says, "There was nothing about it that did not make sense rationally."

In the summer of 1986, therefore, Beatty has much to look forward to. The Oscars for 1986 will be presented on March 30 1987, Warren's fiftieth birthday. *Ishtar* may bring him an extra present. Moreover, in the same span of time, he will have sponsored movies by two American directors, Elaine May and James Toback, known for their talent, independence and difficulty. What a producer he will appear as if he has enabled them to make their best films and their greatest hits.

The business wonders at how, or even whether, *Ishtar* will be promoted by its producer; and whether it will keep that title. There is no hint of what it will be except a double-page picture in the May 1986 *Life* of Beatty and Dustin Hoffman, in Morocco, on a camel – with Hoffman chuckling at a guarded Beatty, clad in blue robe and burnoose, eyes narrowed, as he gazes into the desert.

But then, in late August, as the picture is supposedly being mixed, Columbia take an ad in *Variety*, announcing the national release date for *Ishtar* – May 22 1987.

This delay is not quite as great as six months seems: it is only moving the picture from one peak season to another. Still, there are signs that Columbia has been caught by surprise. A ninety-second trailer for *Ishtar* has already been playing with *Armed and Dangerous*; and a six-month extension on what is said to be a $34 million picture can add $2 million in interest to the budget – or $5 million to the break-even rentals. One Columbia executive speaks of "grave disappointment."

There are reports of coolness between *Ishtar* and Columbia's new chairman, Englishman David Puttnam. Indeed, on the occasion of Oscars night in 1982 (when *Reds* won for direction, but Puttnam's *Chariots of Fire* took best picture), Puttnam has made open comments to the effect that Beatty is not as good a director as *Chariots'* Hugh Hudson. Puttnam's predecessor at Columbia, Guy McElwaine, had had responsibility for *Ishtar* as well as Beatty's fond regard. (In fact, we have met McElwaine already, in 1967: he was the Warner's press agent Rex Reed had to endure to get his interview with Beatty.)

There is no evidence, though, that Columbia has said *Ishtar* is not ready or good enough. Beatty gives a press interview to make it clear that he is protecting his and Elaine May's right to take the proper time and trouble with the picture:

"Elaine is a meticulous director, and it seemed like a shame to force her into a rushed situation. When you're making a movie, you have to keep your eye on the ball and let someone work the way they work best."

As I write, it is the fall of 1986. There is no word of re-shooting on *Ishtar*, in Morocco or in some closer, less dangerous desert. The picture is being refined. And Warren is getting ready for 50. Both *Ishtar* and *The Pick-Up Artist* are scheduled to open in the spring of 1987, not long after the publication of this book.

DICKLESS DEMOCRACY

"... a feature writer from the Associated Press asked Inez what she believed to be the 'major cost' of public life.

"'Memory, mainly,' Inez said . . . 'Things that might or might not be true get repeated in the clips until you can't tell the difference.'

"'But that's why I'm here. I'm not writing a piece from the clips. I'm writing a piece based on what you tell me.'

"'You might as well write it from the clips,' Inez said. Her voice was reasonable. 'Because I've lost track. Which is what I said in the first place.'"
   – Joan Didion, *Democracy* (1984)

*

I really think I'd prefer you not calling, Warren, if and when you read this book. Though I did consider writing such a call for this last chapter, as a way of covering a few things that need to be said. But I don't think I want to meet you, or get to know you, or have you play that game with me. The charm has been in the imagining.

I did ask you once to talk, and you were very doubtful, but you left me waiting for an answer, and so now, years later, you may reproach me for getting on and doing it without you; and you may wonder out loud in your lovely injured innocence how anyone could do such a book without knowing you. But I'm not sure the knowing is possible, and I have a hunch you offer it as a smokescreen, a way of concealing yourself. I suspect you believe you're unknowable because it helps you feel elusive. That's not a challenge or a criticism – I think it's probably vital in an actor and a public figure.

You can write your own book one day, if you will. There could be a dozen books about you and publishers' interest in your own memoirs would only mount. You know this very well, for you have always quietly urged others to write and think about you. And it has worked so well that you now need barely a public word to keep it going. So it's entirely up to you whether you write your book. I guess you won't,

436

because you want to stay secret. I don't just mean you'd rather the public wondered; I think you're happier, freer, if you can go on wondering about it all yourself. The hard facts may be far too cold and blunt for comfort.

That's why I quoted that passage from *Democracy* at the head of this chapter. We can be angry or disturbed that public life dissolves memory. We can say that memory is history, integrity and responsibility. All true. Yet I'm not sure Joan Didion or her Inez are simply angry or devastated at the slippage, and not also a touch curious and enchanted by this slipperiness in public life. For public life digests all the facts and their helpless contradictions and turns them into an atmosphere – a mode that is impossible to recall or pin down accurately, but so hard to forget: it is not the butterfly, but our experience of its flight and its tiny, fragrant wind. That's how I think of you, Warren, not quite as a real man, but the idea of American beauty for men in this time. (Not that women don't think about you too.) And I wrote this book because I like the idea, and I wrote it in the way I did because I was trying to get the idea and the slipstream as well as you.

There's only one thing I'd ask. Don't ever run for any political office, please. It's not that you couldn't do the job, or wouldn't be more capable than many others. It's just that the routine is so actual and tedious, and so wearing; it's not even a true role, let alone a good script; it would bore you and leave you tired and bitter. Look at it this way. Do you really think in this time we're going to vote for a president, or any other public official, with a dick? No, we want the old-timers, the re-tread ghosts, the tepid smilers and those wishful, handsome guys whose eyes seem to have been put in by two different doll-makers.

We must get used to humdrum presidents and problems that are only solved in hand-outs and fireside chats. Before Reagan was elected, Gore Vidal warned of a man whose training had been to stand handsomely in the light and do as he was told. But the fact and the "numbers" of the Reagan years have only shown us how far our political impasses and lobbying interests not only require a stooge, but can hardly persist without one. A thinking leader could collapse or start assassinating his people. So the tedium and the intractability may make for many more actorly leaders ready to speak the tranquilising communiqués.

If you did get to be president now, there's not much to look forward to except those daily photo opportunities, and one day having your colon or your polyps spread across the evening news. So play parts like Bugsy Siegel instead, because, let's face it, if at fifty-plus you play that dashing

437

John Gutmann, *Face Behind Veil*, 1939

hood-killer-loudmouth-fucker, it wouldn't be a tactful run-in for election. America loves its killers and its cocksmen, but it likes them to know their place. (You know the deputy sheriff parts Reagan had to play; you should remember that the time America loved you best was when you started killing us, giving your shit-eating grin to all the sheriffs.)

Be dangerous and seductive – that's your thing. Be the great shy lady-killer of our time. And if the Smithsonian want to measure your dick, let them come to you. Get on with Siegel and all the other wild guys you could be, because you *are* nearly fifty, and I know you hurt your shoulder in Morocco filming *Ishtar*, and you're at an age when the hurt might not go away and you could wake up a year from now knowing you were old and . . .

You see, age is not kind to modern American magic. But the gorgeous young women go on for ever and they have backs like butter. You are already America's man, our most shady, elegant hero, and no one wants to know or see when you can't manage it any longer – not the new women, not America, and least of all you.

Acknowledgments

I have to thank Warren Beatty for withholding himself. If you have been touched, amused or intrigued by this book, you are bound to honor Warren's exceptional refinement and reticence of presence and his Romantic calculation that there was more energy likely to be stirred here by his absence than his presence. Imagine the book that might have found itself having to transcribe his reveries, believe his confessions, and wait for his pauses. Imagine, too, a subsequent editorial process in which he would have had to ask himself if he had said what he meant; and, if he had, whether the book could be safely released.

Tactful and delicate, he left me hanging, and thinking. Perhaps he is inclined to believe that imagining still has more to offer a book than tape-recording. For example, the real Warren might have had to admit glumly, "Well, no, I've not read that." But in my speculations, I can shine up the possibility that he had known (all along) John Berger's book *A Seventh Man*, with its insight into all the lifelike imagery of our time:

> "A friend came to see me in a dream. From far away. And I asked in the dream: 'Did you come by photography or train?' All photographs are a form of transport and an expression of absence."

The presence of Warren Beatty, I believe, has a great deal to do with the melancholy of absence. That is why I have spent time in this book with the detail of the films, and with the suggestion of an unmade movie that might be fit for Warren. Such worlds have a place along with the real context measured by the IRS and *Variety*. This is a book about the way a movie star lives and wonders; and, as such, that involves him listening to us whistling up our imitation of him. If anything keeps Warren from doing something, it is his wondering about doing everything else. And if you care to understand a star and the mist of starriness, knowing them exactly, legally or biographically is not so much out of the question as a distraction from their heartfelt pursuit of metamorphosis.

This book has not talked to everyone alive who has touched Warren. It has sought and talked, here and there, but it has not wanted to be aggressive or intrusive. Actually, it has welcomed those who preferred not to talk. The one thing I have in common with Warren Beatty is shyness – and the worry that shyness is only the ingrowing flamboyance of those who would like to run the show, but cannot bear to be seen doing so.

But I am grateful to these people for varying amounts and degrees of talk and insight: Peter Bogdanovich, Raymond Carney, Helen Chaplin, Francis and Eleanor Coppola, Richard and Mary Corliss, Richmond Crinkley, Clint Eastwood, Roger Ebert, Jeannette Etheredge, Jeffrey Alan Fiskin, Sid Ganis, Frank Gilroy, Lee Goerner, Molly Haskell, Goldie Hawn, Buck Henry, Joe Hyams, Kevin Hyson, Henry Jaglom, Diane Johnson, Phil and Rose Kaufman, Jerzy Kosinski, Edith Kramer, Gavin Lambert, Tom Luddy, Arthur Mayer, Patrick McGilligan, David MacLeod, Mike Mahern, Daniel Melnick, Robin Menken, Monique Montgomery, Alan J. Pakula, Bob Rafelson, Maurice Rapf, Peter Scarlet, Paul Schrader, Martin Scorsese, Harry Dean Stanton, Tom Sternberg, Alan Surgal, Richard Sylbert, James Toback, Robert Towne, Wayne Wang and Debra Winger.

I owe a great deal to the initial instinct and support of Sam Vaughan at Doubleday, to the care and energy of Jim Moser and Heather Kilpatrick at the same house, and to the enthusiasm and insight of Laura Morris at Secker & Warburg, not just a publisher but a friend – always a portrait on the wall.

There have been several people at *California* magazine who have encouraged and assisted this project: Meredith White and Bill Broyles; Harold Hayes and, especially, Andy Olstein.

Then there are those who listen to me, and who had to try to live with me while I was wondering about Warren. Gratitude is such a small part of what they deserve – Kate, Mathew and Rachel Thomson and, above all, Lucy Gray, who has done her own research on living with the ghost of Warren Beatty.

Notes

All quotations from the dialogue in movies are transcribed from the films.

There are these other books on Warren Beatty:

Jim Burke, *Warren Beatty* (New York: Belmont Tower Books, 1976)
Suzanne Munshower, *Warren Beatty: His Life, His Loves, His Work* (New York: St Martin's Press, 1983)
Lawrence J. Quirk, *The Films of Warren Beatty* (Secaucus, N.J.: Citadel Press, 1979)
James Spada, *Shirley & Warren* (New York: Collier Books, 1985)

p.6   "The only way . . ." is from Barbara Leaming, *Orson Welles: A Biography* (New York: Viking, 1985), p.191.
p.7   "was so fascinated . . ." is Leaming, p.191.
p.17   ". . . this amazing business . . ." is F. Scott Fitzgerald to Max Perkins, April 23 1938, from *The Letters of F. Scott Fitzgerald*, ed. Andrew Turnbull (New York: Scribner, 1963), p.278.
p.17   background on Richmond, Virginia, is from Virginius Dabney, *The Last Review: The Confederate Reunion, Richmond, 1932* (Chapel Hill, N.C.: Algonquin Books, 1984).
p.17   "The competition was . . ." is from Shirley MacLaine, *Dancing in the Light* (New York: Bantam, 1985), p.32.
p.19   "My father was . . ." is from Shirley MacLaine, *Don't Fall Off the Mountain* (New York: Norton, 1970), p.2.
p.19   "He spent most . . ." is MacLaine, *Don't Fall*, p.3.
p.20   "He could see . . ." is MacLaine, *Don't Fall*, p.11.
p.21   "Why aren't these windows . . ." is MacLaine, *Don't Fall*, p.149.
p.26   "He'll do something . . ." is MacLaine, *Don't Fall*, p.17.
p.28   "I may be a prejudiced . . ." is quoted in Charles Higham, *Orson Welles: The Rise and Fall of an American Genius* (New York: St Martin's Press, 1985), pp.217–18.
p.29   "I never thought . . ." is Munshower, p.7.
p.30   "Warren would look . . ." is MacLaine, *Don't Fall*, p.4; "acting out his soul . . ." is p.16.

p.30   "I remember he . . ." is quoted in MacLaine, *Dancing in the Light*, p.70.

p.37   "My earliest childhood . . ." is an interview with Joe Hyams, *Show Business Illustrated*, March 1962.

p.39   "practice elocution . . ." is F. Scott Fitzgerald, *The Great Gatsby* (New York: Scribner, 1925).

p.40   "Maybe it has . . ." is Munshower, p.11.

p.40   "Mad Dog Beatty" is John Phillips, *Papa John* (New York: Doubleday, 1986), p.166.

p.40   "Warren would come . . ." is *People*, July 1 1985.

p.40   "a cheerful hypocrite . . ." is *Time*, September 1 1961.

p.49   "A guy actually . . ." is in Rex Reed, "Will the Real Warren Beatty Please Shut Up", *Esquire*, August 1967.

p.55   "I don't think . . ." is MacLaine, *Don't Fall*, p.17.

p.56   "You mean me . . ." is MacLaine, *Don't Fall*, p.21.

p.57   "It was a junk heap . . ." is in Tommy Thompson, "Warren Beatty, the Charmer", *Life*, April 26 1968.

p.61   "I was born tired . . ." is MacLaine, *Dancing in the Light*, p.145.

p.62   ". . . it's something I got . . ." is an interview with Jack Nicholson, *Rolling Stone*, March 29 1984.

p.64   "Alas, his college boy . . ." is Britt Ekland, *True Britt* (Englewood Cliffs, N.J.: Prentice-Hall, 1980), p.135.

p.70   "She equipped me . . ." is Quirk, p.34.

p.79   "I sent for him . . ." is Joshua Logan, *Movie Stars, Real People and Me* (New York: Delacorte Press, 1978), p.269.

p.79   "They worked very hard . . ." is Logan, p.270.

p.86   this and all quotations from *A Loss of Roses* are from the Dramatists Play Service edition, 1963.

p.88   "I have never . . ." is Inge, *A Loss of Roses*, p.5.

p.89   "I have to say . . ." is Spada, p.36.

p.89   "Warren won't listen . . ." is Reed, p.127.

p.89   "Warren is really . . ." is Munshower, p.19.

p.90   "Warren changed lines . . ." is Reed, p.127.

p.90   "sensual around . . ." is Kenneth Tynan, *The New Yorker*, December 12 1959.

p.97   "That boy . . ." is Joan Collins, *Past Imperfect* (New York: Simon & Schuster, 1984), p.159.

p.98   "He was about . . ." is Collins, pp.159–60.

p.100   "We became inseparable . . ." is Collins, p.164.

p.101   "Don't go, Butterfly . . ." is Collins, p.170.

p.101   "He was never happier . . ." is Collins, p.171.

p.102   "He was an excellent . . ." is Collins, p.170.

p.110 "Butterfly, we *can't* . . ." is Collins, p.174.

p.111 "It's your engagement . . ." is Collins, p.181.

p.111 "There's a basic . . ." is Michel Ciment, *Kazan on Kazan* (London: Secker & Warburg, 1973), pp.40–1.

p.113 "I'm better with actresses . . ." is Ciment, p.42.

p.114 "I was in awe . . ." is Lana Wood, *Natalie: A Memoir by Her Sister* (New York: Putnam, 1984), p.61.

p.123 "As for Bud . . ." is Ciment, p.144.

p.136 "because she had squeezed . . ." is Wood, p.61.

p.137 "How to make a . . ." is Collins, pp.183–4.

p.138 "stubborn and aggressive . . ." is Collins, p.179.

p.138 military career: letter from Selective Service System, September 6 1985.

p.139 "expressing his misery . . ." is Collins, p.189.

p.139 "It's show biz . . ." is Collins, p.187.

p.139 "His hair . . ." is Collins, p.192.

p.147 "I walked up to him . . ." is Munshower, p.35.

p.147 "Go home to bed . . ." is Dotson Rader, *Tennessee: Cry of the Heart* (New York: Doubleday, 1985), p.46.

p.147 "the difficulty . . ." is letter from Gavin Lambert, December 26 1984.

p.149 "I found him charming . . ." is Susan Strasberg, *Bittersweet* (New York: Putnam, 1980), p.143.

p.149 "surrounded by . . ." is Strasberg, p.144.

p.150 "I wasn't quite sure . . ." is Strasberg, p.144.

p.158 "It was obvious . . ." is Collins, p.196.

p.158 "Two reasons . . ." is Collins, p.196.

p.164 "All gold . . ." is Wood, p.69.

p.165 "Together in public . . ." is Wood, p.62.

p.165 "Norman Mailer will . . ." is Mailer, *Marilyn* (New York: Grosset & Dunlap, 1973), p.237.

p.165 "They occasionally . . ." is Wood, p.64.

p.167 "He told me . . ." is Wood, p.66.

p.182 "everybody in the story . . ." is Bosley Crowther, *The New York Times*, April 12 1962.

p.183 "Almost against my will . . ." is John Houseman, *Final Dress* (New York: Simon & Schuster, 1983), p.204.

p.183 "In an astonishing . . ." is Houseman, p.204.

p.184 "From the start . . ." is Houseman, p.207.

p.184 "Physically, Beatty . . ." is Stanley Kauffmann, *The New Republic*, April 23 1962.

p.185 "To break another . . ." is Jon Whitcomb, *Cosmopolitan*, February 1962.

p.185 "This young man . . ." is Whitcomb.

p.192 "In the middle 60s . . ." is Michel Ciment, *Conversations with Losey*, (New York: Methuen, 1985), p.191.

p.194 "Actors today . . ." is Reed, p.127.

p.194 "I've given you . . ." is Joseph Laitin, *Saturday Evening Post*, July 14–21 1962.

p.195 "If Natalie knew . . ." is Laitin.

p.201 "that of comparing . . ." is an interview with Robert Rossen, *Cahiers du Cinéma in English*, no. 7, 1967.

p.203 "She's got that flawed . . ." is David Richards, *Played Out: The Jean Seberg Story* (New York: Random House, 1981), p.132.

p.203 "fraternal, very intimate . . ." is Jean Seberg, "Lilith and I", *Cahiers du Cinéma in English*, no. 7, 1967.

p.203 "Warren is a brilliant . . ." is in Richards, p.137.

p.206 "She has a kind of . . ." is J.R. Salamanca, *Lilith* (New York: Simon & Schuster, 1961), p.223.

p.214 "It's not a bad film . . ." is Mike Wilmington and Gerald Peary, Interview with Warren Beatty, *The Velvet Light Trap*, no. 7, winter 1972–3.

p.215 "I spent about . . ." is in William Lee Jackson, "Bye-Bye Beatty", *The Players*, Fall 1964.

p.217 "Beatty gives it . . ." is Archer Winston, *The New York Post*, September 28 1965.

p.222 "It was quite strong . . ." is in Aaron Latham, "Warren Beatty Seriously", *Rolling Stone*, April 1 1982.

p.225 "whenever she wants . . ." is Munshower, p.46.

p.225 "He was considered . . ." is in Latham.

p.231 "Warren was the most . . ." is Ekland, p.132.

p.233 "surrounded by young actresses . . ." is Roger Vadim, *Bardot Deneuve Fonda* (New York: Simon & Schuster, 1986), p.242.

p.233 "That's *Shampoo* . . ." is an interview with Martin Scorsese.

p.240 "Bonnie writes . . ." is David Newman in Dan Yakir, "The 401st Blow", *Film Comment*, February 1985.

p.240 "He likes and . . ." is an interview with Alan Surgal.

p.250 "What do you see . . ." is an interview with Robert Towne.

p.251 "The way he discarded me . . ." is Latham.

p.253 "You know how he is . . ." is in Kevin Thomas, *Los Angeles Times*, July 2 1968.

p.254 "Warren was truly . . ." is an interview with Towne.

p.261 "Back in New York . . ." is Reed.

p.261 "a tiny pink . . ." is Reed.

p.261 "the desperation to be liked . . ." is Reed.

p.261 "There is . . ." is Reed.

p.262 "I don't know . . ." is in Wilmington and Peary.

p.263 "What do you think . . ." is in Wilmington and Peary.

p.279 "a cheap piece of . . ." is Bosley Crowther, *The New York Times*, August 14 1967.

p.279 "the most gruesome carnage . . ." is Joseph Morgenstern, *Newsweek*, August 21 1967.

p.279 "Both Producer Beatty . . ." is *Time*, August 25 1967.

p.280 "is about two . . ." is Penelope Gilliatt, *The New Yorker*, August 19 1967.

p.280 box-office figures are *Variety*.

p.281 "grossly unfair . . ." is Morgenstern, *Newsweek*, August 28 1967.

p.282 "a totally irrelevant exercise . . ." is Stefan Kanfer, *Time*, December 8 1967.

p.282 ". . . in a number of roles . . ." is Pauline Kael, *The New Yorker*, October 18 1967.

p.283 "So I ran up . . ." is Beatty in the film, *George Stevens: A Filmmaker's Journey*, 1984, directed by George Stevens Jr.

p.287 "Duke, I know . . ." is an interview with Niven Busch, *Film Comment*, August 1985.

p.293 "I did my greatest . . ." is MacLaine, *Dancing in the Light*, p.159.

p.293 "He procrastinated . . ." is Roman Polanski, *Roman* (New York: Morrow, 1984), p.250.

p.293 "a stream of . . ." is Polanski, p.305.

p.294 "Like Papillon . . ." is Polanski, p.313; "You're absolutely . . ." is p.314; "I'm not going to . . ." is p.314.

p.295 "Oh, nothing . . ." is Burke, p.159.

p.297 "It was like . . ." is Henry Ehrlich, "Warren and Julie: Together at Last", *Life*, June 1 1971.

p.297 "It became very apparent . . ." is interview with Frank Gilroy.

p.307 "too simple . . ." is Pauline Kael, *The New Yorker*, July 3 1971.

p.308 "I like to play schmucks . . ." is Wilmington and Peary.

p.310 Vancouver: see Ehrlich, *Life*, June 1 1971.

p.311 "Well, actually . . ." is interview with Gore Vidal, *American Film*, April 1977.

p.316 "The American presidency . . ." is in Roland Flamini, *Harper's Bazaar*, November 1972.

p.316 "I don't do . . ." is in Richard Reeves, *Saturday Review*, July 8 1972.

p.316 "He is seldom . . ." is Tommy Thompson, *Life*, April 26 1968.

p.319 "Warren was a . . ." is Munshower, p.89.

p.319 "He took a year out . . ." is Joan Dew, "Warren Beatty: More Than Just a Lover", *Redbook*, May 1974.

p.319 "invented the political concert . . ." is Munshower, p.91

p.321 "A sound and reasonable . . ." is *San Francisco Chronicle*, July 7 1968.

p.322 "has a greater degree . . ." is an interview with Sally Quinn, *The Washington Post*, June 1972.

p.322 "Before Florida and Wisconsin . . ." is Chris Chase, *Life*, June 23 1972.

p.322 "The most desperate feeling . . ." is Ehrlich, *Life*, June 1 1971.

p.322 "I even tried to . . ." is Flamini, *Harper's Bazaar*, November 1972.

p.323 "You drop everything . . ." is Flamini.

p.326 "'Easygoing' is not . . ." is in Frank Rich, "Warren Beatty Strikes Again", *Time*, July 3 1978.

p.326 "What do you have . . ." is Dew, *Redbook*, May 1974.

p.341 "So who do you like . . ." is an interview with Alan J. Pakula.

p.348 "but is wasting . . ." is Gary Arnold, *Washington Post*, December 15 1971.

p.349 "As an artist . . ." is Burke, p.164.

p.349 "Warren's gaze . . ." is Ekland, p.133.

p.349 "I missed you . . ." is Ekland, p.134.

p.350 "Warren is a . . ." is Wood, p.190.

p.351 "He was very angry . . ." is an interview with Robert Towne.

p.364 "Not long after . . ." is an interview with Molly Haskell.

p.364 "There does seem . . ." is Patrick McGilligan, "Warren Beatty Smoother after 'Shampoo'", *Boston Globe*, March 30 1975.

p.370 "The truth is . . ." is Spada, p.170.

p.370 "He feels that . . ." is Spada, p.170.

p.371 "One way to describe . . ." is Spada, p.156.

p.371 "wanted the daughter . . ." is an interview with Paul Schrader.

p.371 "He will always win . . ." is an interview with Schrader.

p.372 "And apparently . . ." is an interview with Schrader.

p.373 "I've been working on it . . ." is *Los Angeles Times*, August 11 1976.

p.380 "wasting time waiting . . ." is in Martin Gottfried, *Jed Harris: The Curse of Genius* (Boston: Little, Brown, 1984), p.256.

p.380 "Warren, I'd like to . . ." is an interview with Peter Bogdanovich.

p.381 "He likes to work . . ." is an interview with Buck Henry.

p.383 gift: see *Time*, May 14 1984.

p.383 "There isn't a whisper . . ." is Pauline Kael, *The New Yorker*, September 25 1978.

p.384 "I've got to read . . ." is in Hollis Alpert, "James Toback: For Love and Money", *American Film*, May 1980.

p.384 "How did you get . . ." is an interview with James Toback.

p.395 "I don't want to . . ." is interview, *American Film*, December 1981.

p.398 "He's got an amazing . . ." is an interview with Richard Sylbert.

p.398 "For me, as a . . ." is Latham, *Rolling Stone*, April 1 1982.

p.398 "You have to worry . . ." is an interview with Jerzy Kosinski.

p.401 "I feel that Warren . . ." is in John Brady, *The Craft of the Screenwriter: Interviews with Six Celebrated Screenwriters* (New York: Simon & Schuster, 1981), p.401.

p.408 "Not one media . . ." is Latham, *Rolling Stone*, April 1 1982.

p.409 Louise Bryant: see Robert A. Rosenstone, *Romantic Revolutionary: A Biography of John Reed* (New York: Knopf, 1975); Elizabeth Hardwick, "A Bunch of Reds", *Bartleby in Manhattan and Other Essays* (New York: Random House, 1983).

p.420 "no disaster . . ." is *Film Comment*, April 1982.

p.420 "A year later" is *Film Comment*, April 1983.

p.421 "It has to do with . . ." is Munshower, p.145.

p.421 "And if he ever delves . . ." is interview with Paul Schrader.

p.423 "They go to see": Herb Caen, *San Francisco Chronicle*, July 25 1984.

p.423 Toronto Film Festival: see Martin Knelman, "Romantic Revolutionary: Mr Beatty Goes to Toronto", *Boston Phoenix*, October 24 1984; Judy Stone, *San Francisco Chronicle*, September 12 1984; Mary Corliss, *Film Comment*, February 1985.

p.424 "They were both . . ." is Jerry Hall, with Christopher Hemphill, "From Rags to Rio", *Vanity Fair*, March 1985.

p.425 "He gathers indirectly": in Dominick Dunne, "Hide-and-Seek with Diane Keaton", *Vanity Fair*, February 1985.

p.425 "It is called *Who* . . .": is an interview with Wayne Wang.

p.428 "The trouble is . . ." is an interview with Martin Scorsese.

p.429 "Those who are demanding . . ." is Larry Leibert, *San Francisco Chronicle*, July 3 1985.

p.430 "irresponsible and intemperate . . ." is editorial, *San Francisco Chronicle*, July 5 1985.

p.431 "I knew every cut . . ." is David T. Friendly, "Blood Lines Drawn on the Cutting-Room Floor", *Los Angeles Times*, June 9 1985.

p.431 "a good cruel sense . . ." is an interview with James Toback.

p.433 "Where's the rest . . ." is an interview with Toback.

p.435 "Elaine is a . . ." is from David T. Friendly, "No Ishtar This Year for Columbia," *Los Angeles Times*, September 4 1986.

p.436 ". . . a feature writer . . ." is Joan Didion, *Democracy* (New York: Simon & Schuster, 1984), pp.50–51.

Filmography

Splendor in the Grass. Produced and directed by Elia Kazan; screenplay by William Inge; photography by Boris Kaufman; music by David Amram; production design by Richard Sylbert; associate producers, William Inge and Charles H. McGuire; make-up by Robert Jiras. With Natalie Wood, WB, Pat Hingle, Audrey Christie, Barbara Loden, Fred Stewart, Zohra Lampert, Joanna Roos, Jan Norris, Gary Lockwood, Sandy Dennis, John McGovern, William Inge (Warner Brothers, 124 mins, opened October 10 1961)

The Roman Spring of Mrs Stone. Produced by Louis de Rochemont; directed by José Quintero; screenplay by Gavin Lambert, from the novel by Tennessee Williams; photography by Harry Waxman; music by Richard Addinsell; production design by Roger Furse. With Vivien Leigh, WB, Lotte Lenya, Coral Browne, Jill St John, Jeremy Spenser, Stella Bonheur, Josephine Brown, Peter Dyneley, Carl Jaffé, Harold Kasket, Viola Keats, Cleo Laine, Bessie Love, Warren Mitchell, Ernest Thesiger, Sarah Miles (Warner Brothers, 104 mins, opened December 28 1961)

All Fall Down. Produced by John Houseman; directed by John Frankenheimer; screenplay by William Inge, from the novel by James Leo Herlihy; photography by Lionel Lindon; music by Alex North; art direction by George W. Davis and Preston Ames. With Eva Marie Saint, WB, Karl Malden, Angela Lansbury, Brandon De Wilde, Constance Ford, Barbara Baxley, Evans Evans, Jennifer Howard, Madame Spivy, Albert Paulson (MGM, 111 mins, opened April 11 1962)

Lilith. Produced and directed by Robert Rossen; screenplay by Rossen from the novel by J. R. Salamanca; photography by Eugen Shufftan; music by Kenyon Hopkins; production design by Richard Sylbert. With WB, Jean Seberg, Peter Fonda, Kim Hunter, Anne Meacham, James Patterson, Jessica Walter, Gene Hackman, Robert Reilly, Rene Auberjonois, Lucy Smith (Columbia, 114 mins, opened September 20 1964)

Mickey One. Produced and directed by Arthur Penn; screenplay by Alan

Surgal; photography by Ghislain Cloquet; music by Eddie Sauter and Stan Getz; production design by George Jenkins; make-up by Robert Jiras. With WB, Alexandra Stewart, Hurd Hatfield, Franchot Tone, Teddy Hart, Jeff Corey, Kamatari Fujiwara, Donne Michelle, Ralph Froody, Norman Gottschalk, Dick Lucas, Benny Dunn (Columbia, 93 mins, opened September 27 1965)

Promise Her Anything. Produced by Stanley Rubin; directed by Arthur Hiller; screenplay by William Peter Blatty, from a story by Arne Sultan and Marvin Worth; photography by Douglas Slocombe; music by Lynn Murray; art direction by Wilfrid Shingleton. With WB, Leslie Caron, Bob Cummings, Hermione Gingold, Lionel Stander, Asa Maynor, Keenan Wynn, Cathleen Nesbitt, Michael Bradley, Bessie Love, Mavis Villiers, Warren Mitchell, Sydney Tafler (Warner Brothers, 98 mins, opened February 22 1966)

Kaleidoscope. Produced by Elliott Kastner; directed by Jack Smight; screenplay by Robert and Jane Howard Carrington; photography by Christopher Challis; music by Stanley Myers; art direction by Maurice Carter; assistant producer Peter Medak. With WB, Susannah York, Clive Revill, Eric Porter, Murray Melvin, George Sewell, Stanley Meadows, John Junkin, Larry Taylor, Yootha Joyce, Jane Birkin, George Murcell, Anthony Newlands (Warner Brothers, 103 mins, opened September 22 1966)

Bonnie and Clyde. Produced by WB; directed by Arthur Penn; screenplay by David Newman and Robert Benton; special consultant, Robert Towne; photography by Burnett Guffey; music by Charles Strouse; art direction by Dean Tavoularis; edited by Dede Allen; costumes by Theadora Van Runkle; make-up by Robert Jiras. With WB, Faye Dunaway, Michael J. Pollard, Gene Hackman, Estelle Parsons, Denver Pyle, Dub Taylor, Evans Evans, Gene Wilder, James Stiver (Warner Brothers, 111 mins, opened August 13 1967)

The Only Game in Town. Produced by Fred Kohlmar; directed by George Stevens; screenplay by Frank D. Gilroy, from his own play; photography by Henri Decaë; music by Maurice Jarre; art direction by Herman Blumenthal and Auguste Capelier. With Elizabeth Taylor, WB, Charles Braswell, Hank Henry (Fox, 113 mins, opened March 4 1970)

McCabe and Mrs Miller. Produced by David Foster and Mitchell Brower; directed by Robert Altman; screenplay by Altman and Brian McKay, from the novel *McCabe* by Edmund Naughton; photography by Vilmos Zsigmond; songs by Leonard Cohen; production design by Leon Ericksen; make-up by Robert Jiras. With WB, Julie Christie, Rene Auberjonois, John Schuck, Bert Remsen, Keith Carradine, William Devane, Corey Fischer, Shelley Duvall,

Michael Murphy, Anthony Holland, Hugh Millais, Manfred Schulz, Jace Vander Veen (Warner Brothers, 120 mins, opened June 24 1971)

$ (Dollars). Produced by Mike Frankovich; directed and written by Richard Brooks; photography by Petrus Schloemp; music by Quincy Jones; art direction by Guy Sheppard and Olaf Ivens; make-up by Ernest Schmekel and Robert Jiras. With WB, Goldie Hawn, Gert Frobe, Robert Webber, Scott Brady, Arthur Brauss, Robert Stiles, Wolfgang Kieling, Robert Herron, Christiane Maybach, Hans Hutter (Columbia, 119 mins, opened December 15 1971)

The Parallax View. Produced and directed by Alan J. Pakula; screenplay by David Giler and Lorenzo Semple Jr, from the novel by Loren Singer; photography by Gordon Willis; music by Michael Small; production design by George Jenkins. With WB, Hume Cronyn, William Daniels, Paula Prentiss, Kelly Thordsen, Earl Hindman, Kenneth Mars, Walter McGinn, Jim Davis, Bill Joyce, Bill McKinney, William Jordan (Paramount, 102 mins, opened June 19 1974)

Shampoo. Produced by WB; directed by Hal Ashby; screenplay by WB and Robert Towne; photography by Laszlo Kovacs; music by Paul Simon; production design by Richard Sylbert; edited by Robert C. Jones. With WB, Julie Christie, Goldie Hawn, Lee Grant, Jack Warden, Tony Bill, Carrie Fisher, Jay Robinson, George Furth, Brad Dexter, William Castle (Columbia, 112 mins, opened February 11 1975)

The Fortune. Produced by Mike Nichols and Don Devlin; directed by Nichols; screenplay by Adrien Joyce; photography by John Alonzo; music by David Shire; production design by Richard Sylbert. With WB, Jack Nicholson, Stockard Channing, Florence Stanley, Richard B. Shull, Tom Newman, John Fiedler, Scatman Crothers, Dub Taylor, Ian Wolfe, Rose Michtom, Brian Avery, Christopher Guest, Kathryn Grody (Columbia, 88 mins, opened May 20 1975)

Heaven Can Wait. Produced by WB; directed by WB and Buck Henry; screenplay by WB and Elaine May; photography by William A. Fraker; music by Dave Grusin; production design by Paul Sylbert; edited by Robert C. Jones and Don Zimmerman; costumes by Theadora Van Runkle, Richard Bruno, Mike Hoffman and Arlene Encell. With WB, Julie Christie, James Mason, Jack Warden, Charles Grodin, Dyan Cannon, Buck Henry, Vincent Gardenia, Joseph Maher, Dolph Sweet, R. G. Armstrong, John Randolph, William Sylvester (Paramount, 101 mins, opened June 28 1978)

Reds. Produced and directed by WB; executive producers, Simon Relph and

Dede Allen; associate producer, David MacLeod; screenplay by WB and Trevor Griffiths; photography by Vittorio Storaro; edited by Dede Allen and Craig McKay; production design by Richard Sylbert; music by Stephen Sondheim and Dave Grusin. With WB, Diane Keaton, Jack Nicholson, Edward Herrmann, Jerzy Kosinski, Paul Sorvino, Maureen Stapleton, Nicolas Coster, M. Emmet Walsh, Ian Wolfe, Bessie Love, MacIntyre Dixon, Pat Starr, Eleanor D. Wilson, Max Wright, George Plimpton, Harry Ditson, Leigh Curran, Kathryn Grody, Brenda Currin, Nancy Duiguid, Norman Chancer, Dolph Sweet, Ramon Bieri, Jack O'Leary, Gene Hackman, William Daniels, Dave King, Joseph Buloff, Josef Sommer, R. G. Armstrong (Paramount, 199 mins, opened December 3 1981)

Ishtar. Produced by WB; directed and written by Elaine May; associate producer, David MacLeod; photography by Vittorio Storaro; edited by Steve Rotter, Bill Reynolds and Richie Cirinzione; production design by Paul Sylbert; music by Dave Grusin; songs by Paul Williams. With WB, Dustin Hoffman, Isabelle Adjani, Charles Grodin, Carol Kane, Tess Harper, Jack Weston (Columbia, about 145 mins, scheduled to open on May 22 1987)

As John Q McCabe (Warner Brothers)

Index